Mom,
A reminder of how
important librarians
are to others.
Love,
Judy & Stan
Christmas 1991

Reading Rooms

Reading
Rooms

Edited by Susan Allen Toth
and John Coughlan

Foreword by Daniel J. Boorstin

D O U B L E D A Y

NEW YORK LONDON TORONTO SYDNEY AUCKLAND

PUBLISHED BY DOUBLEDAY
a division of Bantam Doubleday Dell Publishing Group, Inc.
666 Fifth Avenue, New York, New York 10103

DOUBLEDAY and the portrayal of an anchor with a dolphin are trademarks
of Doubleday, a division of Bantam Doubleday Dell Publishing Group, Inc.

Acknowledgments for permission to quote from copyrighted sources will be
found below.

Typography and binding design by Chris Welch

Library of Congress Cataloging-in-Publication Data
Reading rooms: America's foremost writers celebrate our public libraries
with stories, memoirs, essays, and poems . . . / edited by Susan Allen
Toth and John Coughlan; foreword by Daniel J. Boorstin.—1st ed.
p.   cm.
Includes bibliographical references.
1. Public libraries—Literary collections.   2. Books and reading—
Literary collections.   3. Authors, American—20th century—Books and
reading.   4. American literature—20th century.   5. Books and
reading—United States.   6. Public libraries—United States.
I. Toth, Susan Allen.   II. Coughlan, John.
PS509.P83R4   1991
810.8'0355—dc20   90-13927
CIP

ISBN 0-385-41291-6
Copyright © 1991 by Susan Toth and John Coughlan
Foreword copyright © 1991 by Daniel J. Boorstin
Introductory matter copyright © 1991 by Susan Toth

All Rights Reserved
Printed in the United States of America
April 1991
First Edition
1   3   5   7   9   10   8   6   4   2

ACKNOWLEDGMENTS

Acknowledgment is gratefully made for permission to use or reprint the following:

The introduction was based on a talk given to the Friends of Bracken Library, Ball State University, Muncie, Indiana, on April 14, 1989.

"Library" by Richard Armour, copyright © 1954 by Richard Armour. Reprinted by permission of John Hawkins & Associates, Inc.

Excerpt from *The Happy Bookers* by Richard Armour, copyright © 1976 by Richard Armour. Reprinted by permission of McGraw-Hill Publishing Company.

"The Library Book" from *The Best Mysteries of Isaac Asimov* by Isaac Asimov, copyright © 1986 by Nightfall, Inc. Reprinted by permission of Doubleday, a division of Bantam Doubleday Dell Publishing Group, Inc.

Excerpt from *Go Tell It on the Mountain* by James Baldwin, copyright © 1952, 1953 by James Baldwin. Reprinted by permission of Doubleday, a division of Bantam Doubleday Dell Publishing Group, Inc.

THIS BOOK IS GRATEFULLY DEDICATED TO ALL LIBRARIANS—
ESPECIALLY THE LIBRARIANS OF THE PUBLIC LIBRARIES
IN AMES, IOWA, AND MANKATO, MINNESOTA,
WHO FIRST WELCOMED US AS CHILDREN
INTO THE WONDERFUL WORLD OF BOOKS

FOREWORD

Reading for self-entertainment and enlightenment is one of our oldest and most vital American traditions. Anyone who rides a bus, a train, or an airplane these days can testify that the current obituaries on the book are premature. In 1772, an eminent Anglican minister, Jacob Duché (who became an enemy of the American Revolution), complained, "The poorest labourer upon the shore of the Delaware thinks himself entitled to deliver his sentiments in matters of religion or politics with as much freedom as the gentleman or the scholar. Indeed, there is less distinction among the citizens of Philadelphia, than among those of any civilized city in the world.... Such is the prevailing taste for books of every kind, that almost every man is a reader; and by pronouncing sentence, right or wrong, upon the various publications that come in his way, puts himself upon a level, in point of knowledge, with their several authors." Other Loyalists agreed that this reading habit nourished the subversive sentiments that caused the American Revolution.

If reading has been a congenital American habit, the American public library has been one of our most characteristic institutions. What was probably the earliest American "social library"—not quite a "public" library—was the creation of Benjamin Franklin, in Philadelphia in 1731, where artisans and tradesmen banded together to buy books and exchange them. The American public library, which would be free and open to all, was also a product of burgeoning New World cities.

The public libraries' origins are so numerous and so unchronicled that we cannot say when the first came into being. But we can clearly see their American characteristics. First, because they arose spontaneously here and there. A local, federal product, they were not organized from the center, nor did they ever become a national "system." Laws facilitated the work of communities, but did not inhibit local enthusiasms. This diversity, too, was quite American. The Boston Public Library, in 1848, was the first to be established by act of a state legislature. By 1933 every state had its own law to facilitate the creation of public libraries. Meanwhile private philanthropy was playing its traditional and distinctive American role. The Astor Library, founded by John Jacob Astor and opened to the public in 1854, combined with others in 1895 to form the New York Public Library which still flourishes as a mixed public-private institution.

The Patron Saint of American Public Libraries was, of course Andrew Carnegie (1835–1919), the Scotsman who became a self-made American millionaire and gave some $56 million for the construction of more than 2,500 library buildings. His vision and enthusiasm inspired the American public library movement. Luckily, it remained a "movement" and never became a "system." Few other movements in American history have been so continuously successful in enlisting local pride and energies. Now we have some 8,000 public libraries of every kind, circulating a billion items.

As our public libraries were characteristically American in their ways of creation, they were, too, in their speedy response to local interests, popular enthusiasms, and novel technology. They became repositories for recordings and videotapes, and centers for community action. Most recently, they have embraced the latest electronic technologies for information storage and retrieval. The authoritative *Encyclopaedia of the Social Sciences*, published in 1933, offers an extensive entry about books and readers under the title "Public Libraries." But its counterpart, the monumental *International Encyclopedia of the Social Sciences*, in 1968, on the threshold of the computer age, has no such entry. Instead, "Libraries" are pigeonholed under "Information Storage and Retrieval."

If anything is plain from the lively selections in this volume, it is that visitors to Reading Rooms seldom sought a facility for "Information Storage and Retrieval." Their wonderfully diverse hopes and enthusiasms are hard to catalogue, but they seemed to come mostly for refuge and delight. Refuge from the confusion and noise of the world outside, of the crowded apartment or nuisancy small brothers and sisters. Delight in the adventuring world of books.

They came to a *place* (a Reading Room), to enjoy a *thing* (a book), with the aid of a *person* (a librarian). These Reading Room experiences must leave us puzzled that the prestigious and costly recent White House Conferences on libraries called themselves a conference on "Library and Information Services." The word "book" entered their proceedings only as an afterthought. But the Reading Room visitors whose accounts we here enjoy did not come to have a "service" rendered. On the contrary. They came to a place where, unlike most other places in late-twentieth-century America, their experience depended entirely on themselves—the book they selected, read (without breaks for commercials) at the pace they chose, for as long as they wished, and without background music. Here readers of all ages were fully independent persons, with the assistance only of a librarian to help them be themselves.

A consequence of modern technology, of which these chapters remind us, is to make every place more like every other place—to make our living rooms into movie houses, stadium seats, Amazon tour boats. *Reading Rooms* reminds us, as we need to be reminded, of the meanings of unique places. Mr. Dooley, as usual, was on the mark when he said "A Carnaygie libry is archytechoor, not lithrachoor. Lithrachoor will be riprisinted." Here was not a headquarters for "access," for tapping into electronic hardware or software. Susan Allen Toth and John Coughlan help us recognize that, in the jargon of our computer age, Reading Rooms can be user-friendly places, a comfort to crawl into. We learn from some of our best authors that these are still places where we can concoct our personal antidote to public bewilderments, and find our tonic in bookish dreams. Refuge, delight, and entertainment are more than enough to justify the Reading Rooms. But if we want more, there is more, as Richard Armour observes:

> *Here is where people,*
> *One frequently finds,*
> *Lower their voices*
> *And raise their minds.*

Daniel J. Boorstin
The Librarian of Congress Emeritus

CONTENTS

NINE   ## Democracy in the Library   417

EDITOR'S NOTE

Any anthology is the result of both passionate attachments and hard choices. The idiosyncrasies of this collection probably reflect those of the editors.

We gratefully acknowledge the many suggestions sent to us by other lovers of libraries. We regret that limitations of space and, in a few frustrating cases, the impossibility of obtaining publishers' permissions, forced us to omit certain selections.

We know that a celebration of the American public library is never complete. We hope this book will point readers toward their own recognitions and discoveries.

Reading Rooms

A CELEBRATION OF LIBRARIES

I used to think I had nothing more to remember about libraries. I had relived my own library days so thoroughly in my first book, *Blooming: A Small-Town Girlhood*, that I was convinced I couldn't possibly recall another detail. I was wrong. Like many writers, I had somehow thought, too, that setting down memories of my intense hours in the Ames Public Library was highly original. Wrong again.

I began to learn more about writers and libraries a few years ago when I came to serve on the board of the Friends of the Minneapolis Public Library. There I made a new friend, John Coughlan, a man of Renaissance interests, and we soon discovered a common passion for many books and for almost all libraries. It was John who suggested we compile an anthology about libraries. I think we both envisioned some lighthearted research and then, perhaps, a gracefully slender book. We *did* have fun. But what we thought might be a simple exploration of one vein of material soon turned out to be an exciting but also an exhaustive, time-consuming journey through a vast connected network of tunnels.

I had not been aware of how many writers have chosen libraries as setting and theme. In *Blooming*, when I let myself sink back into the Ames Public Library, with its imposing facade, wide stone steps, and hushed cavernous interior, I wasn't at all sure as I was writing that anyone would find the atmosphere I recalled so clearly very compelling. After all, my memories were of small, ordinary details: the tiny chairs in the children's room, the librarian's office with its locked case, and even the frighteningly dark below-stairs toilets, I had the sense that I might have been the only impressionable, book-loving child who ever fell in love with a library. When curious friends asked me what part of my memoir I was now working on, and I answered, "Oh, a chapter on the Ames Public Library," they looked at me discouragingly. Their expressions said plainly, "Who cares?"

But I quickly learned that many people did care about libraries. When readers wrote to me after my book was published, the chapter they mentioned most often was the one on the library. The letters frequently went on to tell me how they had loved *their* libraries. They too had revered the Head Librarian, tiptoed into the forbidden adult section, and discovered the astonishing extent of the world of books.

Still I didn't realize how many marvelous writers had recorded in different ways their feelings about libraries. When we began our collection, we each could cite some examples—John had a dog-eared folder of favorites and I could sing along with Robert Preston the lyrics of "Marian the Librarian"—but neither of us really understood what literary possibilities lay before us, some treasures, some substantial nuggets, and some gleaming pebbles. What we gradually uncovered felt something like those long-ago days when we, as children, first began to explore, respectively, the Ames, Iowa, and Mankato, Minnesota, public libraries.

Libraries—those temples of learning, those granite-and-marble monuments—do not appear to most people as places of passion or even vital activity. Local newspapers don't cover the library beat as ardently as they do city hall; protests don't usually erupt for television cameras on the library steps; the mayor doesn't invite visiting celebrities to be feted and photographed in the Main Reading Room. For most Americans, the library is a reassuring and stable presence, there when they need it, and until then, to be comfortably taken for granted.

Yet many men and women, not just writers, feel passionately about libraries. When we sent an "author's query" to *The New York Times Book Review*, asking for suggestions of literary passages that celebrated public libraries, we were not sure what to expect. For years, I had flipped past those polite scholarly requests for correspondence, information, and memorabilia. Sometimes, especially when the query seemed quite obscure, I'd idly wondered if anyone ever answered them. Now we found out.

A few days after our note appeared at the bottom of an inside page, four letters arrived. The next day, six. A pause for a day, then four more. At the end of six weeks, we had heard from sixty-five respondents, and an occasional card or letter still trickled in. Our mail came from Connecticut to California, as well as from Angers, France, and Tokyo.

People sent poems, stories, song lyrics, speeches, cartoons, jokes, book-plates, postcards, reproductions of paintings, news clippings, and suggestions for further research.

One man in New York thought we should study the transcripts of hearings of the Board of Estimates in order to glean the impassioned rhetoric of those who plead for library support. Another man wrote to share his outrage at the shocking state of library funding in his town. One woman wrote us a personal anecdote about how a nun had taken her as a child to a library for the first time; another, a retired librarian, sent ("with some embarrassment, at the insistence of my trustees") a glowing dedication an author had written in tribute to her skills and service. What all these letters had in common, besides a generous willingness to share information, was passion. Our correspondents had taken the time and trouble to write to us because, as so many of them said explicitly, they loved libraries.

That love of libraries often goes back to childhood. Our correspondents, and many published writers, were deeply affected as children by the grandeur of libraries. In many small towns, the Carnegie library often had an architectural presence that other ordinary buildings lacked. An alert child could not fail to be impressed by its stern and weighty stone construction, its monumental staircases or porticoes, its classical pediments and columns. The library's rooms were spacious and tall, and light poured in from high windows onto clean and gleaming surfaces. One's house might be small, cramped, and messy, but the library never was.

Many writers have noted the sensuous pleasure they felt then, and often still do, upon entering library. In *A Leak in the Heart* essayist Faye Moskowitz was timorous and reverent: "There, in the cool, softly lit interior, so like the Christian church I had set foot in once on a dare, I tiptoed past the shushing librarian's curved mahogany desk to the book-lined rooms smelling of library paste and canvas bindings." In *A Tree Grows in Brooklyn*, young Francie regards the library with near-religious veneration: "The library was a little old shabby place. Francie thought it was beautiful. The feeling she had about it was as good as the feeling she had about church. . . . She pushed open the door and went in. She liked the combined smell of worn leather bindings, library paste and freshly-inked stamping pads better than she liked the smell of burning incense at high mass."

There it is: that wonderful library smell. How could I have forgotten it? The *feel* of libraries—the way they look, smell, sound—lingers intensely as the memories of a fierce first love. Writers recollect not only the intense physical presence of library buildings, but also the imposing character of the librarians who served and guarded them. In poems, stories, and novels, the librarian—usually a woman—is sometimes dull, mousy, and repressed, but she is also often strong and formidable. For many children who grew up in the not-too-distant past, the town librarian was one of the few women they knew who seemed to exercise professional power. In some smaller towns or neighborhoods, she was, in fact, unique. Women teachers had authority, but they usually reported to male principals or superintendents. A librarian, in a child's view, reported to no one. I could not imagine Miss Davidson, the Ames librarian, asking anyone's permission for anything, accepting rules from a town council or mayor, or defending her decisions to a board. I was sure she ruled her domain single-handedly and absolutely.

A writer often describes the childhood experience of going to the library as a rite of passage, an entrance into a magical world. Novelist Julian Moynahan, analyzing his love of libraries, knows exactly when his passion first began: "I trace it back to a rainy day in Philadelphia when my mother deposited me soaking wet in the Children's Department of the main Public Library while she continued her efficient patriotic sightseeing with my older brother and sister. I dried out slowly while reading a richly illustrated book about a large green frog. Earlier that day I had visited a sodden cemetery thought to contain the remains of Benjamin Franklin. It meant nothing to me at all, whereas the frog book hooked me on libraries for life."

The library is a place where frogs can turn into princes. As a child, I once saw a poster-map of the Land of Make-Believe. It stretched between East of the Sun and West of the Moon, and scattered over the map were whimsical illustrations of various fairy-tale characters, emerging from turreted castles and magical mountains and even Rapunzel's tower. I had early given my wholehearted allegiance to the Land of Make-Believe, and I knew that books led into it. Whenever I entered the Library and began to browse along its shelves, I felt I was about to step through the looking glass right onto that map.

Although children know they can find frog princes and fairy tales in the library, grown men and women often look for fantasies there too. Libraries have been the setting for many literary romances, and I never have trouble wholeheartedly believing in them, for I can easily suppose love lurking in the shadows of the stacks. As a moony college student, I used to dream about meeting my own prince—not a frog—in a library, since I thought any young man who loved books might perhaps love me too. One summer in Cambridge, Massachusetts, I haunted the aisles of the Widener Library at Harvard, hoping to bump into that perfect mate, somewhere between A and Z. But, even when I once caught a glimpse of a golden-haired Harvard student, handsome and yet intellectual-looking, ensconced in a book-laden carrel, I had no idea how to get his attention. What could I say to him? How could I learn his name? He looked older; was he married? For all my helplessness in knowing exactly how to breach the silence of the library, he might have been enveloped in a green cloak and hood, hiding in the Enchanted Woods in the Land of Make-Believe. He may be there still, grayer but craggily attractive, absorbed in his impenetrable research, a Sleeping Prince. Illusions live a long time in the sheltered light of libraries.

While the dark stacks of libraries are ideal rendezvous for lovers, or for those who dream of finding lovers, they also make fine settings for mystery and murder. Perhaps because the library seems such a quiet, controlled, and secure environment, writers have enjoyed placing violent crimes in it. Literary library murders are common enough so that I now explore the lower, darker, uninhabited stacks of the University of Minnesota library rather more carefully than I used to.

Lighthearted love and sensational murder may take place in writers' libraries, but these libraries have inspired much more sober and philosophical treatises as well. The public library is an important symbol of a working democracy, which is founded on the belief that members of the society can make educated decisions about how they are governed. Immigrants to America, and the dispossessed, have often recorded their gratitude to public libraries for the free and accessible education they received there.

Yet as part of an imperfect society, libraries, alas, have not always welcomed those who most want to enter the world of books. Novelist Richard Wright, in his autobiography *Black Boy*, and James Baldwin, in his autobiographical novel *Go Tell It on the Mountain*, write powerfully about how it felt to be excluded from that privileged world, by actual or implied intimidation.

Libraries are perfect places for imaginative musings. Many writers have looked around a library reading room and wondered about the lives of the other readers at those long wooden tables. Poet Randall Jarrell observes a chunky, sleepy college student, with muscular calves, brown braids, and glasses. Under the spell of the reading room, Jarrell soon whisks her back to the mythical worlds of the Nibelung and of Troy. Reading-room reveries perhaps reach their bizarre apogee in Steven Millhauser's "The Library of Morpheus." The god of sleep and dreams escorts the narrator through a fantastic library that offers, among its many strange collections, books that have been planned but never written, lost books, late books by authors who died young—the novel written after *Finnegans Wake*, the poem after the *Aeneid*, the play after *The Tempest*. Such tempting tasks could keep a daydreamer staring at the ceiling of the reading room all afternoon.

Although libraries are usually solemn places, they also provoke laughter in those writers who see the ludicrous side of institutions, and rules and regulations. Readers of Eleanor Estes's children's story *Rufus M.* can delight in her description of how stubborn, irrepressible Rufus gets his first library card. Memorable light verse has also been written about libraries, such as Pyke Johnson's "Annual report to the heads of the town: Circulation is up. Computer is down."

From mystery to laughter, from social analysis to flights of fancy, our prospecting in literature about libraries has brought us many imaginative rewards. Through reading writers on libraries, we both have been able to remember how we felt as children when we entered a library for the first time. We have once again found ourselves lost in the stacks, or at least lost to any sense of the world outside. Once more time slipped away as we sat cross-legged on the tiled or wooden floor in front of a enticing shelf of unknown books. We have vicariously visited many libraries and sat in many reading rooms, where we almost always felt quite at home. By sharing these selections by outstanding writers, we hope others also can once again affirm the love of reading that is so richly nurtured by libraries.

Susan Allen Toth

ONE

Small-Town Libraries

S mall towns have always drawn mixed reactions from American writers. Some eloquently attack the self-satisfied, stultifying atmosphere of small-town life, while others warmly recall its neighborly visits, shared concerns, and long-established community events. So, too, have small-town libraries been memorialized and criticized, evoked both with nostalgia and with bitterness.

Some small-town libraries seem moribund, bereft of both patrons and interesting books, as in Edith Wharton's short novel *Summer*. Wharton's gloomy portrait of the one-room Hatchard Memorial Library, a "ridiculous mausoleum" with its "blotched walls, the discoloured rows of books, and the stern rosewood desk surmounted by the portrait of the young Honorius," suggests the airless, mouldy spirit of the village itself. In Sinclair Lewis's *Main Street*, the library in Gopher's Prairie offers new comer Carol Kennicott neither instruction nor solace. Some fifty years after Lewis's satirical exposé of small-town life, Jon Hassler describes in his novel *Grand Opening* a library just as symbolic of the cramped soul of the tiny town of Plum.

Other writers, like Eudora Welty in her memoir, remember small-town libraries with respect and great affection. Dorothy Canfield Fisher celebrates a small and old-fashioned Vermont library that embodies the New England ideal of communal involvement—until it is replaced by a newer, grander, and less friendly one. In the excerpt from my own memoir *Blooming: A Small-Town Girlhood*, I had originally intended to record just a few brief memories of my hometown library in Ames, Iowa. Finding myself suddenly back in that much-loved quiet place, I ended up with an entire chapter.

Excerpt from *One Writer's Beginnings* by Eudora Welty

Eudora Welty, born in Mississippi in 1909, is one of the most important Southern writers of the twentieth century. With her best-selling memoir, One Writer's Beginnings *(1984), from which the following excerpt is taken, Ms. Welty continued to extend her national audience of readers who respond to her gifts of characterization, sly humor, poignance, and sense of the absurd.*

Ms. Welty is known both for her short stories, which have appeared in volumes like The Golden Apples *(1949) and* The Bride of the Innisfallen *(1955), as well as* Collected Stories *(1980); and for her longer fiction, including* The Robber Bridegroom *(1942);* Delta Wedding *(1946);* The Ponder Heart *(1954);* Losing Battles *(1970); and the Pulitzer Prize—winning* The Optimist's Daughter *(1972).*

Jackson's Carnegie Library was on the same street where our house was, on the other side of the State Capitol. "Through the Capitol" was the way to go to the Library. You could glide through it on your bicycle or even coast through on roller skates, though without family permission.

I never knew anyone who'd grown up in Jackson without being afraid of Mrs. Calloway, our librarian. She ran the Library absolutely by herself, from the desk where she sat with her back to the books and facing the stairs, her dragon eye on the front door, where who knew what kind of person might come in from the public? SILENCE in big black letters was on signs tacked up everywhere. She herself spoke in her normally commanding voice; every word could be heard all over the Library above a steady seething sound coming from her electric fan; it was the only fan in the Library and stood on her desk, turned directly onto her streaming face.

As you came in from the bright outside, if you were a girl, she sent her strong eyes down the stairway to test you; if she could see through your skirt she sent you straight back home: you could just put on another petticoat if you wanted a book that badly from the public library. I was willing; I would do anything to read.

My mother was not afraid of Mrs. Calloway. She wished me to have my own library card to check out books for myself. She took me in to introduce me and I saw I had met a witch. "Eudora is nine years old and has my permission to read any book she wants from the shelves, children or adult," Mother said. "With the exception of *Elsie Dinsmore*," she added. Later she explained to me that she'd made this rule because Elsie the heroine, being made by her father to practice too long and hard at the piano, fainted and fell off the piano stool. "You're too impressionable, dear," she told me. "You'd read that and the very first thing you'd do, you'd fall off the piano stool." "Impressionable" was a new word. I never hear it yet without the image that comes with it of falling straight off the piano stool.

Mrs. Calloway made her own rules about books. You could not take back a book to the Library on the same day you'd taken it out; it made no difference to her that you'd read every word in it and needed another to start. You could take out two books at a time and two only; this applied as long as you were a child and also for the rest of your life, to my mother as severely as to me. So two by two, I read library books as fast as I could go, rushing them home in the basket of my bicycle. From the minute I reached our house, I started to read. Every book I seized on, from *Bunny Brown and His Sister Sue at Camp Rest-a-While* to *Twenty Thousand Leagues under the Sea*, stood for the devouring wish to read being instantly granted. I knew this was bliss, knew it at the time. Taste isn't nearly so important; it comes in its own time. I wanted to read *immediately*. The only fear was that of books coming to an end.

My mother was very sharing of this feeling of insatiability. Now, I think of her as reading so much of the time while doing something else. In my mind's eye *The Origin of Species* is lying on the shelf in the pantry under a light dusting of flour—my mother was a bread maker; she'd pick it up, sit by the kitchen window and find her place, with one eye on the oven. I remember her picking up *The Man in Lower Ten* while my hair got dry enough to unroll from a load of kid curlers trying to make me like my idol, Mary Pickford. A generation later, when my brother Walter was away in the Navy and his two little girls often spent the day in our house, I remember Mother reading the new issue of *Time* magazine while taking the part of the Wolf in a game of "Little Red Riding Hood" with the children. She'd just look up at the right time, long enough to answer—in character—"The better to eat you with, my dear," and go back to her place in the war news.

Excerpt from *Summer* by Edith Wharton

With its powerful evocation of scene, strong emotional content, and relentlessly bleak analysis of its heroine's limited future, Edith Wharton's short novel Summer *(1917) illustrates many of the gifts that have won Wharton a secure place in American literature. Wharton's life (1862–1937) spanned a transitional period in American history; she recorded the decline of Victorian values, the disappearance of old New York society, the effects of World War I, and the jarring contrasts of American and European cultural assumptions. Although she is perhaps best known for her short tragic novel* Ethan Frome *(1911), many readers have their own*

Wharton favorites, such as The House of Mirth *(1905);* The Custom of the Country *(1913);* The Age of Innocence *(1920 Pulitzer Prize); or* Hudson River Bracketed *(1929).*

The following excerpt contains the opening pages of Summer, *the story of Charity Royall, an uneducated but passionate young woman who grows up in an isolated and narrow-minded New England village.*

A girl came out of lawyer Royall's house, at the end of the one street of North Dormer, and stood on the doorstep.

It was the beginning of a June afternoon. The springlike transparent sky shed a rain of silver sunshine on the roofs of the village, and on the pastures and larchwoods surrounding it. A little wind moved among the round white clouds on the shoulders of the hills, driving their shadows across the fields and down the grassy road that takes the name of street when it passes through North Dormer. The place lies high and in the open, and lacks the lavish shade of the more protected New England villages. The clump of weeping-willows about the duck pond, and the Norway spruces in front of the Hatchard gate, cast almost the only roadside shadow between lawyer Royall's house and the point where, at the other end of the village, the road rises above the church and skirts the black hemlock wall enclosing the cemetery.

The little June wind, frisking down the street, shook the doleful fringes of the Hatchard spruces, caught the straw hat of a young man just passing under them, and spun it clean across the road into the duck-pond.

As he ran to fish it out the girl on lawyer Royall's doorstep noticed that he was a stranger, that he wore city clothes, and that he was laughing with all his teeth, as the young and careless laugh at such mishaps.

Her heart contracted a little, and the shrinking that sometimes came over her when she saw people with holiday faces made her draw back into the house and pretend to look for the key that she knew she had already put into her pocket. A narrow greenish mirror with a gilt eagle over it hung on the passage wall, and she looked critically at her reflection, wished for the thousandth time that she had blue eyes like

Annabel Balch, the girl who sometimes came from Springfield to spend a week with old Miss Hatchard, straightened the sunburnt hat over her small swarthy face, and turned out again into the sunshine.

"How I hate everything!" she murmured.

The young man had passed through the Hatchard gate, and she had the street to herself. North Dormer is at all times an empty place, and at three o'clock on a June afternoon its few able-bodied men are off in the fields or woods, and the women indoors, engaged in languid household drudgery.

The girl walked along, swinging her key on a finger, and looking about her with the heightened attention produced by the presence of a stranger in a familiar place. What, she wondered, did North Dormer look like to people from other parts of the world? She herself had lived there since the age of five, and had long supposed it to be a place of some importance. But about a year before, Mr. Miles, the new Episcopal clergyman at Hepburn, who drove over every other Sunday—when the roads were not ploughed up by hauling—to hold a service in the North Dormer church, had proposed, in a fit of missionary zeal, to take the young people down to Nettleton to hear an illustrated lecture on the Holy Land; and the dozen girls and boys who represented the future of North Dormer had been piled into a farm-waggon, driven over the hills to Hepburn, put into a way-train and carried to Nettleton. In the course of that incredible day Charity Royall had, for the first and only time, experienced railway-travel, looked into shops with plate-glass fronts, tasted cocoanut pie, sat in a theatre, and listened to a gentleman saying unintelligible things before pictures that she would have enjoyed looking at if his explanations had not prevented her from understanding them. This initiation had shown her that North Dormer was a small place, and developed in her a thirst for information that her position as custodian of the village library had previously failed to excite. For a month or two she dipped feverishly and disconnectedly into the dusty volumes of the Hatchard Memorial Library; then the impression of Nettleton began to fade, and she found it easier to take North Dormer as the norm of the universe than to go on reading.

The sight of the stranger once more revived memories of Nettleton, and North Dormer shrank to its real size. As she looked up and down it, from lawyer Royall's faded red house at one end to the white church at the other, she pitilessly took its measure. There it lay, a weather-beaten sunburnt village of the hills, abandoned of men, left apart by railway, trolley, telegraph, and all the forces that link life to life in modern communities. It had no shops, no theatres, no lectures, no "business block"; only a church that was opened every other Sunday if the state of the roads permitted, and a library for which no new books had been bought for twenty years, and where the old ones mouldered undisturbed on the damp shelves. Yet Charity Royall had always been told that she ought to consider it a privilege that her lot had been cast in North Dormer. She knew that, compared to the place she had come from, North Dormer represented all the blessings of the most refined civilization. Everyone in the village had told her so ever since she had been brought there as a child. Even old Miss Hatchard had said to her, on a terrible occasion in her life: "My child, you must never cease to remember that it was Mr. Royall who brought you down from the Mountain."

She had been "brought down from the Mountain"; from the scarred cliff that lifted its sullen wall above the lesser slopes of Eagle Range, making a perpetual background of gloom to the lonely valley. The Mountain was a good fifteen miles away, but it rose so abruptly from the lower hills that it seemed almost to cast its shadow over North Dormer. And it was like a great magnet drawing the clouds and scattering them in storm across the valley. If ever, in the purest summer sky, there trailed a thread of vapour over North Dormer, it drifted to the Mountain as a ship drifts to a whirlpool, and was caught among the rocks, torn up and multiplied, to sweep back over the village in rain and darkness.

Charity was not very clear about the Mountain; but she knew it was a bad place, and a shame to have come from, and that, whatever befell her in North Dormer, she ought, as Miss Hatchard had once reminded her, to remember that she had been brought down from there, and hold her tongue and be thankful. She looked up at the Mountain, thinking of these things, and tried as usual to be thankful. But the sight of the young man turning in at Miss Hatchard's gate had brought back the vision of the glittering streets of Nettleton, and she felt ashamed of her old sun-hat, and sick of North Dormer, and jealously aware of Annabel Balch of Springfield, opening her blue eyes somewhere far off on glories greater than the glories of Nettleton.

"How I hate everything!" she said again.

Halfway down the street she stopped at a weak-hinged gate. Passing through it, she walked down a brick path to a queer little brick temple with white wooden columns supporting a pediment on which was inscribed in tarnished gold letters: "The Honorius Hatchard Memorial Library, 1832."

Honorius Hatchard had been old Miss Hatchard's great-uncle; though she would undoubtedly have reversed the phrase, and put forward, as her only claim to distinction, the fact that she was his great-niece. For Honorius Hatchard, in the early years of the nineteenth century, had enjoyed a modest celebrity. As the marble tablet in the interior of the library informed its infrequent visitors, he had possessed marked literary gifts, written a series of papers called "The Recluse of Eagle Range," enjoyed the acquaintance of Washington Irving and Fitz-Greene Halleck, and been cut off in his flower by a fever contracted in Italy. Such had been the sole link between North Dormer and literature, a link piously commemorated by the erection of the monument where Charity Royall, every Tuesday and Thursday afternoon, sat at her desk under a freckled steel engraving of the deceased author, and wondered if he felt any deader in his grave than she did in his library.

Entering her prison-house with a listless step she took off her hat, hung it on a plaster bust of Minerva, opened the shutters, leaned out to see if there were any eggs in the swallow's nest above one of the windows, and finally, seating herself behind the desk, drew out a roll of cotton lace and a steel crochet hook. She was not an expert work-woman, and it had taken her many weeks to make the half-yard of narrow lace which she kept wound about the buckram back of a dis-integrated copy of "The Lamplighter." But there was no other way of getting any lace to trim her summer blouse, and since Ally Hawes, the poorest girl in the village, had shown herself in church with enviable transparencies about the shoulders, Charity's hook had travelled faster. She unrolled the lace, dug the hook into a loop, and bent to the task with furrowed brows.

Suddenly the door opened, and before she had raised her eyes she knew that the young man she had seen going in at the Hatchard gate had entered the library.

Without taking any notice of her he began to move slowly about the long vault-like room, his hands behind his back, his short-sighted eyes peering up and down the rows of rusty bindings. At length he reached the desk and stood before her.

"Have you a card-catalogue?" he asked in a pleasant abrupt voice; and the oddness of the question caused her to drop her work.

"A *what?*"

"Why, you know——" He broke off, and she became conscious that he was looking at her for the first time, having apparently, on his entrance, included her in his general short-sighted survey as part of the furniture of the library.

The fact that, in discovering her, he lost the thread of his remark, did not escape her attention, and she looked down and smiled. He smiled also.

"No, I don't suppose you *do* know," he corrected himself. "In fact, it would be almost a pity——"

She thought she detected a slight condescension in his tone, and asked sharply: "Why?"

"Because it's so much pleasanter, in a small library like this, to poke about by one's self—with the help of the librarian."

He added the last phrase so respectfully that she was mollified, and rejoined with a sigh: "I'm afraid I can't help you much."

"Why?" he questioned in his turn; and she replied that there weren't many books anyhow, and that she'd hardly read any of them. "The worms are getting at them," she added gloomily.

"Are they? That's a pity, for I see there are some good ones." He seemed to have lost interest in their conversation, and strolled away again, apparently forgetting her. His indifference nettled her, and she picked up her work, resolved not to offer him the least assistance. Apparently he did not need it, for he spent a long time with his back to her, lifting down, one after another, the tall cobwebby volumes from a distant shelf.

"Oh, I say!" he exclaimed; and looking up she saw that he had drawn out his handkerchief and was carefully wiping the edges of the book in his hand. The action struck her as an unwarranted criticism on her care of the books, and she said irritably: "It's not my fault if they're dirty."

He turned around and looked at her with reviving interest. "Ah— then you're not the librarian?"

"Of course I am; but I can't dust all these books. Besides, nobody ever looks at them, now Miss Hatchard's too lame to come round."

"No, I suppose not." He laid down the book he had been wiping, and stood considering her in silence. She wondered if Miss Hatchard had sent him round to pry into the way the library was looked after, and the suspicion increased her resentment. "I saw you going into her house just now, didn't I?" she asked, with the New England avoidance of the proper name. She was determined to find out why he was poking about among her books.

"Miss Hatchard's house? Yes—she's my cousin and I'm staying there," the young man answered; adding, as if to disarm a visible distrust: "My name is Harney—Lucius Harney. She may have spoken of me."

"No, she hasn't," said Charity, wishing she could have said: "Yes, she has."

"Oh, well—" said Miss Hatchard's cousin with a laugh; and after another pause, during which it occurred to Charity that her answer had not been encouraging, he remarked: "You don't seem strong on architecture."

Her bewilderment was complete: the more she wished to appear to understand him the more unintelligible his remarks became. He reminded her of the gentleman who had "explained" the pictures at Nettleton, and the weight of her ignorance settled down on her again like a pall.

"I mean, I can't see that you have any books on the old houses about here. I suppose, for that matter, this part of the country hasn't been much explored. They all go on doing Plymouth and Salem. So stupid. My cousin's house, now, is remarkable. This place must have had a past—it must have been more of a place once." He stopped short, with the blush of a shy man who overhears himself, and fears he has been voluble. "I'm an architect, you see, and I'm hunting up old houses in these parts."

She stared. "Old houses? Everything's old in North Dormer, isn't it? The folks are, anyhow."

He laughed, and wandered away again.

"Haven't you any kind of a history of the place? I think there was one written about 1840: a book or pamphlet about its first settlement," he presently said from the farther end of the room.

She pressed her crochet hook against her lip and pondered. There was such a work, she knew: "North Dormer and the Early Townships of Eagle County." She had a special grudge against it because it was a limp weakly book that was always either falling off the shelf or slipping back and disappearing if one squeezed it in between sustaining volumes. She remembered, the last time she had picked it up, wondering how anyone could have taken the trouble to write a book about North Dormer and its neighbours: Dormer, Hamblin, Creston and Creston River. She knew them all, mere lost clusters of houses in the folds of the desolate ridges: Dormer, where North Dormer went for its apples; Creston River, where there used to be a papermill, and its grey walls stood decaying by the stream; and Hamblin, where the first snow always fell. Such were their titles to fame.

She got up and began to move about vaguely before the shelves. But she had no idea where she had last put the book, and something told her that it was going to play her its usual trick and remain invisible. It was not one of her lucky days.

"I guess it's somewhere," she said, to prove her zeal; but she spoke without conviction, and felt that her words conveyed none.

"Oh, well——" he said again. She knew he was going, and wished more than ever to find the book.

"It will be for next time," he added; and picking up the volume he had laid on the desk he handed it to her. "By the way, a little air and sun would do this good; it's rather valuable."

He gave her a nod and smile, and passed out.

The hours of the Hatchard Memorial librarian were from three to five; and Charity Royall's sense of duty usually kept her at her desk until nearly half-past four.

But she had never perceived that any practical advantage thereby accrued either to North Dormer or to herself; and she had no scruple in decreeing, when it suited her, that the library should close an hour earlier. A few minutes after Mr. Harney's departure she formed this decision, put away her lace, fastened the shutters, and turned the key in the door of the temple of knowledge.

The street upon which she emerged was still empty: and after glancing up and down it she began to walk toward her house. But instead of entering she passed on, turned into a field-path and mounted to a pasture on the hillside. She let down the bars of the gate, followed a trail along the crumbling wall of the pasture, and walked on till she reached a knoll where a clump of larches shook out their fresh tassels to the wind. There she lay down on the slope, tossed off her hat and hid her face in the grass.

She was blind and insensible to many things, and dimly knew it; but to all that was light and air, perfume and colour, every drop of blood in her responded. She loved the roughness of the dry mountain grass under her palms, the smell of the thyme into which she crushed her face, the fingering of the wind in her hair and through her cotton blouse, and the creak of the larches as they swayed to it.

She often climbed up the hill and lay there alone for the mere pleasure of feeling the wind and of rubbing her cheeks in the grass. Generally at such times she did not think of anything, but lay immersed in an inarticulate well-being. Today the sense of well-being was intensified by her joy at escaping from the library. She liked well enough to have a friend drop in and talk to her when she was on duty, but she hated to be bothered about books. How could she remember where they were, when they were so seldom asked for? Orma Fry occasionally took out a novel, and her brother Ben was fond of what he called "jography," and of books relating to trade and bookkeeping; but no one else asked for anything except, at intervals, "Uncle Tom's Cabin," or "Opening a Chestnut Burr," or Longfellow. She had these under her hand, and could have found them in the dark; but unexpected demands came so rarely that they exasperated her like an injustice. . . .

She had liked the young man's looks, and his short-sighted eyes, and his odd way of speaking, that was abrupt yet soft, just as his hands were sunburnt and sinewy, yet with smooth nails like a woman's. His hair was sunburnt-looking, too, or rather the colour of bracken after frost; his eyes grey, with the appealing look of the shortsighted, his smile shy yet confident, as if he knew lots of things she had never dreamed of, and yet wouldn't for the world have had her feel his superiority. But she did feel it, and liked the feeling; for it was new to her. Poor and ignorant as she was, and knew herself to be—humblest of the humble even in North Dormer, where to come from the Mountain was the worst disgrace—yet in her narrow world she had always ruled. It was partly, of course, owing to the fact that lawyer Royall was "the biggest man in North Dormer"; so much too big for it, in fact, that outsiders, who didn't know, always wondered how it held him. In spite of everything—and in spite even of Miss Hatchard—lawyer Royall ruled in North Dormer; and Charity ruled in lawyer Royall's house. She had never put it to herself in those terms; but she knew her power, knew what it was made of, and hated it. Confusedly, the young man in the library had made her feel for the first time what might be the sweetness of dependence. . . .

The next day, when Mr. Royall came back to dinner, they faced each other in silence as usual. Verena's presence at the table was an excuse for their not talking, though her deafness would have permitted the freest interchange of confidences. But when the meal was over, and Mr. Royall rose from the table, he looked back at Charity, who had stayed to help the old woman clear away the dishes.

"I want to speak to you a minute," he said; and she followed him across the passage, wondering.

He seated himself in his black horse-hair armchair, and she leaned against the window, indifferently. She was impatient to be gone to the library, to hunt for the book on North Dormer.

"See here," he said, "why ain't you at the library the days you're supposed to be there?"

The question, breaking in on her mood of blissful abstraction, deprived her of speech, and she stared at him for a moment without answering.

"Who says I ain't?"

"There's been some complaints made, it appears. Miss Hatchard sent for me this morning—"

Charity's smouldering resentment broke into a blaze. "I know! Orma Fry, and that toad of a Targatt girl—and Ben Fry, like as not. He's going round with her. The low-down sneaks—I always knew they'd try to have me out! As if anybody ever came to the library, anyhow!"

"Somebody did yesterday, and you weren't there."

"Yesterday?" she laughed at her happy recollection. "At what time wasn't I there yesterday, I'd like to know?"

"Round about four o'clock."

Charity was silent. She had been so steeped in the dreamy remembrance of young Harney's visit that she had forgotten having deserted her post as soon as he had left the library.

"Who came at four o'clock?"

"Miss Hatchard did."

"Miss Hatchard? Why, she ain't ever been near the place since she's been lame. She couldn't get up the steps if she tried."

"She can be helped up, I guess. She was yesterday, anyhow, by the young fellow that's staying with her. He found you there, I understand, earlier in the afternoon; and he went back and told Miss Hatchard the books were in bad shape and needed attending to. She got excited, and had herself wheeled straight round; and when she got there the place was locked. So she sent for me, and told me about that, and about the other complaints. She claims you've neglected things, and that she's going to get a trained librarian."

Charity had not moved while he spoke. She stood with her head thrown back against the window-frame, her arms hanging against her sides, and her hands so tightly clenched that she felt, without knowing what hurt her, the sharp edge of her nails against her palms.

Of all Mr. Royall had said she had retained only the phrase: "He told Miss Hatchard the books were in bad shape." What did she care for the other charges against her? Malice or truth, she despised them as she despised her detractors. But that the stranger to whom she had felt herself so mysteriously drawn should have betrayed her! That at the very moment when she had fled up the hillside to think of him more deliciously he should have been hastening home to denounce her shortcomings! She remembered how, in the darkness of her room, she had covered her face to press his imagined kiss closer; and her heart raged against him for the liberty he had not taken.

"Well, I'll go," she said suddenly. "I'll go right off."

"Go where?" She heard the startled note in Mr. Royall's voice.

"Why, out of their old library: straight out, and never set foot in it again. They needn't think I'm going to wait round and let them say they've discharged me!"

"Charity—Charity Royall, you listen—" he began, getting heavily out of his chair; but she waved him aside, and walked out of the room.

Upstairs she took the library key from the place where she always hid it under her pincushion—who said she wasn't careful?—put on her hat, and swept down again and out into the street. If Mr. Royall heard her go he made no motion to detain her: his sudden rages probably made him understand the uselessness of reasoning with hers.

She reached the brick temple, unlocked the door and entered into the glacial twilight. "I'm glad I'll never have to sit in this old vault again when other folks are out in the sun!" she said aloud as the familiar chill took her. She looked with abhorrence at the long dingy rows of books, the sheep-nosed Minerva on her black pedestal, and the mild-faced young man in a high stock whose effigy pined above her desk. She meant to take out of the drawer her roll of lace and the library register, and go straight to Miss Hatchard to announce her resignation. But suddenly a great desolation overcame her, and she sat down and laid her face against the desk. Her heart was ravaged by life's cruellest discovery: the first creature who had come toward her out of the wilderness had brought her anguish instead of joy. She did not cry; tears came hard to her, and the storms of her heart spent themselves inwardly. But as she sat there in her dumb woe she felt her life to be too desolate, too ugly and intolerable.

"What have I ever done to it, that it should hurt me so?" she groaned, and pressed her fists against her lids. which were beginning to swell with weeping.

"I won't—I won't go there looking like a horror!" she muttered, springing up and pushing back her hair as if it stifled her. She opened the drawer, dragged out the register, and turned toward the door. As she did so it opened, and the young man from Miss Hatchard's came in whistling.

He stopped and lifted his hat with a shy smile. "I beg your pardon," he said. "I thought there was no one here."

Charity stood before him, barring his way. "You can't come in. The library ain't open to the public Wednesdays."

"I know it's not; but my cousin gave me her key."

"Miss Hatchard's got no right to give her key to other folks, any more'n I have. I'm the librarian and I know the by-laws. This is my library."

The young man looked profoundly surprised.

"Why, I know it is; I'm so sorry if you mind my coming."

"I suppose you came to see what more you could say to set her against me? But you needn't trouble: it's my library today, but it won't be this time tomorrow. I'm on the way now to take her back the key and the register."

Young Harney's face grew grave, but without betraying the consciousness of guilt she had looked for.

"I don't understand," he said. "There must be some mistake. Why should I say things against you to Miss Hatchard—or to anyone?"

The apparent evasiveness of the reply caused Charity's indignation to overflow. "I don't know why you should. I could understand Orma Fry's doing it, because she's always wanted to get me out of here ever since the first day. I can't see why, when she's got her own home, and her father to work for her; nor Ida Targatt, neither, when she got a legacy from her step-brother on'y last year. But anyway we all live in the same place, and when it's a place like North Dormer it's enough to make people hate each other just to have to walk down the same street every day. But you don't live here, and you don't know anything about any of us, so what did you have to meddle for? Do you suppose the other girls'd have kept the books any better'n I did? Why, Orma Fry don't hardly know a book from a flat-iron! And what if I don't always sit round here doing nothing till it strikes five up at the church? Who cares if the library's open or shut? Do you suppose anybody ever comes here for books? What they'd like to come for is to meet the fellows they're going with—if I'd let 'em. But I wouldn't let Bill Sollas from over the hill hang round here waiting for the youngest Targatt girl, because I know him . . . that's all . . . even if I don't know about books all I ought to. . . ."

She stopped with a choking in her throat. Tremors of rage were running through her, and she steadied herself against the edge of the desk lest he should see her weakness.

What he saw seemed to affect him deeply, for he grew red under his sunburn, and stammered out: "But, Miss Royall, I assure you . . . I assure you . . ."

His distress inflamed her anger, and she regained her voice to fling back: "If I was you I'd have the nerve to stick to what I said!"

The taunt seemed to restore his presence of mind. "I hope I should if I knew; but I don't. Apparently something disagreeable has happened, for which you think I'm to blame. But I don't know what it is, because I've been up on Eagle Ridge ever since the early morning."

"I don't know where you've been this morning: but I know you were here in this library yesterday; and it was you that went home and told your cousin the books were in bad shape, and brought her round to see how I'd neglected them."

Young Harney looked sincerely concerned. "Was that what you were told? I don't wonder you're angry. The books *are* in bad shape, and as some are interesting it's a pity. I told Miss Hatchard they were suffering from dampness and lack of air; and I brought her here to show her how easily the place could be ventilated. I also told her you ought to have some one to help you do the dusting and airing. If you were given a wrong version of what I said I'm sorry; but I'm so fond of old books that I'd rather see them made into a bonfire than left to moulder away like these."

Charity felt her sobs rising and tried to stifle them in words. "I don't care what you say you told her. All I know is she thinks it's all my fault, and I'm going to lose my job, and I wanted it more'n anyone in the village, because I haven't got anybody belonging to me, the way other folks have. All I wanted was to put aside money enough to get away from here sometime. D'you suppose if it hadn't been for that I'd have kept on sitting day after day in this old vault?"

Of this appeal her hearer took up only the last question. "It *is* an old vault; but need it be? That's the point. And it's my putting the question to my cousin that seems to have been the cause of the trouble." His glance explored the melancholy penumbra of the long narrow room, resting on the blotched walls, the discoloured rows of books, and the stern rosewood desk surmounted by the portrait of the young Honorius. "Of course it's a bad job to do anything with a building jammed against a hill like this ridiculous mausoleum: you couldn't get a good draught through it without blowing a hole in the mountain. But it can be ventilated after a fashion, and the sun can be let in: I'll show you how if you like. . . ." The architect's passion for improvement had already made him lose sight of her grievance, and he lifted his stick instructively toward the cornice. But her silence seemed to tell him that she took no interest in the ventilation of the library, and turning back to her abruptly he held out both hands. "Look here—you don't mean what you said? You don't really think I'd do anything to hurt you?"

A new note in his voice disarmed her: no one had ever spoken to her in that tone.

"Oh, what *did* you do it for then?" she wailed. He had her hands in his, and she was feeling the smooth touch that she had imagined the day before on the hillside.

He pressed her hands lightly and let them go. "Why, to make things pleasanter for you here; and better for the books. I'm sorry if my cousin twisted around what I said. She's excitable, and she lives on trifles: I ought to have remembered that. Don't punish me by letting her think you take her seriously."

It was wonderful to hear him speak of Miss Hatchard as if she were a querulous baby: in spite of his shyness he had the air of power that the experience of cities probably gave. It was the fact of having lived in Nettleton that made lawyer Royall, in spite of his infirmities, the strongest man in North Dormer; and Charity was sure that this young man had lived in bigger places than Nettleton.

She felt that if she kept up her denunciatory tone he would secretly class her with Miss Hatchard; and the thought made her suddenly simple.

"It don't matter to Miss Hatchard how I take her. Mr. Royall says she's going to get a trained librarian; and I'd sooner resign than have the village say she sent me away."

"Naturally you would. But I'm sure she doesn't mean to send you away. At any rate, won't you give me the chance to find out first and let you know? It will be time enough to resign if I'm mistaken."

Her pride flamed into her cheeks at the suggestion of his intervening. "I don't want anybody should coax her to keep me if I don't suit."

He coloured too. "I give you my word I won't do that. Only wait till tomorrow, will you?" He looked straight into her eyes with his shy grey glance. "You can trust me, you know—you really can."

All the old frozen woes seemed to melt in her, and she murmured awkwardly, looking away from him: "Oh, I'll wait."

Excerpt from *Main Street* by Sinclair Lewis

Sinclair Lewis (1885–1951) was the first American author to win a Nobel Prize (1930) for distinction in world literature. Although he wrote several books after that, Lewis's great work was done early: Main Street (1920), from which an excerpt follows; Babbitt (1922); Arrowsmith (1925); and Dodsworth (1929). Lewis, who was born in Minnesota, wrote with acid humor about the hypocrisies and vagaries of Midwestern provincial life. The title character of Babbitt was so acutely drawn that the name has become a generic label for a crass and bourgeois American businessman. Likewise, Main Street is often mentioned as the quintessential description of the narrowness and materialism inherent in small towns. Into such a town, Carol Kennicott, a former librarian who marries the local doctor, tries to bring culture and enlightenment, with depressing results.

In a month Carol's ambition had clouded. Her hesitancy about becoming a teacher had returned. She was not, she worried, strong enough to endure the routine, and she could not picture herself standing before grinning children and pretending to be wise and decisive. But the desire for the creation of a beautiful town remained. When she encountered an item about small-town women's clubs or a photograph of a straggling Main Street, she was homesick for it, she felt robbed of her work.

It was the advice of the professor of English which led her to study professional library work in a Chicago school. Her imagination carved and colored the new plan. She saw herself persuading children to read charming fairy tales, helping young men to find books on mechanics, being ever so courteous to old men who were hunting for newspapers—the light of the library, an authority on books, invited to dinners with poets and explorers, reading a paper to an association of distinguished scholars.

The last faculty reception before commencement. In five days they would be in the cyclone of final examinations.

The house of the president had been massed with palms suggestive of polite undertaking parlors, and in the library, a ten-foot room with a globe and the portraits of Whittier and Martha Washington, the student orchestra was playing "Carmen" and "Madame Butterfly." Carol was dizzy with music and the emotions of parting. She saw the palms as a jungle, the pink-shaded electric globes as an opaline haze, and the eye-glassed faculty as Olympians. She was melancholy at sight of the mousey girls with whom she had "always intended to get acquainted," and the half dozen young men who were ready to fall in love with her.

But it was Stewart Snyder whom she encouraged. He was so much manlier than the others; he was an even warm brown, like his new ready-made suit with its padded shoulders. She sat with him, and with two cups of coffee and a chicken patty, upon a pile of presidential overshoes in the coat-closet under the stairs, and as the thin music seeped in, Stewart whispered:

"I can't stand it, this breaking up after four years! The happiest years of life."

She believed it. "Oh, I know! To think that in just a few days we'll be parting, and we'll never see some of the bunch again!"

"Carol, you got to listen to me! You always duck when I try to talk seriously to you, but you got to listen to me. I'm going to be a big lawyer, maybe a judge, and I need you, and I'd protect you—"

His arm slid behind her shoulders. The insinuating music drained her independence. She said mournfully, "Would you take care of me?" She touched his hand. It was warm, solid.

"You bet I would! We'd have, Lord, we'd have bully times in Yankton, where I'm going to settle—"

"But I want to do something with life."

"What's better than making a comfy home and bringing up some cute kids and knowing nice homey people?"

It was the immemorial male reply to the restless woman. Thus to the young Sappho spake the melon-venders; thus the captains to Zenobia; and in the damp cave over gnawed bones the hairy suitor thus protested to the woman advocate of matriarchy. In the dialect of Blodgett College but with the voice of Sappho was Carol's answer:

"Of course. I know. I suppose that's so. Honestly, I do love children. But there's lots of women that can do housework, but I—well, if you *have* got a college education, you ought to use it for the world."

"I know, but you can use it just as well in the home. And gee, Carol, just think of a bunch of us going out on an auto picnic some nice spring evening."

"Yes."

"And sleigh-riding in winter, and going fishing—"

Blarrrrrr! The orchestra had crashed into the "Soldiers' Chorus"; and she was protesting, "No! No! You're a dear, but I want to do things. I don't understand myself but I want—everything in the world! Maybe I can't sing or write, but I know I can be an influence in library work. Just suppose I encouraged some boy and he became a great artist! I will! I will do it! Stewart dear, I can't settle down to nothing but dish-washing!"

Two minutes later—two hectic minutes—they were disturbed by an embarrassed couple also seeking the idyllic seclusion of the overshoe-closet.

After graduation she never saw Stewart Snyder again. She wrote to him once a week—for one month.

A year Carol spent in Chicago. Her study of library-cataloguing, recording, books of reference, was easy and not too somniferous. She reveled in the Art Institute, in symphonies and violin recitals and chamber music, in the theater and classic dancing. She almost gave up library work to become one of the young women who dance in cheese-cloth in the moonlight. She was taken to a certified Studio Party, with beer, cigarettes, bobbed hair, and a Russian Jewess who sang the Internationale. It cannot be reported that Carol had anything significant to say to the Bohemians. She was awkward with them, and felt ignorant, and she was shocked by the free manners which she had for years desired. But she heard and remembered discussions of Freud, Romain Rolland, syndicalism, the Confédération Générale du Travail, feminism vs. haremism, Chinese lyrics, nationalization of mines, Christian Science, and fishing in Ontario.

She went home, and that was the beginning and end of her Bohemian life.

The second cousin of Carol's sister's husband lived in Winnetka, and once invited her out to Sunday dinner. She walked back through Wilmette and Evanston, discovered new forms of suburban architecture, and remembered her desire to recreate villages. She decided that she would give up library work and, by a miracle whose nature was not very clearly revealed to her, turn a prairie town into Georgian houses and Japanese bungalows.

The next day in library class she had to read a theme on the use of the *Cumulative Index*, and she was taken so seriously in the discussion that she put off her career of town-planning—and in the autumn she was in the public library of St. Paul.

Carol was not unhappy and she was not exhilarated, in the St. Paul Library. She slowly confessed that she was not visibly affecting lives. She did, at first, put into her contact with the patrons a willingness which should have moved worlds. But so few of these stolid worlds wanted to be moved. When she was in charge of the magazine room the readers did not ask for suggestions about elevated essays. They grunted, "Wanta find the *Leather Goods Gazette* for last February." When she was giving out books the principal query was, "Can you tell me of a good, light, exciting love story to read? My husband's going away for a week."

She was fond of the other librarians; proud of their aspirations. And by the chance of propinquity she read scores of books unnatural to her gay white littleness: volumes of anthropology with ditches of foot-notes filled with heaps of small dusty type, Parisian imagistes, Hindu recipes for curry, voyages to the Solomon Isles, theosophy with modern American improvements, treatises upon success in the real-estate business. She took walks, and was sensible about shoes and diet. And never did she feel that she was living.

She went to dances and suppers at the houses of college acquaintances. Sometimes she one-stepped demurely; sometimes, in dread of life's slipping past, she turned into a bacchanal, her tender eyes excited, her throat tense, as she slid down the room.

During her three years of library work several men showed diligent interest in her—the treasurer of a fur-manufacturing firm, a teacher, a newspaper reporter, and a petty railroad official. None of them made her more than pause in thought. For months no male emerged from the mass. Then, at the Marburys', she met Dr. Will Kennicott. . . .

[She marries Will and moves with him to Gopher Prairie, Minnesota, a small town she finds narrow-minded and suffocating. She tries to find evidence of cultural life in the library.]

"We haven't seen you at the library yet," Miss Villets reproved.

"I've wanted to run in so much but I've been getting settled and— I'll probably come in so often you'll get tired of me! I hear you have such a nice library."

"There are many who like it. We have two thousand more books than Wakamin."

"Isn't that fine. I'm sure you are largely responsible. I've had some experience, in St. Paul."

"So I have been informed. Not that I entirely approve of library methods in these large cities. So careless, letting tramps and all sorts of dirty persons practically sleep in the reading-rooms."

"I know, but the poor souls— Well, I'm sure you will agree with me in one thing: The chief task of a librarian is to get people to read."

"You feel so? My feeling, Mrs. Kennicott, and I am merely quoting the librarian of a very large college, is that the first duty of the *conscientious* librarian is to preserve the books."

"Oh!" Carol repented her "Oh." Miss Villets stiffened, and attacked:

"It may be all very well in cities, where they have unlimited funds, to let nasty children ruin books and just deliberately tear them up, and fresh young men take more books out than they are entitled to by the regulations, but I'm never going to permit it in this library!"

"What if some children are destructive? They learn to read. Books are cheaper than minds."

"Nothing is cheaper than the minds of some of these children that come in and bother me simply because their mothers don't keep them home where they belong. Some librarians may choose to be so wishy-washy and turn their libraries into nursing-homes and kindergartens, but as long as I'm in charge, the Gopher Prairie library is going to be quiet and decent, and the books well kept!"

Carol saw that the others were listening, waiting for her to be objectionable. She flinched before their dislike. She hastened to smile in agreement with Miss Villets, to glance publicly at her wrist-watch, to warble that it was "so late—have to hurry home—husband—such nice party—maybe you were right about maids, prejudiced because Bea so nice—such perfectly divine angel's-food. Mrs. Haydock must give me the recipe—good-by, such happy party—"

[Carol keeps trying. She decides to pay a visit to the library, even though Miss Villets' remarks have warned her about what she will find.]

In the afternoon she scampered to the public library.

The library was open three afternoons and four evenings a week. It was housed in an old dwelling, sufficient but unattractive. Carol caught herself picturing pleasanter reading rooms, chairs for children, an art collection, a librarian young enough to experiment.

She berated herself, "Stop this fever of reforming everything! I *will* be satisfied with the library! The city hall is enough for a beginning. And it's really an excellent library. It's—it isn't so bad. . . . Is it possible that I am to find dishonesties and stupidity in every human activity I encounter? In schools and business and government and everything? Is there never any contentment, never any rest?"

She shook her head as though she were shaking off water, and hastened into the library, a young, light, amiable presence, modest in unbuttoned fur coat, blue suit, fresh organdy collar, and tan boots roughened from scuffling snow. Miss Villets stared at her, and Carol purred, "I was so sorry not to see you at the Thanatopsis yesterday. Vida said you might come."

"Oh. You went to the Thanatopsis. Did you enjoy it?"

"So much. Such good papers on the poets." Carol lied resolutely. "But I did think they should have had you give one of the papers on poetry!"

"Well— Of course I'm not one of the bunch that seem to have the time to take and run the club, and if they prefer to have papers on literature by other ladies who have no literary training—after all, why should I complain? What am I but a city employee!"

"You're not! You're the one person that does—that does—oh, you do so much. Tell me, is there, uh— Who are the people who control the club?"

Miss Villets emphatically stamped a date in the front of "Frank on the Lower Mississippi" for a small flaxen boy, glowered at him as though she were stamping a warning on his brain, and sighed:

"I wouldn't put myself forward or criticize anyone for the world, and Vida is one of my best friends, and such a splendid teacher, and there is no one in town more advanced and interested in all movements, but I must say that no matter who the president or the committees are, Vida Sherwin seems to be behind them all the time, and though she is always telling me about what she is pleased to call my 'fine work in the library,' I notice that I'm not often called on for papers, though Mrs. Lyman Cass once volunteered and told me that she thought my paper on 'The Cathedrals of England' was the most interesting paper we had, the year we took up English and French travel and architecture. But— And of course Mrs. Mott and Mrs. Warren are very important in the club, as you might expect of the wives of the superintendent of schools and the Congregational pastor, and indeed they are both very cultured, but— No, you may regard me as entirely unimportant. I'm sure what I say doesn't matter a bit!"

"You're much too modest, and I'm going to tell Vida so, and, uh, I wonder if you can give me just a teeny bit of your time and show me where the magazine files are kept?"

She had won. She was profusely escorted to a room like a grand-mother's attic, where she discovered periodicals devoted to house-decoration and town-planning, with a six-year file of the *National Geo-graphic*. Miss Villets blessedly left her alone. Humming, fluttering pages with delighted fingers, Carol sat cross-legged on the floor, the magazines in heaps about her.

She found pictures of New England streets: the dignity of Falmouth, the charm of Concord, Stockbridge and Farmington and Hillhouse Avenue. The fairy-book suburb of Forest Hills on Long Island. Devonshire cottages and Essex manors and a Yorkshire High Street and Port Sunlight. The Arab village of Djeddah—an intricately chased jewel-box. A town in California which had changed itself from the barren brick fronts and slatternly frame sheds of a Main Street to a way which led the eye down a vista of arcades and gardens.

Assured that she was not quite mad in her belief that a small American town might be lovely, as well as useful in buying wheat and selling plows, she sat brooding, her thin fingers playing a tattoo on her cheeks. She saw in Gopher Prairie a Georgian city hall: warm brick walls with white shutters, a fanlight, a wide hall and curving stair. She saw it the common home and inspiration not only of the town but of the country about. It should contain the court-room (she couldn't get herself to put in a jail), public library, a collection of excellent prints, rest-room and model kitchen for farmwives, theater, lecture room, free community ballroom, farm-bureau, gymnasium. Forming about it and influenced by it, as medieval villages gathered about the castle, she saw a new Georgian town as graceful and beloved as Annapolis or that bowery Alexandria to which Washington rode.

All this the Thanatopsis Club was to accomplish with no difficulty whatever, since its several husbands were the controllers of business and politics. She was proud of herself for this practical view.

She had taken only half an hour to change a wire-fenced potato-plot into a walled rose-garden. She hurried out to apprize Mrs. Leonard Warren, as president of the Thanatopsis, of the miracle which had been worked. . . .

[Even joining the Library Board proves to be a dead end.]

She was unexpectedly appointed to the town library-board by Ole Jenson, the new mayor. The other members were Dr. Westlake, Lyman Cass, Julius Flickerbaugh the attorney, Guy Pollock, and Martin Mahoney, former livery-stable keeper and now owner of a garage. She was delighted. She went to the first meeting rather condescendingly, regarding herself as the only one besides Guy who knew anything about books or library methods. She was planning to revolutionize the whole system.

Her condescension was ruined and her humility wholesomely increased when she found the board, in the shabby room on the second floor of the house which had been converted into the library, not discussing the weather and longing to play checkers, but talking about books. She discovered that amiable old Dr. Westlake read everything in verse and "light fiction"; that Lyman Cass, the veal-faced, bristly-bearded owner of the mill, had tramped through Gibbon, Hume, Grote, Prescott, and the other thick historians; that he could repeat pages from them—and did. When Dr. Westlake whispered to her, "Yes, Lym is a very well-informed man, but he's modest about it," she felt uninformed and immodest, and scolded at herself that she had missed the human potentialities in this vast Gopher Prairie. When Dr. Westlake quoted the "Paradiso," "Don Quixote," "Wilhelm Meister," and the Koran, she reflected that no one she knew, not even her father, had read all four.

She came diffidently to the second meeting of the board. She did not plan to revolutionize anything. She hoped that the wise elders might be so tolerant as to listen to her suggestions about changing the shelving of the juveniles.

Yet after four sessions of the library-board she was where she had been before the first session. She had found that for all their pride in being reading men, Westlake and Cass and even Guy had no conception of making the library familiar to the whole town. They used it, they passed resolutions about it, and they left it as dead as Moses. Only the Henty books and the Elsie books and the latest optimisms by moral female novelists and virile clergymen were in general demand, and the board themselves were interested only in old, stilted volumes. They had no tenderness for the noisiness of youth discovering great literature.

If she was egotistic about her tiny learning, they were at least as much so regarding theirs. And for all their talk of the need of additional library-tax none of them was willing to risk censure by battling for it, though they now had so small a fund that, after paying for rent, heat, light, and Miss Villets's salary, they had only a hundred dollars a year for the purchase of books.

The Incident of the Seventeen Cents killed her none too enduring interest.

She had come to the board-meeting singing with a plan. She had made a list of thirty European novels of the past ten years, with twenty important books on psychology, education, and economics which the library lacked. She had made Kennicott promise to give fifteen dollars. If each of the board would contribute the same, they could have the books.

Lym Cass looked alarmed, scratched himself, and protested, "I think it would be a bad precedent for the board-members to contribute money—uh—not that I mind, but it wouldn't be fair—establish precedent. Gracious! They don't pay us a cent for our services! Certainly can't expect us to pay for the privilege of serving!"

Only Guy looked sympathetic, and he stroked the pine table and said nothing.

The rest of the meeting they gave to a bellicose investigation of the fact that there was seventeen cents less than there should be in the Fund. Miss Villets was summoned; she spent half an hour in explosively defending herself; the seventeen cents were gnawed over, penny by penny; and Carol, glancing at the carefully inscribed list which had been so lovely and exciting an hour before, was silent, and sorry for Miss Villets, and sorrier for herself.

She was reasonably regular in attendance till her two years were up and Vida Sherwin was appointed to the board in her place, but she did not try to be revolutionary. In the plodding course of her life there was nothing changed, and nothing new.

Excerpt from *Grand Opening* by Jon Hassler

Jon Hassler's reputation as a thoughtful, sharp-eyed and very readable novelist has grown steadily since the publication of Staggerford *(1977), a story centering on a Minnesota high-school English teacher. It was followed by* Simon's Night *(1979);* The Love Hunter *(1981);* Green Journey *(1985);* Grand Opening *(1987) and* North of Hope *(1990). In 1981 a critic wrote in* The New York Times Book Review, *"Jon Hassler is a writer good enough to restore your faith in fiction."*

Hassler, himself a former high school teacher who has also taught at several Minnesota colleges, writes with perceptive familiarity about his Minnesota characters and landscape. In the excerpt from Grand Opening *that follows, the Fosters have moved from Minneapolis to the small town of Plum, Minnesota, where they have bought one of the town's two grocery stores. Catherine Foster, a cultivated and sociable woman, finds the town almost as constricting and deadening as Carol Kennicott found Gopher Prairie, Minnesota, in Sinclair Lewis's* Main Street. *Catherine soon discovers that the town "library" is really a one-room private fiefdom, reflecting the constable's sister's hypochondriacal tastes.*

F acing her at the end of the hallway was a third door.

LIBRARY

Wipe Your Feet

It was locked. She retraced her steps and put her head in at the mayor's office.

"Excuse me."

The mayor, a gray-haired, gray-faced man in a starched shirt, raised his head from his bookwork, removed his glasses, and peered at her with ice-blue eyes.

"Will the library be open this afternoon?"

He shook his head.

"Tomorrow?"

"Saturday," he said, putting on his glasses and lowering his nose to his ledger.

As she backed into the hallway, chilled, the constable's door opened behind her and a tall, middle-aged man leaned out with a smile. "Hello, I'm the constable. Can I help you?" His back was severely bent—injury to the spine in World War One, according to Wallace. Offering Catherine his hand (knobby, arthritic knuckles, razor-nicked fingers) he said, "I'm Charles Heffernand, and you're the grocer's wife. My sister Melva pointed you out in church."

"Catherine Foster. And I'm also the grocer's partner."

"Are you interested in aeroplanes? Step in and take a gander at my Japanese Zero."

She went in. The upper half of his high-ceilinged office was thick with model airplanes hanging on strings. A long table was covered with blueprints and planes in various stages of construction. Taped to the walls were newspaper photos of planes and their pilots. On his desk she saw tiny bits of wood he had been shaving with a razor blade.

"Ever since Pearl Harbor I've been building Jap and German aeroplanes and setting them afire. Bombers, transports, fighters. It gives home-front morale a big boost. Here's my Zero. There's this rubber band attached to the propeller so it actually flies—see it here? When it's finished I'll put a notice in the paper and at the appointed time I'll take her up on the roof of the village hall and turn the propeller tight and set a match to the wing and let her go. She'll zip out over the street trailing smoke and flames and crash like the planes in the newsreels. You'll want to see it, Mrs. Foster. There's always a good crowd. I do it during noon hour so the school children don't have to miss it. Jack Sims from the *Plum Alert* always comes with his camera and puts the picture on the front page of the next issue. Last year a reporter came from Rochester and covered it for the *Post-Bulletin*."

Catherine made several appreciative remarks, then asked about the library.

"The library? You want to see the library? Here, I can let you in this way." He opened a door at the far end of his office. "Library's open only on Saturday from one till four, but I can let you have a look-see. Watch your step."

The library was a small, stuffy room with one window. Its holdings were a hundred books, a buffalo head, and a collection of janitorial supplies—brooms, dustpans, buckets of paint and detergent. A few books were laid out on a table beneath the buffalo head; the rest stood in two small bookcases flanking the window. Catherine recognized none of the titles on the table. The two she picked up, *The Blind Jurist* and *The One-Armed Apothecary*, were written by someone named Edward Hodge Fleet.

"Oh, oh," said the constable, hurrying to the window and pulling down the dark brown shade, "the janitor must have raised the shade. My sister Melva says books hate the sun."

"They hate dryness too," Catherine told him, imagining all the cracked spines in this airless room. "Why do you open only on Saturdays?"

"My sister Melva's librarian, and during the week she's telephone central. I take over the switchboard for her on Saturdays so she can open up the library, and on Sundays so she can sing in church. We've got the switchboard in our living room. It was our father who brought the telephone system to Plum back in the teens, and we've kept it in the family."

Crossing to the small bookcases beside the window, Catherine recalled the solo voice that emanated from the choir loft during High Mass, an off-key quaver which together with the croaks of the old priest made for an unholy mixture of sour sounds. Now that she thought about it, it was the same voice that said "Number please" when you picked up the phone. She asked, without much interest in the answer, "Who takes over as constable while you take over the switchboard?"

"Nobody. No need for it. Nothing much happening on weekends around here, or any other day either. Stray dog now and again. Or maybe somebody having a stroke and needing a ride to the Mayo Clinic."

She examined the titles in the bookcase on the left. The few she recognized were insipid romances of ten or fifteen years ago. The shelves on the right held the collected works of Edward Hodge Fleet. She drew out a volume and turned it over in her hands. "Who *is* this?"

"Ah, our pride and joy. We're one of the few libraries in Minnesota with a complete set of Edward Hodge Fleet. When we bought the twenty-fifth book his publisher awarded us that plaque." He pointed to a small copper plate hanging on the wall. "And this special bookcase to hold his books. He's an inspiration."

"I've never heard of him."

"That's because he's only now becoming known west of the Mississippi. Culture comes from the East, my sister Melva says, and it was Mayor Brask and his wife who brought the first Fleet books with them when they moved here from Chicago."

She examined the book. The embossed binding was elegant. The paper was cheap, the print coarse. She looked at the front matter. The Tisdale Press, Chicago. Dozens of titles by the same author, all suggesting physical impairment.

"A new volume is sent to us every three months and the Christmas volume is free. Last Christmas it was *The Hobbling Cobbler*. It's a particular favorite of the mayor's. Come with me, you'll want to meet the mayor."

"I think I've met him."

"He's a literary man, come with me."

She returned to the bookcase on the left, searching desperately for a name she knew—Hawthorne, Cather, Galsworthy—but there was none. She felt a little dizzy. The heat in the room was oppressive. She called to mind Wallace's smirk, which she now understood. Dropping the Fleet book on the table, she followed the constable out of the room.

The mayor, as before, raised his eyes reluctantly from his ledger and removed his glasses. He seemed no more pleased than last time. It occurred to Catherine that getting acquainted in Plum was like learning your way through a zoo—an odd new specimen at every turn, vertebrates like yourself but not the kind you can communicate with.

"Mrs. Foster, Mayor Brask," said the constable. "Mayor Brask, the new woman in town."

The mayor stood up from his padded leather chair. He was chunky, solidly packed, shorter than the constable by six or eight inches. "Will you be attending one of our fine churches?" were the first words out of his mouth. He was quite sure of her answer, but he liked to verify hearsay.

"Yes, we're Catholic."

Rotten luck, his expression seemed to say. He cleaned his glasses on his necktie. "How many others in your family, Mrs. Foster?"

"My husband, my son, and my father."

He was relieved when she stopped after three. Not quite enough to tip Plum's religious balance. Now the risky issue:

"Is your husband politically inclined, Mrs. Foster?"

"Not at all."

He nodded approvingly as he returned his glasses to his face, using both hands to hook the bows carefully over his ears.

"But I am," she added.

The mayor turned away, frowning. The constable, a peace-loving man, wished she had not said that. The mayor, he knew, was upset by the very idea of political-minded women. Whiling away long afternoons in the village hall, the mayor had often told the constable about his running for the school board in Chicago and being defeated by a woman. Political women were dangerous, and it was schools they usually tampered with. Besides being mayor, Harlan Brask was chairman, ex officio, of the five-member Plum school board, on which there were two Lutherans besides himself—a majority nearly offset by the influence of the superintendent, who was Catholic.

"The Fosters have taken over Kermit's Grocery," said the constable.

The mayor said, "I see," not admitting that on recent afternoons he had stood in Legget's Grocery across the street from Hank's Market and watched the Fosters at work. His friend Louie Legget, always one to put the worst face on things, cursed whatever fate had brought him this ambitious competitor, who was sure to drain off all the Catholic trade Legget had gained through Kermit's decline.

Because this too was obviously an unhappy topic, the constable shifted to books. "She's a reader, Harlan. I showed her our Fleet collection."

The mayor brightened, looking her over. "Pain is gripping, don't you think?"

"Gripping? Pain?"

"In books, I mean. Don't you like reading about pain?"

"No, not as a rule."

"Edward Hodge Fleet is a master of pain. There's pain in all his work. Sometimes even mutilation and dismemberment. And it's always followed by happiness."

"Yes," said the constable, "my sister Melva says Fleet's got the sequence correct. Pain comes first and happiness follows."

"Inspiring," said the mayor.

"You bet," said the constable. "His books have done wonders for the war effort nationwide."

There were noises from both men, upper respiratory noises of satisfaction as they recalled passages of pain and the happiness that followed.

Catherine excused herself, claiming to be needed at the store. The mayor said goodbye, and the constable accompanied her down the hall to the front door.

"Tell the men in your family that most likely I'll burn my Zero two weeks from Monday."

As she returned slowly to the store, her shoulders drooping in discouragement, Catherine advised herself to forget about finding friends and books in this outpost and concentrate instead on caring for her family and building up the market. She would be satisfied with Plum, she vowed, as long as her men were satisfied, and as long as Plum bought their groceries.

"Library Scene, Small Town, 1941" by John R. Nixon, Jr.

Born in Batesville, Virginia, John R. Nixon, Jr., has lived for many years in Virginia. His poetry has appeared in many magazines, including The New Yorker, Saturday Review, The New Republic, Commonweal, Arizona Quarterly, The Washingtonian, *and in* The Christian Science Monitor. *For sixteen years he edited* The Lyric. *Nixon has received the Bellamann Award for his poetry. "Library Scene, Small Town, 1941" originally appeared in* Mississippi Review.

She took in "La Corbeille," a lady's journal,
and the "Sylphe Des Salons."

Flaubert, it seemed, was not for teen-aged males.
Indeed, the gaunt librarian confided,
The book was one of several sordid tales

Recently found unsuitable for gentle
Library patrons; it had been withdrawn
From circulation. Now the proper mental

And moral stimulation for a lad
Could be derived from (here she searched the shelves)—
"By the way, Bovary's about a bad

Woman—here 'tis: The Americanization
of Edward Bok!" She never pointed out
That wholesome Mr. Bok had vended fashion

Pictures like those that urged poor Emma, sick
Of all dull things in her provincial world,
To Boulanger, Rouen, and arsenic.

"Hillsboro's Good Luck" by Dorothy Canfield Fisher

It is particularly fitting that a story by Dorothy Canfield Fisher (1879–1958) appears in this anthology, because the Book-of-the-Month Club, on whose editorial board she served, established in her memory annual awards to public libraries in small-town communities.

Although born in Kansas, Dorothy Canfield (the maiden name under which she wrote many novels) is also associated with Vermont, where she lived after 1907. Her earlier work, like The Bent Twig (1915), draws on Midwestern backgrounds; other works, including a collection of stories, Hillsboro People (1915), and a nonfiction work, Vermont Tradition (1953), focus on Vermont.

When the news of Hillsboro's good fortune swept along the highroad there was not a person in the other three villages of the valley who did not admit that Hillsboro' deserved it. Every one said that in this case Providence had rewarded true merit, Providence being represented by Mr. Josiah Camden, king of the Chicago wheat pit, whose carelessly bestowed bounty meant the happy termination of Hillsboro's long and arduous struggles.

The memory of man could not go back to the time when that town had not had a public library. It was the pride of the remote village, lost among the Green Mountains, that long before Carnegie ever left Scotland there had been a collection of books free to all in the wing of Deacon Bradlaugh's house. Then as now the feat was achieved by the united efforts of all inhabitants. They boasted that the town had never been taxed a cent to keep up the library, that not a person had contributed a single penny except of his own free will; and it was true that the public spirit of the village concentrated itself most harmoniously upon this favorite feature of their common life. Political strife might rage in the grocery stores, religious differences flame high in the vestibule of the church, and social distinctions embitter the Ladies' Club, but the library was a neutral ground where all parties met, united by a common and disinterested effort.

Like all disinterested and generous actions it brought its own reward. The great social event of the year, not only for Hillsboro', but for all the outlying country, was the annual "Entertainment for buying new books," as it was named on the handbills which were welcomed so eagerly by the snow-bound, monotony-ridden inhabitants of the Nec-ronsett Valley. It usually "ran" three nights so that every one could get there, the people from over Hemlock Mountain driving twenty miles. There was no theatre for forty miles, and many a dweller on the Hemlock slopes had never seen a nearer approach to one than the town hall of Hillsboro' on the great nights of the "Library Show."

As for Hillsboro' itself, the excitement of one effort was scarcely over before plans for the next year's were begun. Although the date was fixed by tradition on the three days after Candlemas (known as "Wood-chuck Day" in the valley), they had often decided what the affair should be and had begun rehearsals before the leaves had turned. There was no corner of the great world of dramatic art they had not explored, borne up to the loftiest regions of endeavor by their touchingly unworldly ignorance of their limitations. As often happens in such cases they believed so ingenuously in their own capacities that their faith wrought miracles.

Sometimes they gave a cantata, sometimes a nigger-minstrel show. The year the interior of the town hall was changed, they took advantage of the time before either the first or second floor was laid, and attempted and achieved an indoor circus. And the year that an orchestra conductor from Albany had to spend the winter in the mountains for his lungs, they presented *Il Trovatore*. Everybody sang, as a matter of course, and those whose best efforts in this direction brought them no glory had their innings the year it was decided to give a play.

They had done *East Lynne* and *Hamlet, Uncle Tom's Cabin* and *Macbeth*, and every once in a while the local literary man, who was also the undertaker, wrote a play based on local traditions. Of course they gave *The Village School* and *Memory's Garland*, and if you don't remember those delectable home-made entertainments, so much the worse for you. It is true that in the allegorical tableau at the end of *Memory's Garland*, the wreath, which was of large artificial roses, had been made of such generous proportions that when the Muses placed it on the head of slender Elnathan Pritchett, representing "The Poet," it slipped over his ears, down over his narrow shoulders, and sliding rapidly towards the floor was only caught by him in time to hold it in place upon his stomach. That happened only on the first night, of course. The other performances it was perfect, lodging on his ears with the greatest precision.

It must not be supposed, however, that the responsibilities of Hillsboro' for the library ended with the triumphant counting out of the money after the entertainment. This sum, the only actual cash ever handled by the committee, was exclusively devoted to the purchase of new books. It was the pride of the village that everything else was cared for without price, by their own enterprise, public spirit, and ingenuity. When the books had overflowed the wing of Deacon Bradlaugh's house, back in 1869, they were given free lodging in the rooms of the then newly established and flourishing Post of the G. A. R. In 1896 they burst from this chrysalis into the whole lower floor of the town hall, newly done over for the purpose. From their shelves here the books looked down benignly on church suppers and sociables, and even an occasional dance. It was the centre of village life, the big, low-ceilinged

room, its windows curtained with white muslin, its walls bright with
fresh paper and colored pictures, like any sitting-room in a village home.
The firewood was contributed, a load apiece, by the farmers of the
country about, and the oil for the lamps was the common gift of the
three grocery stores. There was no carpet, but bright-colored rag rugs
lay about on the bare floor, and it was a point of honor with the Ladies'
Aid Society of the church to keep these renewed.

The expense of a librarian's salary was obviated by the expedient of
having no librarian. The ladies of Hillsboro' took turns in presiding over
the librarian's table, each one's day coming about once in three weeks.
"Library Day" was as fixed an institution in Hillsboro' as "wash day,"
and there was not a busy housewife who did not look forward to the
long quiet morning spent in dusting and caring for the worn old books,
which were like the faces of friends to her, familiar from childhood.
The afternoon and evening were more animated, since the library had
become a sort of common meeting-ground. The big, cheerful, sunlighted
room full of grown-ups and children, talking together, even laughing
out loud at times, did not look like any sophisticated idea of a library,
for Hillsboro' was as benighted on the subject of the need for silence
in a reading-room as on all other up-to-date library theories. If you
were so weak-nerved and sickly that the noise kept you from reading,
you could take your book, go into Elzaphan Hall's room and shut the
door, or you could take your book and go home, but you could not
object to people being sociable.

Elzaphan Hall was the janitor, and the town's only pauper. He was
an old G. A. R. man who had come back from the war minus an arm
and a foot, and otherwise so shattered that steady work was impossible.
In order not to wound him by making him feel that he was dependent
on public charity, it had been at once settled that he should keep the
fire going in the library, scrub the floor, and keep the room clean in
return for his food and lodging. He "boarded round" like the schoolteacher, and slept in a little room off the library. In the course of years
he had grown pathetically and exasperatingly convinced of his own
importance, but he had been there so long that his dictatorial airs and
humors were regarded with the unsurprised tolerance granted to things
of long standing, and were forgiven in view of his devotion to the best
interests of the library, which took the place of a family to him.

As for the expenses of cataloguing, no one ever thought of such a thing. Catalogue the books? Why, as soon hang up a list of the family so that you wouldn't forget how many children you had; as soon draw a plan of the village so that people should not lose their way about. Everybody knew what and where the books were, as well as they knew what and where the fields on their farms were, or where the dishes were on the pantry shelves. The money from the entertainment was in hand by the middle of February; by April the new books, usually about a hundred in number, had arrived; and by June any wide-awake, intelligent resident of Hillsboro' would have been ashamed to confess that he did not know the location of every one.

The system of placing on the shelves was simplicity itself. Each year's new acquisitions were kept together, regardless of subject, and located by the name of the entertainment which had bought them. Thus, if you wished to consult a certain book on geology, in which subject the library was rich, owing to the scientific tastes of Squire Pritchett, you were told by the librarian for the day, as she looked up from her darning with a friendly smile, that it was in the "Uncle Tom's Cabin section." The Shakespeare set, honorably worn and dog's-eared, dated back to the unnamed mass coming from early days before things were so well systematized, and was said to be in the "Old Times section;" whereas Ibsen (for some of Hillsboro's young people go away to college) was bright and fresh in the "East Lynne section."

The books were a visible and sincere symbol of Hillsboro's past and present. The honest, unpretending people had bought the books they wished to read, and every one's taste was represented, even a few French legends and pious tales being present as a concession to the Roman Catholic element among the French Canadians. There was a great deal of E. P. Roe, there was all of Mrs. Southworth—is it possible that anywhere else in the world there is a complete collection of that lady's voluminous productions?—but beside them stood the Elizabethan dramatists and a translation of Dante. The men of the town, who after they were grown up did not care much for fiction, cast their votes for scientific treatises on agriculture, forestry, and the like; and there was an informal history club, consisting of the postmaster, the doctor, and the druggist, who bore down heavily on history books. The schoolteacher, the minister, and the priest had each, ex officio, the choice of ten books with nobody to object, and the children in school were allowed another ten with no advice from elders.

It would have made a scientific librarian faint, the Hillsboro' system, but the result was that not a book was bought which did not find readers eager to welcome it. A stranger would have turned dizzy trying to find his way about, but there are no strangers in Hillsboro'. The arrival even of a new French-Canadian lumberman is a subject of endless discussion.

It can be imagined, therefore, how electrified was the village by the apparition, on a bright June day, of an automobile creaking and wheezing its slow way to the old tavern. The irritated elderly gentleman who stepped out and began blaming the chauffeur for the delay, announced himself to Zadok Foster, the tavern-keeper, as Josiah Camden of Chicago, and was electrified in his turn by the calmness with which that mighty name was received.

During the two days he waited in Hillsboro' for the repair of his machine, he amused himself first by making sure of the incredible fact that nobody in the village had ever heard of him, and second by learning with an astounded and insatiable curiosity all the details of life in this forgotten corner of the mountains. It was newer and stranger to him than anything he had seen during his celebrated motor-car trip through the Soudan. He was stricken speechless by hearing that you could rent a whole house (of only five rooms, to be sure) and a garden for thirty-six dollars a year, and that the wealthiest man in the place was supposed to have inherited and accumulated the vast sum of ten thousand dollars. When he heard of the public library he inquired quickly how much it cost to run *that*! Mr. Camden knew from experience something about the cost of public libraries.

"Not a cent," said Zadok Foster proudly.

Mr. Camden came from Chicago and not from Missouri, but the involuntary exclamation of amazed incredulity which burst from his lips was, "Show *me*!"

So they showed him. The denizen of the great world entered the poor, low-ceilinged room, looked around at the dreadful chromos on the walls, at the cheap, darned muslin curtains, at the gaudy rag rugs, at the shabby, worn books in inextricable confusion on the shelves, and listened with gleaming eyes to the account given by the librarian for the day of the years of patient and uncomplaining struggles by which these poverty-stricken mountaineers had secured this meagre result. He struck one hand into the other with a clap. "It's a chance in a million!" he cried aloud.

When his momentous letter came back from Chicago, this was still the recurrent note, that nowadays it is so hard for a poor millionaire to find a deserving object for his gifts, that it is the rarest opportunity possible when he really with his own eyes can make sure of placing his money where it will carry on a work already begun in the right spirit. He spoke in such glowing terms of Hillsboro's pathetic endeavors to keep their poor little enterprise going, that Hillsboro', very unconscious indeed of being pathetic, was bewildered. He said that owing to the unusual conditions he would break the usual rules governing his benefactions and ask no guarantee from the town. He begged therefore to have the honor to announce that he had already dispatched an architect and a contractor to Hillsboro', who would look the ground over, and put up a thoroughly modern library building with no expense spared to make it complete in equipment; that he had already placed to the credit of the "Hillsboro' Camden Public Library" a sufficient sum to maintain in perpetuity a well-paid librarian, and to cover all expenses of fuel, lights, purchase of books, cataloguing, etc.; and that the Library School in Albany had already an order to select a perfectly well-balanced library of thirty thousand books to begin with.

Reason recoils from any attempt to portray the excitement of Hillsboro' after this letter arrived. To say that it was as if a gold mine had been discovered under the village green is the feeblest of metaphors. For an entire week the town went to bed at night tired out with exclaiming, woke in the morning sure it had dreamed it all, rushed with a common impulse to the post-office where the letter was posted on the wall, and fell to exclaiming again.

Then the architect and contractor arrived, and with the jealous instinct of New Englanders to hide emotions from outsiders, Hillsboro' drew back into its shell of sombre taciturnity, and acted, the contractor told the architect, as though they were in the habit of having libraries given them three times a week regularly.

The architect replied that these mountaineers were like Indians. You *couldn't* throw a shock into them that would make them loosen up any.

Indeed, this characterization seemed just enough, in view of the passive way in which Hillsboro' received what was done for it during the months which followed. It was the passivity of stupefaction, however, as one marvel after another was revealed to them. The first evening the architect sketched the plans of a picturesque building in the old Norse style, to match the romantic scenery of the lovely valley. The next morning he located it upon a knoll cooled by a steady breeze. The contractor made hasty inquiries about lumber, labor, and houses for his men, found that none of these essentials were at hand, decided to import everything from Albany; and by noon of the day after they arrived these two brisk young gentlemen had departed, leaving Hillsboro' still incredulous of its good fortune.

When they returned ten days later, however, they brought solid and visible proof in the shape of a train-load of building materials and a crowd of Italian laborers, who established themselves in a boarding-car on a side-track near the station.

"We are going," remarked the contractor to the architect, "to make the dirt fly."

"We will make things hum," answered the architect, "as they've never hummed before in this benighted spot."

And indeed, as up to this time they had never hummed at all, it is not surprising that Hillsboro' caught its breath as the work went forward like Aladdin's palace. The corner-stone was laid on the third of July, and on the first of October the building stood complete. By the first of November the books had come, already catalogued by the Library School and arranged in boxes so that they could be put at once upon the shelves; and the last details of the interior decoration were complete. The architect was in the most naïve ecstasy of admiration for his own taste. The outside was deliciously unhackneyed in design, the only reproduction of a Norwegian *Stave-Kirke* in America, he reported to Mr. Camden; and while that made the interior a little dark, the quaint wooden building was exquisitely in harmony with the landscape. As for the interior, it was a dream! The reading-room was like the most beautiful drawing-room, an education in itself, done in dark oak, with oriental rugs, mission furniture, and reproductions of old masters on the walls. Lace sash-curtains hung at the windows, covered by rich draperies in oriental design, which subdued the light to a delightful soberness. The lamps came from Tiffany's.

When the young-lady librarian arrived from Albany and approved enthusiastically of the stack-room and cataloguing, the architect's cup of satisfaction fairly ran over; and when he went away, leaving her installed in her handsome oak-finished office, he could hardly refrain from embracing her, so exactly the right touch did she add to the whole thing with her fresh white shirt-waist and pretty, business-like airs. There had been no ceremony of opening, because Mr. Camden was so absorbed in an exciting wheat deal that he could not think of coming East, and indeed the whole transaction had been almost blotted from his mind by a month's flurried, unsteady market. So one day in November the pretty librarian walked into her office, and the Hillsboro' Camden Public Library was open.

She was a very pretty librarian indeed, and she wore her tailor suits with an air which made the village girls look uneasily into their mirrors and made the village boys look after her as she passed. She was moreover as permeated with the missionary fervor instilled into her at the Library School as she was pretty, and she began at once to practice all the latest devices for automatically turning a benighted community into the latest thing in culture. When Mrs. Bradlaugh, wife of the deacon and president of the Ladies' Aid Society, was confined to the house with a cold, she sent over to the library, as was her wont in such cases, for some entertaining story to while away her tedious convalescence. Miss Martin sent back one of Henry James's novels, and was surprised that Mrs. Bradlaugh made no second attempt to use the library. When the little girls in school asked for the Elsie books, she answered with a glow of pride that the library did not possess one of those silly stories, and offered as substitute, *Greek Myths for Children*.

Squire Pritchett came, in a great hurry, one morning, and asked for his favorite condensed handbook of geology, in order to identify a stone. He was told that it was entirely out of date and very incomplete, and the library did not own it, and he was referred to the drawer in the card catalogue relating to geology. For a time his stubbed old fingers fumbled among the cards, with an ever-rising flood of baffled exasperation. How could he tell by looking at a strange name on a little piece of paper whether the book it represented would tell him about a stone out of his gravel-pit! Finally he appealed to the librarian, who proclaimed on all occasions her eagerness to help inquirers and she referred him to a handsome great Encyclopedia of Geology in forty-seven volumes. He wandered around hopelessly in this for about an hour, and in the end retreated unenlightened. Miss Martin tried to help him in his search, but, half-amused by his rustic ignorance, she asked him finally, with an air of gentle patience, "how, if he didn't know *any* of the scientific names, he expected to be able to look up a subject in an alphabetically arranged book?" Squire Pritchett never entered the library again. His son Elnathan might be caught by her airs and graces, he said rudely enough in the post-office, but he was "too old to be talked down to by a chit who didn't know granite from marble."

When the schoolboys asked for Nick Carter she gave them those classics, *The Rollo Books*; and to the French Canadians she gave, reasonably enough, the acknowledged masters of their language, Voltaire, Balzac, and Flaubert, till the horrified priest forbade from the pulpit any of his simple-minded flock to enter "that temple of sin, the public library." She had little classes in art criticism for the young ladies in town, explaining to them with sweet lucidity why the Botticellis and Rembrandts and Dürers were better than the chromos which still hung on the walls of the old library, now cold and deserted except for church suppers and sociables, which were never held in the new reading-room, the oriental rugs being much too fine to have doughnut crumbs and coffee spilled on them. After a time, however, the young ladies told her that they found themselves too busy getting the missionary barrels ready to continue absorbing information about Botticelli's rhythm and Dürer's line.

Miss Martin was not only pretty and competent, but she was firm of purpose, as was shown by her encounter with Elzaphan Hall who had domineered over two generations of amateur librarians. The old man had received strict orders to preserve silence in the reading-room when the librarian could not be there, and yet one day she returned from the stack-room to find the place in a most shocking state of confusion. Everybody was laughing, Elzaphan himself most of all, and they did not stop when she brought her severe young face among them. Elzaphan explained, waving his hand at a dark Rembrandt looking gloomily down upon them, that Elnathan Pritchett had said that if *he* had such a dirty face as that he'd *wash* it, if he had to go as far as from here to the Eagle Rock Spring to get the water! This seemed the dullest of bucolic wit to Miss Martin, and she chilled Elnathan to the marrow by her sad gaze of disappointment in him. Jennie Foster was very jealous of Miss Martin (as were all the girls in town), and she rejoiced openly in Elnathan's witticism, continuing to laugh at intervals after the rest of the room had cowered into silence under the librarian's eye.

Miss Martin took the old janitor aside and told him sternly that if such a thing happened again she would dismiss him; and when the old man, crazily trying to show his spirit, allowed a spelling-match to go on, full blast, right in library hours, she did dismiss him, drawing on the endless funds at her disposal to import a young Irishman from Albany, who was soon playing havoc with the pretty French-Canadian girls. Elzaphan Hall, stunned by the blow, fell into bad company and began to drink heavily, paying for his liquor by exceedingly comic and disrespectful imitations of Miss Martin's talks on art.

It was now about the middle of the winter, and the knoll which in June had been the centre of gratefully cool breezes was raked by piercing north winds which penetrated the picturesquely unplastered, wood-finished walls as though they had been paper. The steam-heating plant did not work very well, and the new janitor, seeing fewer and fewer people come to the reading-room, spent less and less time in struggling with the boilers, or in keeping the long path up the hill shoveled clear of snow. Miss Martin, positively frightened by the ferocity with which winter flings itself upon the high narrow valley, was helpless before the problem of the new conditions, and could think of nothing to do except to buy more fuel and yet more, and to beseech the elusive Celt, city-trained in plausible excuses for not doing his duty, to burn more wood. Once she remarked plaintively to Elnathan Pritchett, as she sat beside him at a church supper (for she made a great point of "mingling with the people"), that it seemed to her there must be something the *matter* with the wood in Hillsboro'.

Everybody within earshot laughed, and the saying was repeated the next day with shameless mirth as the best joke of the season. For the wood for the library had had a history distinctly discreditable and as distinctly ludicrous, at which Hillsboro' people laughed with a conscious lowering of their standards of honesty. The beginning had been an accident, but the long sequence was not. For the first time in the history of the library, the farmer who brought the first load of wood presented a bill for this service. He charged two dollars a cord on the scrawled memorandum, but Miss Martin mistook this figure for a seven, corrected his total with the kindest tolerance for his faulty arithmetic, and gave the countryman a check which reduced him for a time to a paralyzed silence. It was only on telling the first person he met outside the library, that the richness of a grown person knowing no more than that about the price of wood came over him, and the two screamed with laughter over the lady's beautifully formed figures on the dirty sheet of paper.

Miss Martin took the hesitating awkwardness of the next man presenting himself before her, not daring to ask the higher price and not willing to take the lower, for rustic bashfulness, and put him at his ease by saying airily, "Five cords? That makes thirty-five dollars. I always pay seven dollars a cord." After that, the procession of grinning men driving lumber-sleds towards the library became incessant. The minister attempted to remonstrate with the respectable men of his church for cheating a poor young lady, but they answered roughly that it wasn't her money but Camden's, who had tossed them the library as a man would toss a penny to a beggar, who had now quite forgotten about them, and, finally, who had made his money none too honestly.

Since he had become of so much importance to them they had looked up his successful career in the Chicago wheat pit, and, undazzled by the millions involved, had penetrated shrewdly to the significance of his operations. The record of his colossal and unpunished frauds had put to sleep, so far as he was concerned, their old minute honesty. It was considered the best of satires that the man who had fooled all the West should be fooled in his turn by a handful of forgotten mountaineers, that they should be fleecing him in little things as he had fleeced Chicago in great. There was, however, an element which frowned on this shifting of standards, and, before long, neighbors and old friends were divided into cliques, calling each other, respectively, cheats and hypocrites.

Hillsboro' was intolerably dull that winter because of the absence of the usual excitement over the entertainment, and in the stagnation all attention was directed to the new joke on the wheat king. It was turned over and over, forwards and back, and refurbished and made to do duty

again and again, after the fashion of rustic jokes. This one had the
additional advantage of lining the pockets of the perpetrators. They
egged one another on to fresh inventions and variations, until even the
children, not to be left out, began to have exploits of their own to tell.
The grocers raised the price of kerosene, groaning all the time at the
extortions of the oil trust, till the guileless guardian of Mr. Camden's
funds was paying fifty cents a gallon for it. The boys charged a quarter
for every bouquet of pine-boughs they brought to decorate the cold,
empty reading-room. The wash-woman charged five dollars for "doing-
up" the lace sash-curtains. As spring came on, and the damages wrought
by the winter winds must be repaired, the carpenters asked wages which
made the sellers of firewood tear their hair at wasted opportunities.
They might have raised the price per cord! The new janitor, hearing
the talk about town, demanded a raise in salary and threatened to leave
without warning if it were not granted.

It was on the fifth of June, a year to a day after the arrival of Mr.
Camden in his automobile, that Miss Martin yielded to this last extortion,
and her action made the day as memorable as that of the year before.
The janitor, carried away by his victory, celebrated his good fortune in
so many glasses of hard cider that he was finally carried home and
deposited limply on the veranda of his boarding-house. Here he slept
till the cold of dawn awoke him to a knowledge of his whereabouts,
so inverted and tipsy that he rose, staggered to the library, cursing the
intolerable length of these damn Vermont winters, and proceeded to
build a roaring fire on the floor of the reading-room. As the varnished
wood of the beautiful fittings took light like a well-constructed bonfire,
realization of his act came to him, and he ran down the valley road,
screaming and giving the alarm at the top of his lungs, and so passed
out of Hillsboro' forever.

The village looked out of its windows, saw the wooden building
blazing like a great torch, hurried on its clothes, and collected around
the fire. No effort was made to save the library. People stood around
in the chilly morning air, looking silently at the mountain of flame which
burned as though it would never stop. They thought of a great many
things in that silent hour as the sun rose over Hemlock Mountain, and
there were no smiles on their faces. They are ignorant and narrow

people in Hillsboro', but they have an inborn capacity unsparingly to look facts in the face.

When the last beam had fallen in with a crash to the blackened cellar-hole, Miss Martin, very pale and shaken, stepped bravely forward. "I know how terribly you must be feeling about this," she began in her carefully modulated voice, "but I want to assure you that I *know* Mr. Camden will rebuild the library for you if——"

She was interrupted by the chief man of the town, Squire Pritchett, who began speaking with a sort of bellow only heard before in exciting moments in town-meeting. "May I never live to see the day!" he shouted; and from all the tongue-tied villagers there rose a murmur of relief at having found a voice. They pressed about him closely and drank in his dry, curt announcement: "As selectman I shall write Mr. Camden, tell him of the fire, thank him for his kindness, and inform him that we don't want any more of it." Everybody nodded. "I don't know whether his money is what they call tainted or not, but there's one thing sure, it ain't done us any good." He passed his hand over his unshaven jaw with a rasping wipe and smiled grimly as he concluded, "I'm no hand to stir up law-breakin' and disorder, but I want to say right here that I'll never inform against any Hillsboro' man who keeps the next automobile out of town, if he has to take a axe to it!"

People laughed, and neighbors who had not spoken to one another since the quarrel over the price of wood, fell into murmured, approving talk.

Elnathan Pritchett, blushing and hesitating, twitched at his father's sleeve. "But father— Miss Martin— We're keeping her out of a position."

That young lady made one more effort to reach these impenetrable people. "I was about to resign," she said with dignity. "I am going to marry the assistant to the head of the Department of Bibliography at Albany."

The only answer to this imposing announcement was a giggle from Jennie Foster, to whose side Elnathan now fell back, silenced.

People began to move away in little knots, talking as they went. Elzaphan Hall stumped hastily down the street to the town hall, and was standing in the open door as the first group passed him.

"Here, Mis' Foster, you're forgittin' somethin'," he said roughly, with his old surly, dictatorial air. "This is your day to the library."

Mrs. Foster hesitated, laughing at the old man's manner. "It seems foolish, but I don't know why *not!*" she said. "Jennie, you run on over home and bring me a dusting-cloth and a broom for Elzaphan. The books must be in a *nawful* state!"

When Jennie came back, a knot of women stood before the door, talking to her mother and looking back at the smouldering ruins. The girl followed the direction of their eyes and of their thoughts. "I don't believe but what we can plant woodbine and things around it so that in a month's time you won't know there's been anything there!" she said hopefully.

"Bookworm," from *Blooming: A Small-Town Girlhood* by Susan Allen Toth

Susan Allen Toth was born in 1940 in Ames, Iowa, the setting for her first memoir, Blooming (1981), about growing up in a small town in the 1940s and 1950s. Ivy Days: Making My Way Out East (1984) carries the narrator through her years at Smith College and ends in the early 1960s. How To Prepare For Your High-School Reunion and Other Mid-life Musings (1988) is a collection of personal and autobiographical essays. Her latest book is A House of One's Own (1990, written with her husband, architect James Stageberg.

Ms. Toth, who is a professor of English at Macalester College in St. Paul, Minnesota, has published stories and essays in, among others, Harper's, Redbook,

Vogue, Self, Ms., The North American Review, The New York Times, and The Washington Post.

"I'll make you a deal," I said craftily to Jennifer. "If you'll go to the grocery store and dry cleaner's with me, I'll take you afterward to the library."

"But I don't want to go to the library, Mom," she said, waiting for a better offer. "You can't keep library books. You have to take them back. I don't think libraries are any fun."

Libraries not fun? I looked unbelievingly at Jennifer. How could a daughter of mine not want to go to the library? When I was pregnant, I had a hard time picturing myself as a mother, doing the things they all do, baking brownies, sewing Halloween costumes, concocting vaporizer tents. But I comforted myself with a vision of reading to my child, the two of us tucked up under a quilt, as I enthralled her with stories I had once loved, Babar, Millions of Cats, Make Way for Ducklings. Some soon-to-be mothers go out and buy Carter's Jamakins; my first purchase was a hard-bound copy of The Little Engine That Could. Alas, Jennifer never liked it. Babar bored her, and once through the Millions of Cats was enough. She did like some stories: Cinderella, Sleeping Beauty, Snow White, anything that ended with a beautiful maiden marrying a handsome prince. Unfortunately, I easily tired of all that happily-ever-after, not to mention the insipid heroines who could only faint and wait. I wanted to read to her instead about monsters, genies, flying horses, and bewitched frogs. They were the magical creatures who had lived, I thought, in the library of my childhood.

When I do take reluctant Jennifer to the library near us, we enter a shiny new building with a pop-art plastic sign outside. Inside it is brightly carpeted, well lit, hung with carefully lettered directions about where to find everything you need. This library is always busy, two or three people taking most of the room at the magazine table, others clustered at the almost-bare new-arrivals shelf, a short line waiting at the checkout counter. I am sure this pleases the library board. But I can see why Jennifer does not respond to the lure of this place and why she does not see it as a secret cave to which I have given her the key.

It is so unlike the library I remember. That was a marble sanctuary, ruled absolutely by a white-haired high priestess, whose initiates, also women, found themselves sworn to whispers and lifelong devotion. In the Ames Public Library we learned to worship the world of books. I gave myself to it so completely that I came to believe it had to correspond, if sometimes obliquely, to the world of *real life. Sisters ought to be loving and playful, like the March girls; nurses were selfless and devoted, like Sue Barton; dogs were nicer than people, like Lad of Sunnybank; unhappy children found rich protectors, as did Sara Crewe; somewhere around a corner anyone might stumble upon her own secret garden. I was convinced that every locked door would open to a magic password. Even today, when I see a certain kind of Oriental rug, I can feel a momentary belief that at night it flies. So when I enter a library, even a commonplace one, I still have a reassuring sense that it is going to tell me all I need to know.*

Whenever I hear the words *inner sanctum* I think of the Ames Public Library. It was a massive stone temple, with imposing front steps that spread on either side into two flat ledges, overhung by evergreens. Waiting for my mother to pick me up, I could sit almost hidden on the cool stone blocks, surveying passing cars with a removed superiority. Safely perched on my pedestal, surrounded by my stacks of new books, I always felt unusually serene, bolstered by the security of the library behind me and the anticipation of the books beside me. Even to the moment of leaving it, my visits to the library were high occasions.

Entering the Ames Public Library I could feel its compelling power immediately. Inside the front doors a split staircase climbed elaborately to the main entrance on the second floor, and trudging up the marble steps I was enveloped by the cavernous space. A chilly breeze always seemed to be blowing up my back. Few buildings in Ames had such grandeur; the only one that reminded me of the library was the college's Memorial Union, which had an entrance hall dedicated to the dead of World War I and inlaid with tablets of granite you weren't supposed to walk on. The library, and the Union Hall, seemed to be places where things lay precariously at rest, just below the surface, waiting to be summoned up again.

I always worried when I went to the library that I might have to go to the bathroom. That meant getting a key from the front desk and descending the staircase again, but turning this time down one more flight of steps into darkness. The locked toilets were in the basement, a storage area known to no one but the janitor and Miss Jepson, the head librarian. Shadows lurked everywhere down there, steps echoed noisily, the light switch was impossible to find. Once I felt the door and fumbled with the key, it didn't always turn right in the lock, and I often had to go back upstairs, embarrassed, to ask an annoyed librarian to come down and try. When the heavy door of the ladies' toilet finally swung shut after I got inside, I was afraid that it might lock itself again. As the day wound on, no one would hear my cries for help behind that wooden block, and night would find me alone and helpless in the dark bowels of the library. I tried to avoid all this by not going to the bathroom. Sometimes I had to cross my legs and pinch myself in the car in order to make it home safely.

But if I didn't have to go down to the basement, I was seldom as happy anywhere as I was at the library. It was a place in which you always knew exactly where you belonged. At the entrance stood a circular wooden enclosure, only entered by librarians, who flipped up a small wooden shelf. There all books were checked in and out. When you came in the door, the librarian on duty glanced up and mentally checked you in as well. Directly behind the librarians' sentry post was adult fiction, both on the main floor and on a dark mezzanine above. For a long time I wasn't allowed up there. To the left was the map, newspaper and periodical room, where I seldom ventured either. Grown-ups who worked downtown sometimes came and ate their lunches at the big tables there, surrounded by spread-out newspapers whose rustlings blended with the quiet sounds of munched lettuce. My world lay to the right.

The west wing of the library was divided into sections for Children and Juniors. At first I nested happily in the Children's Room, with its small round tables and equally small chairs. I liked knowing that adults looked ridiculous trying to squat on those chairs, though of course that was also why a few years later I was ready to escape to the Junior Room, which had adult-sized chairs that didn't make you feel as though you were a baby. Besides its coziness and small scale, the Children's Room held two of the most important places in the whole library. One was the curtained door to Miss Jepson's office, which you never entered unless you were going to have a Serious Talk with her. The other was a window, a three-sided display case at child's-eye level that held a changing miniature diorama. I always rushed to see it before I went anywhere else in the library. All children did. Usually it was a scene from a familiar book, like *Goldilocks* or *Rumpelstiltskin*, though sometimes I had to guess. Nobody I knew had miniatures like the library's tiny kettles, braided rugs, hand-knit doll aprons, and I could stand for fifteen minutes admiring the elaborate sets. It was like a small theatre with the actors all frozen into a single moment. Like a theatre, it had a small velvet curtain that was kept drawn when the scene was being changed. Its inner doors, or backstage, were entered from inside Miss Jepson's office, although she personally never had anything to do with the actual changing of displays. That, like most menial tasks, was left to Mrs. Erhard and her assistants.

The Children's collection was not a large one, and before long I roamed through it confidently. I gorged myself on books, lugging home piles as high as I could carry, sometimes begging for Mrs. Erhard's permission because she was so sure I couldn't read them all in a week. But I could. At home I read before school, after school, with a book on my lap at dinner, and at night before I went to bed. I read with equal avidity about Horton hatching an egg and about East of the sun and West of the moon. I moved without pausing from Rabbit Hill to the tower of the Little Lame Prince. It was like having a box of assorted chocolates, all tempting, with unknown centers. I wanted to bite into each one right away to see what it was like.

About this time I first heard myself called a bookworm. One of the boys in my class saw me struggling off the city bus on a day when my mother hadn't been able to pick me up at the library. "Whaddya think ya are, a bookworm or something?" he said with a sneer. I had my chin on the top of my stack of books to keep them steady, so I couldn't open my mouth very far to respond. "I am NOT," I said defiantly, as the stack quivered. But I felt caught, labeled with something dirty and unpleasant. I didn't like worms. After that I looked around carefully when I was carrying a load of books, and if a friend was with me I made her carry part of mine. But not even the fear of being known as a bookworm could stop my reading.

As I looked ahead to the Junior Room, I could see that it held at least four times as many books as did Children's. I worried about how I was going to tackle such a task; I felt the order and serenity that emanated from the library dictated that I approach my reading in a suitably controlled way. So in third grade I decided to compile a min-iature card catalogue, like the library's, for each book I read. My mother bought me a pile of index cards and a small metal file box. Now I felt official, part of the library itself, as I sat down at a polished maple table and importantly spread out my stack of cards. On each card I noted author, title, and one or two sentences of plot summary so I could remember what I'd read. Then I created an elaborate series of abbre-viations, which today I can barely decipher, like "N.G." for "No Good," or "Exc." for "Excellent," as well as a series of numbers which must have been an attempt to compare each book with the others. I can no longer remember why *Caddie Woodlawn* might have been a "2," let alone "G," as opposed to *The Five Little Peppers*, which was "3" and "V.G." Soon I was spending more time making notes and inventing annotations than I was reading, a fact which Mrs. Erhard pointed out to me one day. She looked at a few of my cards and laughed. My feelings were hurt. I had thought of myself as preparing for a job like hers. Not long afterward I put the card catalogue away.

When I moved to the Junior Room, probably at the age of ten or eleven, I decided, like many omnivorous readers, to begin with the A's and read through to the Z's. I thought this was obviously the best way of making sure I didn't miss anything. Though three walls of this large room were lined with books, I didn't think it would be impossible to cover it all. The Ames Public Library did have a human scale to it. I might have done so, too, except I found somewhat to my surprise that I was developing tastes. I didn't really like books about horses. I wasn't very interested in boy detectives. I didn't want to read anything if the author was trying too hard to be educational. I was happy through the B's, where I found *Sue Barton, Rural Nurse; Sue Barton, Public Nurse*; and *Sue Barton, Superintendent of Nurses*; but after that I bogged down quickly. I skipped ahead to the L's, where I had discovered Maud Hart Lovelace's sequential adventures of Betsy, Tacy, and Tib, and promised myself I would someday return to the C's. But I never did.

When I abandoned my plan of methodically reading everything in the library, I was stimulated by new freedom of choice. I began to explore the nonfiction sections, which had never interested me before, and gradually I realized that within the walls of the Ames Public Library could probably be found the answers to any questions I would ever have. All my problems could be solved if I could only find the right book. At twelve, when *The Teen-Agers' Complete Guide to Beauty* fell into my hands, I thought I had found just such an authority. It was written, its cover assured me, by a successful New York teen-age model named Barbie Betts, whose unfamiliar face and name didn't deter me from believing every word she had to say. I checked out her book and renewed it twice, until Mrs. Erhard said I would have to ask Miss Jepson to change the rules if I wanted to renew it again. Then I reluctantly released it back to the shelves.

My mother hated *The Teen-Agers' Complete Guide to Beauty*. It upset our home for weeks. I fervently believed that if I followed all its instructions, I would be transformed into the girl of my dreams, thin, graceful, well dressed and well groomed. Barbie Betts felt especially strongly about the importance of good grooming, a phrase I had previously connected only with horses. She suggested that I make my evening bath a beauty routine, buy a pumice stone for the rough skin on my elbows, soak my cuticles in olive oil, powder carefully between my toes. Although my mother muttered loudly that she couldn't see anything wrong with the way I looked, I disappeared each night for an hour into the bathroom with a tray of beauty aids and soaked, scrubbed, powdered. I got wrinkles from staying so long in the water and the places I scrubbed turned very pink, but I didn't look different at all. Nobody ever stopped to admire my cuticles or tell me how nice my elbows felt. I eventually gave up and only continued halfheartedly to brush my hair one hundred strokes a night.

Then I turned my full attention to the problem of being well dressed. Barbie Betts said that the key to a successful wardrobe was not money but organization. I tried to follow her directions about sorting my clothes, coordinating them into interchangeable outfits, and then color-coding each outfit with markers in the closet. This took days of heaped clothes on the floor, disastrous experiments with colored paper glued to hangers, and hours of frustrated weeping when I discovered I lacked several crucial essentials of the master plan, like a wide black leather belt and a white wool skirt, which my mother said we couldn't afford. Near despair, I thought perhaps I could transform my environment even if

I myself remained a lump of raw material. I studied intently Barbie Betts's pictures of model bedrooms, which were frilly and feminine, and asked my mother if we could at least buy a headboard and make a canopy. She sighed. I wept again. I gradually realized that I could never carry out Barbie Betts's full-scale plans, and I was convinced halfway measures wouldn't work. I was doomed to a life of unmatched sweaters and tufted chenille bedspreads.

But when my dream of beauty failed, I retreated, as always, to other dreams. The Ames Public Library had an unending supply of them. I was too old by now for *The Blue Fairy Book* and *The Green Fairy Book*, but for solace I soon found Elizabeth Goudge. For at least a year I wandered blissfully through English cathedral towns and country inns, where I met benevolent grandfathers with spiritual secrets and freckled fun-loving boys who grew up into gentle sweethearts. If only I had lived a hundred years ago in England, I thought, how satisfying life would have been.

As I moved toward high school, I began to consider what I was going to be when I grew up, a question I felt it was time I took seriously. Despite my attraction to Sue Barton, I doubted whether I would make a good nurse. The only one I knew in real life was at school, a cross-faced tough-jawed woman who didn't believe you were sick unless you threw up copiously in the hall. Then she grumbled, took your temperature, and sent you home. I would have to be pretty lucky to escape that kind of life and find one like Sue Barton's, who married her Doctor Bill in the end. For a long while I thought I could be a foreign correspondent, since I liked to write and loved the idea of travel, but the career guides I began to read assiduously all seemed discouraging about a woman's chances as a reporter. My inevitable choice was the career I had been nurturing in my bones since my first trip up those marble steps. I decided to become a librarian.

Although librarians didn't make much money, my career guides warned me, they had something else that appealed to me as much as constant proximity to all those books. They had power. Not many women in Ames visibly wielded that, but Miss Jepson did. Even her deputy, Mrs. Erhard, had a derived air of stern authority. Miss Jepson, whose white hair and wrinkled pink skin made her seem agelessly preserved, was a definite-minded woman whose tongue had an almost audible snap. Whenever she submitted a budget request to the Ames City Council, she was able to get almost everything she wanted. No one dared to argue long with Miss Jepson. She personally selected each book the library ordered and gave the impression that she had read them all first. No detail of the library's operation escaped her inspection; she knew it so well I thought for a long time she must live there, in a secret suite connecting to her office.

The most impressive symbol of Miss Jepson's power was her locked glass case. This was a small cabinet in her office where she kept books whose literary or scholarly worth was unquestioned but whose text or illustrations she deemed obscene. Only Miss Jepson had the key. If you wanted to read one of Those Books, you had to knock at Miss Jepson's curtained door, enter when you heard her gruff voice, and then sit down facing her to explain why you felt it necessary to check out that particular book. If your reasons were unsatisfactory, it stayed in the locked case.

If I ever wanted a book in that case, I don't remember what it was. But I did have several uncomfortable conversations in Miss Jepson's office. One was the culmination of my struggles with her deputy, Mrs. Erhard, who had to enforce Miss Jepson's edicts. The rule that got me into trouble was the strict age limitation placed upon moving from the Junior to the Adult collection. Although sometimes Mrs. Erhard might stretch a year or two to let a child take something from Juniors', she was not going to yield so much as a month when it came to Adults'. I think the dividing line for Adults' was entrance into the downtown high school; whatever it was, it came too late for me. I was impatient to be exploring the stacks of novels on the mezzanine long before Mrs. Erhard thought I should. We would stand at the checkout desk and argue over my confiscated books, as I pointed out that my mother let me read everything in her library at home. Mrs. Erhard said what my mother did at home was her business, but in the Ames Public Library I was not yet an adult and could not check out adult books. Besides, she asked slyly, had I read every single book in the Junior section? I admitted I hadn't. With a triumphant smile, Mrs. Erhard lifted her wooden drawbridge and left. A few minutes later she was back, holding a small pile of Junior books. Had I read any of these? She could recommend them all highly.

I agreed ungraciously to try them. But I had no intention of giving in. Back home, I complained vehemently to my mother, until she agreed to call Miss Jepson for a little chat. Whatever my mother said must have worked. The next week Mrs. Erhard glared at me and told me to report to Miss Jepson's office. There Miss Jepson looked me up and down, asked me a few questions about books, impressed upon me the rarity of exceptions to the library's rules, and told me from now on I could check out three adult books a week.

After that I wandered freely among the adults, though I tried to choose checkout times when a student assistant was replacing Mrs. Erhard. I was afraid she might veto some of my choices. I remember trembling when I carried *The Empress of Byzantium* from its shelf to the desk, hoping Mrs. Erhard hadn't read it. I had already seen enough to know she wouldn't approve. *The Empress of Byzantium*, whose author I had never heard of, should have been in Miss Jepson's locked case. I discovered it by accident, as I often uncovered marvels in the library, pulling down books because of their elegant gold lettering or well-worn bindings or unusual color. Adult fiction was particularly suited for this kind of browsing, since the mezzanine had narrow aisles just wide enough to brace your back against one shelf while you sat on the rubber-tiled floor and ruffled through the books opposite. Whatever first attracted me to *The Empress of Byzantium* soon fled my mind when I saw what the book held inside: sex, sadism, and a graphic style that left little to my active imagination. I remember nothing about the plot, but I do recall one particular scene that galvanized me. The heroine, who had recently given birth, was in bed with her husband. He resented the child, I think, and they had some kind of argument followed by what I could dimly recognize as lovemaking. He grabbed her, began to nibble on her nipples until little drops of milk leaked out, and sucked until she managed to push him away. She was shocked; so was I. I couldn't remember seeing anyone breastfeed a baby, but I thought husbands were probably repelled by it. I read greedily through as much of the book as I could manage that afternoon, brought it home and hid it in my closet, and then carried it furtively back to the library the next week. I looked at Mrs. Erhard with a new respect. If she had read all the books in the adult section, she probably knew all about sex too.

Not only did librarians have access to all important knowledge, but in the Ames Public Library they had social power as well. It was not that either Miss Jepson or Mrs. Erhard attended coffee parties, played bridge, or belonged to the Country Club, but rather that they carefully used their ability to select student assistants. Miss Jepson's hand-picked band, chosen from high-school applicants after a long screening process culminating in an intensive interview behind her curtained door, were dedicated to becoming future librarians. They had to be serious, devoted, and of high moral character. The training they received from Miss Jepson and Mrs. Erhard was supposed to be the equivalent of a library degree; in return the student assistants had to agree to work a steady number of hours after school and weekends all through high school. Like dedicating yourself to a convent, you knew that to withdraw from this agreement after acceptance, and worse, after months of training, was to fail disgracefully.

When I was just beginning junior high school, I desperately admired Miss Jepson's student librarians. One of them was Shelley McNulty, the oldest daughter of one of the most respected families in town. Her dignified father served communion at our church, and her mother played golf regularly with the wife of the head of the Leichner Clinic. Shelley herself was gravely beautiful, with warm dark eyes and softly curling short hair. She was quiet, graceful, assured, all the things I had given up hope of being after abandoning Barbie Betts's optimistic teen-age program. Only the best boys were permitted to take her out, and she never went steady with any of them, not because they didn't ask her, but because her parents didn't approve. Everyone in high school knew how special she was; Shelley had already been Homecoming Queen and was an obvious shoo-in for Senior Sweetheart in her last year. If Shelley McNulty was going to be a librarian, I could hardly have aspired to any career more socially sanctioned.

As I grew older, however, and Shelley eventually moved on to college and away from the library, I found to my dismay that my dedication to her model began to waver. My future had seemed quite set. By the time I was in eighth grade, I had already had one serious talk with Miss Jepson about becoming an assistant when I was a sophomore. But as the time approached, although I still loved the library, I was no longer quite so sure that I could give up all my after-school hours and weekends. In ninth grade, I tried being a student helper in our school library, and I was disappointed. Although I enjoyed shelving books, finding the infinitesimally exact Dewey decimal numbers between which to sandwich each volume, noting with pride the tidiness of the arrangement when I had finished, I found that within a day all the books were messed up again. Other people kept taking them out. I had always thought of the library as a personal possession, and I wasn't altogether comfortable about sharing it. Since nobody asked me questions about where things were, I didn't get a chance to show off my superior knowledge either. Mainly I sat on a high stool behind the one-drawer card catalogue and guarded the checkout slips. It was against the rules to read while you were being a student helper. Not many kids wandered back to the library to talk, and none of them were boys. My volunteer hours became duller, and shorter.

When Miss Jepson called me into her office as a new sophomore, to check her list of promised disciples, I had to tell her that I was too busy. I said I wanted to work on the high-school newspaper, act in some plays, and attend all the out-of-town football games. As I faintly concluded this feeble list, Miss Jepson's eyes seemed to crackle and give off small sparks of light. "All I can say is that I'm disappointed in you, Susan," she said, her firm mouth tightening even more. "I hope you have made the right choice. You know your decision will close the door here to you permanently. I'm sorry because I think you would have been a fine librarian." I had no reply. I backed out of her office and left the library that day without even checking out any books.

Although I tended to avoid Miss Jepson for a while after that, I certainly didn't give up the library. I continued my regular visits there during high school, and while in college I managed to squeeze trips to the library into my brief vacations home. I sought it out increasingly as a place of quiet more than as a source of knowledge. Although I was now aware that other libraries had more books and more impressive buildings, the Ames Public Library was my own private refuge. If I had a difficult paper to write, I knew I could spread it out on the shiny maple tables in the Junior Room. I would make notes, sort piles of paper, look out the tall windows at the elm trees, and take little breaks to wander past the familiar shelves, plucking out old friends that seemed like once-loved dolls carefully packed away for someone else. Few people came into the library when I spent my afternoons there, and I would be lulled by the soft padding of the librarians' feet, the gentle thud of the heavy front door, the rare whispers from the Children's Room next door. Sometimes during college vacations I would just go there to write letters. Miss Jepson nodded at me then and asked me how I liked Smith; I smiled at her as one adult to another. Eventually I no longer even wondered about the books in her little glass case. Perhaps now I had read them all.

But although the Ames Public Library eventually became simply a pleasant place to visit, I still think of it at odd times. When something troubles me, I feel an urge to go to the library to get a book on it, though now that I can afford to buy books occasionally, I sometimes go to the bookstore instead. My crowded shelves hold all the books I thought would help: advice and guidance on needlepoint, cats, England, loneliness, parenting, and antique jewelry. Last spring, when I decided it was time for me to get my body in shape, I went downtown in a self-satisfied glow to outfit myself for exercise. I had planned to buy some properly cushioned shoes. But I passed by a bookstore first, stopped to browse, and spent my money instead on *The Complete Book of Running*. I thought I had better read about running first to see whether I would like it.

TWO

City Libraries

Writers who grew up in big cities remember their libraries with as much affection and vivid attention as do writers from small towns, though their memories sometimes differ in significant ways. City libraries, like smaller ones, serve as temporary shelters, but the range of possible patrons is naturally wider in a big city. Many writers' memoirs of city libraries, like Alfred Kazin's in *New York Jew*, focus on the fascinating human panorama that passes before an alert reader who looks up from his seat in the reading room. Kazin shows us "street philosophers, fanatics, advertising agents, the homeless—passing faces in the crowd," as well as individual patrons like "the little man with one slice of hair across his bald head, like General MacArthur's."

Nowhere is that diversity of patrons more concentrated than at the New York Public Library on Fifth Avenue and Forty-second Street. Its solemn stone lions seem like totems of New York itself, as in E. B. White's poem "A Library Lion Speaks."

Inside, perhaps the most often remembered parts of the New York Public Library are Room 315 and the Reading Rooms, described here by Alfred Kazin, William Cole, Elizabeth Hardwick, and Henry Miller, as well as in some later selections in Chapter 8, "Reading-Room Reveries." In his poem, "Reading Room," E. B. White promises that "books are the door of escape from the forest." The forest also becomes a metaphor for Edmund Wilson in his poem "Response of the Gentle Scholars," which is a satiric comment on a letter written to *The Saturday Review of Literature*. In this letter, an unidentified reader complained bitterly about the "rag-tail and bob-tail," "the rabble," the "down-and-outers" who might drive away the "gentle scholars" from the sheltering walls of the New York Public Library. The letter-writer provoked Wilson to a memorable reply.

Blocks north, memoirist Kate Simon evokes her Bronx childhood, when Ida Liebowitz read *goyish* library books on her fire escape, safely secluded from the eyes of her father. In another big city, Hamlin Garland recalls the Boston of his youth, when he sought refuge in the public library from a cramped and semistarved existence. In her poem "Poetry Reading in the Downtown Library," Cathy Stern shows a city library serving as an unusual connection between poets and the dispossessed. For all of these writers, the city library is a precious resource.

Except from *New York Jew* by Alfred Kazin

When Alfred Kazin published his provocative and ground-breaking work on American literature On Native Grounds, *in 1942, he established a reputation as a challenging and knowledgeable critic that has continued to the present day. Other literary essays appear in* The Inmost Leaf *(1955);* Contemporaries *(1962); and* Bright Book of Life *(1973). In 1988 he published* A Writer's America: Landscape in Literature. *Kazin has also edited a number of important studies of major American writers.*

Although Kazin has taught at American colleges and universities across the country, from Smith College to the University of California, he is most associated with the literary life of New York City. He was born in Brooklyn in 1915 and attended the College of the City of New York and Columbia.

Kazin has published three autobiographical memoirs about his life in New York: A Walker in the City *(1951);* Starting Out in the Thirties *(1965);* New

York Jew *(1978)*. *Anatole Broyard, writing in* The New York Times Book Review *about Kazin's text for a book of photographs by David Finn,* Our New York *(1989), commented: "Mr. Kazin is one of the last of that generation who searched the city streets for meaning, 'looking for my future,' as Bernard Malamud put it. . . . Mr. Kazin has produced many of American literature's best thoughts during almost 50 years of exploring New York." (For a New York story by Malamud, see Chapter 9, "Democracy in the Library.")*

> *Anything can happen now that we've slid over this bridge, I thought, anything at all.*
> *——The Great Gatsby*

One dreamlike week in 1942 I published my first book, *On Native Grounds*, became an editor of *The New Republic*, and with my wife, Natasha, moved into a little apartment on Twenty-fourth Street and Lexington. Its casement windows looked out on a shop that sold everything you could possibly need for your horse. From across the street the shop seemed to gleam with silver rein buckles, brightly polished saddles and bridles. In front of the shop stood a prancing, thoroughly affable wooden horse painted bright yellow.

I had never lived in Manhattan before. In those first few weeks of my "arrival" in the big city I went between my home, my publishers at Lexington and Twenty-eight and *The New Republic* at Forty-ninth and Madison in a dizzy exaltation mixed with the direst suspicion of what might happen next. Riding away from the office at the "violet hour" in the sudden opulence of wartime, when the incomparable autumn light of New York still hung over the buildings that would soon be shadowed by the faint wartime brownout, I could feel, when the taxi skidded around the circular passageway under the ramp of Grand Central into Fourth Avenue, sensations of personal deliverance that came and went like the light between the arches. I was stupefied by the advance interest in my book, which would soon give me a considerable boost at *The New Republic*; I loved working in the center of New York and living in Manhattan. Riding home at the rush hour, I could taste all the wild distraction of New York in wartime like a first martini. But I missed my long solitary days in the Forty-second Street Library, I was expecting at every moment to be called into the Army, and I was not prepared for so much good fortune.

I had begun my book in our single room in Brooklyn Heights soon after our wedding at City Hall. It was 1938. We were twenty-three, we had known each other two weeks, Natasha was taking her doctorate in bacteriology at Bellevue, and we were both in a terrible rush to get away from everything we had grown up with. Beginning my book in a mood of great husbandly contentment, I soon knew that thanks to an idle suggestion from Carl Van Doren, who liked my first reviews and literary essays, I had found my natural subject. Van Doren wondered why there had never been a study of the "new" American writing in the twentieth century that would also be a historical explanation of its emergence.

For almost five years I had worked toward the book in the great open reading room, 315, of the New York Public Library, often in great all-day bouts of reading that began when the place opened at nine in the morning and that ended only at ten at night. With my friend Richard Hofstadter, who was writing *Social Darwinism in American Thought* for his doctorate at Columbia, I would snatch my lunch in the Automat across the street from the Library, run up Fifth Avenue in the "brownout" for exercise, find a pool parlor off Times Square for a hurried game of Ping-Pong, then return to the great yellow tables in 315, somehow always smelling of fresh varnish and piled with our books, on which we had left little notes saying "BACK SOON, DO NOT DISTURB." We spent an afternoon every week in the Trans-Lux Newsreel Theatre on Broadway and solemnly congratulated each other the day we were privileged to look at lines of heavy tanks lumbering off the Detroit assembly lines like new automobiles. War, blessed war, had come to the rescue of my generation, and nothing would ever be the same.

I had written my book at the kitchen table in Brooklyn Heights; on Forty-first Street near the El in Long Island City; at Provincetown in the summer of 1940; and the last summer at Yaddo in Saratoga, where, as I saw Natasha walking away down Union Avenue to her train, I was blinded by my tears and the grief that was to come. For almost five years I had lived in a state of scholarly innocence, of unexpected intellectual assurance that floated my book home on the radical confidence of the 1930s. I had gone back and forth between the subway and 315, between Bryant Park and 315, between the Automat's coffee spigot and 315, between Natasha's influenza lab at Bellevue and 315.

There it was, as soon as you walked up the great marble steps off Fifth Avenue. "ON THE DIFFUSION OF EDUCATION AMONG THE PEOPLE REST THE PRESERVATION AND PERPETUATION OF OUR FREE INSTITUTIONS." It said that to you as you entered the great hall, in gold letters on the pylons facing the Fifth Avenue entrance. The entrance also read: "THE LIBRARY IS OPEN EVERY DAY OF THE YEAR 9 A.M.—10 P.M., MONDAY—SATURDAY. 1—10 SUNDAY."

Year after year I seemed to have nothing more delightful to do than to sit much of the day and many an evening at one of those great golden tables acquainting myself with every side of my subject. Whenever I was free to read, the great Library seemed free to receive me. Anything I had heard of and wanted to see, the blessed place owned: first editions of American novels out of those germinal decades after the Civil War that led to my theme of the "modern"; old catalogues from long-departed Chicago publishers who had been young men in the 1890s trying to support a little realism; yellowing, crumbling, but intact sets of the old *Masses* (1911–1918), which was to the Stalinist *New Masses* what St. Francis is to the Inquisition; the old *Delineator*, under the brief editorship of the disgraceful failed novelist Theodore Dreiser, which cravenly opposed the vile sexual immorality that had wrecked *Sister Carrie*; the *Smart Set*, which was "not for the boneheads," said Mencken and Nathan when they took it over in 1914; *The Chap-Book*, which was published in Chicago in the yellow nineties, yellow especially in Chicago, and whose honesty about the local scene explained why so many strong novels would soon come out of Chicago; forgotten pamphlets by genteel lady hacks of 1900 still attacking Henry James for *his* un-American immorality in permitting a splendid American type like Daisy Miller to walk in the Colosseum at night with a greaser; every possible item bearing on Randolph Bourne, Eugene Victor Debs, Max Eastman, Art Young and the many other Socialists and writers collared by the government for opposing what Dos Passos would call "Mr. Wilson's War"; the endless medical advice by Upton Sinclair on how rice cured his headaches and on how to avoid the death by drink suffered by armies of American writers; the opinions on practically everything by James Huneker, Henry Mencken, Willard Huntington Wright, Irving Babbitt, Paul Elmer More, Edmund Wilson, R. P. Blackmur, Allen Tate, their followers and their followers' followers.

So between 1938 and 1942 I would many a morning and evening make my way across Fifth Avenue to the main door under the inscription "BUT ABOVE ALL THINGS TRUTH BEARETH AWAY THE VICTORY," past the great hall with its tantalizing display of Renaissance maps, incunabula, letters by Dickens; and since I was too intent on 315 to wait for the elevator, would dash up those steps whose exhilaratingly smooth marble was so much a part of the lordly building designed in 1898 by Carrère & Hastings, past the enormous wall painting "Blind Milton Dictating *Paradise Lost* to His Daughters," through the third-floor halls lined with the many prints of old New York fires and firemen collected by Isaac Newton Phelps Stokes for his iconography of New York City, and finally arrive at the great catalogue room lined wall to wall with trays of endlessly thumbed cards.

I was my own staff researcher, a totally unaffiliated free lance and occasional evening college instructor who was educating himself in the mind of modern American by writing, in the middle of the Great Depression, a wildly ambitious literary and intellectual history. 315 was my intellectual armory. My privacy was complete. No one behind the information desk ever asked me *why* I needed to look at the yellowing, crumbling, fast-fading material about insurgent young Chicago and San Francisco publishing houses in 1897. No one suggested that I might manage whatever-it-was-I-was-doing with something more readily available than the very first issue of *Poetry* in 1912; *The New Republic* in 1914; muckraking *Collier's* in the Theodore Roosevelt era; material showing President Nicholas Murray Butler's displeasure with Professor Charles A. Beard's *An Economic Interpretation of the Constitution of the United States*; Professor Beard's resignation from Columbia when President Butler sharply discouraged objections to "Mr. Wilson's War"; the attacks of John S. Sumner's anti-vice league on Theodore Dreiser's The *"Genius"*; Alfred A. Knopf persuading cowardly booksellers to show the new American and European novelists he was publishing; Eugene O'Neill's experiences living a season on the Provincetown dunes near the old Peaked Hill Bar Coast Guard station facing the Atlantic.

As one of "the people" in the New York Public Library, I could get the story of Mrs. Frank Doubleday getting Mr. Frank Doubleday to suppress Doubleday, Page & Co.'s edition of *Sister Carrie*; Frank Norris's efforts as an editor at Doubleday to sneak out review copies of that wicked book; the 1918 propaganda by "literary" people that H. L. Mencken was "pro-German," attacks so personal that by 1940 Mencken was defending Hitler; the founding of new magazines, publishing houses, experimental theaters by "new people" who were radicals, sexual and political, even in the ivy-dead American universities. . . . I came to know what Edmund Wilson thought of his classmate Scott Fitzgerald when they were both at Princeton and how that dogged libertarian John Dos Passos was so horrified by the Communist execution of anarchists and Socialists during the Spanish Civil War—and his friend Hemingway's indifference to these murders—that Dos Passos turned sharp right.

"There's my Middle West," Fitzgerald crooned in the last slow movement of *The Great Gatsby*. Years before I saw Chicago, I learned what hope, élan, intellectual freshness came with those pioneer realists out of the Middle West who said there was no American literature but the one *they* were rushing to create. My subject had to do with the "modern" as democracy; with America itself as the modern; with the end of the nineteenth century as the great preparation: in lonely small towns, prairie villages, isolated colleges, dusty law offices, national magazines, and provincial "academies" where no one suspected that the obedient-looking young reporters, law clerks, librarians, teachers would turn out to be Willa Cather, Robert Frost, Sinclair Lewis, Wallace Stevens, Marianne Moore. The new literature was being created inside an old century—proud, stormy, yet elegant. The elegance was still in those great halls of the Library; up those marble stairs; always surrounded by pictures of the mid-century reservoir that had been replaced by the Library, the old fire fighters in their red wagons, the traditional view from the Battery. These put me right back into the turn of the century that saw the building of the Library—and the intellectual insurgence and radical hope that bedrocked my book. Even the spacious twin reading rooms, each two blocks long, gave me a sense of the powerful amenity that I craved for my own life, a world of power in which my own people had moved about as strangers.

It fascinated me, in those days of our easy radicalism before the war—and only the war—ended the Great Depression, to do my reading and thinking in that asylum and church of the unemployed; of crazy ideologists and equally crazy Bible students doggedly writing "YOU LIE!" in the reference books on the open shelves; of puzzle fans searching every encyclopedia; of commission salesmen secretly tearing address lists out of city directories.

Whatever happened to the little man with one slice of hair across his bald head, like General MacArthur's, the little man who was always there every day I ever went in between 1938 and 1942, poring with a faint smile over a large six-column Bible in Hebrew, Greek, Latin, English, French, German? Or the bony, ugly, screeching madwoman who reminded me of Maxim Gorky's "Boless," the anguished old maid who had a professional scribe take down passionate letters to a lover and then asked the scribe to make up letters from the lover to her? She invariably accused the man reading next to her of trying to pick her up. She would cry out with a madly contented smile—"This is a library, Buster! A place to read in! Get it, Buster?"

Street philosophers, fanatics, advertising agents, the homeless—passing faces in the crowd. I liked reading and working out my ideas in the midst of that endless crowd walking in and out of 315 looking for *something*; that Depression crowd so pent up, searching for puzzle contests, beauty contests, clues to buried treasure off Sandy Hook; seeking lost and dead rich relatives in old New York books of genealogy and Pittsburgh telephone books. Reading in the midst of this jumpy Depression crowd, I, too, was seeking fame and fortune by sitting at the end of a long golden table next to the sets of American authors on the open shelves. I could feel on my skin the worry of all those people; I could hear day and evening those restless hungry footsteps; I was entangled in the hunger of all those aimless, bewildered, panicky seekers for "opportunity." I must have looked as mad to them as they did to me: jumping up with excitement and walking about the great halls as I discovered that just for the asking I could obtain all the books anyone would ever want to read by William Dean Howells, Henry James,

Stephen Crane, Joseph Kirkland, Robert Herrick, Ed Howe, Henry Blake Fuller, Frank Norris, Theodore Dreiser, Jack London. I could read the mind behind each book. I felt connected with the text. There was some telepathy working between me and the invisible person, the omnipresent mind, that had put down these words. I was hungry for it all, hungry all the time. I was made so restless by the many minds within my reach that no matter how often I rushed across to the Automat for another bun and coffee, to fuel up at those stand-up tables for New Yorkers too harried to eat their food sitting down, I could never get back to my books and notes, "BACK SOON, DO NOT DISTURB," without the same hunger pains tearing me inside. There was something about the vibrating empty rooms early in the morning—light falling through the great tall windows, the sun burning the smooth tops of the golden tables as if they had been freshly painted—that made me restless with the need to grab up every book, press into every single mind right there on the open shelves. My book was building itself. The age was with me. "ON THE DIFFUSION OF EDUCATION AMONG THE PEOPLE REST THE PRESERVATION AND PERPETUATION OF OUR FREE INSTITUTIONS."

"A Library Lion Speaks" by E. B. White

Although E. B. White (1899–1985) wrote enough poems to fill most of a book (Poems and Sketches, 1981), he is not primarily known for his verse. In his preface to that collection, he admits that he has no "accreditation papers" as a poet and goes on to rejoice that he thus feels "no obligation to mingle with other writers of verse to exchange sensitivities, no compulsion to visit the 'Y' to read from his own works, no need to travel the wine-and-cheese circuit, where the word 'poet' carries the aroma of magic and ladies creep up from behind carrying ballpoint pens and sprigs of asphodel."

It is just this indefinably idiosyncratic tone, this lilt in his prose, this delightful sense of humor that continues to win such a large audience for White's essays. Many significant American writers credit White with teaching them how to find and hone a personal voice; his brilliant style remains inimitable. White's prose appeared for many years in The New Yorker *and in* Harper's; *it is collected in several volumes, including* One Man's Meat *(1944);* The Second Tree from the Corner *(1954); and* The Points of My Compass *(1962). Many readers know him best for his children's books, especially* Stuart Little *(1945) and* Charlotte's Web *(1952).*

I

*I do not care what hours have slipped
Since April's torrid lovers tripped
Along these steps; for all that while
I've worn my supercilious smile,
And now, with snow upon my jowl,
Through storms that chill and winds that howl,
In attitude unchanged I hear
Music of the departing year—
A paragon, as you'll agree,
Of imperturbability.*

II

*Through summer's fall, through winter's spring,
I see the peoples journeying:
The goers south, the goers north,
The comers home, the farers forth,
Each little man who thinks he knows
The dancer that's inside his clothes.
And I—with nothing else to do—
I try to look as though I knew!
Which helps explain, it seems to me,
My imperturbability.*

III

I mark the bright expectant looks
Of those who come to read in books:
The graybeard, at his soul's behest
Exploring life's unanswered jest;
The stripling knight astride a dream,
His eyes alight, his spurs agleam——
The library! There's nothing there
Not found upon my thoroughfare.
Which quite excuses, as you see,
My imperturbability.

IV

I read each day, at even-fall,
The mightiest poem of them all:
The city, at the edge of night,
Hung in a pale and trembling light,
Sung to the quick, the listening ears,
Scrawled with a pen first dipt in tears,
The city where I crouch in state,
Aware that I have long to wait.
Which vindicates, to some degree,
My imperturbability.

V

Nor have I brooded here in vain
And heard low songs made in the rain:
I've seen how men will feed a dove
Who have not any other love,
I know the hope that somehow lies
In almost any pair of eyes,
I know that April comes once more
And lovers skipping through her door——
Things which have almost torn from me
My imperturbability!

"The Heart of the Heart of the Library" by William Cole

William R. Cole, born in 1919, has been involved with books and publishing for most of his life, serving as publicity director and editor at Alfred A. Knopf and at Simon and Schuster; publishing books at Viking Press under the William Cole Books imprint; and writing and editing sixty books and anthologies of his own. He has also been active in writers' organizations, serving on the executive or governing boards of International P.E.N., Poets and Writers, and the Poetry Society of America.

An enthusiastic anthologizer, Cole has edited such varied collections as The Best Cartoons from Punch *(1952);* The Fireside Book of Humorous Poetry *(1959);* The Most of A. J. Leibling *(1963);* Eight Lines and Under: An Anthology of Short, Short Poems *(1967);* The Dog in Stories, Reminiscences, Poems and Cartoons *(1967);* An Arkful of Animals *(1978);* The Poetry of Horses *(1979);* Monster Knock Knocks *(1988);* New York: A Literary Companion *(1989); and many more.*

The heart of the New York Public Library has always seemed to me to be Room 315.

Many years ago, when I first entered the library and asked where I should go to look something up, I was told "Room 315." Well, it seemed silly to call it a room; it was more a *place*, an acreage. And I still never enter it without being awed by its spacious dignity and air of no-nonsense utility.

The heart of the heart of Room 315 is the Information Desk, a 700-square-foot enclosure within which work 20 busy librarians—11 men and nine women—each of whom is particularly skilled in ready reference. To work on the Desk is the ultimate for any librarian who is attracted to research; it is to a librarian what working at Bellevue would be to a young doctor, such is the range, variety and volume. The Desk, this card-file-lined room and the adjacent reading rooms are under the direction of James G. Tobin, a quietly efficient man in his early sixties, whose title is Chief of the General Research and Humanities Division.

About 2,000 people pass through Room 315 daily. There are no guided tours; but many New Yorkers, such as myself, looking for something impressive to show out-of-town visitors, will parade them through this three-story high room with its ornate ceiling into the still more impressive Reading Rooms, which extend for two whole city blocks. (The Reading Rooms—North Hall and South Hall—are really one long room divided by a book delivery area.)

But it is Room 315 itself, and more specifically its Information Desk, that has always fascinated me. The mind boggles at the information these librarians can make available to the man-from-the-street. Here is a room lined with 10,000 card trays, containing 10 million cards. In this room and the adjoining ones are 40,000 reference books available on open shelves. And all this is backed up by seven floors of stacks, holding 2½ million books, one of which can (ideally) be put into a reader's hands in 20 minutes.

There are four librarians "up front" at the Desk at any given moment. Each is an hour at this post, handling an average of 30 questions, and is then rotated with the other librarians. When not up front, the librarians are assigned other positions within the enclosure. One stint is answering telephone queries, about 150 daily; this used to figure much larger in their schedule until last year, when the nearby Mid-Manhattan Library established a separate telephone reference room which handles about 1,000 calls daily. Now the questions that come to the Desk are only those fielded to them by Mid-Manhattan, questions they are not equipped to handle.

Another assignment is answering mail queries from the public, from scholars and from other libraries; these letters range from a request for the text of James Whitcomb Riley's "The Passing of the Backhouse" to aid in tracking down a 13th-century manuscript. You will always find one librarian working on a "snag" as Mr. Tobin calls it; these are extremely tough questions that the librarians look on as challenges. They admit that they don't *always* get their man, but almost always. And then a great deal of time is taken up with ordering books, the point being to keep the research library as up-to-date as possible; someone is always poring over catalogues, book-trade publications and library listings from all over the world.

The librarians up front are the ones on the firing line. Their customers come in waves:

At one moment the four librarians will be standing four abreast behind the Desk, one tapping his pencil absently, another two exchanging a few words, the fourth catching a glance at a literary review. Then, the next moment, they'll be beseiged, with readers lining up behind one another impatiently.

Most of the questions are routine: Someone filled out a call-slip wrong, forgot to put down an asterisk or a plus sign or filled out a slip for a book that is to be found only in one of the library's specialized collections. Others can't quite remember the title of a book or got it a bit wrong —the librarians still remember a request for Darwin's "Oranges and Peaches." Many want information on the city's social services, on schools or biographical information about an author. The librarians are trained not so much to answer questions as to point the reader in the direction of a reference tool that will.

Over the years Mr. Tobin has found that the books most likely to be stolen or mutilated are those containing hard, practical information. Outstanding victims are such titles as "Practice for the Armed Forces Tests," "Hotel and Motel Red Book" "Resumés that Get Jobs" (easier to tear out a page than to copy a whole resumé) and "The Foundation Directory." These, even for quick, on-the-spot consultation at the Desk, have to be signed for. The librarians keep their reference books up-to-the-minute. The day after Padraic Colum died, I happened to pick up "Twentieth Century Writing" at the desk. It fell open to his biography; and the day, month and year of his death had already been neatly penciled in. Snooping among the ready reference books I was surprised to see "The Joy of Cooking" over the telephone reference desk. Sure, they use it; someone has lost a recipe, or run out of an ingredient in mid-recipe, and what should he substitute?

There are 300 to 400 books within the enclosure available to the librarians for "stand-up" questions. These are supplemented by what Mr. Tobin calls the "scrapbox." This is a file of Manila folders, each of which pertains to frequently asked questions. Looking through it, I came across folders for "Water Dowsing," "The Bible," "Phobias," "Peace Symbols," "Draft" (which contained, among other things, a pamphlet called "Manual for Draft-Age Immigrants to Canada"). The librarians really get to know what fads and current concerns of the public are, and have recently built up files on organic food, communes, astrology, parapsychology, group therapy and, happily, ecology and urban planning.

It is only in recent years that the library schools have originated courses in the handling of reader's questions. What's the quickest way to really find out what a reader wants to know? Some readers are reluctant to come to the point and will begin with a general question, such as, "How are the catalogue files arranged?" The librarians train themselves to do a "quick take." "A reader asks, 'Do you have anything on pattern-cutting?' and I have to figure is he after dress patterns or sheet-metal patterns? If the question is about Indians, is he after American Indians or Indian Indians?" There are a certain number of pests, and some lonely people who just want some human communication.

The librarians are asked to hold each questioner down to a maximum of five minutes. "Sometimes that's hard to do," said one librarian. "I get interested in the subject and want to find out more about it myself." There is an air of genteel camaraderie within the enclosure; if the librarians notice that someone up front is having trouble with a reader who is a time-waster or is hard to understand, they'll come to his assistance. They share 12 languages among them, and one recalls the case of a reader she simply couldn't understand. After a few minutes of this non-communication, she asked, "Pardon me, sir, but what is your language?" "Lingwitch! Lingwitch!" he burst out, "Inklitsch!"

One day, after browsing around the room looking at the catalogue, I had a question of my own. "Why," I asked Mr. Tobin, "under all those headings for 'World War,' is there nothing for World War I? It's all World War II!" "Well," he replied, "at the time of World War I, we didn't *know* it was World War I. You'll find it under 'European War.' "

Over the years, the librarians have noted down some of the more unusual, even looney, questions that come to them. Some are poignant: "Is there a law in New York City where a child can become unrelated to his parents if they don't like each other?" Some have an eerie logic about them: "If self-preservation is the first law of nature, what's the second?" and "Can you give me a list of historical characters who were at the right place at the right time?" Others stagger the imagination: "Can mice 'throw up'?" and "Does the female human being belong to the mammal class?" Yet others are little comic dramas:

Q. "What is the natural enemy of the duck?"

A. "I don't quite understand your question."

Q. "Well, I have this swimming pool, and a flock of ducks landed on it. I went out and waved a broom at them, but they just looked at me and quacked. I want to know what kind of animal I can get who's their natural enemy."

And this hysterical monologue which came in over the phone:

Q. "How do I put up wallpaper? I have the paper, I have the paste. What do I do next? Does the paste go on the wall or on the paper? I've tried both, and it doesn't seem to work."

As is true of any other public facility, a certain number of eccentrics can be found in Room 315. Derelicts come in out of the cold; young men find it a place for pick-ups; occasionally a real crazy has to be ejected. I suppose the passing thousands represent as good a cross section of New York as you'd find anywhere. I watched the people for a half hour one afternoon: There's an elderly man in a three-piece suit whose secretary is helping him go through a file; over in the corner are two bearded poets I know huddled over a file drawer working on a poetry anthology; through the door comes a handsome, bra-less girl whose appearance untracks half the research in the room; there's a nattily-dressed black man carrying a dispatch case and a tennis racquet; there's a young man wearing what seems to be a horse blanket. Every kind of fashion can be seen, from mod to mess.

Mr. Tobin tells me that there is a kind of seasonal migration observable; Christmas, when the schools are out, is the maddest time, a time for the serious researcher to stay away. In the fall the fashion academy students come in droves; at midyear gray-clad young men from the police academy come in pairs, like nuns. In the late spring the college instructors and young professors appear, full of beans for their summer projects, knowing they must publish early lest they perish.

Over the years, the librarians get to notice the "regulars," outstanding among whom is Mr. Norbert Pearlroth. Mr. Pearlroth is the researcher for the syndicated feature, "Believe It or Not," and should qualify for inclusion in it himself, having been in the library almost every day for the past 50 years. I spoke with this record-holder, who is a spry 74, with white hair and black eyebrows. "When they cut down on the open days, it was a catastrophe for me," he said. "I used to come in seven days a week." Mr. Pearlroth always sits at the same table in the South Hall. "You can tell where I am because I always put the reading light out, I prefer to read by natural light." A good testimony from a man who doesn't wear glasses.

Mr. Pearlroth is the only man I ever heard of who researches by serendipity. Shortly after 10 in the morning, he enters Room 315 and selects a file drawer at random, preferring one that is already out and sitting on a table. He then goes rapidly through the cards, selecting, with what he calls a second sense, a dozen books that sound promising. It doesn't really matter what language they're in—he reads a dozen. He puts the call slips in, three at a time, during the morning, and sets to work. When I visited his reading table, he was surrounded by a dozen books, each of which either had "Kirch . . ." as the beginning of its title or whose author was named Kirch. He'd been in a "K" file. In German there was a book on poisons, one on noted Berlin women and a long treatise on the Swiss town of Kirchberg.

There were nine books in English, including a history of the Roan Schools and a book on whales. "I average 24 books a day—I don't eat lunch—and I'm lucky if I find three usable items." Occasionally he gets stuck in a book, to his annoyance—usually a book about World War I, in which he served in the Austrian Army. He finds local histories the most promising mines, and travel books by Frenchmen, who seem to have a flair for the strange and unusual. Travel books by South Americans are useless. "Too much about churches," he says. His technique is to skim rapidly, paying particular attention to pictures, the most interesting of which he has reproduced in the Photographic Services Room at the end of each day. He figures he has gone through 7,000 books a year, making a grand total of 350,000 books. What does Mr. Pearlroth do when he goes home at night? "Sometimes I read."

Another regular was a woman who earned the distinction of having worked her way methodically through every one of the 10,000 card trays in Room 315. She was after every listed French translation of American works. This woman always worked at a particular seat in the South Hall, near the French reference books, and claimed squatter's rights to it. If she found anyone else in her seat, she firmly asked them to move.

And then there's Timothy Dickinson, a young Englishman who is in the way of being a professional polymath. I had met him socially a couple of times and thought of him as a kind of ambulatory encyclopedia. Mention any subject, particularly history or literature, and he would come forth with dates, places, incidents and a list of secondary sources. The indelible impression that this makes on people is reinforced by his individualistic style: striped trousers, what appears to be a morning coat, and *pince-nez*. Mr. Dickinson is frequently to be found in the library doing freelance research for publishers of scholarly reprints and reference books. The librarians know him, of course, and when I asked them whether or not he put many questions to them, the reply was, "Not really—but sometimes he's very helpful to *us*. He's given us some good leads."

It's easy to see that the librarians in Room 315 take pride and pleasure in their work. They are genuinely pleased when they can supply an answer to a question; and the harder the question, the more pleasure. They weren't really offended by the wording of a question that one of them remembers from last year: "Is this the place where I ask questions I can't get the answers to?"

Excerpt from *Plexus* by Henry Miller

Plexus *(1953) is part of Henry Miller's memoir* The Rosy Crucifixion, *which also includes* Sexus *(1949) and* Nexus *(1960). The exuberance, energy, and lyrical rush of this excerpt are typical of Miller's work, most of which celebrates his intense life.*

Miller (1891–1980), who became one of America's most famous literary expatriates, achieved notoriety with Tropic of Cancer, *published in France in 1934 but not in America until 1961. Because of its sexual material,* Tropic of Cancer *became the focus of fierce debate about the relationship between, and definitions of, pornography and art. This debate caused one critic to summarize Miller's career thus: "His role in American cultural history generally overshadowed his place in American literature." Two other memoirs published in France in the 1930s then appeared in America,* Tropic of Capricorn *in 1962, followed by* Black Spring *in 1963.*

Miller wrote many other books, such as The Air-Conditioned Nightmare *(1945);* Big Sur and the Oranges of Hieronymus Bosch *(1957); and* Just Wild About Harry *(1963), a play. Miller, who was a major influence on the Beat movement, might have been surprised to find himself represented in an anthology celebrating such a respectable institution as the American public library.*

Following out the plan I had laid down for myself I was busier than the busiest executive in the industrial world. Some of the articles I had elected to write demanded considerable research work, which was never an ordeal for me because I loved going to the library and have them dig up books that were hard to find. How many wonderful days and nights I spent at the 42nd Street Library, seated at a long table, one among thousands, it seemed, in that main reading room. The tables themselves excited me. It was always my desire to own a table of extraordinary dimensions, a table so large that I could not only sleep on it but dance on it, even skate on it. (There *was* a writer, once, who worked at such a table, which he had placed in the centre of a huge, barren room—my ideal as a work place. His name was Andreyev, and needless to add, he was one of my favourites.)

Yes, it gave one a good feeling to be working amidst so many other industrious students in a room the size of a cathedral, under a lofty ceiling which was an imitation of heaven itself. One left the library slightly dazed, often with a holy feeling. It was always a shock to plunge into the crowd at Fifth Avenue and 42nd Street; there was no connection between that busy thoroughfare and the peaceful world of books. Often, while waiting for the books to come up from the mysterious depths of the library. I would stroll along the outer aisles glancing at the titles of the amazing reference books which lined the walls. Thumbing those books was enough to set my mind racing for days. Sometimes I sat and meditated, wondering what question I could put to the genius which presided over the spirit of this vast institution that it could not answer. There was no subject under the sun, I suppose, which had not been written about and filed in those archives. My omnivorous appetite pulled me one way, my fear of becoming a book-worm the other way.

It was also enjoyable to make a trip to Long Island City, that most woe-begone hole, to see at first hand how chewing gum was manufactured. Here was a world of sheer lunacy—efficiency, it is usually called. In a room filled with a choking powder of sickenly sweet stench hundreds of moronic girls worked like butterflies packing the slabs of gum in wrappers; their nimble fingers, I was told, worked more accurately and skilfully than any machine yet invented. I went through the plant, a huge one, under an escort, each wing as it opened up to view presenting the aspect of another section of hell. It was only when I threw out a random query about the chicle, which is the base of chewing gum, that I stumbled on to the really interesting phase of my research. The *chicleros*, as they are called, the men who toil in the depths of the jungles of Yucatan, are a fascinating breed of men. I spent weeks at the library reading about their customs and habits. I got so interested in them, indeed, that I almost forgot about chewing gum. And, of course, from a study of the *chicleros* I was drawn into the world of the Mayans, thence to those fascinating books about Atlantis and the lost continent of Mu, the canals which ran from one side of South America to another, the cities which were lifted a mile high when the Andes came into being, the sea traffic between Easter Island and the western slope of South America, the analogies and affinities between the Amerindian culture and the culture of the Near East, the mysteries of the Aztec alphabet, and so on and so forth until, by some strange detour I came upon Paul Gauguin in the centre of the Polynesian archipelago and went home reeling with *Noa Noa* under my arm. And from the life and letters of Gauguin, which I had to read *at once*, to the life and letters of Vincent Van Gogh was but a step.

No doubt it is important to read the classics; it is perhaps even more important to first read the literature of one's own time, which is enormous in itself. But more valuable than either of these, to a writer at least, is to read whatever comes to hand, to follow his nose, as it were. In the musty tomes of every great library there are buried articles by obscure or unknown individuals on subjects ostensibly of no importance, but saturated with data, ideas, fancies, moods, whims, portents of such a calibre that they can only be likened, in their effect, to rare drugs. The most exciting days often began with the search for the definition of a new word. One little word, which the ordinary reader is content to pass over unperturbed, may prove (for a writer) to be a veritable gold mine. From the dictionary I usually went to the encyclopaedia, not just one encyclopaedia but several; from the encyclopaedia, to all manner of reference books; from reference books to hand-books, and thence to a nine day debauch. A debauch of digging and ferreting, digging and ferreting. In addition to the reams of notes I made I copied out pages and pages of excerpts. Sometimes I simply tore out the pages I needed most. Between times I would make forays on the museums.

The officials with whom I dealt never doubted for a moment that I was engaged in writing a book which would be a contribution to the subject. I talked as if I knew vastly more than I cared to reveal. I would make casual, oblique references to books I had never read or hint of encounters with eminent authorities I had never met. It was nothing, in such moods, to give myself scholastic degrees which I had not even dreamed of acquiring. I spoke of distinguished leaders in such fields as anthropology, sociology, physics, astronomy, as though I had been intimately associated with them. When I saw that I was getting in too deep I had always the wit to excuse myself and pretend to go to the toilet, which was my word for 'exit'. Once, deeply interested in genealogy, I thought it a good idea to take a job for a space in the genealogy division of the public library. It so happened that they were short a man in this division the day I called to make application for a job. They needed a man so badly that they put me to work immediately, which was more than I had bargained for. The application blank which I had left with the director of the library was a marvel of falsification. I wondered, as I listened to the poor devil who was breaking me in, how long it would take for them to get on to me. Meanwhile my superior was climbing ladders with me, pointing out this and that, bending over in dark corners to extract documents, files, and such like, calling in other employees to introduce me, explaining hurriedly as best he could (whilst messengers came and went as in a Shakespearean play) the most salient features of my supposed routine. Realizing in a short time that I was not in the least interested in all this jabberwocky, and thinking of Mona waiting for me to lunch with her, I suddenly interrupted him in the midst of a lengthy exposition of something or other to ask where the toilet was. He looked at me rather strangely, wondering, no doubt, why I hadn't the decency to hear him out before running to the lavatory, but with the aid of a few grimaces and gestures, which conveyed most patently that I had been caught short, might do it right there on the floor or in the waste basket, I managed to get out of his clutches, grab my hat and coat which fortunately were still lying on a chair near the door, and run as fast as I could out of the building. . . .

The dominant passion was the acquisition of knowledge, skill, mastery of technique, inexhaustible experience, but like a sub-dominant chord there existed steadily in the back of my head vibration which meant order, beauty, simplification, enjoyment, appreciation. Reading Van Gogh's letters I identify myself with him in the struggle to lead a simple life, a life in which art is all. How glowingly he writes about this dedication to art in his letters from Arles, a place I am destined to visit later though reading about it now I don't even dream of ever seeing it. To give a more *musical* expression to one's life—that is how he puts it. Over and over again he makes reference to the austere beauty and dignity of the life of the Japanese artist, dwelling on their simplicity, their certitude, their naturalness. It is this Japanese quality which I find in our love-nest; it is this bare, simple beauty, this stark elegance, which sustain and comfort me. I find myself drawn to drawn to Japan more than to China. I read of Whistler's experience and fall in love with his etchings. I read Lafcadio Hearn, everything he has written about Japan, especially what he gives of their fairy tales, which tales impress me to this day more than those of any other people. Japanese prints adorn the walls; they hang in the bathroom as well. They are even under the glass on my writing table. I know nothing about Zen yet, but I am in love with the art of Jujitsu which is the supreme art of self-defence. I love the miniature gardens, the bridges and lanterns, the temples, the beauty of their landscapes. For weeks, after reading Loti's *Madame Chrysanthemum*, I really feel as if I were living in Japan. With Loti I travel from Japan to Turkey, thence to Jerusalem. I become so infatuated with his *Jerusalem* that I finally persuade the editor of a Jewish magazine to let me write something about Solomon's Temple. More research! Somewhere, somehow, I succeeded in finding a model of the temple, showing its evolution, its changes—until the final destruction. I remember reading this article I wrote on the Temple to my father one evening; I recall his amazement that I should possess such a profound knowledge of the subject. . . . What an industrious worm I must have been!

"Back Issues"
by Elizabeth Hardwick

The fact that Elizabeth Hardwick was a founder of The New York Review of Books, *the thoughtful and intellectual periodical in which "Back Issues" first appeared, is an index to the important place she has long held in New York— and national—literary life. She is known not only as an essayist but also as a novelist, memoirist, and critic. Her first novel was* The Ghostly Lover *(1945), her most recent,* Sleepless Nights *(1979), about which critic John Leonard wrote: "Again and again, Miss Hardwick's prose compares favorably with the prose of the masters." Her essays have been collected in* A View of My Own *(1962);* Seduction and Betrayal: Women and Literature *(1974); and* Bartleby in Manhattan *(1983).*

Dark, cold, and misty in January of this year, 1981. Bloomingdale's did better than expected in the Christmas sales and heaven knows it was filled with a mystical spirit for the whole month of December and Fifth Avenue shone with a great light and all was well with the buying and selling of clothes. The army of clothes paraded in the streets and there was impressive national power in the boots, expecially that pair of tan leather trimmed in lizard and costing $600. What luck to find them caressing a shinbone since they were certain to cost more next year.

Splendid *sportif* raccoon coats pacing the avenues, sniffing, fearless night beauties, with small, happy faces peering out of the ruff at the neck, faces with dabs of purplish red on the cheekbones. On the streets you understand that the greatness of winter is to wear woolen shawls, big as a shepherd's cloak, little knit caps, fur-lined gloves, plaid skirts with two dozen pleats, suede pants, and leather vest—and in the evening, velvet.

But the brilliance of this warm display is suddenly snubbed by the impatient appearance of resort clothes, light little things slipped into the windows in the stealth of night, ready for the 2nd of January as if a hot wind had blown them up from the storage basement. Bathing suits and shorts, cotton dresses with spaghetti straps; sunburns and surfboards, tennis rackets and green turf for golf, black waiters and seafood. On Madison Avenue, roses and bougainvillea and the lowly hibiscus; blue swimming pools, strawberries and cream. Overnight, what sun-splattered health in the January slush.

So much for the landscape and the defiant calendar of merchandise. A step on the way to the New York Public Library, the castle of stone and Vermont marble backed by its stone-bench park of infamous as-signations. No reason to doubt the Library, "Modern Renaissance more or less in the style of Louis XVI," has survived the night and its treasures, its flakey books, parcels of such peculiarity, will move back and forth from stack to hand like the tide going in and out.

Forty-second Street does not appear this morning to have enjoyed a particularly good Christmas season. Instead it has the thick and thuggish air of having endured the predicted slump of the times. And it is not on its way to the Caribbean. No need for that since there is something hot and tropical about shoddy, dusty, fatigued little business places in which the winter air seems rich with summer flies.

They say Forty-second Street will be reclaimed and that means many familiar, unpromising things will be deflected. Not unlike the way the state highway department decides upon a new road, makes its plans, and the plans cut through the middle of an old widow's house, tottering there in her own yard, with the rotting barn, its roof beautifully smashed in like a felt hat, and the cracked oval windows of the hayloft. All of it collapse, desuetude that you might call irreplaceable. Goodbye. Off the widow goes to the trailer park where her "assessment" buys a cozy, oblong piece of tin fitted together in the early 1950s. At least there she is in another rural environment and soon at night she can hear the trucks, magnificent transcontinental donkeys carrying hard tomatoes across the country on their backs.

The bar of the Hotel Astor, heart of Times Square not so long ago. Scene of many misadventures owing to double doses of the Manhattan cocktail, wrongly named because of its sweetness. Neat, squeamish girls floating on New Year's Eve into the streets, for history, for city experience—and the men pushing into them, nearly penetrating as it were.

Everywhere there is much respect for the honorable suicide of old buildings tired of the haul up and down, exhausted by patched-up arteries and expensive surgery. The moonlight on ten stories of a sand-stone building with Gothic pediments: for that you go down to the archives like men in rubber suits searching for jewel cases left in the *Andrea Doria*. Cheap sunlight on an empty right-hand corner. There is some of that in empty, dead Main Streets, streets with the ashamed gaze of nude manikins in a shop window at night. Here, in Manhattan, an excavation deep in the middle of Fiftieth Street is as awesome as a crypt in a cathedral and a certain quiet wonder about the nature of things can be observed on the faces of strollers staring down into the hole.

If they reclaim Times Square the squalid pornography houses, the public scene of the private, will then move on, find another ground elsewhere for the onanistic seed. But what about the orange drinks in large, round, glass vessels which swirl the liquid around as if there were many goldfish inside needing circulation? And the record shops, providing through the open doors sounds that grab the arm like a companion suddenly come upon? And the Brazilian shoes with their dagger heels tilted on little pieces of plastic in the display window? They fit someone, just right. And the cafeterias with chopped liver, tunafish, and egg salad brought in at dawn from some sinister kitchen? Yes, the tenacity of disreputable avenues; and yet all is possible and the necessary conditions may arrive and bottles and pencils, hats and condoms will go to their grave.

. . .

The New York Public Library—not much to be done with that. You would not want to say that it has the smell of the tomb of its steady, underpaid clerks; but it does have the smell of a tomb and that is not unpleasant for a day of study. Damp winter shrouds on the backs of chairs. Bright, determined scholars, using the minutes, the hours, and the bibliographies, the footnotes falling into line obediently, like little soldiers in the ranks of documentation.

The others, the others. There at the front table in the left gallery is one of them, a fair-skinned old lady, a true American, daily researching her genealogy—an indefatigable digger, burrowing in the holes of Virginia and Massachusetts. Yes, you see me here in the scum of Manhattan, but my blue eyes and this yellowing white hair go back to Josiah Somebody, a man of great importance in the American Revolution, and I will soon know precisely where the old homestead stood. It was very near to that of his dear friend, the great General John Stark of New Hampshire.

Displaced widow of New York City, what are you doing here, with your pocketbook full of the American Revolution, your house keys, a few dollars, your Senior Citizen bus pass, and your Unitarian memories? Will you not budge, you blue-eyed remainder? Will you never go back to that place where you met your husband in high school, where you went to Normal School to learn to teach reading and arithmetic? There is room back there among the town hall records, the village library, the Grange meetings, the church fair, the waving flags, and the graves. No, she is not going anywhere, is never to be severed; she will not part from thee, Manhattan. She is part of some irrevocable trust, signed and notarized years ago. And now a pretty tortoise-shell comb falls from the bun of her white hair. It falls without sound to the floor, but in its passage it is observed by a young woman who picks it up, puts it in the pocket of her red cable-knit cardigan, and ever so swiftly moves to a table at the back of the room. Another keepsake gone.

Ah, well, the library is a hallowed spot. (Ten men were killed in the building of it, along with twenty or thirty seriously injured.) My university was the New York Public Library, some left-wing intellectuals used to say, singing it out in a *"Deutschland über Alles"* rhythm, the same Hail! rhythm used by the universities themselves.

In the library there can be found Back Issues, old copies of our literary magazines. Quarterlies they were for the most part, inspirations of the vernal equinox and winter solstice. Long and short memorials to the thoughts of many therein. More hours of these lives were spent on book reviews than on lovemaking or even on making a living. Married, divorced, two children, won Pulitzer Prize, suffered torments which at last appeared in print—an emanation, a sign with a name attached to it, as Halley predicting a natural phenomenon claimed as his own the swooning, remarkable flash in the sky. Back Issues, a candy store, small business. Poems and stories, politics, reversals and discoveries, individually packed by hand and some, as they say, moving faster than others.

For this day at the library I took with me the first notebook at hand: a nice object, cherry-colored, flecked with white and bound in a black strip: A-Plus Notebook made by Eaton Paper Division of Textron. There inside were reminders of sloth or perhaps despair of idea—scattered notes for an unwritten article on George Gissing. Part of life, these notes, no different from a large bill in the morning, a Chinese dinner in the evening—real life, set aside like pennies in a dish.

"This ink-stained world."

"The reading-public—oh, the reading public!" p. 200.

And on p. 79 of *New Grub Street*, the terrible cry of: "Don't be foolish, dear. What is to prevent your writing?" What is to prevent? What is to prevent?

Sitting on the bench, awaiting the Back Issues, alongside a beautiful man. Write it down just as male authors write of "the haunting face across the room of a beautiful woman."

He is not an American, certainly not. His genealogy is filled with martyrs, black-eyed, black-haired oppressed peoples, mowed down, starved. Perhaps he comes from some hated minority booted about by an overbearing conqueror; an Armenian perhaps.

The waits at the book desk are an extended intermission, like a queue at a betting place. No matter, quite a few are pleased to pass the time here in warmth, safety, quiet, and best of all in the chapel rectitude of merely "being at the library." The pale green paper lampshades, replacing the old green glass, the worn gloss of the wooden tables, the expert sense of which number directs to the left and which to the right, the world-renowned card catalogue, the free slips of paper, the chutes into which they drop. This place is an occupation with its bits of skill and familiarity with the position of the lavatories.

The beautiful man from the race of martyrs was dressed well enough in the style of modest indoor occupations. He was wearing a white shirt—out of step with the times there—a dark blue or black suit and a black tie. That was rather clerkly and hopeless for midday at Forty-second and Fifth—but see the lustrous black eyes, the tall, thin body, and the hard-edged perfection of nose, cheekbone, and chin. No surprise to observe the foreign, oppressed people's patience in his sitting without sighs, without a crumpled newspaper. At last his number appeared and he received a large volume and the out-of-date quarterlies followed soon.

At our different tables it was possible to see him slowly turning pages. The time passed, he left his place for a moment and I, slipping past the large book, made out the title: *Nervous Diseases*. Yes, yes, he is "nervous," unhappy. There is something wrong with his mind and no one can tell him just what it is. He is in the Public Library researching his misery, his confusion, his sorrow.

Diseases and litigious frenzies, tumors and fits, money owed and great corporations befouling an obscure, solitary person's dreams: Forty-second and Fifth is the roost of these afflictions and who knows but what a great speckled egg of amelioration or revenge lies buried in the stacks or down in the basement of the seldom-called-for. The trouble is that abstract knowledge does not quite fit the personal case with its galling concreteness and its nasty distance from the universal. Con Edison will not refund, the old employer will never rehire, the ringing in the ear will not cease tolling out its dizzying suspicions.

The Summer Issue. Who does not remember that it arrived when the besotted fall leaves were thick in the gutters, providing plenty of time for the unseasonal pages to lie upon the desk until January, when the Autumn Issue appeared in the mails?

1964: "Our judgment of Hawthorne may have to be that he is not for us today, or perhaps not even tomorrow. He is, in Nietzsche's phrase, one of the spirits of yesterday—and the day after tomorrow."

The dash (—) is beautiful. And with what grace it prepares for "and the day after tomorrow."

Now, where does the despised and rejected Armenian live and on what? That's the question of Manhattan, isn't it, for the darkly handsome and for the fair retiree of old American stock?

Reviews of first novels and late novels, poems, stories from some who died young and some who ceased to write, suffering thereby lifelong as from a liver complaint. The touch of the Muse, brushing the cheek like a breeze one day in youth—beware.

Now, here is a first novel, *The Avalanches of Summer*, by a young American, new as a fresh-born kitten, noticed by a critic now wearing as many medals as a Hohenzollern in honor of his notable, fearless displeasures. But wait. The critic finds this young novel brilliant, astonishing, an achievement of the highest sort, and more than that, more than anything to be hoped for, *significant*, actually *about something*.

The climbers, who fall under the avalanche, are two young men and their girlfriends, creatures of post-war Germany, the land of restored opera houses and speeding demons on the Autobahn, a country glowing once more in the brightness of "Munich blue." Their parents, survivors of a thousand cruel ambiguities, do not know that the ice will reach them at last, burying their children who are guilty only of a sporting holiday, the holiday of post-war German prosperity, with its hidden glaciers of guilty ice which no summer sun can melt.

But where is the author and where is his novel? Sank without a trace, in the murderous phrase. What right, you might ask, has the monstrous sea of pages to engulf the young man as if he were a third-class passenger on the arrogant *Lusitania*, watching through the porthole, as he sank, the half-empty lifeboats? Of course it is always possible the critic's pleasure unhinged him, but who can bear to think of the diseases of happiness?

Many brilliant names on the magazine covers arousing a palsy of anticipation. The romance of names, as if one were to say, I met him at a party and that is how it started. Fall in love in the middle of a Winter Issue. Or suffer a disillusionment, make several telephone calls, as if to a doctor or a druggist, to ask: What do you make of that? My head aches from the wrong turning at the end.

It's only words, the druggist says.

Worms?

No, words.

Spring Issue, 1958: "There remains the case of the forcibly Sovietized countries of Eastern Europe, whose plight we cannot recognize as definite." That was good news for us of the anti-Stalinist left.

At mid-afternoon the sun, slipping through the mist, made a bright stripe across the face of the handsome man. His skin had the sallow tintings of so many interesting peoples. But there was nothing of shah or sheik or pasha in his black-suited diffidence. Perhaps just a shade of flirtatiousness that comes from life as a beauty and being noticed—a sort of lifting of the head.

In another Back Issue a translation from the French:

But novels are written *by* men and *for* men. In the eyes of God, Who cuts through appearances and goes beyond them, there is no novel, no art, for art thrives on appearances. God is not an artist. Neither is M. Mauriac.

Appearances has several meanings. The face of the handsome foreigner is not to the point here.

Nothing much to report about him. Activities at the library table have their dramatic limits. *Nervous Diseases* has been abandoned, pushed to the side. Now he seems to be writing a letter with its thoughtful pauses for reflection followed by a steady, rhythmical sweep across the sheet of paper.

The pages of the purple or cherry-colored notebook ripple back to jottings about George Gissing. "He wanted home life and found a slattern." That was Edith, the second Mrs. Gissing, the second fatality. Such a "selfish and coarse nature" he chose, even after his youthful marriage to the alcoholic prostitute, Nell, the best of the two. Nell died at thirty-one, and at last, at last, in a fearful scene, freezing in fever in her light dirty dress on a filthy, miserable bed. "The trade of the damned" appears as a quotation, but it is not about poor Nell; it is about Gissing at his writing desk or one of his writing characters.

In the old magazines there are early opinions, what you might call thin ones, and now twenty or so years later the opinions of some have expanded like the size of the waistband.

The advertisements on the back covers linger there like gossip. What was born that year that did not exist the year before? "I am inclined to believe that John Berryman's 77 Dream Songs will in the long run be seen as more important than his brilliant Homage to Mistress Bradstreet."—Allen Tate. Well, that was true. Across the board.

No one in the Public Library today brings to mind the early John B. peering over his large, glinting eyeglasses from the stage of the YMHA, the temple of poetry readings. There he was then, spare, intense, and learned; there he was in a smart tweed jacket, there before the faithful girls of New York. High style infatuation. In the vestibule where white wine completed the evening, the poet could be seen skating as if on one toe over the oil slick of questions, diverting away from his own lines to *The Winter's Tale* and gorgeous Perdita, left to the wind and the waves, and the parenthetical paranoias of Leontes. Another evening. That's what we're here for, the filing cabinet of first and last performances.

Of course you never know who is about in the library. The pretty, plump girl smiling like intelligence itself as she reads. . . . Time to leave. Gather up the Gissing class-bloodied world, a clot of unsuccess. Leave the magazine essays and their seashell precocity.

He too rose and there he is at the stairs and then again at the cloakroom. Outside a cold, heavy rain annoys hundreds who begin to scream for taxis even though there are none to be seen with the light on. But scream away just in case there has been an electrical shortage in the engine and half the cabs are indeed free. People from the street crowd under the narrow ledge of the Forty-second Street entrance. A fury of restless vexation addressed to the weather. High heels drown in the splash at the curb and the mean West Side wind from the Hudson blows about as carelessly as crime. Nothing special—just a skirmish with time, time as scarce as old shoe buckles for the busy and the idle.

Think of the courage of the new Hotel Hyatt down the street at Grand Central. Millions and millions of dollars of faith, each dollar a pilgrim. The intrepid gleam of its brass and glass, its Alpine waterfall splashing over three long, flat concrete steps, and the pastoral, bay-windowed restaurant, cozy as a cottage garden, hanging over Forty-second Street. Down below our third world mysteries and wonders of bus exhausts, blowing garbage, and blind newsdealers to salute the Japanese. Fortunately they are accustomed to the Asiatic.

And here is my man, unrolling a large black umbrella of genuine cloth. With his black cap of curls, his careful courtesy, he now has the look of a seminarian. As companions from the bookshelf and reading room, he holds the umbrella over my head and we begin to converse. People sometimes meet each other in the library, although that is not the romance of the noble building. It is not a suitable landscape for the enrichment of social experience, no. The single persons it claims are far too singular and the encounters struck up are likely to be as unfortunately surprising as the meeting of a homosexual and a detective in the subway toilets.

After we agree that it is raining, he asks: Where do you live, you American?

A reassuring accent, a nice, lilting, slightly askew knowledge of the language, the attractive flow of someone who has learned English abroad.

I live here in Manhattan.

Manhattan. More than a million and a half.

We are each one of more than a million.

What is the occupation of your life? he continues. A little rote learning in that perhaps. Once long ago I looked over the shoulder of a young man on a train in Europe in order to discover his *Nervous Diseases*, as it were. He was studying an English grammar, working on a sentence which read: "Can you tell me, sir, where I can purchase a pair of plus-fours?" So, a bit of plus-fours in the black beauty's English.

My occupation? I find myself occupied as a teacher.

A pause, a brief, dry cough and then: Now, I am sad. In my other life I was a teacher. That was also my occupation in life and so we are engaged in a coincidence, you and I.

What is your occupation in life now?

And suddenly there in the freezing rain, the rain of a thousand annoyances not to be endured without multitudinous protests and curses of betrayal, the true black-suited man appeared. Whence cometh thou, new immigrant standing on the steps of the New York Public Library?

I am Greek. In my black suit and black tie I work in a Greek restaurant tonight and every night except Sunday.

The sad dark Greek in a dark Greek restaurant. Unfair, unfair, since it has been said time and time again that the quality of Greek light is one of the land's greatest treasures.

His is a family story, a condensation of history: Many of my relations, relatives—which is it, the word?—are here. My brother is driving a taxi. My aunt, one uncle, and two cousins are in the streets all day. They are occupied with selling Sabrett hot dogs. Down at the corner you will see a woman dressed in ten layers of clothing and standing in the rain. My mother's sister and a very strong woman. But the Sabrett is not much in life, is it, would you say? . . . Still, I don't know. It is a question for philosophers. You make a little list of this and that and the head becomes dizzy.

Oh the Greeks in the Manhattan streets. One in felt boots, wrapped up like a mummy, showing her red, gap-toothed face, face like roughened hide with a bright hole in it. She moves her cart from the Fifty-ninth Street subway station entrance, on down to Fifty-seventh, following the market. The thin, hawk-nosed seller outside the ABC building floats into my memory and mingles with the nerve-wrung Greek beside me.

And the library with the people huddling to escape the rain seemed like an old monastery surrounded by beggars waiting for alms. Only we, the man and I, a prelate and a nun, stand under our papal umbrella.

The restaurant?

Just another *ethnic*. I like that word ethnic, Greek root, although I never heard it in my country. We have a belly-dancer on the weekend. That's Turkish, not Greek, but what's the difference? *Danse du ventre* on Friday and Saturday. Most of the dancers are American. They say they are college girls. Can you tell me true if they are college girls?

Probably not. Topless college girls. College call-girls. Another question.

I look up at the handsome Greek waiter and he smiles, showing perfect white teeth to complete his square, fleshless jaw. And what did he teach in Greece? Ah, he said, don't be amused. It was English I taught. Of course my Greek education is not sufficient for a profession here, not sufficient in the least way. And I am finished back there, out of the system, because I got it in my head to come to the States.

So, this man with his striking perfections has in his circle of choices become a whole. He is a completed form, awaiting the content of the future. Youth, foot over foot on the rungs of the ladder of the teaching bureaucracy, breathing the uncertain air of a respectable possibility. No getting drunk in taverns—and also a cautious purity perhaps, avoiding the trap of many children. Black plastic briefcase, the girdle of Adonis.

The rain let up and down came the umbrella. I am off to the unspeakable restaurant, he said with a bow. And for me the crosstown bus braked to a stop on the corner of Sixth Avenue. And there he was talking with a woman standing under the Sabrett yellow and blue umbrella. She was standing like a thoughtful animal in its winter stall.

No special surprise when he telephoned a few nights later, one teacher of English to another, the occupied and the disoccupied, bound together by one of our great public institutions. There was the question of his knowing my name and he said that it was found on a slip of paper left at the reading desk. It was his idea that the curious could discover what they wished.

In accord with that it was possible to ask: If you taught English why aren't you reading novels instead of *Nervous Diseases*?

Novels? I can't understand novels . . . no more than a sheep.

Can you understand medical books?

The one I was looking at had nothing to say about my condition in life. A disappointment.

In the background there was the noise of the restaurant and he stopped now and then to speak aside in Greek.

Explaining himself to me he said, in a matter-of-fact way apparently so clear and unalterable to him it was without regret: I don't know anything about English culture. I just happened to be able to learn the language, like singing. Maybe it turned out to be a pity. A bad Greek fate. I am ignorant, deeply ignorant.

Of course this admission made me trust him without reserve. No need to imagine harassment from such an abyss of self-examination.

Also, I can't talk about Seferis or Kazantzakis . . . or even Aeschylus.

His correct Greek pronunciation bejeweled the already glittering consonants and vowels of the names of his countrymen. After a pause he said: Do not be disturbed. I am not fantastical. I have no fantasies.

What a pity, the Mediterranean voyager.

I have looked for him from time to time near the library. It would be nice to see him standing at the door, with the sun on his "classical" nose and all the storehouse of the Age of Pericles behind him in the dark vaults.

At Easter I heard from him again and for the last time. He said he was getting married to a well-to-do Greek-American who came as a customer to the restaurant.

Oh, the bitch.

It turned out that "well-to-do" was the result of a divorce settlement. I said: Watch out. She may have to give that up if she marries again.

He said, no, his understanding was that she was well-to-do from a *lump sum*. And he asked if that was the correct phrase and I said yes, a lump sum was quite acceptable.

And what will you do when you have married the lump sum?

He said: I will speak English to it.

That is all about my Greek exile, now a New Yorker, all about one of those "incomplete, sensitive men," as the phrase has it in my Gissing notes. Such notes and phrases and quotations all day long attach themselves to real people like a handshake.

I think of him when I hear the wheels of the hot dog cart pushing up the street early in the morning, pushing all the way it now seems to me from a Greek village to midtown Manhattan, and with no amazement at what, covered with boiled onions or mustard, we will eat for breakfast.

I will remember him in the conservative black and white so well suited to a displaced martyr, a teacher of English. Not the heart to imagine the bright closet of turtleneck jerseys and zippered jackets he may be wearing out there in Queens, known as the borough of cemeteries.

And the Back Issues pile up in front of and behind experience, wedging the sandwich of real life in between. Pages are existence and the eye never stops on its lookout for the worm, the seed, the fish beneath the water, the next meal.

It is summer now and yesterday I crashed into a tree in order to avoid a deer on a June morning so foggy the deer perhaps thought it was dusk. An unusual happening, a drama, terrible, a trauma. But in the evening my injured shoulder and the awesome closeness to death gave way. A Back Issue from England, one of a month or so ago, told me that in France the population had in a hundred years risen by 25 percent but "the number of art students from 1,000 to 191,600." The conclusion was that "such numbers lead to devaluation." An interesting idea, displacing for a time shoulder, deer, death, and, in our creative usage, my "totaled" car.

"Reading Room" by E. B. White

Although in later life E. B. White lived in Maine, he knew and loved New York City and its famous Public Library. Of the following poem, White commented that it was "inspired by hours spent in the New York Public Library, where I often went not to read but to write. . . . I still feel a sentimental attachment to the Library, still have a sense of indebtedness."

Sadness and languor along the oak tables
Steady the minds of the sitters and readers;
Sleep and despair, and the stealth of hunters,
And (in the man at the end of the row) anger.

Books are the door of escape from the forest,
Books are the wilderness, too, for the scholar;
Walled in the past, drowning in fables,
Out of the weather we sit, steady in languor.

Which are the ones that belong, properly?
Which are the hunters, which the harried?
Break not the hush that surrounds this miracle—
Mind against mind, coupling in splendor—
Step on no twig, disturbing the forest.
Enter the aisles of despair. Sit down and be quiet.

"Response of the Gentle Scholars" by Edmund Wilson

Any attempt at identifying Edmund Wilson (1895–1972) must suggest his vast knowledge and his continuing reputation as perhaps the preeminent American man of letters in the twentieth century. Poet, novelist, literary critic and historian, essayist, editor, playwright, and lecturer, he wrote on subjects as diverse as Symbolist literature (Axel's Castle, *1931); the European revolutionary tradition (*To the Finland Station, *1940);* The Dead Sea Scrolls, 1947–1969 *(1969); the history of the American Indian Confederacy (*Apologies to the Iroquois, *1959); literature of the American Civil War (*Patriotic Gore, *1962); Russian literature and language (*A Window on Russia, *1972).*

Wilson published three books of poetry. "Response of the Gentle Scholars" is taken from Notebooks of Night *(1942).*

"**N**ow the public libraries, particularly the Forty-second Street one, are simply loathsome. All the chairs in the Magazine Room and Newspaper Room are filled with down-and-outers, the overflow from

Bryant Park and Central. All the marble seats on the stairs are filled with more down-and-outers, their feet swathed in newspapers. Besides the down-and-outers, Communists with mops of hair like black moss gabble in the corridors, or engage in amorous dalliance on the stairs. . . . I think it is the smell I resent the most rather than the actual presence of these people, nauseating as that is. . . . Open the Morgan Library and who will throng its halls, pushing the gentle scholars away, ruining the silence for readers to whom Shelley, Pope and Ben Jonson are not dehumanized? The rag-tail and bob-tail. The rabble. The down-and-outers. The feeble-minded. . . . Interesting to a historian, perhaps, but not to a bibliophile longing for the gentle peace that is to be found only in woods and libraries."

—From a letter to *The Saturday Review of Literature.*

They reach you then, the great, the grim,
  Like mediums murmuring from swoons
In chambers carpeted and dim,
  Where Cromwell or Napoleon croons,
Becoming as a little child:
  "This place is peaceful! never fear!"
Shakespeare, Mark Twain and Oscar Wilde
  Declare, "We are so happy here!"
They lull you then, they leave you calm:
  Ben Jonson's hardness and Pope's hate?
You never flush nor feel a qualm
  At Shelley's rage against the great?
—We gentle students of the dead,
  We've known them long and marked them well—
Who seek among the books a bed,
  Ill-shod, unshaven, foul to smell;
And marked you others, better-shod,
  Among the books who beg to creep
To planes of being chaste but odd:
  Not literature nor life nor sleep.
And we, alas!—we mayn't ignore,
  Among the books, that you, poor friends,

And they have both been seen before
    In junctures doomed to desperate ends,
Wherein you did perforce endure
    —So Time's depressing record tells—
Much tumult, much discomfiture,
    And even more unpleasant smells.
For you and us and all we cherished,
    "Silence" was "ruined" then indeed—
And even libraries have perished
    From bibliophiles who failed to read.

These funny muffled woods; the rusted stream
Scarce rustling in the hollow; stifled weather;
An airplane dimly humming; dull as March—
In summer warmth the darkling light of autumn;
The very colors of the wood subdued.

    You are alone—
The woods are dumb with the dead.

The crows of March are barking in the wood
Alarmed they haarch-haarch and yar-yar-yar
They have their exits and their entrances
And one crow in his life plays several parts
One crow mounts guaard-guaard in a tree
Gives yar-yar-yarning: all the parts are plain.
So once in these sparse woods before the dark
All lonely, wild and lyric twanged their calling.
At morning now who sleepless long have lain,
Loveless, nervous, tired, torn,
Almost I envy sentinel and sleeping host
Almost I envy voices grown coarse-coarse that caw the morn.
The days and nights—pressure and relief—
    Outlast them both—wake till the snow is white—
Desire pales and dies—that heat is brief—
    The day was here like night—outlast the night!

For only when distaste and lust, and bright and dark—
    Silence and noise, the quiet and the quick—
Are spent against the will like waves, the rock, the Ark,
    Survives the surf that laps the crumbled brick.

Now the garage shows green—the servant wakes—
    My mistress sleeps—she dreams of nothing now—
But I, my thoughts stay while all the ground shakes.

—My dear,
                    My dear, you cough in your sleep—
    You say you gave me rock and ark, and I had forgotten how.

Excerpt from *Bronx Primitive* by Kate Simon

Kate Simon (1912–90), who was born in Poland, came to America with her family in steerage at the age of four. She wrote in Bronx Primitive: Portraits in a Childhood *(1982) about her childhood in the Tremont section of the Bronx. Ms. Simon was an editor and book reviewer as well as a well-known author of numerous travel books, including* Mexico: Places and Pleasures *(1963);* Italy: The Places In Between *(1970); and* England's Green and Pleasant Land *(1974); and* A Renaissance Tapestry: The Gonzaga of Mantua *(1988). She also wrote a best-selling guide to New York,* New York Places and Pleasures: An Uncommon Guidebook *(1959).*

Following Bronx Primitive, *Ms. Simon published* A Wider World: Portraits in Adolescence *(1986), a memoir about her teenage years. Robert Pinsky in* The New York Times *praised her "clean and unpretentious prose style, her aristocratic disdain for cant and her frank worldliness." These qualities are evident in the following selection from* Bronx Primitive.

My family arrived on Lafontaine the summer before I was six and ready to be enrolled in the first grade, my brother in kindergarten. As I had learned to do in European trains and stations, in inns, on the vastness of the ship *Susquehanna* when I was an immigrant four-year-old, I studied every landmark, every turning of our new surroundings.

On the day we registered for school, P.S. 58 on Washington Avenue at 176th Street, my mother pointed out each turn, the number of blocks to the left or right and here we were at the big red building, the school, across from the little white building, the library. On the first day of school we went unaccompanied—hold his hand, don't talk to strange men. He complained that I was squeezing his hand and I probably was, tense and worried, avidly searching for the places I had marked out on our route: first to Tremont Avenue and right to the cake store, cross Third Avenue under the El, pass the butcher's with the pigs' feet in the window, cross Tremont at the bicycle shop to the barber's pole, continue on to the white library, and cross Washington Avenue to the school. . . .

Immediately to the left of us lived the Silverbergs. Manya Silverberg was dashing and pretty, younger than my mother and more stylish, with an impressive repertory of clothing that she made herself. She cooked well and made cookies that were more "American" than my mother's little pockets of hard tack known as cheese cookies. Like my mother, she was soft-spoken, a reader and a learner; both moved like debased aristocrats through the slatternly street of dented garbage cans on their way to English classes at the local public library. I loved Mrs. Silverberg as I loved Lillian Gish, as I loved the pretty young aunts, still in Warsaw, in the photographs I stared at for long times, trying to invent voices for them, improvising dialogues with them. She became a substitute aunt. . . .

The lower landings were more remote, shaping their own looser tribes. A number of our friends lived in various sections of the house and we knew some of their parents, of little consequence to us unless they were unusually hospitable or unusually forbidding. The only fourth-floor family that steadily interested me were the Liebowitzes. Ida Liebowitz, who was in my class, wore long stockings and long sleeves winter and summer, a cruel piece of religious fanaticism according to the other mothers. She had no skates, wasn't permitted to go to the movies, ever, and on Saturdays read her library books on her fire escape away from the eyes of her father, Yontiff ("Holiday"), who would not permit the handling of *goyish* books on the Sabbath. He once caught her at it and tore the book out of her hands, thrusting it far onto the empty lot. There were fierce, unspecified punishments for losing library books, a sin as terrible as stealing or playing doctor. Ida might be sent to prison or left back in school or made to stay in every afternoon writing a hundred times "I must not lose library books." We all worried. Ida was not permitted to leave her house, the free-roaming boys would not stoop to search for a girl's book, and the girls, eager for the drama of the search, were told to "stay home and mind your own business." In any case, we hadn't much time. Last night's gefilte fish wrapped in its quivering coat of jelly and the chunks of *challa* were already on the table to be gobbled fast so we could get to the Belmont movie theatre when it opened.

We almost immediately lost interest in the book and in the Liebowitzes, who soon moved to what the women called a more "kosher" neighborhood, with more piety, fewer *goyim*, and fewer of the even more dangerous Jewish *goyim* who let their children skate on Saturday and go to libraries and movies on Saturday, handling money to view the abominations of Sodom and Gomorrah. . . .

The ticker tape in my head busily clicking observations about power and vanity, theirs and mine, and yet knowing nothing, I went on the day of my graduation from elementary school to change my child's library card for one that permitted me to use the downstairs room for adults. Some writer there would tell me what Louisa May Alcott couldn't, nor Dickens nor the children's biographies of Mozart and Beethoven. Where the titles came from I don't know but I had ready a mental list of books to take from the adult shelves and found them: Knut Hamsun's *Hunger*, Hugo's *Les Misérables*, Nietzsche's *Thus Spake Zarathustra*, the plays of Chekhov. Armed with these mighty weapons, I would know, I would understand. The clotted brambles would melt away from the secret door and I would be in the adult garden of clean colors and shapes where everything had its own unchanging name; white-petaled truth always truth, the slender trees with silvery bark always promises kept, the mazes of love and sex clearly marked, brilliantly illustrated and immutable. Anyhow, it was a proud thing to be turning the pages of such great thoughts and emotions, and although they didn't teach me enough—just what was it Zarathustra was preaching? why were all those people mooning and yearning for Moscow?—they were pushing me, little by little, I hoped, toward that garden of crystal clarity. The books grew heavier, some not helpful at all—Dostoevski's brothers Karamazov were as irrational as the people around me—some, like Chekhov's stories, confirming in whispers things I almost half knew about people.

As I was reading Chekhov's "The Darling" one morning, envying her fullness of devotion, contemptuous of her dopiness, I felt as if I were losing urine, without the usual warning sensations except a heaviness in my lower belly. When I took off my bloomers in the bathroom, I saw a few red drops of blood on them and on my thigh. I called to my mother, astonished and frightened; maybe this, not going blind or crazy, was the result of masturbating. She said, smiling, that it was my monthlies and slapped me hard on the face. She had not been particularly friendly since my practicing on the new piano had diminished, but she hadn't seethed or boiled like my father. So why hit me now, what had I done? Was this some sort of punishment? For not practicing enough? For reading instead of going to the grocery store? For not watching my little sister carefully enough? For running after Sal? Why? I was back, slapped back from the growing confidence of being over thirteen to the be-wilderments of eight and nine. It was months later, after I had learned to use and wash, reuse and rewash the strips of torn sheet she gave me, that she explained the slap; it was to restore a girl's circulation and all mothers did it in the Old Country. I was relieved but unforgiving; she could have told me sooner, and what was this Old Country junk in a woman who scorned so many of its practices?

It was a day in May. I had achieved my first menstrual period, my white wedding dress tree on 179th Street had covered its sky with blossoms. In the library that Saturday morning were my two favorite librarians, the young woman with long blond hair twisted in a satiny band around her head who spoke English as Miss Bender did, as I was determined to, even though my friends called me a "show-off" and "teacher's pet"; the word "affected" was not in their vocabulary. The other favorite librarian was a short woman who always wore a brown dress with a lace collar and brown shoes. She had puffs of brown hair and round brown eyes and I thought of her as one of the plump brown birds I saw in Crotona Park. She spoke with a slight accent, nothing like the cadences I heard on Lafontaine, not marked enough to mimic. She was intensely interested in what I was selecting, what I had chosen to take home. *War and Peace?* She looked doubtful, but said to try it anyway. *The Great God Brown*, maybe not, but it, too, was worth trying. She never said absolutely no; a good pedagogue, she let me glean what I could out of any choice I made. She must have sensed, as well, how proud I was to be carrying these ponderous works by masters through the street, not on skates anymore, but on foot, like the college student I meant to be mistaken for.

Excerpt from *A Son of the Middle Border* by Hamlin Garland

Hamlin Garland (1860–1940) is one of the best-known chroniclers of Midwestern farm life, a subject much less celebrated in American literature than, say, life in New York City. Born in Wisconsin, he lived also on farms in Iowa and South Dakota before moving for a time to Boston (a journey that is the subject of the following excerpt). His stories were collected in Main-Travelled Roads *(1891), probably his best-known book;* Prairie Folks *(1893);* Wayside Courtships *(1897); and* Boy Life on the Prairie *(1899).*

Garland's novels, like Jason Edwards: An Average Man *(1892) and* Rose of Dutcher's Coolly *(1895), were often written with the unashamed intention of bettering the lives of the hardworking and impoverished rural people he knew. In a book of essays,* Crumbling Idols *(1895), he explained his theories of "veritism," a socially oriented realism. He also wrote many volumes of memoirs, of which the best regarded are* A Son of the Middle Border *(1917) and* A Daughter of the Middle Border *(1921), which won a Pulitzer Prize.*

I t took me thirty-six hours more to get to Boston, and as I was ill all the way (I again rode in the smoking car) a less triumphant Jason never entered the City of Light and Learning. The day was a true November day, dark and rainy and cold, and when I confronted my cloud-built city of domes and towers I was concerned only with a place to sleep—I had little desire of battle and no remembrance of the Golden Fleece.

Up from the Hoosac Station and over the slimy, greasy pavement I trod with humped back, carrying my heavy valise (it was the same imitation-leather concern with which I had toured the city two years before), while gay little street cars tinkled by, so close to my shoulder that I could have touched them with my hand.

Again I found my way through Haymarket Square to Tremont Street and so at last to the Common, which presented a cold and dismal face at this time. The glory of my dream had fled. The trees, bare and brown and dripping with rain, offered no shelter. The benches were sodden, the paths muddy, and the sky, lost in a desolate mist shut down over my head with oppressive weight. I crawled along the muddy walk feeling about as important as a belated beetle in a July thunderstorm. Half of me was ready to surrender and go home on the next train but the other half, the obstinate half, sullenly forged ahead, busy with the problem of a roof and bed.

My experience in Rock River now stood me in good hand. Stopping a policeman I asked the way to the Young Men's Christian Association. The officer pointed out a small tower not far away, and down the Tremont Street walk I plodded as wretched a youth as one would care to see.

Humbled, apologetic, I climbed the stairway, approached the desk, and in a weak voice requested the address of a cheap lodging place.

From the cards which the clerk carelessly handed to me I selected the nearest address, which chanced to be on Boylston Place, a short narrow street just beyond the Public Library. It was a deplorably wet and gloomy alley, but I ventured down its narrow walk and desperately knocked on the door of No. 12.

From this sunless nook, this narrow niche, I began my study of Boston, whose historic significance quite overpowered me. I was alone. Mr. Bashford, in Portland, Maine, was the only person in all the east on whom I could call for aid or advice in case of sickness. My father wrote me that he had relatives living in the city but I did not know how to find them. No one could have been more absolutely alone than I during that first month. I made no acquaintances, I spoke to no one.

A part of each day was spent in studying the historical monuments of the city, and the remaining time was given to reading at the Young Men's Union or in the Public Library, which stood next door to my lodging house.

At night I made detailed studies of the habits of the cockroaches with which my room was peopled. There was something uncanny in the action of these beasts. They were new to me and apparently my like had never before been observed by them. They belonged to the shadow, to the cold and to the damp of the city, whereas I was fresh from the sunlight of the plain, and as I watched them peering out from behind my wash-basin, they appeared to marvel at me and to confer on my case with almost elfish intelligence.

Tantalized by an occasional feeble and vacillating current of warm air from the register, I was forced at times to wear my overcoat as I read, and at night I spread it over my cot. I did not see the sun for a month. The wind was always filled with rain or sleet, and as the lights in Bates' Hall were almost always blazing, I could hardly tell when day left off and night began. It seemed as if I had been plunged into another and darker world, a world of storm, of gray clouds, of endless cold.

Having resolved to keep all my expenses within five dollars per week, I laid down a scientific plan for cheap living. I first nosed out every low-priced eating place within ten minutes' walk of my lodging and soon knew which of these "joints" were wholesome, and which were not. Just around the corner was a place where a filling dinner could be procured for fifteen cents, including pudding, and the little lunch counter on Tremont Street supplied my breakfast. Not one nickel did I spend in carfare, and yet I saw almost every celebrated building in the city. However, I tenderly regarded my shoe soles each night, for the cost of tapping was enormous.

My notion of studying at some school was never carried out. The Boston University classes did not attract me. The Harvard lectures were inaccessible, and my call upon the teacher of "Expression" to whom Mr. Bashford had given me a letter led to nothing. The professor was a nervous person and made the mistake of assuming that I was as timid as I was silent. His manner irritated me and the outburst of my resentment was astonishing to him. I was hungry at the moment and to be patronized was too much!

This encounter plunged me into deep discouragement and I went back to my reading in the library with a despairing resolution to improve every moment, for my stay in the east could not last many weeks. At the rate my money was going May would see me bankrupt.

I read both day and night, grappling with Darwin, Spencer, Fiske, Helmholtz, Haeckel—all the mighty masters of evolution whose books I had not hitherto been able to open. For diversion I dived into early English poetry and weltered in that sea of song which marks the beginnings of every literature, conning the ballads of Ireland and Wales, the epics of Ireland, the early German and the songs of the troubadours, a course of reading which started me on a series of lectures to be written directly from a study of the authors themselves. This dimly took shape as a volume to be called *The Development of English Ideals*, a sufficiently ambitious project.

Among other proscribed books I read Whitman's *Leaves of Grass* and without doubt that volume changed the world for me as it did for many others. Its rhythmic chants, its wonderful music filled me with a keen sense of the mystery of the near at hand. I rose from that first reading with a sense of having been taken up into high places. The spiritual significance of America was let loose upon me.

Herbert Spencer remained my philosopher and master. With eager haste I sought to compass the "Synthetic Philosophy." The universe took on order and harmony as, from my five cent breakfast, I went directly to the consideration of Spencer's theory of the evolution of music or painting or sculpture. It was thrilling, it was joyful to perceive that everything moved from the simple to the complex—how the bowstring became the harp, and the egg the chicken. My mental diaphragm creaked with the pressure of inrushing ideas. My brain young, sensitive to every touch, took hold of facts and theories like a phonographic cylinder, and while my body softened and my muscles wasted from disuse, I skittered from pole to pole of the intellectual universe like an impatient bat. I learned a little of everything and nothing very thoroughly. With so many peaks in sight, I had no time to spend on digging up the valley soil.

My only exercise was an occasional slow walk. I could not afford to waste my food in physical effort, and besides I was thinly dressed and could not go out except when the sun shone. My overcoat was considerably more than half cotton and a poor shield against the bitter wind which drove straight from the arctic sea into my bones. Even when the weather was mild, the crossings were nearly always ankle deep in slush, and walking was anything but a pleasure, therefore it happened that for days I took no outing whatsoever. From my meals I returned to my table in the library and read until closing time, conserving in every way my thirty cents' worth of "food units."

In this way I covered a wide literary and scientific territory. Humped over my fitful register I discussed the Nebular Hypothesis. My poets and scientists not merely told me of things I had never known, they confirmed me in certain conceptions which had come to me without effort in the past. I became an evolutionist in the fullest sense, accepting Spencer as the greatest living thinker. Fiske and Galton and Allen were merely assistants to the Master Mind whose generalizations included in their circles all modern discovery.

It was a sad change when, leaving the brilliant reading room where my mind had been in contact with these masters of the scientific world, I crept back to my minute den, there to sit humped and shivering (my overcoat thrown over my shoulders) confronting with scared resentment the sure wasting of my little store of dollars. In spite of all my care, the pennies departed from my pockets like grains of sand from an hourglass and most disheartening of all I was making no apparent gain toward fitting myself for employment in the west.

Furthermore, the greatness, the significance, the beauty of Boston was growing upon me. I felt the neighboring presence of its autocrats more definitely and powerfully each day. Their names filled the daily papers, their comings and goings were carefully noted. William Dean Howells, Oliver Wendell Holmes, John G. Whittier, Edwin Booth, James Russell Lowell, all these towering personalities seemed very near to me now, and their presence, even if I never saw their faces, was an inspiration to one who had definitely decided to compose essays and poems, and to write possibly a history of American Literature. Symphony concerts, the Lowell Institute Lectures, the *Atlantic Monthly*—(all the distinctive institutions of the Hub) had become very precious to me notwithstanding the fact that I had little actual share in them. Their nearness while making my poverty more bitter, aroused in me a vague ambition to succeed—in something. "I won't be beaten, I will not surrender," I said.

Being neither a resident of the city nor a pupil of any school I could not take books from the library and this inhibition wore upon me till at last I determined to seek the aid of Edward Everett Hale who had long been a great and gracious figure in my mind. His name had been among the "Authors" of our rainy-day game on the farm. I had read his books, and I had heard him preach and as his "Lend-a-hand" helpfulness was proverbial, I resolved to call upon him at his study in the church, and ask his advice. I was not very definite as to what I expected him to do, probably I hoped for sympathy in some form.

The old man received me with kindness, but with a look of weariness which I quickly understood. Accustomed to helping people he considered me just another "Case." With hesitation I explained my difficulty about taking out books.

With a bluff roar he exclaimed, "Well, well That is strange! Have you spoken to the Librarian about it?"

"I have, Dr. Hale, but he told me there were twenty thousand young students in the city in precisely my condition. People not residents and with no one to vouch for them cannot take books home."

"I don't like that," he said. "I will look into that. You shall be provided for. Present my card to Judge Chamberlain; I am one of the trustees, and he will see that you have all the books you want."

I thanked him and withdrew, feeling that I had gained a point. I presented the card to the librarian whose manner softened at once. As a protégé of Dr. Hale I was distinguished. "I will see what can be done for you," said Judge Chamberlain. Thereafter I was able to take books to my room, a habit which still further imperilled my health, for I read fourteen hours a day instead of ten.

Naturally I grew white and weak. My Dakota tan and my corn-fed muscle melted away. The only part of me which flourished was my hair. I begrudged every quarter which went to the barbers and I was cold most of the time (except when I infested the library) and I was hungry *all* the time.

I knew that I was physically on the down-grade, but what could I do? Nothing except to cut down my expenses. I was living on less than five dollars a week, but even at that the end of my *stay* in the city was not far off. Hence I walked gingerly and read fiercely.

"Poetry Reading in the Downtown Library" by Cathy Stern

Cathy Stern's work has been published in The New Republic *and* Shenandoah, *and some of her poems and an interview appeared in the anthology* A Wider Giving: Women Writing After a Long Silence *(Chicory Blue Press, 1988). She teaches English and creative writing at the University of Houston-Downtown. "Poetry Reading in the Downtown Library" was first published in* The Bayou Review.

About this poem Ms. Stern has commented: "There was a derelict who had come in out of the rain at a poetry reading I gave during the Houston Festival. I thought, I would like to deal with this, but how? . . . I had a lot of trouble with the last two lines because there was a little shadow of condescension in there and I had to get it out. I changed 'I open the slim / folder of my poems and I read to him' to 'I open my slim / folder of poems and I read them to him,' just a fine line of difference."

In this rain, I wouldn't have come myself

but I'm one of the readers. So I'm here
crossing the lobby, going past the shelf
of bestsellers, down the escalator

to the blue-carpeted room where a few
friends, shaking out raincoats, seem glad to see
me. I'm glad to see them, I'll tell you.
I thought my husband and mother might be

the audience, plus a couple of friends
of Jim's—he's reading after me. But now I'm
up at the mike, there's a strange old man's
bleary, unshaven face in the back row,

empty eyes on me. I open my slim
folder of poems and I read them to him.

for Jim Ulmer

THREE

The Librarian

Librarians are such an essential part of the American public library that they appear as characters in every section of this anthology. They introduce children to the world of books, they are influential local citizens, they provide patient and complex services, they fall in love, they solve mysteries, they are the subject of humor, and they struggle to maintain the place of an open and free library in a strong democracy.

Yet, despite their importance, librarians have an image that is often as dusty and out-of-date as a book no one has taken from the shelf for years. Librarians know this, and their professional journals are full of unavailing complaint about how they traditionally are taken for granted, misrepresented, and even abused in print.

The selections here illustrate some of the different ways writers have viewed librarians. Many remember the librarians of their childhood with a mixture of awe, respect, and affection. Howard Wilson evokes an especially memorable librarian in "*Growing Up with a Past.*" With her orangey red hair and odd color of dress, Wilson's Miss Louise is a dramatic figure. Yet she is also warm and approachable, sought as a confidante, and highly respected.

Miss Louise, as her honorific indicates, never marries. The single female librarian is pervasive in library fiction, with some historical basis in the days when the few professions open to women were sometimes restricted, culturally if not officially, to those who were unmarried. A representative example is lonely Lucy Wallis of *Centerville U.S.A.*, a drab contrast to lively Miss Louise.

Although "Marian the Librarian" is single, she will not remain so much longer. The heroine of Meredith Willson's beloved musical *The Music Man*, Marian is a woman of such beauty, spirit, and independence that it is no wonder Harold Hill, the smooth-talking con man, wants to win her. Readers who remember the play or the film will have to imagine Robert Preston, who brought irresistible charm and magnetism to the role of Harold, waving his paper bag of marbles, intoning his outrageous rhymes, and beginning a successful wooing of Miss Marian.

A librarian's life is not, of course, mainly love and laughter. In the last chapter of this book, "Democracy in the Library," many selections attest to the critical role librarians play in maintaining the heritage and continuing the growth of libraries. Here, in Nikki Giovanni's "The Library," a young black girl wants to learn about black history from the local library—the *black* library. The librarian, who seems at first a pleasant but conventional woman, is gradually transformed into a figure of magical power, who permits the girl to learn about both her past and future—at her peril.

The librarian in Joanne Greenberg's "Gloss on a Decision of the Council of Nicaea," published in 1966 and reflecting the social and political climate of that era, is transformed by her own actions. Myra, a rather sheltered woman, suddenly leaves her segregated library and joins a small group of black demonstrators in the street. Later, in jail, she says: "I don't know anything about the struggle between the races. I know about the library and the books that are in the library; and I know that it is wrong for the library to deny its treasures to those who want them." Her ringing affirmation would be echoed by most of the librarians American writers have chosen to commemorate.

Excerpt from *Betsy and Tacy Go Down Town* by Maud Hart Lovelace

Maud Hart Lovelace (1892–1980) wrote so believably about Betsy Ray, her friends Tacy Kelly and "Tib" Mueller, and their immediate families, that several generations of girls have grown up feeling they know all about life in Mankato, Minnesota ("Deep Valley") in the early 1900s. Lovelace wrote ten books that constitute the Betsy-Tacy series, as well as three others with related themes, and these books form a complete picture of Betsy, Tacy, and Tib as they grow up, succeed at careers, and marry. Though Lovelace wrote knowingly about the pangs of seeking popularity, looking for direction in life, and falling in love, she also believed in happy endings. Her books radiate warmth and belief in family ties. Among her Betsy-Tacy titles are Betsy-Tacy *(1940);* Betsy Tacy and Tib *(1941);* Over the Big Hill *(1942);* Down-Town *(1943), reissued in 1961 as* Betsy and Tacy Go Down Town; Heaven to Betsy *(1945); and* Betsy and Joe *(1948).*

BETSY'S DESK

Betsy, Tacy, and Tib did not give *The Repentance of Lady Clinton*. Winona understood. She understood so well that she never even mentioned it. They gave plenty of plays that year, and Winona was in them, but they did not give that one.

Mrs. Muller cleaned her downstairs without the satisfaction of having it mussed up first. Uncle Keith's costumes were aired and put away without having had their hour on the boards. Betsy helped her mother fold the garments and lay them in the flat-topped trunk. As they worked she asked questions, for since seeing *Uncle Tom's Cabin* she had a new interest in her actor-uncle.

"He'll come home sometime," Mrs. Ray said. "He must want to see me again, just as I want to see him. He was awfully hurt and angry when he left. And he doesn't know that our stepfather has gone out to California with mother."

"Do you think he's still an actor, mamma?"

"Yes, I do. Of course he went into the Spanish War. But if anything had happened to him the government would have told us. He must be just trouping, waiting for the big success he wanted to have before he came home.

" 'I'll come home, Jule, when I have a feather in my cap.' That's what he said when he said good-by to me" Betsy's mother paused in folding a Roman toga, and her face grew sad with the old sad memory of the night Keith ran away.

"What did he look like, mamma?" asked Betsy, although she had heard a hundred times.

"He looked like me," Mrs. Ray answered. "That is, he was tall and thin with a pompadour of red wavy hair. His eyes were brighter than mine, so full of fun and mischief. And he had the gayest smile I ever saw. None of you children look like him. You look like your father and his sisters. You get plenty of talents from your Uncle Keith, though."

Mrs. Ray's voice lifted proudly. She finished folding the Roman toga and laid it into the trunk.

"Does Julia get her reciting from him?" asked Betsy, knowing the answer well.

"Yes, she does. And her beautiful singing voice. And her gift at the piano. How Keith could make the piano keys fly, though he never had a lesson in his life! He could play and sing as well as act and he could draw and paint and model and write . . ."

"Write!" cried Betsy. She always loved to hear about the writing part.

"Yes, write. He wrote poems, plays, stories, everything. He was always scribbling, just as you are. And that reminds me, Betsy. Isn't it getting pretty cold to write up in the maple tree?"

Mrs. Ray knew all about the office in the maple tree. She had given

Betsy the cigar box. Betsy's mother was a great believer in people having private places.

"Yes, it is," said Betsy, "I haven't been writing lately."

"You must bring your papers indoors then. Your father and I are very proud of your writing. We want you to keep at it. You ought to have a desk but we can't afford one yet. I'll find a place for your things, though."

Mrs. Ray smoothed the last costume into place and closed the trunk.

"Rena will help me lift this into the garret," she said. "Come on into your room, Betsy."

Betsy followed her mother into the front bedroom. It was a small room with low tentlike walls. There was a single window at the front looking across to Tacy's house and the trees and the sunsets behind it. The big bed for Julia and Betsy, the small bed for Margaret, the chest of drawers, and the commode for wash bowl and pitcher filled the room.

Mrs. Ray pulled out the drawers in the chest. They were all crammed full. She looked around in some perplexity.

"I could make a place for your things in the back parlor," she said. "But I've noticed that you like to get away by yourself when you write."

"Yes, I do," said Betsy.

"It's got to be here then," Mrs. Ray answered. She tapped her lips thoughtfully.

"I have it!" she cried after a moment, her eyes flashing as brightly as she had said that Uncle Keith's used to flash.

"What?" asked Betsy.

"The trunk. Uncle Keith's trunk. You may have that for a desk. It can fit here under the window out of the way. It's just the thing."

She ran back into Rena's room and Betsy followed. They opened the trunk again. Swiftly her mother stowed the articles filling the tray into the bottom compartment.

"You can have the tray for your papers," she told Betsy happily. "Just wait until I get it fixed up!"

Mrs. Ray loved to fix things up around her house. And when she got started, Mr. Ray often said, she didn't let any grass grow under her feet.

She called down the stairs to Rena.

"Will you come up, please? Bring some shelf paper with scalloped edging. And my old brown shawl. And a couple of pillows."

"What are the shawl and pillows for?" asked Betsy, dancing about with excitement.

"They're to make a little window seat out of the trunk when you're not writing. When you feel like writing, you'll put the pillows on the floor and sit on them and open your desk. It's much nicer than an ordinary desk, because it's a real theatrical trunk."

Betsy thought so too.

Rena came up the stairs on a run. She was used to Mrs. Ray's lightning ideas. They carried the trunk into the front bedroom and placed it beneath the window. Mrs. Ray started papering the tray.

"I'll go out to get my things," said Betsy joyfully.

She ran down the stairs and out the door and waded through golden leaves to the back-yard maple.

When she reached the crotch where the cigar box was nailed, she looked out on a scene rivaling Little Eva's Heaven. The maples of Hill Street were golden clouds; and the encircling hillside made a backdrop of more clouds, copper colored, wine-red and crimson. The sky was brightly blue.

It was a sight to make one catch one's breath, but there was a chill in the air. Betsy brushed the dead leaves off the cigar box and opened it. A squirrel had already entered claim to possession. Six butternuts were there.

Hurriedly Betsy gathered up her belongings. Those tablets marked "Ray's Shoe Store. Wear Queen Quality Shoes," in which her novels were written. Two stubby pencils. An eraser. Some odds and ends of paper on which she had made verses. Leaving the Spanish lady to guard the butternuts, she wriggled down the tree.

She rushed eagerly into the kitchen and started up the stairs two at a time. Halfway up, she slowed her pace a little. It occurred to her to wonder whether her mother would notice the titles of her books.

Her mother did not read Betsy's writing without express permission. And she did not allow anyone else to do so. She was very particular about it. But these titles were printed out so big and bold. She could hardly help seeing them. And if she did, she would know that Betsy had been reading Rena's novels.

Betsy walked slowly with a suddenly flushed face into the front bedroom.

"It's all ready," her mother called cheerfully. Rena, Betsy saw, was gone. "I've finished papering it. Doesn't it look pretty?"

It did.

"Here is a case for your pencils. I'll ask papa to bring you fresh ones, and an eraser, and a little ten-cent dictionary. Perhaps you would like to put in a book or two? The Bible and Longfellow?"

"Yes, I would," said Betsy. Her mother noticed her changed voice. She looked up quickly and saw that Betsy was hugging her tablets secretively to her breast.

"You can put the tablets right into this corner," Mrs. Ray said. "Don't think I might ask to read them, dear. I won't. Keith was just like you about that. He never wanted anyone to read what he was writing until he was through with it, and sometimes not then. Whenever you show anything you've written to papa or me, we're interested and proud. But never feel that you have to."

Betsy threw the tablets roughly into the trunk.

"I don't care if you read them."

"But I don't want to read them," said her mother, looking troubled, "unless you want me to. The whole idea of this desk is to give you privacy. There is even a key to it, you know."

"Read them," said Betsy crossly. She turned away and scowled.

Mrs. Ray gathered up the tablets. The titles flashed past. *Lady Gwendolyn's Sin. The Tall Dark Stranger. Hardly More than a Child.*

For quite a while she did not say a word. She did not open the books. She just stacked them into a pile which she shaped with her hands, thoughtfully.

Betsy stole a glance at her mother's profile, fine and straight like George Washington's. It did not look angry, but it looked serious, grave.

"I think," said Mrs. Ray at last, "that Rena must have been sharing her dime novels with you."

Betsy did not answer.

"Betsy, it's a mistake for you to read that stuff. There's no great harm in it, but if you're going to be a writer you need to read good books. They train you to write, build up your mind. We have good books in the bookcase downstairs. Why don't you read them?"

"I've read them all," said Betsy.

"Of course," said her mother. "I never thought of that."

She took her hands away from the neat pile. The tray of the trunk, with its lining of scalloped blue paper looked fresh and inviting. Betsy felt ashamed.

"I'll throw those stories away if you want me to," she said.

"No," answered her mother. "Not until *you* want to." She still looked thoughtful. Then her face lighted up as it had when she thought of using Uncle Keith's trunk for a desk.

"I have a plan," she said. "A splendid plan. But I have to talk it over with papa."

"When will I know about it?"

"Tonight, maybe. Yes, I think you will know tonight before you go to bed."

Smiling, Mrs. Ray jumped up and closed the trunk. She and Betsy arranged the brown shawl and the pillows.

"It's almost like a cozy-corner," Mrs. Ray said.

She and Betsy ran downstairs and told Julia and Margaret about the new desk. Betsy ran outdoors to find Tacy and Tib and tell them. She brought them in to see it, and they liked it very much.

She kept wondering what the plan was. And after supper she found out. She had been playing games out in the street with the neighborhood children. Julia and Katie didn't play out any more. They were too grown up or too busy or had too many lessons or something. Margaret and the Rivers children played, and Paul and Freddie and Hobbie, and somehow the street seemed to belong to them even more than it did to Betsy, Tacy, and Tib.

When Margaret and Betsy went into the house, Julia was writing to Jerry. Their father and mother were reading beside the back-parlor lamp. Their father was reading a newspaper and their mother was reading a novel. It wasn't a paper-backed novel like Rena's. It was called *When Knighthood Was in Flower*.

Margaret climbed up on her father's lap and he put down his newspaper. Mrs. Ray put down her novel. She smiled at her husband.

"Papa has that plan all worked out," she said. "Tell her about it, Bob."

Mr. Ray crossed his legs, hoisted Margaret to a comfortable position and began.

"Well, Betsy," he said, "your mother tells me that you are going to use Uncle Keith's trunk for a desk. That's fine. You need a desk. I've often noticed how much you like to write. The way you eat up those advertising tablets from the store! I never saw anything like it. I can't understand it though. I never write anything but checks myself."

"Bob!" said Mrs. Ray. "You wrote the most wonderful letters to me before we were married. I still have them, a big bundle of them. Every time I clean house I read them over and cry."

"Cry, eh?" said Mr. Ray, grinning. "In spite of what your mother says, Betsy, if you have any talent for writing, it comes from her family. Her brother Keith was mighty talented, and maybe you are too. Maybe you're going to be a writer."

Betsy was silent, agreeably abashed.

"But if you're going to be a writer," he went on, "you've got to read. Good books. Great books. The classics. And fortunately . . . that's what I'm driving at . . . Deep Valley has a new Carnegie Library, almost ready to open. White marble building, sunny, spick and span, just full of books."

"I know," Betsy said.

"That library," her father continued, "is going to be just what you need. And your mother and I want you to get acquainted with it. Of course it's way down town, but you're old enough now to go down town alone. Julia goes down to her music lessons, since the Williamses moved away, and this is just as important."

He shifted his position, and his hand went into his pocket.

"As I understand it," he said, "you can keep a book two weeks. So, after the library opens, why don't you start going down . . . every other Saturday, say . . . and get some books? And don't hurry home. Stay a while. Browse around among the books. Every time you go, you can take fifteen cents." He gave her two coins. "At noon go over to Bier-bauer's Bakery for a sandwich and milk and ice cream. Would you like that?"

"Oh, papa!" said Betsy. She could hardly speak.

She thought of the library, so shining white and new; the rows and rows of unread books; the bliss of unhurried sojourns there and of going out to a restaurant, alone, to eat.

"I'd like it," she said in a choked voice. "I'd like it a lot."

Julia was as happy as Betsy was, almost. One nice thing about Julia was that she rejoiced in other people's luck.

"It's a wonderful plan, papa," she cried. "I've thought for ages that Betsy was going to be a writer."

"I thought Betsy learned to write a long time ago," said Margaret, staring out of her new English bob.

Everyone laughed, and Mrs. Ray explained to Margaret what kind of writer Betsy might come to be.

Betsy was so full of joy that she had to be alone. She ran upstairs to her bedroom and sat down on Uncle Keith's trunk. Behind Tacy's house the sun had set. A wind had sprung up and the trees, their color dimmed, moved under a brooding sky. All the stories she had told Tacy and Tib seemed to be dancing in those trees, along with all the stories she planned to write some day and all the stories she would read at the library. Good stories. Great stories. The classics. Not like Rena's novels.

She pulled off the pillows and shawl and opened her desk. She took out the pile of little tablets and ran with them down to the kitchen and lifted the lid of the stove and shoved them in. Then she walked into the back parlor, dusting off her hands.

"Papa," she said, "will you bring me some more tablets? Quite a lot of them, please."

A TRIP TO THE LIBRARY

Early in November Betsy made her first expedition to the library.

It was a windy day. Gray clouds like battleships moved across a purplish sea of sky. It looked like snow, Mrs. Ray remarked as she and Julia stood on the front porch seeing Betsy off. She looked a little doubtfully at Betsy's Sunday hat, a flowered brim that left her ears perilously exposed.

"Oughtn't you to wear your hood, Betsy?"

"Mamma! Not when I'm going down town to the new Carnegie Library!"

"You'd better put on leggins and overshoes though."

"There isn't a speck of snow on the ground."

Mrs. Ray looked at the thick woolen stockings, the stout high shoes.

"All right. Just button your coat. But if it snows, walk over to the store and ride home with papa."

"I will," Betsy promised.

She tried to act as though it were nothing to go to the library alone. But her happiness betrayed her. Her smile could not be restrained, and it spread from her tightly pressed mouth, to her round cheeks, almost to the hair ribbons tied in perky bows over her ears.

Julia had loaned her a pocket book to hold her fifteen cents. It dangled elegantly from a chain over Betsy's mittened hand. Betsy opened it and looked inside to see that her money was safe. She closed it again and took the chain firmly into her grasp.

"Good-by," she said, kissing her mother and Julia.

"Good-by," she waved to Rena, who was smiling through the window.

"Good-by," she called to Margaret, who was playing on the hill as the small girls of Hill Street did on a Saturday morning. Betsy could remember well when she used to do it herself. (It was only last Saturday.)

Tacy ran across the street to walk to the corner with her. It was a little hard, parting from Tacy. They were so used to doing everything together.

"I wish you were coming too," Betsy said.

"I'll be all right. I'm going to play with Tib."

"Some Saturday soon you'll be coming."

"Sure I will."

In spite of her brave words Tacy sounded forlorn. She looked forlorn, bareheaded, the wind pulling her curls.

But at the corner she hugged Betsy's arm. She looked into Betsy's eyes with her deep blue eyes that were always so loving and kind.

"I *want* you to go," she said. "Why, I've always known you were going to be a writer. I knew it ahead of everyone."

Betsy felt all right about going then. She kissed Tacy and went off at a run.

The big elm in Lincoln Park, bare and austere, pointed the way down town. She entered Broad Street, passing big houses cloaked in withered vines against November cold. She passed the corner where she usually turned off to go to her father's store and kept briskly on until she reached the library.

This small white marble temple was glittering with newness. Betsy went up the immaculate steps, pulled open the shining door.

She entered a bit self-consciously, never having been in a library before. She saw an open space with a big cage in the center, a cage such as they had in the bank, with windows in it. Behind rose an orderly forest of bookcases, tall and dark, with aisles between.

Betsy advanced to the cage and the young lady sitting inside smiled at her. She had a cozy little face, with half a dozen tiny moles. Her eyes were black and dancing. Her hair was black too, curly and untidy.

"Are you looking for the Children's Room?" she asked.

Betsy beamed in response.

"Well, not exactly. That is, I'd like to see it. But I may not want to read just in the Children's Room."

"You don't think so?" asked the young lady, sounding surprised.

"No. You see," explained Betsy, "I want to read the classics."

"You do?"

"Yes. All of them. I hope I'm going to like them."

The young lady looked at her with a bright intensity. She got down off her stool.

"I know a few you'll like," she said. "And they happen to be in the Children's Room. Come on. I'll show you."

The Children's Room was exactly right for children. The tables and chairs were low. Low bookshelves lined the walls, and tempting-looking books with plenty of illustrations were open on the tables. There was a big fireplace in the room, with a fire throwing up flames and making crackling noises. Above it was the painting of a rocky island with a temple on it, called *The Isle of Delos*.

"That's one of the Greek islands," said Miss Sparrow. Miss Sparrow was the young lady's name; she had told Betsy so. "There's nothing more classic than Greece," she said. "Do you know Greek mythology? No? Then let's begin on that."

She went to the shelves and returned with a book.

"*Tanglewood Tales*, by Nathaniel Hawthorne. Mythology. Classic," she said.

She went back to the shelves and returned with an armful of books. She handed them to Betsy one by one.

"*Tales from Shakespeare*, by Charles and Mary Lamb. Classic. *Don Quixote*, by Miguel de Cervantes. Classic. *Gulliver's Travels*, by Jonathan Swift. Classic. *Tom Sawyer*, by Mark Twain. Classic, going-to-be."

She was laughing, and so was Betsy.

"You don't need to read them all today," Miss Sparrow said.

"May I get a card and take some home?"

"You may have a card, but you'll have to get it signed before you draw out books. You may stay here and read though, as long as you like."

"Thank you," Betsy said.

Miss Sparrow went away.

Betsy took off her hat and coat. She was the only child in the room. Others came in shortly, but now she was all alone.

She seated herself in the chair nearest the fire, piled the books beside her and opened *Tanglewood Tales*. But she did not start to read at once. Before she began she smiled at the fire, she smiled at her books, she smiled broadly all around the room.

When the Big Mill whistle blew for twelve o'clock, she was surprised. She got up and put on her things.

"Did you have a good time?" Miss Sparrow asked, as Betsy passed the desk.

"Yes. I did."

"Be sure to come again."

"Oh," said Betsy, "I'll be back just as soon as I eat."

"But I thought you lived way up on Hill Street?"

"I do. But I'm eating at Bierbauer's Bakery. My father gave me fifteen cents. I'm going to eat there every time I come to the library," Betsy explained. "It's so I can take my time here, browse around among the books."

Miss Sparrow regarded her with the brightly intent look that Betsy had observed before.

"What a beautiful plan!" Miss Sparrow said.

Eating at Bierbauer's Bakery was almost as much fun as reading before the fire. It was warm in the bakery, and there was a delicious smell. Betsy bought a bologna sandwich, made of thick slices of freshly baked bread. She had a glass of milk too, and ice cream for dessert. But she decided that she wouldn't always have ice cream for dessert. Sometimes she would have jelly roll. It looked so good inside the glass counter.

Betsy couldn't help wondering if the other people in the bakery weren't surprised to see a girl her age eating there all alone. Whenever anyone looked at her she smiled. She was smiling most of the time.

On the way back to the library she looked eagerly for snow. She hoped she would have to call for her father. She loved visiting the store, riding the movable ladders from which he took boxes from the highest shelves, helping herself to the advertising tablets, talking to customers. But there wasn't a flake in the air. The battleships had changed to feather beds, hanging dark and low in the purplish sky.

Betsy returned to her chair, took off her coat and hat, opened her book and forgot the world again.

She looked up suddenly from *The Miraculous Pitcher* to see flakes coming past the window. They were coming thick and fast. She ran to look outdoors and saw that they had been coming for some time. Roofs and branches and the once brown lawns were already drenched in white.

"Now I've got to go to the store," she thought with satisfaction. She hurried into her wraps, said good-by to Miss Sparrow.

"It's too bad," said Miss Sparrow, "to take that pretty hat out into the snow."

"I haven't far to go," said Betsy. "I'm going to the store to ride home with my father. I'll see you in two weeks."

"Good-by," Miss Sparrow said.

Betsy's shoes made black tracks on the sidewalk. But the snow covered them at once. Filmy flakes settled on her coat and mittens. Soon she was cloaked in white. The air was filled with flakes, coming ever thicker and faster. Betsy ran and slid and slid again. She longed for Tacy and Tib. It was the first snow of the winter and demanded company.

She was soon to have it.

At the Opera House she paused to stare up at the posters. She wondered if there were a matinee coming. Winona would take them if there were. Then she noticed Mr. Poppy's horseless carriage, standing in front of the livery stable, blanketed in snow. She had not seen it since the day Tib took her ride, and she ran to inspect it.

A soft ball hit the back of her head. She whirled around. It was the worst thing she could have done. A snowball broke in her face.

She stooped blindly to mold a ball herself.

"All dressed up in her Sunday hat," somebody yelled.

A volley hit her hat, knocking it off. Snow oozed down the collar of her coat.

Her assailants were boys she had never seen before. She was one to three or four, and never any good at snowballs. Besides, she was handicapped by holding Julia's pocket book. She grabbed her hat and started to run.

She slipped on the soft snow. Swish! her feet went up!

Bang! she clattered down.

Yelling fiendishly, the boys ran away.

A little man came out of the livery stable and helped her to her feet. Behind him came a very large lady whose fur coat breathed a sweet perfume. Sunny Jim and Mrs. Poppy helped Betsy to her feet.

"Did you hurt yourself?" asked Mrs. Poppy.

"No ma'am. Not a bit." Betsy winked back the tears of which she was ashamed.

"They were bad boys."

"If I knew who they were," said Betsy, shaking off snow, "I'd bring Tacy and Tib and come back. Tib would fix them. She can throw snowballs better than any boy."

"Tib?" asked Mrs. Poppy. "My little friend Tib?"

"That's right. We waved to you from the box at *Uncle Tom's Cabin.* Tib and Tacy and Winona and me."

"Of course. I know you. But I don't know your name."

"Betsy Ray."

"Her pa runs Ray's Shoe Store," said Sunny Jim. "I know him well."

"I'm on my way to the shoe store now," said Betsy. "To ride home with my father." She shook the snow from her hat and put it on her head, grasped Julia's pocket book firmly. "Thank you for helping me," she said.

Mrs. Poppy was looking down at Betsy's feet.

"Speaking of shoes," she said, "yours are very wet, and your stockings are sopping. Why don't you come over to the hotel and dry out? I can telephone your father."

"Why . . . why . . . I'd love to," said Betsy.

"We'll have some hot chocolate with whipped cream," said Mrs. Poppy. She spoke fast and eagerly, like a child planning a party.

Her face alight, she turned to Sunny Jim.

"Just tell Mr. Poppy I won't wait. Tell him I've gone on home. It's just a step."

"Yes, Mrs. Poppy," said Sunny Jim respectfully.

Mrs. Poppy took Betsy's hand. They started toward Front Street through waving curtains of snow. The visit to the Carnegie Library raced into Betsy's past before a future which held hot chocolate at the Melborn Hotel.

"Growing Up with a Past" by Howard A. Wilson

Howard A. Wilson is an Emeritus Professor of English at Knox College, where he taught from 1946 until 1980. He was born in New Harmony, Indiana, in 1913 and reports, "I get back there once or twice a year. I always stop in at The Workingmen's Institute Library." His essay "Growing Up with a Past" first appeared in Yale Review *in 1977.*

Some of my friends insist that when I meet new faculty members I always manage to steer the conversation to New Harmony and to judge them on whether or not they have heard of my home town.

Maybe I do, but it seems a perfectly good way of gauging my treatment of someone I've just met. If he has not heard of New Harmony I do not, as my friends maintain, decide that we cannot possibly have anything in common. Instead I feel it my duty to fill in a part of his education that for some reason has been neglected. One thing I learned when I was growing up in New Harmony was that every educated adult knows something about New Harmony. There is no excuse not to. One runs across references to it all the time.

It didn't surprise me therefore when I opened the July 1975 issue of *In Britain* to discover in an article called "Not-so-Satanic Mills" that one of the chief British interests for the Architectural Heritage Year in Europe was Robert Owen's model industrial town of New Lanark, Scotland, which he began in 1800. What disappointed me was that though the author gave Owen credit for some of the first industrial city planning and for an enlightened attitude toward his workers, he did not mention Owen's more ambitious project for complete social reform in southern Indiana.

In 1825 Owen bought an entire village and 20,000 acres of land on the Wabash River as the site for his new experiment. The town of Harmonie had been established eleven years earlier by George Rapp, the leader of a German communal society. The Rappites—or Harmonists, as they were properly called—had prospered, but for one reason or another had decided to sell their town and move back to Pennsylvania, where they had first settled after coming from Germany. Owen, in partnership with William Maclure, bought Harmonie and its environs as the site for establishing his New Moral World and Community of Equality. Here a hundred years later the history of the two communities was something that I never really had to learn.

Miss Louise M. Husband was the Assistant Librarian of the Workingmen's Institute Library when I was growing up in New Harmony. Mrs. Fretageot (pronounced Fru táyz yu in New Harmony) was the Librarian, but it was Miss Louise who was usually at the desk in the Reading Room and who stamped our books for us. It was almost always she who gave casual visitors from out of town a brief history of the Rappite and Owenite communities, identified the famous people whose portraits hung on the walls, and sent them upstairs to see the art gallery and the museum with its skeleton of Old Fly, the horse Mr. Barrett had ridden through the Civil War, and the skull of my grandfather Wilson's monkey, Jack.

I can't remember when I didn't know Miss Louise. I can remember when I got my library card though I can't remember how old I was— eight or nine probably, because Miss Louise explained that she was giving me my mother's number, 16; and my mother had died when I was seven and a half. The Library was only a half block from our house and I spent a lot of time there, even in summer, when there were likely to be groups of out-of-town visitors almost every day.

I might be reading *St. Nicholas* or looking through *Judge* or the old *Life* or *The Illustrated London News*, but Miss Louise's talks to the visitors never really bothered me. Whether she had at one time prepared them or whether they had developed through many repetitions I never thought to ask myself. Either way, they had taken their proper form, which rarely varied, and she had found her proper tone. Miss Louise was good at declaiming poetry (though not as popular as Aunt Phoebe Elliott, whose "Destruction of Sennacherib" was a favorite at school assemblies). Miss Louise was in her early forties when I first remember her, but her age was something I never thought about. During all the time I knew her it never seemed to change. She had a good "robust" figure and orangey red hair which she wore piled about her head. She usually wore sweaters and skirts at the Library, browns, bottle greens, rusts, and often a scarf of mauve, saffron, or coral. Some people thought she didn't have a very good sense of what colors went together, but I found her costumes interesting and imaginative. There was something dramatic about her and about her dress. When I was a boy she always went to the annual masqued ball given by St. Stephen's Guild. She had acted in amateur theatricals and "entertainments" all her life. In one of the entertainments, "A Vision of Fair Women," my mother had been Evangeline. Miss Louise had been the director and reader, and although I have no memory of seeing the production I am sure that Longfellow's dactylic hexameter was a meter that Miss Louise could do justice to. At St. Stephen's she was the one whose voice always led the rest of the congregation in the suffrages and psalms. It was strong, and for me at least musical, and she spoke clearly and distinctly. As she declaimed to the visitors, what she said seemed a fitting background for my reading, a kind of bardic recital of history I had always known.

After a while I knew her talks almost by heart and could anticipate her inflection when she pointed out the portraits of Dr. and Mrs. Murphy, "the generous donors of our building." Dr. Murphy, she would continue, "had come to New Harmony a barefoot boy from Cork, Ireland." He had been discovered peering in at the window of one of the community buildings where the Owenites were having a ball and the community had taken him in and given him a home. In his old age, having decided "to do something for the town that had befriended him," he had built this home for the Library of the Workingmen's Institute and had generously endowed it. Upstairs in the art gallery, Miss Louise would point out, was a bronze urn containing his and Mrs. Murphy's ashes, surrounded by the copies of the famous paintings he had bought when he and Mrs. Murphy had taken their European tour. . . .

By the time I was in high school Miss Louise had become not only my good friend but my confidante. Miss Louise was interested in everything about me, I thought, just as she was interested in everybody in town. Many people confided in her, adults as well as teenage boys. At her desk in the Library she exchanged news with almost everyone who came in. And yet I never thought of her interest in news as gossip. New Harmony was her home town and she liked to know what was happening to the people who lived there.

While I was in college Mrs. Fretageot died and Miss Louise became Librarian. Aunt Phoebe Elliott, who for years had written most of the obituaries for the *Times*, died too and Miss Louise took over her task. Her obituaries were tender and loving tributes, for she knew and loved everybody she wrote about. It was at this time also that she began to write a column for the *Times* which she called quite simply "Comments on Things That Interest Me."

Every summer there were visitors to the Library who came to do research on New Harmony's history. When I was in college Richard Leopold, who was only a few years older than I, was there for two or three summers doing research for his Harvard dissertation which later became the definitive biography of Robert Dale Owen. Miss Louise loved to help anyone who was doing research on New Harmony, but she also knew that scholars needed to be left alone and she never intruded on Mr. Leopold where he worked in the small room that housed the Special Collection. Yet a genuine friendship grew up between them, and Mr. Leopold kept her up to date during the winters on the progress of his dissertation. I remember how proud she was when she told me that he had written to tell her that it was to be published.

Another scholar who came during the summers when I was home from graduate school was Professor Teitlebaum. Mr. Teitlebaum was an older scholar than Mr. Leopold, a professor of education at the University of Pittsburgh. He had come to do research on Joseph Neef, the Pestalozzian teacher in the Owen school. Mr. Teitlebaum returned several summers, and in the course of his visits a friendship developed between him and Miss Louise that I sensed was different from the friendship she had for Mr. Leopold. One summer when I was home I learned—from whom I no longer remember—that Mr. Teitlebaum had proposed to Miss Louise. She had, I was told, considered the proposal quite seriously and in the end had accepted it—on one condition: that Mr. Teitlebaum move to New Harmony. Although this brought the proposal to an impasse the two remained good friends and Miss Louise always spoke warmly and affectionately of Mr. Teitlebaum to me.

Next year when I was home for Christmas vacation she saw me passing her house and called me in to see her Christmas presents. She lived alone in a red brick vaguely Federalist house on Church Street that she had inherited from her half-brother Harry, who had married my Uncle Field Robb's sister. Although in many ways I knew Miss Louise better than I knew Miss Anne and although through Uncle Field I was in a way related to her—at least by marriage—I had never been inside her house. She took most of her meals at Mrs. Bailey's Dew Drop Inn, and I think she didn't do much cooking.

Her presents were on display in great profusion on the library table, on top of the square piano, and some had spilled over to the chairs. I can't remember what they were—handkerchiefs, scarves, books, toilet water, fancy work, candy, a fruit cake, homemade pickles, a sweater perhaps. I recollect that I was mildly curious about why she had called me in to see them, though keeping one's Christmas presents on display until New Year's was a good New Harmony custom.

She waited for me to admire and comment on each present and to examine the gift tag with each one. Then, with a fine sense of someone who has kept the best for last, she said, "Now come into the bedroom and see what Mr. Teitlebaum sent me."

He had sent her a lavender chenille bedspread and a lavender chenille robe.

"When I unwrapped them," she told me, "I put the spread on the bed, put on the chenille robe, flung myself on the bed, and felt just like Cleopatra."

Miss Louise died in 1944. She was sixty-seven. I was teaching at the Naval Training School at Indiana University and could not get home for her funeral. A long, heartfelt obituary appeared in the *Times*, but I could not help thinking that she was the only person who could have written it properly. I decided to do what I could, so I wrote and sent off a tribute to Miss Louise which the editor printed. For the next four weeks there were always two and sometimes three tributes to Miss Louise in the paper. They came from former residents, from boys in the service, from scholars whom she had helped in the Library, from the Librarian of the Crerar Library in Chicago. It seemed fitting that Miss Louise should have not one obituary but a dozen.

Mrs. Fretageot, Miss Anne, Aunt Phoebe Elliot had all died while I was in college. But with Miss Louise's death I knew that my strongest connection with a part of my past was gone. Miss Aline, Miss Fauntleroy remained, but I had never known them in the way I knew Miss Louise. It had been Miss Louise who on those mornings in the Library had helped me create my past.

"Lucy Wallis," from *Centerville, U.S.A.* by Charles Merz

Charles Merz (1893–1977) was an influential journalist who, as editor of The New York Times *(1938–61), both observed and commented on many aspects of American life. Besides* Centerville, U.S.A. *(1924), based on his childhood in Sandusky, Ohio, Merz published a collection of essays on the American scene,* The Great American Bandwagon *(1928), and* The Dry Decade *(1931), a study of Prohibition, and he edited a volume of* Times *editorials,* Days of Decision *(1941).*

"Lucy Wallis" is a chapter in Centerville, U.S.A., *which links the lives of many people in a quintessential American small town. One contemporary critic commented that it was "a book full of tears and laughter and that strange beauty which is in some etchings of dingy, tumbledown houses."*

I

Some people stumble into romance, and other people chart the countryside and try to run it down. Take Lucy Wallis, for example, and the young man with the eye-shade.

Lucy Wallis had been dedicated to some useful, cultivated labor from the start; her family had done its best to see that she would never go to seed or lose herself in easy pleasure. She had gone without a hitch through school and college; kept on afterward, from the force of her momentum, to win herself a graduate degree. She talked of doing social work, of teaching school, of going out to some warm Eastern land to help the church spread gospel. In the end she chose to stay with books, went back to school again, and finished one last course of training as a librarian. It was pure chance that when it came her turn to find an opening, the Fates decreed her Centerville.

Not for long, before this opportunity arrived, had books in Centerville possessed a home that they could call their own. For years "the library" had been a room above a shoe store: so closely guarded on one flank by the Scylla of a moving-picture show, and on the other by Charybdis in the guise of Malley's combination candy and cigar store, that only the most determined seekers after book-lore found the straight and narrow path between. The scene had shifted by the time the new librarian arrived. Thanks to the last will and testament of Henry Nesbit, Sr., the literary heritage of Centerville had come to rest in a low-roofed mausoleum of its own.

Lucy Wallis found a place to live, around the corner from this job of hers, boarding with a family of pioneers. She came to work at nine o'clock, and stayed at night until eight thirty. At noon and suppertime she had an alternate to take her place. The rest of the day the four-room building was her own. There was a reading-room—with a file of index-cards and two racks of magazines hung up like chickens in a market by their necks; a stack-room—cases of non-fiction backed against the farther wall, at bay before advancing hordes of romance; a "children's room," so called, Lucy Wallis was ready to decide, at the end of her first week of work, because occasionally the children ran through it when they used the halls for tag.

This was all, down-stairs; three rooms closely crowded. But overhead, reserved for special Sundays in the winter months, and then thrown open for the afternoon, the attic sheltered a Museum. Portraits, here, of Henry Nesbit—of George Loring, the town's first mayor—of Matthew Kent, who came back from the Cuban war a major. Authentic bits of early Centerville displayed in glass-topped cases: a chart of the town in '43, a deed of land for its first school, a draft-list from the days of Chickamauga. Here and there a gift less highly prized, but difficult to spurn without offense to kindly giver: an arrow-head, a stone run down and trampled by the glaciers, a crochet portrait of McKinley, a lump of lava from Mount Etna.

Which one of these four rooms most closely touched the lives of people in the town, Lucy Wallis wasn't certain. The stack-room pumped a steady flood of fiction through perhaps three hundred homes. The Museum had its special friends, who came to see what comments their own gifts brought forth. The children's room had possibilities.

But tact alone would not make Mother Goose and Lives of Great Inventors as popular as hunting through the picture-books and tearing out the lions.

II

Time, meanwhile, had kept the promises it made when Lucy Wallis was a child. In these days of Centerville there was nothing of the elf about her; no foibles and no shams. She was as plain and manifestly to be trusted, and if the truth be told as uncompelling to the eye, as when, a little girl of four, her parents brought her in before the guests assembled in the parlor.

She was about thirty now; a tall girl with ruddy hair that might have carried off successfully some gayer bangle than the 2B pencil she would stick above her ear when she was cataloguing books. Her skin was smooth and softly colored; but only an indulgent uncle, years ago, had called her handsome. Her cheeks were thin; her lips were pale; her eyes were handicapped by thick round lenses that struggled with astigmatism. She had been taught, as a child, that bright colors did not go with red hair and a sense of duty. Her dresses were a serviceable gray.

Not that it made much difference, in the run of things, what clothes she wore: provided they were warm enough or cool enough, and not so dark or light that they would show the dust that covered Burke and Boswell's Johnson. She didn't know the sort of people here who entertained at parties. She didn't easily make friends. Of those she had, the most familiar was a woman with a shawl who came to read a paper from Chicago. She used to live there, she explained, and liked to read the ads and see what bargains she'd have had if she had stayed. Another regular was a veteran of '61 who brought his own book with him when he came, and read it in a corner. There was a school-boy launched on

Kipling, and a girl who copied first-aid data from the magazines. And then there was the young man with the eye-shade.

Lucy Wallis had found out what there was to know of him before he came the second time. "Professor" was his title in the town. Like herself, he was a stranger here. He was teaching mathematics in the high school: a young man—sandy-haired, square-faced, immensely serious. He would bring a leather brief-case with him, and sometimes spread its contents on a table in the reading-room and start correcting papers. Lucy Wallis decided he was quite as lonely in his boarding-house as she felt in her own.

He would come in quietly, close the door as softly as though this were a sick-room, put his bag down on a table, hang his hat behind the door, and disappear into the stack-room. Usually it took him quite a time to find the book he wanted. Then he would come back across the reading-room again, this time on tiptoe, and, because his shoes creaked, not so quietly. He would choose a chair as near a light as he could get and hook an eye-shade on his ears. From that time forth there was no disturbing him until the hour came to dim the lights.

Lucy Wallis never knew what book this silent man was reading. He always put it back in its right stall before he left the building. She used to watch, when he was working, to see if he would steal a glance her way. She never caught him doing it, and never drew from him a more responsive greeting than a nod. She was sorry that was so. He was a student. He was lonely. There was a good deal they might have talked about, a good many interests they might share. More interests than she had in common with the Chicago lady or the people in her boarding-house or the high-school boys who came to her in search of topics for their essays.

It was a little dreary in the evenings after half-past eight. Lucy Wallis was well schooled in the indifference of men. They had been hanging their hats behind the door and nodding their good evenings from across the room for fifteen years. But here was a lost waif like herself. Friendship, and a break in the routine of empty evenings: surely that much lay within the bounds of reason.

III

There was always an even chance that the reading-room would be deserted after seven forty-five, and to-night the place was quiet. Lucy

Wallis and the young man with the eye-shade had it to themselves. A clock above the rack of papers raked the room with even ticks. The young man was reading; he had been sitting there since half-past six, elbows on the table, eyes intent upon the slowly turning pages underneath the light.

Lucy Wallis had a book she liked; but she had watched this man uneasily for half an hour. And now she slid the top drawer of her desk half open, let the book slip into it, and walked across the room.

"I'm sorry to disturb you—" she began.

The young man rose, unhooked his eye-shade from his ears, and peered at her through glasses quite as prepossessing as her own.

"A new book came to-day," she said. "I thought I'd speak to you about it. You might want to read it. It's Bertrand Russell on the theory of the atom."

He cleared his throat. It was a book, he said, that he would read with pleasure. The atom was an interesting subject. A very interesting subject. He was glad that she had let him know.

He told her this in heavy whispers, as though the room were filled with sleepers and the hour late.

"There's no one in the building," she suggested. "I don't think you need to talk that way."

He agreed that this was true. It was the force of habit in that room.

For a moment he looked down, and Lucy Wallis sent her glance along with his. She couldn't read the title of his book. It lay upon its face, as if it, too, considered safety lay in numbers.

It was more than she had planned, but she drew a chair up to the table. "You read a great deal, don't you?" she observed.

"I like to read when I can find good books," he said. "And then, you see, I don't know many people here."

She nodded. —Did he see that she was sitting down? He was still standing there behind his straight-backed chair, and seemed to be deciding whether he could roll his eye-shade flat enough to make it lie inside a pocket.

"There's nothing like a good book," she agreed. "So many people waste their time. Dancing every night, and moving pictures."

She was wondering if he ever danced. What did he think of picture shows?

He kept his feet well on the highway of a literary conversation. "Of course, teaching in the public schools, I have to read a good deal, anyway," he said. "Sort of keep abreast of things, you know."

There was a sandy lock of hair that hung down on his forehead. Probably, she thought, if he didn't comb it straight so often it would curl.

"What do you read most nights in here?" she asked him.

"Oh—different things. I go out in the stacks and find them."

"I know," she said. "I've seen you. You're about the only one who comes in here and picks out his own books. Most people ask me where to find them."

He looked his guilt. "Of course, if there's a rule—"

"Oh, no. There isn't any rule. Most people just don't know which way the numbers go."

"I see. I rather like to hunt around myself. I read different sorts of things, you see. And sometimes I don't know just what I want until I see the title."

"Don't you?" She was surprised at that. "You always look as if you had your mind made up. I mean, when you go out there to the stack-room. I've always thought—I've thought when I was sitting at the desk and saw you—that you knew just what you wanted from the start."

"I like to look around a little, first. I guess you know the way I mean. I've noticed you do quite a bit of reading, too."

He had observed that much, at any rate, she thought. That eye-shade must be made with a transparent brim.

"You see, I don't know many people either," she suggested. —His hair would be presentable enough if he would comb it right. —"And then, it's a treat to read something worth while now and then. You know, most people who come in here for books read fiction all the time. The lightest sort of fiction. After I've been helping them hunt stories all day long I like to do a little reading of my own."

"Philosophy? That sort of thing?"

She nodded.

"That's fine," he said. "There's nothing like a book to keep your mind on edge. I don't meet many people of that sort out here."

She smiled. Perhaps this much would do them for a starter. She rose, and pushed the chair back to the table.

"I'm glad you told me of that book," he told her. "What was it—atoms, I believe you said?"

"Yes. Bertrand Russell. —And would you mind if I said something? I like to talk with people who really care for books—I mean, books that matter."

He nodded; cleared his throat again, and stretched his wings to pay her back the compliment.

She left him, went back to her desk, took out her book again. Across the room he buckled on his eye-shade.

Together, while the clock ticked, they sat reading.

He, "The Girl of the Limberlost."

She, the desert story of "The Sheik."

"Marian the Librarian" by Meredith Willson

Meredith Willson (1902–84) had a long and varied musical career, as a composer, conductor, lecturer, and author, but most Americans know his name as creator of the popular and award-winning musical The Music Man, *first produced on Broadway in 1957 and then made into an equally successful movie. In addition to many honors garnered as a Broadway musical (the Drama Critics Circle Award for best musical, best music and best lyrics, five Tony awards, and more), the musical score won both an Academy Award and a Grammy.*

Willson also wrote several books, including three autobiographical memoirs: And There I Stood with My Piccolo *(1948);* Eggs I Have Laid *(1955); and* "But He Doesn't Know the Territory" *(1959). He composed both* symphonies and songs (one perennial favorite is "It's Beginning to Look Like Christmas.") Willson was gifted with both musical and verbal skills, as the delightful song "Marian the Librarian" illustrates.

MARIAN THE LIBRARIAN

(*Music starts before lights come up.*)
(*Dialogue starts after lights come up.*)
HAROLD: It's all right. I know everything. . . .
(*dialogue until*)
Cue: HAROLD: (*Whispering*) The librarian. You're not listening, Marian. Look! (*He holds up paper bag of marbles.*)
HAROLD: Marbles, Six steelies, eight aggies, a dozen peewees, and one big glassie with an American flag in the middle. I think I'll drop 'em.
MARIAN: No!
HAROLD: Shhh!

Madam librarian. What can I do, my dear, to catch your ear?
I love you madly, madly, Madam librarian,
Marian Heaven help us, if the library caught on fire,
and the volunteer hosebrigademen had to whisper the news to Marian, Madam librarian.
What can I say, my dear, to make it clear?
I need you badly, badly, Madam librarian, Marian.
If I stumbled, and I busted my what-you-ma-call-it,
I could lie on your floor unnoticed, 'til my body had turned to carrion.
Madam librarian.

Now in the moonlight
A man could sing it
in the moonlight
And a fellow would know that his darling had heard ev'ry word of his song
with the moonlight helping along.

But when I try, in here, to tell you, dear,
I love you madly, madly, Madam librarian,
Marian, it's a long lost cause I can never win,
for the civilized world accepts as unforgivable sin
any talking out loud with any librarian,
such as Marian, Madam librarian.

But when I try, in here,
to tell you, dear,
I love you madly, madly, Madam librarian,
Marian, it's a long lost cause I can never win,
for the civilized world accepts as unforgivable sin
any talking out loud with any librarian,
such as Marian, Madam librarian.

HAROLD: The ladies' dance committee meets Tuesday night. Marsh-
mallow?

MARIAN THE LIBRARIAN

(Music starts before lights come up.)
(Dialogue starts after lights come up.)
HAROLD: It's all right. I know everything....
(dialogue until)
Cue: HAROLD: *(Whispering)* The librarian. You're not listening, Marian.
Look! *He holds up paper bag of marbles.*

Moderate 4

Piano

pp   [safety repeat]

Piano, Cello,
Bsn., Drums

HAROLD:

Ma ——————————— ri - an.

HAROLD: Marbles. Six steelies, eight aggies, a dozen peewees, and one big glassie with an American
flag in the middle. I think I'll drop 'em.
MARIAN: No!
HAROLD: Shhh!

[safety repeat]

Ma - dam li - bra ——————————— ri -

an.   What can I

do, my dear, to catch your ear? I love you mad-ly, mad-ly, Ma-dam li-

brar-i - an, Mar - i - an Hea-ven help us, if the li - bra - ry caught on

fi - re, and the vol - un - teer hose - bri - gade-men had to whis-per the news to

Mar _____ i - an,

86

"The Library" by Nikki Giovanni

Poet, essayist, lecturer, and professor, Nikki Giovanni (born in 1943) has received recognition not only for her poetry but also for her sensitive and informed contributions to an understanding of black American culture. First recognized as an important writer in the 1960s black literary renaissance, Ms. Giovanni has since been awarded many prizes, fellowships, and honorary degrees. Her books of poetry have included, Black Feeling, Black Talk *(1968) and* Black Judgment *(1969);* The Women and the Men *(1975);* Cotton Candy on a Rainy Day *(1978);* Those Who Ride the Night Wind *(1983); and* Spin a Soft Black Song *(1985). She is also known for several albums of poetry recorded to music, such as the best-selling* Truth Is on Its Way *(1971); and a highly praised memoir,* Gemini: An Extended Autobiography on My First Twenty-Five Years of Being a Black Poet *(1971). A collection of autobiographical essays and articles,* Sacred Cows . . . & Other Edibles, *was published in 1986.*

Ms. Giovanni has contributed to many newspapers, magazines and anthologies. The story we include here, "The Library," is taken from Brothers and Sisters: Modern Stories by Black Americans *(1970).*

A lot of folks ask me about that and I really haven't thought about it a whole lot. You know how you just go along and try not to get on folks' nerves and never think about it much anymore 'cause it'll just make you unhappy. When I was real little nobody much was talking bout Black is Beautiful and Black Power and Think Black and stuff. Nobody even talked about White Power or how the system could maybe be wrong and how much it hurts to be lynched and burned and to lose your father in a war that you don't even understand way away from home and then the government in Washington gives you a couple of thousand dollars for him but he won't be back to play with you or even to fuss at your mommy. No, when I was a little girl, we just were unhappy by ourselves and we tried not to let anybody know how unhappy we were 'cause America was the land of the brave and we wanted to be the bravest of them all. So we never talked about our History at all except sometimes during Brotherhood Week or Negro History Week and sometimes, if you lived in a hometown like mine, we celebrated Emancipation Day and THEY let us go to WhiteWash, the big amusement park.

I would hear Mommy and Aunt Bertha saying that Negroes don't know nothing about themselves, so I wasn't completely dumb about us 'cause I knew that I didn't know anything and that's really a good thing to know, I think. And once during a really phosphoresce period—I think that's what they called it, you know, during The Teapot Dome Scandal and all—there was this man named Andrew Carnegie who gave lots of money for libraries 'cause he had been dumb once himself and he wanted everybody to have an equal chance like he didn't have. In my hometown the Carnegie library is for COLORED ONLY so Mommy took me there one day after I was pestering her to tell me something about Negroes. The first thing the librarian did was to give us a book called *Up from Slavery* which was by a very great man named Booker T. Washington. He pulled himself up by practically nothing at all to be the biggest and most important Negro in maybe the whole world. And he told us not to fool with politics and stuff but to lay our burden down, I mean to put our loaves afloat—that is, to cast the first stone where we were and the Southern people would be good to us and understand that we were just like their children. My mommy liked Dr. Washington very much and was a truly great follower of his, 'cause she worked two jobs every day and a half a day on Sunday. Dr. Washington said if we worked really hard and didn't get on anybody's nerves we would soon live in peace and comfort. When I read him and the big speech he gave in Atlanta, Georgia, I just laughed and laughed 'cause I knew how hard my mommy worked and we not only didn't have nothing but we didn't have no peace! And honest, we never meant to get on anybody's nerves; but as Mommy would say, Folks are just naturally mean and some folks are just naturally meaner than others. So no matter how hard we tried we just never had no peace.

I went back to the library by myself and told the librarian that I didn't like that book 'cause he didn't tell the whole truth. I mean, if it would've been the whole truth we would've been living in peace and comfort 'cause not Mommy or Daddy or even Gram and Granpapa ever bothered anybody except for that time Deacon Wright stole the church money and you couldn't say we were wrong for getting upset 'bout folks mistreating God! Or folks mistreating folks for that matter. I heard Mommy talking 'bout Daddy going over to fight Hitler for rights that we didn't have and Double V and all 'cause war is awful and if we can't get something good out of a war we shouldn't fight anyway. That's what Mommy said. So I went and got a book by a real smart man named Dr. DuBois. He said we must fight for our manhood rights and learn about politics and Africa 'cause these were the most important things in the world. He said Dr. Washington had political power already and was just being selfish if he didn't let other Negroes get political power. Dr. DuBois started The National Association for Colored People to Advance By and then THEY got mad at him and he left home and lived in Africa. I liked him a lot but we still were in a lot of trouble 'cause we were trying to prove by science methods that we were human and it doesn't seem the sort of thing that we can prove. I mean, how can you prove that you are human and all when you are there talking to folks and they are talking to you? Plus they sure passed a lot of laws that said we couldn't do stuff that only humans could do. Like Dr. Frederick Douglass said, why would they pass a law saying that we couldn't marry them if we weren't human? 'Cause a bull couldn't marry them, could he? I mean, not to really live with them and raise a family and go to church and all.

So I wanted to know lots more about us and I asked the librarian what she thought would be real good. She looked at me real hard, then shook her head . . . then looked real hard again and scratched her head and started mumbling 'bout what an old fool she is. Then told me to come back about closing time. I went down to the drugstore and bought a *Screen Stories* and went back to the lawn area and read it until it was time to see her. When I went back in she asked if anyone had seen me come in. I said no. Then she closed up the library and looked around again. She asked me if I would promise not to tell anyone what she was going to show me. And I promised and crossed my heart three times while facing east. So we went down to the basement where Mommy's Lodge used to hold meetings. She had a flashlight so that we could see. Right there where the TV sat was a door. She took the key off the wall and we went into the door. She told me the door was a part of the underground railroad which was not in use at this time. We walked about five minutes in the tunnel and I must admit it was a bit scary. I had read about Harriet Tubman, how she was my friend and all but it was still cold and scary down there. Then we came to another door and the librarian stopped and looked at me and asked me again if I would promise not to tell what she was about to show me. I swore on the Bible that Dr. Sweet Daddy Grace once used and she started chanting:

> *Ole Nat Turner still alive*
> *Got him one, wants to get five*
>
> *Denmark Vesey sitting nifty*
> *Got one hundred wants one fifty*
>
> *Gabriel, Gabriel, you our man*
> *If you don't get them Garvey can*

And all the while she was talking her hair was turning fuzzy on her head and wasn't long like it had been, and all the makeup was disappearing from her face and the dress she had on turned to a gunny-sack dress and then to a long gown that looked real strange to me. Her shoes went away and she looked like an African or something. Now, I really did want another book to read but I was scared about all the funny things that were going on and I was getting ready to run home. Just then the door opened and she pushed me inside. The room was huge like a museum and all around on the walls were books, higher than I could ever reach. She told me this was the Black Museum that held *The Great Black Book*. Most of the books the people didn't even know about 'cause they wouldn't be published 'til much later when we were ready for them. Some others had already been outside but THEY had tried to destroy them and books have feelings like everybody else. So they had come home 'til we were ready for them. The librarian had shown this room to only one other person and that's the one we call Crazy Butch, 'cause he just mumbles to himself all the time and people don't understand him. It gave me a real queasy feeling to be there. There were books about Africa and Asia and South America and China. There were books by Ronald Fair and John Killens and Lerone Bennett and LeRoi Jones. Ed Bullins and Larry Neal and Etheridge Knight and Diane Oliver and lots and lots of people. There were big picture books with lots of maps and there were books with lots of writing without anything to see but the words. There were children's books and grown-up books and books about cooking the kind of foods we like to eat. And just every book in the world that we would ever write. And then there was *The Great Black Book*. I asked if I could touch it. It was taller than me and it sat all by itself in a corner on the floor. I wiped my hands on my dress and touched it once. It opened to the year when I was born and there was everything that had happened to us in that year. It didn't say anything about me but I still liked it. Then it flipped ten years and showed everything that was happening then. I started to turn to see what would happen in the future but the librarian stopped me to warn me. If you look in the future of *The Great Black Book* wherever you are in the real world will be where you stay. Like if you are ten years old then you will always act like a ten-year-old on the outside even though you could know what will happen in the next century. I thought about Crazy Butch for a little minute and I knew what was wrong with him. It's because he knows everything and nobody else understands that. I guess that's how come people say too much learning will drive you crazy. But I wanted to know 'cause I think it's very important that you know as much as you can. Plus, when the year gets to where you stopped reading in the future all of a sudden you will be making sense on the outside and people will quit laughing at you. So I read all the way up to 1970 and boy! You should see what will happen. I read about Floyd McKissick and a little boy named Stokely Carmichael. I read about The Black, Shining Prince and Rap Brown. I read all about how they would help us a whole lot. And then there are these people called Vietnamese who will fight with the US and a little puppet called Tshombe who will have to run a lot 'cause he won't act nice at home. Plus there are some really funny stories about the 35th President and how the 36th got to take his place. Boy! You should see those. But I can't talk anymore 'cause it's time for us to pack up and move on. I don't mind being in a circus, I guess, but I really wish they'd let me out of this cage every now and then.

"Gloss on a Decision of the Council of Nicaea" by Joanne Greenberg

Joanne Greenberg, born in 1932, is known not only for the novels published under her own name but also for an autobiographical novel, I Never Promised You a Rose Garden, *published in 1964 under the pseudonym Hannah Green. She is known as a writer of passionate convictions and psychological acuity. One critic has said of her work, "Greenberg clearly believes in traditional values, along with such old-fashioned themes as good and evil, but there is humor and compassion in her treatment of both, making her always a joy to read."*

Greenberg's novels include The King's Persons *(1963);* The Monday Voices *(1965);* In This Sign *(1968);* Founder's Praise *(1976);* A Season of Delight *(1981);* The Far Side of Victory *(1983); and* Simple Gifts *(1986). Her short stories have been collected in* Summering *(1966), from which the following story is taken;* Rites of Passage *(1971); and* High Crimes and Misdemeanors *(1979).*

The major schisms of the Church. A list of the Bishops of Sarum. She knew a great deal about medieval church politics. With luck and God's help, knowledge would save her. Because the jail was so terrifying.

She had seen the demonstrators out there in front of the library, and she had watched them for a few minutes, unemotionally, and then she had gone into her little office and scratched out some words on a piece of cardboard for a sign. Then she had walked out of the library and down the steps to stand with the demonstrators. She had made no conscious decision to do this. Her heart was exploding its blood in rhythmic spasms of panic, but she paid no attention to it; and this frightened Myra, because she had always weighed her choices carefully and measured feeling against propriety.

Now she was standing in a jail cell. What was there to be afraid of? Jails haven't changed much since the Middle Ages; the properties of a jail—the dirt, discomfort, lack of privacy, and ugliness—were the same. Being a student of history, she had pondered many imprisonments. Except for the electric lights, Tugwell's county jail might have been anywhere at any time; and for Myra, who had always respected fighters for a cause, prison had meant Boethius' great hour, Gottschalk, the Albigensian teachers, and John of the Cross. She now understood that the worst, the most horrifying feature of their imprisonment had eluded her; and in her own moment, its sudden presence was almost too much to stand. Captors hate. How could she have missed so plain a fact? Captors hate. When the sheriff had come to "protect" them from the hecklers, she had started forward, trying to get to him. "These Negroes and I are protesting an unjust . . ."

But he had turned, reaching to take her and the girl next to her, and he had looked at them with a look that stopped the words in her mouth. At the jail, as they went past him into the cell, she saw the look again, a loathing, an all-pervading contempt. Before the wave of fear and sickness had passed, the door was closed and he was gone.

There were no statements taken, no charges made. She had wasted the first hours mustering answers from an array of imprisoned giants, the brilliant, searing words of men whose causes, once eclipsed and darkened, were now the commonplace truths of our civilization.

After a while Myra had looked around and counted. There are eight of us. The young men had been taken somewhere else. Eight girls, two beds—an upper and lower bunk—one spigot, two slop buckets, one bare wall, and two square yards of floor to sit on. That was all. The girls had gone to the bunks in an order that seemed natural: two rested or slept on the lower, four sat on the upper bunk, leaving the floor for the remaining two. When anyone had sat or rested enough, she would move and a girl on the floor would take her place.

She had expected choices. There were none, not even a list of rules that they could obey or refuse to obey. It underlined the sheriff's look. One doesn't give choices to an animal; the sheriff, giving such choices, would be recognizing the humanity of his prisoners and their right to make some disposition of their own lives. So, Miss Myra, the careful librarian of Tugwell, who walked in the crosswalks and did not spit where it said *No Spitting*, was forced to put her own boundaries to her day. She decided to spend the mornings mentally recounting history, braiding popes and synods and the heresies they sifted. Perhaps they would shed light on the evolution of secular law, in which she had done a good deal of reading. In the afternoon she would have to find a way to get some exercise, to get a letter out, to wash her clothes. . . . The girls talked a little now and then, the random exchanges of people waiting. Myra sensed that they didn't have her need for formed, measured bits of time, for routines and categories. They seemed to hang free within the terms of imprisonment, simply waiting.

On the evening of the second day Matilda Jane asked her, "Miss Myra, how you come to be with us?"

The others looked over at her, some smiling, no doubt remembering the scene of themselves as they stood and sang in front of the library, hoping they could keep their voices from quavering. They had watched the door, certain of the nose of a gun or the tip of a firehose as it slowly opened. Instead, there had grown only the tiny white edge of Myra's quickly lettered sign, giving them a word at a time: OPEN LIBRARY TO ALL! IGNORANCE IS NOT BLISS. Then, Myra herself had come, slowly, very much alone. It was as if in the expectation of a cannon, they had been shocked by a pop gun. Some of them had even laughed.

"I'd never thought about it, I mean about colored people not using the library, not until Roswell Dillingham came. After that, I had to—well—to protest."

"*Roswell?*" And the other girls sat up, surprised, interested, waiting for something rich. "Heber's little brother?"

"Hey, she mean Sailor."

They laughed.

"What Sailor done now?"

"I didn't know his nickname," Myra said, and Lalie, who was sitting on the bed beside her, guffawed. "Lord, yes! Great big mouth, blowin' an' goin' all the time, two big ears a-flappin', ma'am; you be with Sailor, you ain' need no boat!" And they all wanted to know what Sailor had done now. They were all eager to hear Roswell's latest, all except Delphine, who was stretched out on the bed dozing.

"Well," Myra said, "there's not much to tell, really. You see, when Mrs. Endicott left and I took over as county librarian, she simply told me that you—I mean that Negroes—just didn't use the library, but that when a Negro needed to look something up, why he would come to me and I would take the book out myself. I know it will seem odd to you —it does to me now—but before that it had never occurred to me that there were no Negroes coming into the library. Anyway, one day this spring, I was locking up and Roswell came and asked me for a book. I just followed Mrs. Endicott's instructions—I got it for him on my card. In three days he was back. Soon he started asking me to recommend books for him to read. Two or three books every week. I started combing lists for things I thought he would like, and the more he read, the more foolish it seemed not to have him come and browse around and pick out the books for himself. When I told him to come, he looked at me as if I had told him to fly like a bird. Negroes were forbidden to use the library.

"*The library!* That business of my getting the books for him had been designed to make me ask him why he wanted them, and then to decide that he wasn't responsible! I wrote an inquiry to the county commission and never got an answer. I never dreamed of demonstrating. I have to be honest and say that, but *the library*—well—I just couldn't consent to that. So, I suppose it was Roswell who got me to come out."

M.J. looked away and there was silence while everyone groped for a new, less dangerous subject.

Loretta whistled softly and said, "Kin you beat that damn Roswell?"

No getting away now; there it was. "What's the trouble?" Myra asked.

"You in here with us, Miss Myra," M.J. said, "so I'm gonna tell you truly what Roswell been doin'. He been makin' money offa them books."

"I don't see how. They were returned on time and in good shape."

"Ma'am, he been liftin' offa them books."

"I'm sorry, M.J., I just don't understand . . ."

"I'm in here in this jail, an' I got to be ashame' for that bigmouth! He takes them books, an' he reads 'em, an' then he take an' make 'em into a play. Then he go an' puts up a sign down to Carters' store an' he an' Fernelle an' one or two of 'em, they acts it out, see. Ten cents a person. He get almost everyone to come an' bring the kids an' make a night out. He ain' stop there. I know there's whole parts of the play that he have just graff right out of the book. I could tell it. Don't shake your head, Lalie, you know good as I do, ain' no words like that come out o' Roswell bigmouth! He lays them words down so nice—an' *powerful*! Miss Myra, he been gettin' maybe five, six dollars clear every Saturday, just showin' *your* books in the meetin' hall of the Hebron Funeral Home!"

Echo of Boethius, calling out of a sixth century cell, "Come, Goddess Wisdom, Come, Heart-ravishing Knowledge . . ." Roswell Dillingham, bootlegger of knowledge, echoed that day when knowledge was an absolute and its conquest as sure as the limits of a finite heaven. Myra wished she could tell them about Boethius, broken and condemned, and crying in his agony: "Earth conquered gives the stars!" It would only embarrass them. She said, "Do the people like the plays?"

"Well—yes, they do. See, Roswell's plays—they're about us, about colored people. It's a' interestin' play, an' folks don' have to go all the way in to Winfiel' Station, sit in the balcony. My granmaw say, she gets to see a play she understan', an' they's nobody drinkin', swearin', runnin' aroun' in they underwear. Roswell plays—I mean *your* plays— they about what happen to our people. Like las' week, he had one call *Oliver Twiss*. Everybody cry in that one. Before that he had one call *Two Cities*."

Myra heard Dickens' story about how Sydney Carton gave himself up to the sheriff, back in the thirties, when the K.K.K. rode patrol out of Tugwell.

"Kite my books, will he . . . I wish I'd known. There's a fine one about a Civil Rights worker who got too rich and comfortable, name of Julius Caesar; one about a girl named Antigone, the freedom play of all time."

There was a snort from the bed. Delphine stretched and then swung her legs over the side and grunted again. "*Miss* Myra, we don't need white stories made over for black people."

"I wasn't patronizing. The books I gave Roswell were good books. They weren't 'white' stories. They were about people—any people . . ."

"No, *ma'am*, Miss Myra, *ma'am*, not while you got 'em piled up and stored away in the white-only library."

"That's why I was glad about Roswell." Myra looked down at Delphine. The two girls on the floor shifted a little, ready to use their bed places. Delphine got up slowly, and Myra got down, and they stood together in the cell.

From the beginning Delphine was the only one with whom Myra knew she could have no more than an armed truce. Delphine knew it too, probably. They seldom spoke to one another directly; when they had to speak, they used an agonizingly elaborate etiquette, which Myra noted had just gone over into parody. Delphine had a hard, absolute way of speaking that Myra found irritating; but Myra knew that Delphine must find life in the cramped cell more difficult with her there. Delphine was their leader. She had been in protests and sit-ins, and jailed four times. She spoke with hard-won, frightening knowledge.

"Next time, wear pedal-pushers like I got on, plaid or check. They hold up good an' they don't show the dirt."

"When they're going to hit you, the muscles by their eyes cinch up. You can always tell. Never take the smack, let the smack take you. Go with it."

If she had been an Albigensian under the Question, Myra knew that Delphine would wake great admiration in her. She was strong and intelligent; she could duck a blow, parry a question, and make her silence ring with accusation. Somehow, the heroine was also an arrogant bitch. Myra wondered if some straying grain of her own prejudice made

Delphine's virtues seem so much like faults. As the pressures built up in the shares of water, slop bucket, and stench, Myra could see, from her neatly labeled and scheduled mental busy-work, that Delphine was trying to separate her from the rest of the girls.

They waited for three days. On the morning of the fourth, the sheriff came around with his notebook. As he stopped on the other side of the bars, Myra spoke to him. They had been arrested and jailed without being given their legal rights, she said. Would this be remedied?

The sheriff looked up slowly from his book, feigning a courteous confusion. "Why you're the little lady works over to the library, ain't you?" Then he let his gaze sift slowly over the others in the cell and come back to her, the expression now one of sympathetic reproof. (Now, look at what you have caused to happen to you.)

She had a sudden, terrifying vision of him in all his genial Southern courtesy cutting away their justice, their law, their lives.

"Oh, ma'am, it's a shame! The commissioners only decided last week that we got to do Comminists the same as we do niggers. Comminist wants to live with niggers, why we ain' gonna stop 'em. But, ma'am, I seen you over in church on Sunday, an' all the bazaars, an' you was servin' donuts at the Legion parade." He looked at her earnestly. "It must be a mistake. I'm sure you ain' one of them Comminists."

Myra had never thought of herself as being a perceptive person. A narrow and careful life had never made it a necessity. Sensitivity can be a frightening gift. It was better to depend on more tangible things: hard work, reasonableness, and caution. Now, in the quiet, fear-laced minute, she suddenly knew that this contemptuously play-acting man was offering her a way out. She had only to weep and tell him how confused she was, to ask for his protection. (Lonely spinster-woman—everybody knows how notional they get. A woman, being more took up with the biological part of things, why, if she don't get to re-lize that biological part of her nature, it's a scientific fact she'll go to gettin' frusterated. Women, why they're *cows*!) It was as if she heard his mind form words. When he did speak, the words were so close that she was dumfounded.

"I guess you kinda got turned around here, all this niggers rights business. I guess you just got confused for a bit. I sure hate to see you in here like this. It sure is a pity." White women are ladies, the code said. You crush ladies not with violence but with pleasant contempt.

She didn't want to leave the girls in the cell. She looked at the sheriff, but she did not speak. The "lady" dealt with, he turned his attention to the others, and his voice hardened and coarsened as the code demanded when speaking to Them.

"We got a list here. You answer to your name when I call it." Then he read the names, stopping between each syllable to allow for their slow black wits to apprehend his meaning. The girls answered in the way Delphine had taught them: their voices cool and level, their eyes straight on him. Myra had been in Tugwell for only three years, having come in answer to a wildly exaggerated ad in the *Library Journal*, and staying because she had liked the town. She had never had any dealings with Tugwell's Negroes, except for Roswell; but she knew somehow that this was not the usual way for Negroes to react to authority in Tugwell. She couldn't trace this knowledge—she had never seen it directly or heard mention of it—it was just there, a certitude that their look was treason and would damn them. She also knew that from that judgment anyway, she was exempt. She might face down the sheriff and be called an old-maid eccentric, but she wouldn't be hurt. Another line of difference had been drawn, excluding her; and for a long moment of the sheriff's passing by, she was overwhelmed with a loneliness so keen that she found herself shivering and on the verge of tears.

She tried to close this separation. To do it, she had to appeal to Delphine. "Four days!" she said. "There must be a way we can get hold of a lawyer . . ."

But Delphine stepped back from the line that the sheriff had helped to set between them. "You aren't Miss Myra here; you aren't ma'am. Not with us. Not for giving us white-man heroes or white-man lawyers either. *You* get *your* lawyer. Let him get *you* out."

"Look, Delphine, I don't know anything about the struggle between the races. I know about the library and the books that are in the library; and I know that it is wrong for the library to deny its treasures to those who want them. I know about books and reading. That's what I know about, where I am strong and where I will fight."

But Delphine had turned her back and gone toward a space on the bed which Myra realized shouldn't have been there. It was there for Delphine. She was the complete leader now. She would always have a seat on the bed or a space to lie down on the bed when she wanted it. Having measured the sheriff, the others had chosen his adversary— tyrant for tyrant. Delphine went to rest on "her" bunk, to claim her compensation. "Her" places would now be offered to others only at her discretion. It was wrong. Myra saw it denying the very equality for which they were risking so much; because Myra now knew that her cellmates were facing the sons of the men who had broken Gottschalk's bones. If only she could give them some of his or Boethius' passionate and simple poetry to have when the time came. They might be strengthened by the words of great prisoners whose causes had been so much like their own. They would need grandeur. That sheriff was one who, to the end, would follow the Customs of the Country.

Later, she was sitting next to M.J. on the floor and they were talking quietly about wonderful food they had eaten. After Myra had dismembered a large, delicately broiled lobster and dipped the red claw carapace full of its vulnerable meat into a well of butter, M.J. leaned close and whispered, "Hey, Myra—uh—you ain' a Comminist or nothin', are you?"

Myra turned in wonder from the fading lobster. "What? Whatever gave you that idea?" Some words scurried across her mind in a disorderly attempt to escape being thought.

"I didn' mean to hurt your feelin's," M.J. murmured, "but, see, Delphine don' trust you, because if you was another kind of different person—well—it wouldn' be like it was one of the regular whites comin' over to our side; it would be like you was arguin' for your own difference, see?"

"M.J., you tell Delphine that all I want is to have the Tugwell library open to everybody, regardless of race, creed, color, or national origin."

"I don' think Delphine is really agains' you."

"Where does she come from?" Myra asked, and M.J. said quickly, "Oh, she from here . . ." And then she looked down. "It's the schoolin' make her talk so much nicer, that's all. Her folks don't live but a street away from us. Her daddy work on the railroad, though, made steady money."

"It's not the way she talks," Myra said, stumbling over that other barrier between them. How could she have read the sheriff so well that his predicted words followed like footprints, and yet not be able to show herself to this girl who had the face and voice of a friend? "Delphine is different from you other girls, she . . ."

"It's the same with us as with the white," M.J. said, and she fingered her torn sleeve in a little nervous gesture that Myra had seen her begin to use after the sheriff's visit. "Some people, you fit 'em in with the rest; it don't bother 'em none. Some, they got to be just one an' the mold broke. Delphine, she like that. She always did feel sharp for things that was done wrong to her. I think she felt hurts more, say, than me. It's cause she's smarter; she got more person to hurt. You know, she went up North to the college."

"I didn't know that."

"I can remember her sayin' all the time how learnin' and education was goin' to get her free. Our grade school here in Tugwell, it ain' hardly one-legged to the white school; an' our high school ain' but a butt-patch to the white. Oh, Myra, an' we didn't know it! Delphine come out of Booker T. Washington High all proud an' keen. She made the straight A. Then she went up North to the college. An' all of a sudden, here she was, bein' counted by white folks measure—an' put down, put way low. It shamed her. The white-school diploma she got cost her a extra year just to fill in on what ol' Booker T. High didn' think a Negro had to know."

"But she did succeed . . ."

"That's what I wonder at—why she come back afterward, here to Tugwell, where she ain't no different from any of us that never done what she did. I can't see how anybody that got the college degree would come back here to be put down low again."

"The fight and the fighter have to be close to each other," Myra murmured.

"What?"

Myra felt a gnawing in her mind that was strange to her. She had to wait until it became plain, and then she recognized that it was her mind moving, feeling blindly toward one of its own motives. It came bumping against something, won the shape from the darkness, and with the shape, a meaning. "Not pretty or smart or gifted, but I had one thing that was mine. The pretty and smart ones had the future; the rich ones had the present. I had the past. In a way, in 'having,' I 'owned.' The history and literature were mine to give when I opened that library door every morning. . . . When Roswell told me that Negroes couldn't use the library, I was mad because the town had no right, no right to deny what wasn't theirs to give or withhold. In a way, Delphine and I are alike." Then she said to M.J., "Delphine has a calling; there's no doubt about that."

Why can't I like her? Myra looked at the leader over the soggy bread in her dinner plate. She has everything I've always reverenced. Watching Delphine at the spigot. . . . not running away, standing, as Boethius stood, and Gottschalk and John. The courage is in knowing exactly what will happen, where the wound will gall most cruelly, and still, standing. . . . But the arrogance in Delphine, who was beginning to posture like Savonarola silhouetted by the light of his own fire, made Myra wince. Delphine's arrogance reached into Myra's thoughts and began to move toward all of the heroes Myra had stored there. She began to worry for the giants she venerated, for years of her pity and love. Was courage only the arrogance used to an enemy?

The next morning the sheriff began.

Tactical blunder: He took Delphine first. She came back sick, the brown color of her face grayed. She was bloody and puffy-faced and harder than ever. Now, anyone who followed would have to come to Delphine before and after, and would be judged. When Loretta went in the afternoon and returned still retching, she was greeted by Delphine's wry smile and the slow unfolding of Delphine's bones, one by one, to make a place for her on the bunk throne of honor. The next day Dilsey and Lalie went. They came back trembling and exhausted, embarrassed at where their hurts were, and with a rumor that things were going to be speeded up because the legal machinery was slowly lumbering in to help. In the night, counting the heretics she knew, burned between 890 and 1350 in France, Myra could hear M.J. quietly sobbing with fear.

It had been hardest for M.J., who had seen all the hurts and heard the accumulating voices in their nightmares. Now the untried ones had the floor all the time. Myra crawled over to M.J. and put a hand on her thin back in a forlorn gesture of comfort. M.J.'s back stopped heaving and the crying stopped or, rather, retreated inward. Myra began to feel that someone was observing her; another silence was there, one that seemed to fill its space instead of being there by default of sound. She turned and saw Delphine looking at them from a seat on the top bunk, her face showing nothing in the dimness. She was awake, all right, watching, listening, as if she were waiting to pounce. It made Myra feel guilty of something. She looked down at M.J., who hadn't moved and was pretending to be asleep, and then she stood up. It was painfully slow; she grunted with the effort and the pain; her legs had been bent against the concrete floor for a long time. When she finally stood, her eyes were at the level of Delphine's kneecaps.

"Help M.J. You know, Delphine, we can't all be as tough as you." She realized immediately that such a plea for M.J. was wrong and stupid.

Crying weakness to Delphine was like asking sympathy from a tornado. Were all heroes so frighteningly impersonal? Damn her! Why couldn't that precious martyrs' firelight extend its warmth and radiance to cover M.J., who had waited all these days while the terror grew?

"Listen, Delphine, I know something about you."

Delphine's impassive face did not move. Damn her, I'll make it move.

"I know, for instance," she continued slowly, whispering a word at a time, "that whatever you took from the sheriff, it didn't hurt as much as theirs did . . ." And she gestured around the cell at the sleepers who were shielding their ugly dreams from the forty-watt light that burned in the corridor outside the cell. "Maybe you didn't feel it at all."

"How come?" Delphine said, fastidiously disinterested.

"You knew it before you went in," Myra went on. "It's a nice secret, too, Delphine, because the welts are real and no one can prove they didn't hurt. Maybe they don't even hurt now."

"No!" Delphine hissed. "Nothing hurts! It's the black skin. Makes you immune. Tougher than the white! Less sensitive!"

"Come off it. It's the anger or the hate that makes you immune. Your anger and hate are better than morphine for shielding you from pain. You were dressed up to the eyes in hate, and you walked in with it to the sheriff and took your licks and came back bleeding. You didn't even have to lie. Did it make you feel superior to the other girls who had to take it raw, without hate?"

That hit. Myra could see it going in to burn behind Delphine's slowly blinking eyes. She was standing close to Delphine, whispering, but they were both aware that M.J. and maybe others were awake and would hear them if their voices got any louder.

Delphine began to negotiate. "What are you going to do about it?"

"You help M.J. to take what she's going to have to take or I'll tell what I know about you."

Delphine laughed, a silent mouth-laugh, whose mirth died long before it reached her eyes.

"I know they won't believe me," Myra said, "but maybe there'll be a minute of doubt, just enough to force you to come right out and claim that bed space and that first drink in the morning."

Delphine sat there, surprised, and Delphine's surprise was a source of pain to Myra. She had no style and she knew it. Her courage looked silly. Nevertheless, she had gotten to Delphine, and Delphine wasn't used to being gotten to.

"I don't want you here!" she hissed. "I don't want what you have to give us! Get your white face out of this cell and let us, for once, do something all by ourselves!"

"I'm here and my white face is here, and you can either like it or lump it."

Where had the words and the strength come from? She had always been a sheltered person, and three years as Miss Myra, the toy librarian in this toy white town of antimacassars and mint tea hadn't done any more than confirm her opinion. Who had she been a week ago that she could be so far from that self right now? Like a rocket, she thought, that had veered a millionth of a degree from the center of its thrust. She had, on the 14th of April, asked a question of a boy named Roswell Dillingham. It was only the smallest shift, a millionth of a degree, and that smallest change was measuring her path at tangent, thousands of miles into strange darkness, to end lost, perhaps, in uncharted spaces that she could not imagine.

Delphine was muttering curses, and Myra turned back to her place on the floor and sat down. Delphine didn't want her, and she had said so. Why not? What did Myra, and by extension white people, have that Delphine couldn't accept? If Delphine hadn't been to college up North, it might have been a falsely exalted picture of American history, a Parson

Weems history that no Negro in slave-holding country could take seriously. It wasn't that. Delphine had read enough and learned enough to know that white men also searched their souls occasionally. Myra knew that she had to get at it, whatever it was, because she needed everything she could use against Delphine's arrogance. She found herself staring at the slop bucket, riveted on it. Exhausted, she thought.

Hard floors and groping, needs and angers, mine and hers, and barely knowing where to separate mine and hers. Why is *she* in this cell? Then she found herself staring at Lalie's back as if to bore through it, and Lalie shifted and moaned so that Myra pulled her eyes away. I have the past. . . . I have the past and two enemies, who both seem to say "nothing personal." It really isn't, I suppose. They are enemies to my history. What a couple they would make: the sheriff, with his fake past, and Delphine, with her fake . . .

It was there, somewhere near, elusive but near, in Delphine's idea of a future. She became alert, groping to more purpose now. It was in a future of which Delphine dreamed, a world that made "white" history irrelevant and Myra a danger. She looked over the sleeping girls. Delphine had given up too, and was curled in a ball, her arm protectively over her face. The only ones who merely pretended to sleep were the two whose turn it would be to go with the sheriff tomorrow. Myra knew that she would not be beaten, and that the law was slowly lumbering toward her. If only Delphine had let it happen, she might have given them a thousand years of prison humor and two thousand years of resistance to the tyrant, eloquent, proud resistance, face to face, as Delphine would have liked it.

And *I* wanted to be in the history too! she thought. Oh, my God, it was as simple as that! I wanted to be in the history even more than I wanted to fight over Roswell's reading. I wanted to come forward where the fire was, feeling that in the fire, I would not be so alone. . . . The thoughts that she had sent out walking for Delphine's weakness had found hers instead. Does it hurt and sear and shatter, that thought? Is it as hard as the sheriff's blows? No, not so hard as that. She wasn't going to be in the history, even though she was in the fire. In the fire, but no less alone. Delphine had fixed that. A segregated fire. She would have to work at not hating Delphine. This cause was right and the cause should take precedence over its leaders. Heaven knows it was an old argument. It showed up as the Montanist Controversy; and it was put to a rule in 325 A.D.: Decision of the Nicene Council, valid sacraments by a lapsed bishop. Very good. It was a comfort to know that the early Church had ruled on Delphine's case.

M.J. rolled over, but her eyes were closed, and she was still pretending to be asleep. She was a nice girl. If Delphine had allowed it, they could have been, all of them, friends together in this cause. Her mind yearned toward M.J. in the night. There were thousands of men and women before you in that room, a thousand rooms, acts, moments. Don't be afraid. You are neighbored all around by people who have screamed or been silent, wept or been brave—all the nations are represented, all the colors of man. Don't be afraid of pleading, of weeping. You are with some shining names.

At the window there was a little gray light coming. The window was almost hidden by the bunks which had been pushed against its bars, but from where Myra sat on the floor, she could see up into a tiny square of the changing sky. The cell looked even worse in the muddy yellow of the electric bulb.

I suppose I shouldn't stop at the heroes of the Middle Ages. There are more recent slaves and conquerers. Dachau and Belsen—they, too, had men who stood in their moment and said, "I am a person; you must not degrade me." Her eye wandered around the cell and fixed on the slop bucket again, and she tried to ease her aching body on the floor. Dachau and Belsen.

In 1910, technology was going to make everybody free and freedom was going to make everybody good. The new cars had rolled up to the gates of death camps. Dreams of the perfecting of man ended in the gas chambers and behind the cleverly devised electric fences. Didn't everybody dream that dream? Didn't we *all*?

Maybe all but one. Is man imperfect by nature? Maybe only white man? There it was. Delphine was answering to everyone who had ever told her that she and hers were outside the elm-street-and-steeple dream of democracy. If the black heroes weren't in the history books, then they were also not included in the Albigensian Crusade and the ride to Belsen. The possibility of perfection—that was being girded, all right. If Delphine took her blows in hate and in the belief that *her* people could be perfect, not in some millennium but soon, and by her own good efforts, what would be, could be given her, what pain could she endure that wasn't worth it? Not for freedom, not for friendship, certainly not for the right of ingress to the Tugwell library. Oh, God, who will help M.J. take her hurting now, when all that M.J. wants is to include in her God-blesses before bed all the misery-running, sorrow-spawning world of white and black?

It was morning. M.J. was trembling quietly on the floor. She looked exhausted and ill, and she hadn't even gone yet. Myra got up, and the aching numbed to her every bone. She went to where Delphine was perched, sleeping.

"Delphine?"

"What-do-you-want?" It was the too-clear enunciation of an educated Negro to a white who will call him Rastus if he slurs a letter.

"You've got to do something to help M.J."

"I bet you're happy, white gal. If it wasn't for your people putting us down, she wouldn't *be* scared now!"

So it was true. The blind would see and the halt would rejoice. No cowards, no sinners, no wrongs. In the jubilee. In the great jubilee. "Help her, Delphine. The sheriff is looking for weakness. If he finds it, he might kill her with his hands or with her own shame. Help her, or I'm going to start talking about you, Delphine. I'm going to start asking questions that the others have never asked."

Myra could see the gains and losses ticking off in Delphine's head. Her eyes were clinical and her expression detached as an Egyptian funerary statue. Delphine, at the height of her concentration, was intensely, breathtakingly beautiful. She stayed in her place for a minute, two. Then she stretched and the odds and possibilities arranged themselves before her. With elaborate, lithe ease she swung down to the floor, yawning, and bent to where M.J. lay. They began to whisper. Myra was glad she couldn't hear them. For a moment her eye strayed to the vacant place, Delphine's place on the bed. She had a sudden urge to climb up and take it and make Delphine fight to get it back. The place would be comfortable for a little nap; she was sore all over from the floor. The place would be dark against the back wall; she could sleep for a while.

No, Delphine was the leader, the place was her place. Only Delphine, however fanatical and blind, could lead the girls through all the questions, the licks and the lawyers. She found her eyes fixed again. What was so fascinating about that slop bucket! We're both on the floor, she thought.

"I wish to record an opinion," she said to it quietly. "In 325 the Council of Nicaea decided that sacraments at the hands of a lapsed bishop were valid where the intent of the communicant was sincere. The baptisms of these bishops stood. I always wondered about that decision. It smacked too much of ends justifying means. I hereby make my statement to the estimable theologians of the Council of Nicaea: 'Avé, fellas, Salvé, fellas, Congratulations and greetings from the Tugwell jail.' "

FOUR

Children in
the Library

A child often sees a library as a magical place. Its doors open into a world of make-believe, romance, and fairy tales. For a child who becomes a passionate reader, the library holds the enticing promise of adventure, entertainment, and comfort that will last a lifetime, held in an inexhaustible supply of books. To some children, like Matthew in Rose Blue's *A Quiet Place,* the library is a haven where a thoughtful child can find rare space and silence.

Libraries can also be fearsome. That huge, echoing space; such awesome quiet; those dark aisles in the stacks—the library looms large in a child's imagination. Who hasn't momentarily wondered what might happen if he or she were forgotten and left in the library all night? In *Thimble Summer,* Elizabeth Enright confronts that possibility and gives it a happy ending.

But a city child may experience a library as a place of security. Young Ben in Stephen King's horror classic finds refuge from bullies in the library. Pete Hamill recalls the tough Brooklyn neighborhood of his childhood, with its youth gangs, "homeless rummies," and "sallow-faced characters with gray fedoras and pinkie rings who carried guns under their coats." Young Hamill was understandably afraid of them: "But I knew one big thing: none of them ever came to the library." What he found in the library, besides safety, was a new center for his life, "a place where most of the things I came to value as an adult had their beginnings."

Adult memoirs and fiction also tell us how, for many children, libraries were inextricably mixed with the difficult process of growing up. A first visit to a library or perhaps a first library card is often an important rite of passage into the adult world. Many well-known writers have documented those moments in their autobiographies or autobiographical fiction, as Betty Smith does here.

Dots on a literary map of writers' well-loved libraries would cover the whole country. Reading these memoirs often tells us something about the place as well as the library. Annie Dillard's memories of the Homewood branch of Pittsburgh's Carnegie Library are focused on her city-dweller's lament that, reading with fascination *The Field Book of Ponds and Streams,* she could not imagine "where I personally might find a pond, or a stream."

The library is the right place to escape into distant lands, both real and imaginary. The magic that libraries hold for children is perhaps nowhere better illustrated than in Edward Eager's books. In the excerpt from *Half Magic,* a visit to the library places three children on an enchanted path that transforms their ordinary small-town life. As the selections in this section illustrate, for many children enchanted paths have often begun in the library.

Excerpt from *A Quiet Place* by Rose Blue

A former teacher and a lyricist of popular songs, Rose Blue is best known for her children's books, which include Black, Black, Beautiful Black *(1969);* Grandma Didn't Wave Back *(1972);* We Are Chicano *(1973);* Cold Rain on the Water *(1979);* My Mother the Witch *(1981); and several others. She has also written books for a high-interest, low-reading-level series. Born in 1931, Ms. Blue lives in New York City.*

The following excerpt is from A Quiet Place *(1969), written, she has said, when she was taking a course in children's literature and found available books about children inadequate. "I feel that more sensitive, perceptive books dealing with realities of life and feelings of children are essential to children's literature. I have attempted to contribute this in my work."*

Matthew jumped as a light went off. They were getting ready to close the library for the day. Matthew looked down at the book open on his lap. It was about a boy who lived a long time ago in the West. There were seventy pages and Matthew was up to page 57. He had read only a few pages today. He would come to the library early tomorrow and finish the book. It was too hard to read in his room with Baby Stevie there. Another light went out and Matthew thought of home, where the kitchen was so bright and cozy. It was almost suppertime. Matthew got up and pulled his white T-shirt down over his jeans. He tucked the book under his arm and left the library, walking briskly through the noisy, crowded streets—past the brownstones and tenements, past the people sitting on the stoops, past the overflowing garbage cans, across the avenue, and down the city block.

"Hey, who's that struttin' down the street?" somebody was singing in a teasing voice. Matthew looked and saw the big kid they called Duke standing by the boarded-up house near the corner. In a minute, Duke and a whole bunch of kids were standing around Matthew, clapping and singing.

"Matthew's struttin' down the street," another boy sang in the same beat.

"Struttin', struttin', with his book," Duke chimed in.

"Hey you, what you gonna do with the book?" one of the group asked.

"He's gonna look at the book," Duke sang, and they all laughed.

Matthew swallowed hard and wished Claudia and her friends were there. They were lots bigger than these kids. "Hey, you guys, get lost," Matthew said, trying to sound as tough as he could.

But now all of Duke's friends were standing around Matthew, clapping and singing, like little kids playing circle games in school.

Matthew did a quick hop-skip and ducked under a big kid's arm and out of the circle. He kept walking as fast as he could, trying to look cool, and went up his front stoop two steps at a time, whistling so the big kids wouldn't think he was scared. When the front door closed behind him he held his book tight and walked slowly up two flights of the five-story house to home.

A delicious smell of something cooking led Matthew into the kitchen where Mama was standing at the stove, stirring a great big pot of stew.

Mama turned, said "Hello, Matthew, honey," and kept stirring without losing the rhythm.

"Hello, Mama," Matthew said quietly. He leaned against the refrigerator awhile, not saying a word.

Mama watched him closely for a long minute. "Anything wrong, Matthew?" she asked.

He shook his head.

"Where you been all day?"

"At the library, Mama," Matthew said softly. "It's closing tomorrow."

Mama stopped stirring. "So that's it," she said, kind of to herself. . . .

Matthew took his book, left the bathroom, and went out the front door. He stood outside for a few minutes, just leaning against the door, and then he climbed the stairs, all the way up to the roof. He pushed open the heavy door and stepped onto the tar-covered floor. Three ladies were hanging clothes on the line and talking, and in a corner two big boys were sitting, playing a radio very loud. The roof was no better for reading and sitting quiet than home was, so Matthew went down again, down all the steps and out to the street.

He went up and down the streets, in and out of alleys, searching for a quiet place. But he found none. His school was across the avenue and down three blocks. He walked by it and wandered around till he came to the park. He passed mothers with baby carriages, children playing in the playground, big kids playing ball. He crossed a path, and kept going until he saw a high, sloping, grassy hill near the back of the park.

He climbed up to the top, where there was a great big leafy tree with four smaller trees around it. The trunk of the big tree made a chair and Matthew sat on it. When he looked down he saw people

walking on the path, but they looked far away, and he could hardly
hear them. When he looked up he saw a ceiling of leaves with little
patches of sky and sunlight showing through.

He sat there, just watching the breeze move the leaves around, till
a stronger chill wind came and made the leaves shudder as the sun hid
behind a dark cloud. A shiver ran through him, and though the wind
stopped and the sun came out once more, Matthew felt no warmer. It
was almost autumn, and after autumn came winter and the snow would
cover his tree. Winter would come and where would he go?

Matthew huddled against his tree trunk, holding his book, and then
he thought of another boy, the boy in the book he had just finished,
the boy who lived way out West, a long, long time ago. He thought
how that boy had gone looking for new places and traveled far when
the way was hard. Yet the little boy kept looking, even though the
winter was bitter cold. The little boy in the West was hungry lots of
times and had to find his own food. Matthew felt lucky—it was still
summer now, with time to look for a new place and still be warm. And
tomorrow Matthew's mama would give him a great, big, hot breakfast.
Tomorrow, right after breakfast, Matthew would go place-hunting. He
would find a quiet place and have it all ready for winter. He would
start with his own basement, and if that wasn't right, he'd search on.
He had found an outside place. He could find an inside one. And then
after autumn and winter, spring would come round again and Matthew
could come back to his tree.

Matthew rolled over on his tummy and lay flat on the soft grass. He
put his book down on the ground with the front cover facing him, and
with his finger he traced the picture of the boy. Then he leaned his
elbow on the grass, rested his chin in his hand, and opened to page 1.

Excerpt from *Thimble Summer* by Elizabeth Enright

Although she published several volumes of stories for adults, Elizabeth Enright (1909–68) is today remembered for her children's books, which a contemporary critic has called "among the select few that are timeless and enduring." Many grown readers still recall fondly her series of books about the Melendy family, The Saturdays *(1955);* The Four-Story Mistake *(1955);* Then There Were Five *(1956); and* Spiderweb for Two *(1956).*

The following excerpt is from her Newbery award–winning book Thimble Summer *(1939). Garnet Linden, the ten-year-old heroine, is living on a farm in Wisconsin during the Great Depression. The book describes Garnet's simple but appealing adventures during one hot summer. Admirers of* Thimble Summer *feel that it poignantly evokes Midwestern rural and small-town life in those dry, sometimes desperate years.*

Garnet sighed. "You always tell stories about people that are grown up and fall in love. I like stories about children and wild animals and explorers." She sat up suddenly. "I know what. Let's go to town to the library and read. It's still early and it's going to rain anyway."

Citronella objected for a minute or two because she said she didn't feel like walking all that way just to read a book. But Garnet was sure they could get a ride with someone and soon persuaded her to come.

As luck would have it the moment they went out of the gate they saw Mr. Freebody's truck clattering down the road towards them. They waved and called and Mr. Freebody stopped and opened the door to let them in. He was going to town to buy feed.

"We'd rather ride outside, if you don't mind," said Garnet, and the two girls scrambled into the back of the truck and stood up holding onto the roof over the driver's seat.

It was fun to ride like that because as soon as he got on the highway Mr. Freebody drove very fast and the wind blew so hard against them that Garnet's pigtails stuck straight out behind, and Citronella's bang stood up on end like a hedge. They felt as though their noses were blown flat against their faces, and when they spoke their words flew away from them.

"I feel like a thing on the front of a boat," shouted Garnet. "A figurehead, I think it's called."

Citronella had never heard of figureheads and it was hard to explain because you had to yell so; the wind roared and Mr. Freebody's truck was a very loud one. Also if you opened your mouth too wide lazy beetles on the wing were apt to be swept into it.

They watched the truck swallow up the flat ribbon of road like a tape-measure; the little grey town of Blaiseville flew towards them. There it was, all just as usual: the courthouse with its tower and gilded dome, the gasoline station, and the red painted depot, and Mrs. Elson's yellow house with clothes leaping on the line; unusually big clothes they were as Mrs. Elson and her husband were both immensely fat. There was Opal Clyde, the doctor's daughter, bouncing a ball on the walk in front of her house, and there was Junior Gertz pulling his dog along in a little express wagon. Garnet and Citronella waved as they rode grandly by. Mr. Freebody drew up in front of the Farm Bureau; the truck coughed hoarsely once or twice and subsided into stillness. The girls jumped down.

"How you two little girls going to git home?" asked Mr. Freebody.

"Oh, we'll walk maybe," answered Garnet. "Or get a ride with someone," added Citronella hopefully.

They thanked him and walked up the Main Street past the blacksmith's and the drugstore and the post office. There was a bulletin in the post-office window that said: "Big Hollow Ladies Annual Picnic Next Sunday.

Come One, Come All!" Garnet giggled at this notice, seeing in her mind a group of huge balloonlike creatures in dresses eating sandwiches under a tree. Of course she knew that the Big Hollow Ladies were simply ladies that lived in Big Hollow, but it had a funny sound all the same. They went on up the street past the store full of straw hats and overalls, and the shoe store, and the "Sweet Eat Shop" where the mechanical piano was making a noise like an old hurdy-gurdy in a boiler factory.

Finally on the outskirts of the town they came to the library, an old-fashioned frame building set back from the road among thick-foliaged maple trees.

Garnet loved the library; it smelled deliciously of old books and was full of stories that she had never read. Miss Pentland, the librarian, was a nice little fat lady who sat behind an enormous desk facing the door.

"Good afternoon, Citronella," she said, smiling. "Good afternoon, Ruby."

Miss Pentland always called Garnet Ruby by mistake. There were so many little girls in Blaiseville with names like jewels that it was very confusing. There were Ruby Schwarz, Ruby Harvey, and Rubye Smalley, Pearl Orison and Pearl Schoenbecker, Beryl Schultz, and little Opal Clyde.

Garnet and Citronella poked about among the books until each had found the one she wanted and then they settled down on a broad window seat between two tall cases of large old volumes that looked as if they hadn't been opened by anyone for fifty years.

Garnet had THE JUNGLE BOOK, and Citronella with a sigh of pleasure began to read a wonderful story called DUCHESS OLGA; OR THE SAPPHIRE SIGNET.

Many times the screen door of the library creaked and closed with a muffled bang as people came and went; other children and grown people, old ladies looking for books on crocheting and boys wanting stories about G-men. For a while rain splintered against the window beside the two girls but they scarcely heard it. Garnet was thousands of miles away with Kotick, the white seal, swimming the wide seas to find a safe island for his people; and Citronella was in a ballroom lighted by a hundred chandeliers and crowded with beautiful ladies and gentle-men in full evening dress.

Garnet finished "The White Seal" and went on to "Toonai of the

Elephants." Once she looked up and stretched. "My, it's quiet," she whispered. "I wonder if it's late."

"Oh, we haven't been here long," said Citronella impatiently. She had reached the most exciting part of the book where Duchess Olga was being lowered on a rope down the face of a huge cliff. The trouble was that the man who held the rope didn't like Duchess Olga and was planning to let her drop at any minute. Citronella thought everything would turn out all right in the end but she wasn't sure.

By the time that Garnet had re-read "Rikki-Tikki-Tavi," and Duchess Olga had been rescued pages back and safely returned to the ballroom, the light began to fade.

"What does the word 'insidious' mean?" asked Citronella, but Garnet didn't know.

"My, it is kind of still here," she went on. "I'll ask Miss Pentland what time it is." She disappeared behind the bookcases.

"Garnet!" she called loudly the next moment. "Miss Pentland's gone! Everyone's gone!"

Garnet leaped from the window seat. It was true; there was no one there. They ran to the door, but it was firmly locked. The back door was locked too; and the heavy glass windows had not been opened in years; they stuck in their frames as if set in cement. It was impossible to move them.

"Good night!" moaned Citronella. "We're locked in!" She was on the verge of tears.

But Garnet felt pleasantly excited.

"Citronella," she said solemnly, "this is an adventure. Things like this happen to people in books; we'll be able to tell our children and grandchildren about it. I hope we stay here all night!"

"Oh gee," sobbed Citronella. She wished with all her heart that she hadn't read DUCHESS OLGA; it was too scary. She simply had no courage left. If only she had picked out a good peaceful book about boarding school girls or something, she wouldn't be so frightened now. Suddenly she had such a terrible thought that she stopped crying.

"Garnet!" she cried. "Do you know what day it is? Saturday! That means we'll be here till day after tomorrow. We'll starve!"

Garnet's excitement went flat. It would be awful to stay in here as long as that.

"Let's bang on the windows," she suggested. "Maybe someone will come."

They banged on the glass and shouted at the tops of their lungs. But the library was some distance from the street, and the thick maples deadened the noise they made. Blaiseville people were peacefully eating their suppers and never heard a sound.

Slowly the dusk sifted into the room. The bookcases looked tall and solemn, and the pictures on the wall were solemn too: steel engravings of Napoleon at Elba, and Washington Crossing the Delaware.

There was no telephone in the library and no electric light. There were gas fixtures but Garnet and Citronella could not find any matches. They rummaged through Miss Pentland's desk but it was full of useless things like filing cards, rubber stamps, elastic bands and neat little rolls of string.

Citronella pounced upon a chocolate bar in a pigeonhole.

"We won't starve right away anyhow," she said, brightening a little. "I don't think Miss Pentland would mind if we ate it, do you?"

"We'll buy her another when we get out," said Garnet; so they divided it and stood, sadly munching, at the window nearest the street.

The twilight deepened.

"Who is that!" cried Garnet suddenly. They saw a dim, small figure slowly approaching on the cement walk that led to the library door. The person seemed to be bowing.

Citronella began thumping on the window joyously. "It's Opal Clyde, bouncing her ball," she said. "Yell, Garnet. Yell, and bang."

They both yelled and banged; and Opal after a scared glance at the dark window scurried down the path as fast as she could go, without coming nearer to see what was making the noise.

"Do you think she'll tell someone?" asked Citronella anxiously.

"Oh, she thought it was a spook," said Garnet in disgust. "Probably no one will believe her if she does."

They watched hopefully. All over Blaiseville the street lamps blossomed suddenly with light, but only a faint gleam penetrated the maple leaves. The two girls heard cars coming and going and faint shouts of children playing in back yards. They pounded and called till they were hoarse and their knuckles ached. But nobody came.

After a while they gave it up as a bad job and returned to the window seat.

The room was very dark now; strange, unknown and filled with shadows. It was as though it wakened at nightfall; as though it breathed and wakened and began to wait. There were tiny creaking sounds and rustlings, and airy scamperings of mouse feet.

"I don't like it," whispered Citronella. "I don't like it all: My own voice scares me. I don't dare talk out loud."

"Neither do I," murmured Garnet. "I feel as if all those books were alive and listening."

"I wonder why our folks don't come after us," said Citronella.

"They don't know where we are, that's why!" answered Garnet. "They don't even know we came to town: and we didn't tell Mr. Freebody that we were going to the library."

"I wish I'd never learned to read," sighed Citronella. "I wish I was some kind of animal and didn't have to be educated."

"It might be fun to be a panther," agreed Garnet, "Or a kangaroo, or a monkey."

"Or a pig, even," said Citronella. "A safe, happy pig asleep in its own pen with its own family!"

"One that had never seen a library and couldn't even spell pork," added Garnet, and giggled. Citronella giggled too, and they both felt much better.

Outside the night wind stirred among the trees, and a maple scratched at the window glass with a thin finger; but inside it was close and still except for the small mysterious sounds that can be heard in all old houses after dark.

Garnet and Citronella huddled together and whispered. They heard the court-house clock strike eight, then nine; but when it struck ten they were both sound asleep.

At a little before midnight they were wakened by a tremendous pounding and shouting.

"Who? What's that? Where am I?" shrieked Citronella in a panic, and Garnet, her heart thumping, said, "In the library, remember? Someone's at the door."

She ran forward in the dark, barking her shins and whacking her elbows on unfamiliar surfaces.

"Who's there?" she called.

"That you, Garnet? Thank the Lord we've found you at last," said a voice that was unmistakably Mr. Freebody's. "Is Citronella with you? Fine! Both your dads are scouring the town for you. Open the door!"

"But we're locked *in*, Mr. Freebody," called Garnet. "Miss Pentland has the key."

"I'll get it. I'll get it," shouted Mr. Freebody excitedly. "You wait there."

"We can't do anything *but* wait," said Citronella crossly. She was always cross when she first woke up.

In a little while they heard rapid footsteps on the front walk, and voices, and then the lovely sound of a key turning in the lock. Miss Pentland, with her hat on sideways, rushed in and embraced them.

"You poor little things!" she cried. "Such a thing has *never* happened before; I always make sure everyone's gone before I lock up. I can't understand how I missed you!"

"That's all right, Miss Pentland," said Garnet. "It was an adventure. And we ate your chocolate!"

"Covert Street" by Michael Waters

Michael Waters teaches at Salisbury State University on the Eastern Shore of Maryland. He has published four volumes of poetry: Fish Light *(1975);* Not Just Any Death *(1979);* Anniversary of the Air *(1985); and* The Burden Lifters *(1989).*

> The boy who lived in the library
> slept among the stacks, behind long rows
> of reference, awakening now and then to peek
> from a gap in the book-bricked wall, one eye

gleaming across the marble floors or
his paste-scented breath feathering my neck
where I stood choosing three books from the profusion
ranging the stained and oaken shelves.

Three books were all the librarian would allow
a boy to carry home, only three
fingered from the festooned section for Young Readers,
yellow streamers framing their glossy spines.

I'd spend hours browsing those books, frowning
like the Hasidic fathers who suffered endless rounds
of chess in the park, rocking my bent body back
and forth till I finally made my choice.

I took my time because I loved the silence,
the scrubbed, glimmering aisles, the smell of lemon wax,
and the dust motes drifting through pillars of light
like snow through synagogue windows in the Carpathians.

A boy could breathe there, and never be bored.
He could learn to love his mother, those mournful
vowels, and his father, the harsh consonants,
then tender their names in a luminous language.

He could leave the library, as I did, as twilight
deepened, to begin the familiar walk home
with three books bracing his arm,
and count off each street, those eternal,

Brooklyn blocks he'd never forget
—Hancock, Halsey, Eldert—, then pause
when he came to his own, Covert Street
hushed in the breeze bowing the sycamores.

Excerpt from *IT* by Stephen King

This excerpt from a best-selling horror novel is a reminder of the wide variety of writers who have been inspired by or in libraries. When a reader thinks of Stephen King, he or she thinks of screams, terror, demonic forces, gore—not of libraries. Yet in this excerpt, King clearly shows his affection for libraries and familiarity with them.

King, born in 1947, had his first blockbuster success with Carrie *(1974), followed by* Salem's Lot *(1975);* The Shining *(1977);* The Stand *(1978); and almost annual novels in succeeding years, including* Christine *(1983);* Pet Sematary *(1983);* The Dark Tower: The Drawing of the Three *(1987); and* The Dark Half *(1989). A complete and* uncut *edition of* The Stand *was published in 1990.*

Ben loved the library.

He loved the way it was always cool, even on the hottest day of a long hot summer; he loved its murmuring quiet, broken only by occasional whispers, the faint thud of a librarian stamping books and cards, or the riffle of pages being turned in the Periodicals Room, where the old men hung out, reading newspapers which had been threaded into long sticks. He loved the quality of the light, which slanted through the high narrow windows in the afternoons or glowed in lazy pools thrown by the chain-hung globes on winter evenings while the wind whined outside. He liked the smell of the books—a spicy smell, faintly fabulous. He would sometimes walk through the adult stacks, looking at the thousands of volumes and imagining a world of lives inside each one, the way he sometimes walked along his street in the burning smoke-hazed twilight of a late-October afternoon, the sun only a bitter orange line on the horizon, imagining the lives going on behind all the windows—people laughing or arguing or arranging flowers or feeding kids or pets or their own faces while they watched the boobtube. He liked the way the glass corridor connecting the old building with the Children's Library was always hot, even in the winter, unless there had been a couple of cloudy days; Mrs. Starrett, the head children's librarian, told him that was caused by something called the greenhouse effect. Ben had been delighted with the idea. Years later he would build the hotly debated BBC communications center in London, and the arguments might rage for a thousand years and still no one would know (except for Ben himself) that the communications center was nothing but the glass corridor of the Derry Public Library stood on end.

He liked the Children's Library as well, although it had none of the shadowy charm he felt in the old library, with its globes and curving iron staircases too narrow for two people to pass upon them—one always had to back up. The Children's Library was bright and sunny, a little noisier in spite of the LET'S BE QUIET, SHALL WE? signs that were posted around. Most of the noise usually came from Pooh's Corner, where the little kids went to look at picture-books. When Ben came in today, story hour had just begun there. Miss Davies, the pretty young librarian, was reading "The Three Billy Goats Gruff."

"Who is that trip-trapping upon my bridge?"

Miss Davies spoke in the low, growling tones of the troll in the story. Some of the little ones covered their mouths and giggled, but most only watched her solemnly, accepting the voice of the troll as they accepted the voices of their dreams, and their grave eyes reflected the eternal fascination of the fairy tale: would the monster be bested . . . or would it feed?

Bright posters were tacked everywhere. Here was a good cartoon kid who had brushed his teeth until his mouth foamed like the muzzle of a mad dog; here was a bad cartoon kid who was smoking cigarettes

(WHEN I GROW UP I WANT TO BE SICK A LOT, JUST LIKE MY DAD, it said underneath); here was a wonderful photograph of a billion tiny pinpoints of light flaring in darkness. The motto beneath said:

ONE IDEA LIGHTS A THOUSAND CANDLES.
—Ralph Waldo Emerson

There were invitations to JOIN THE SCOUTING EXPERIENCE. A poster advancing the idea that THE GIRLS' CLUBS OF TODAY BUILD THE WOMEN OF TOMORROW. There were softball sign-up sheets and Community House Children's Theater sign-up sheets. And, of course, one inviting kids to JOIN THE SUMMER READING PROGRAM. Ben was a big fan of the summer reading program. You got a map of the United States when you signed up. Then, for every book you read and made a report on, you got a state sticker to lick and put on your map. The sticker came complete with info like the state bird, the state flower, the year admitted to the Union, and what presidents, if any, had ever come from that state. When you got all forty-eight stuck on your map, you got a free book. Helluva good deal. Ben planned to do just as the poster suggested: "Waste no time, sign up today."

Conspicuous amid this bright and amiable riot of color was a simple stark poster taped to the checkout desk—no cartoons or fancy photographs here, just black print on white poster-paper reading:

REMEMBER THE CURFEW.

7 P.M.

DERRY POLICE DEPARTMENT

Just looking at it gave Ben a chill. In the excitement of getting his rank-card, worrying about Henry Bowers, talking with Beverly, and starting summer vacation, he had forgotten all about the curfew, and the murders.

People argued about how many there had been, but everyone agreed that there had been at least four since last winter—five if you counted George Denbrough (many held the opinion that the little Denbrough boy's death must have been some kind of bizarre freak accident). The first everyone was sure of was Betty Ripsom, who had been found the day after Christmas in the area of turnpike construction on Outer Jackson Street. The girl, who was thirteen, had been found mutilated and frozen into the muddy earth. This had not been in the paper, nor was it a thing any adult had spoken of to Ben. It was just something he had picked up around the corners of overheard conversations.

About three and a half months later, not long after the trout-fishing season had begun, a fisherman working the bank of a stream twenty miles east of Derry had hooked onto something he believed at first to be a stick. It had turned out to be the hand, wrist, and first four inches of a girl's forearm. His hook had snagged this awful trophy by the web of flesh between the thumb and first finger.

The State Police had found the rest of Cheryl Lamonica seventy yards farther downstream, caught in a tree that had fallen across the stream the previous winter. It was only luck that the body had not been washed into the Penobscot and then out to sea in the spring runoff.

The Lamonica girl had been sixteen. She was from Derry but did not attend school; three years before she had given birth to a daughter, Andrea. She and her daughter lived at home with Cheryl's parents. "Cheryl was a little wild sometimes but she was a good girl at heart," her sobbing father had told police. "Andi keeps asking 'Where's my mommy?' and I don't know what to tell her."

The girl had been reported missing five weeks before the body was found. The police investigation of Cheryl Lamonica's death began with a logical enough assumption: that she had been murdered by one of her boyfriends. She had lots of boyfriends. Many were from the air base up Bangor way. "They were nice boys, most of them," Cheryl's mother said. One of the "nice boys" had been a forty-year-old Air Force colonel with a wife and three children in New Mexico. Another was currently serving time in Shawshank for armed robbery.

A boyfriend, the police thought. Or just possibly a stranger. A sexfiend.

If it was a sexfiend, he was apparently a fiend for boys as well. In late April a junior-high teacher on a nature walk with his eighth-grade class had spied a pair of red sneakers and a pair of blue corduroy rompers protruding from the mouth of a culvert on Merit Street. That end of Merit had been blocked off with sawhorses. The asphalt had been bulldozed up the previous fall. The turnpike extension would cross there as well on its way north to Bangor.

The body had been that of three-year-old Matthew Clements, re-ported missing by his parents only the day before (his picture had been on the front page of the Derry News, a dark-haired little kid grinning brashly into the camera, a Red Sox cap perched on his head). The Clements family lived on Kansas Street, all the way on the other side of town. His mother, so stunned by her grief that she seemed to exist in a glass ball of utter calm, told police that Matty had been riding his tricycle up and down the sidewalk beside the house, which stood on the corner of Kansas Street and Kossuth Lane. She went to put her washing in the drier, and when she next looked out the window to check on Matty, he was gone. There had only been his overturned trike on the grass between the sidewalk and the street. One of the back wheels was still spinning lazily. As she looked, it came to a stop.

That was enough for Chief Borton. He proposed the seven o'clock curfew at a special session of the City Council the following evening; it was adopted unanimously and went into effect the next day. Small children were to be watched by a "qualified adult" at all times, according to the story which reported the curfew in the News. At Ben's school there had been a special assembly a month ago. The Chief went on stage, hooked his thumbs into his gunbelt, and assured the children they had nothing at all to worry about as long as they followed a few simple rules: don't talk to strangers, don't accept rides with people unless you know them well, always remember that The Policeman Is Your Friend . . . and obey the curfew.

Two weeks ago a boy Ben knew only vaguely (he was in the other fifth-grade classroom at Derry Elementary) had looked into one of the stormdrains out by Neibolt Street and had seen what looked like a lot of hair floating around in there. This boy, whose name was either Frankie or Freddy Ross (or maybe Roth), had been out prospecting for goodies with a gadget of his own invention, which he called THE FABULOUS GUM-STICK. When he talked about it you could tell he thought about it like that, in capital letters (and maybe neon, as well). THE FABULOUS GUM-STICK was a birch branch with a big wad of bubble-gum stuck on the tip. In his spare time Freddy (or Frankie) walked around Derry with it, peering into sewers and drains. Sometimes he saw money—pennies mostly, but sometimes a dime or even a quarter (he referred to these latter, for some reason known only to him, as "quay-monsters"). Once the money was spotted, Frankie-or-Freddy and THE FABULOUS GUM-STICK would swing into action. One downward poke through the grating and the coin was as good as in his pocket.

Ben had heard rumors of Frankie-or-Freddy and his gum-stick long before the kid had vaulted into the limelight by discovering the body of Veronica Grogan. "He's really gross," a kid named Richie Tozier had confided to Ben one day during activity period. Tozier was a scrawny kid who wore glasses. Ben thought that without them Tozier probably saw every bit as well as Mr. Magoo; his magnified eyes swam behind the thick lenses with an expression of perpetual surprise. He also had huge front teeth that had earned him the nickname Bucky Beaver. He was in the same fifth-grade class as Freddy-or-Frankie. "Pokes that gum-stick of his down sewer-drains all day long and then chews the gum from the end of it at night."

"Oh gosh, that's bad!" Ben had exclaimed.

"Dat's wight, wabbit," Tozier said, and walked away.

Frankie-or-Freddy had worked THE FABULOUS GUM-STICK back and forth through the grate of the stormdrain, believing he'd found a wig. He thought maybe he could dry it out and give it to his mother for her birthday, or something. After a few minutes of poking and prodding, just as he was about to give up, a face had floated out of the murky water in the plugged drain, a face with dead leaves plastered to its white cheeks and dirt in its staring eyes.

Freddy-or-Frankie ran home screaming.

Veronica Grogan had been in the fourth grade at the Neibolt Street Church School, which was run by people Ben's mother called "the Christers." She was buried on what would have been her tenth birthday.

After this most recent horror, Arlene Hanscom had taken Ben into the living room one evening and sat beside him on the couch. She picked up his hands and looked intently into his face. Ben looked back, feeling a little uneasy.

"Ben," she said presently, "are you a fool?"

"No, Mamma," Ben said, feeling more uneasy than ever. He hadn't the slightest idea what this was about. He could not remember ever seeing his mamma look so grave.

"No," she echoed. "I don't believe you are."

She fell silent for a long time then, not looking at Ben but pensively out the window. Ben wondered briefly if she had forgotten all about him. She was a young woman still—only thirty-two—but raising a boy by herself had put a mark on her. She worked forty hours a week in the spool-and-bale room at Stark's Mills in Newport, and after workdays when the dust and lint had been particularly bad, she sometimes coughed so long and hard that Ben would become frightened. On those nights he would lie awake for a long time, looking through the window beside his bed into the darkness, wondering what would become of him if she died. He would be an orphan then, he supposed. He might become a State Kid (he thought that meant you had to go live with farmers who made you work from sunup to sunset), or he might be sent to the Bangor Orphan Asylum. He tried to tell himself it was foolish to worry about such things, but the telling did absolutely no good. Nor was it just himself he was worried about; he worried for her as well. She was a hard woman, his mamma, and she insisted on having her own way about most things, but she was a good mamma. He loved her very much.

"You know about these murders," she said, looking back at last.

He nodded.

"At first people thought they were . . ." She hesitated over the next word, never spoken in her son's presence before, but the circumstances were unusual and she forced herself. ". . . sex crimes. Maybe they were and maybe they weren't. Maybe they're over and maybe they're not. No one can be sure of anything anymore, except that some crazy man who preys on little children is out there. Do you understand me, Ben?"

He nodded.

"And you know what I mean when I say they may have been sex crimes?"

He didn't—at least not exactly—but he nodded again. If his mother felt she had to talk to him about the birds and bees as well as this other business, he thought he would die of embarrassment.

"I worry about you, Ben. I worry that I'm not doing right by you."

Ben squirmed and said nothing.

"You're on your own a lot. Too much, I guess. You—"

"Mamma—"

"Hush while I'm talking to you," she said, and Ben hushed. "You have to be careful, Benny. Summer's coming and I don't want to spoil your vacation, but you have to be careful. I want you in by suppertime every day. What time do we eat supper?"

"Six o'clock."

"Right with Eversharp! So hear what I'm saying: if I set the table and pour your milk and see that there's no Ben washing his hands at the sink, I'm going to go right away to the telephone and call the police and report you missing. Do you understand that?"

"Yes, Mamma."

"And you believe I mean exactly what I say?"

"Yes."

"It would probably turn out that I did it for nothing, if I ever had to do it at all. I'm not entirely ignorant about the ways of boys. I know they get wrapped up in their own games and projects during summer vacation—lining bees back to their hives or playing ball or kick-the-can or whatever. I have a pretty good idea what you and your friends are up to, you see."

Ben nodded soberly, thinking that if she didn't know he had no friends, she probably didn't know anywhere near as much about his boyhood as she thought she did. But he would never have dreamed of saying such a thing to her, not in ten thousand years of dreaming.

She took something from the pocket of her housedress and handed it to him. It was a small plastic box. Ben opened it. When he saw what was inside, his mouth dropped open. *"Wow!"* he said, his admiration totally unaffected. *"Thanks!"*

It was a Timex watch with small silver numbers and an imitation-leather band. She had set it and wound it; he could hear it ticking.

"Jeez, it's the coolest!" He gave her an enthusiastic hug and a loud kiss on the cheek.

She smiled, pleased that he was pleased, and nodded. Then she grew grave again. "Put it on, keep it on, wear it, wind it, mind it, don't lose it."

"Okay."

"Now that you have a watch you have no reason to be late home. Remember what I said: if you're not on time, the police will be looking for you on my behalf. At least until they catch the bastard who is killing children around here, don't you dare be a single minute late, or I'll be on that telephone."

"Yes, Mamma."

"One other thing. I don't want you going around alone. You know enough not to accept candy or rides from strangers—we both agree that you're no fool—and you're big for your age, but a grown man, particularly a crazy one, can overpower a child if he really wants to. When you go to the park or the library, go with one of your friends."

"I will, Mamma."

She looked out the window again and uttered a sigh that was full of trouble. "Things have come to a pretty pass when a thing like this can go on. There's something ugly about this town, anyway. I've always thought so." She looked back at him, brows drawn down. "You're such a wanderer, Ben. You must know almost everyplace in Derry, don't you? The town part of it, at least."

Ben didn't think he knew anywhere near all the places, but he did know a lot of them. And he was so thrilled by the unexpected gift of the Timex that he would have agreed with his mother that night if she had suggested John Wayne should play Adolf Hitler in a musical comedy about World War II. He nodded.

"*You've* never seen anything, have you?" she asked. "Anything or anyone . . . well, suspicious? Anything out of the ordinary? Anything that scared you?"

And in his pleasure over the watch, his feeling of love for her, his small-boy gladness at her concern (which was at the same time a little frightening in its unhidden unabashed fierceness), he almost told her about the thing that had happened last January.

He opened his mouth and then something—some powerful intuition—closed it again.

What was that something, exactly? Intuition. No more than that . . . and no less. Even children may intuit love's more complex responsibilities from time to time, and to sense that in some cases it may be kinder to remain quiet. That was part of the reason Ben closed his mouth. But there was something else as well, something not so noble. She could be hard, his mamma. She could be a boss. She never called him "fat," she called him "big" (sometimes amplified to "big for his age"), and when there were leftovers from supper she would often bring them to him while he was watching TV or doing his homework, and he would eat them, although some dim part of him hated himself for doing so (but never his mamma for putting the food before him—Ben Hanscom would not have dared to hate his mamma; God would surely strike him dead for feeling such a brutish, ungrateful emotion even for a second). And perhaps some even dimmer part of him—the far-off Tibet of Ben's deeper thoughts—suspected her motives in this constant feeding. Was it just love? Could it be anything else? Surely not. But . . . he wondered. More to the point, she didn't know he had no friends. That lack of knowledge made him distrust her, made him unsure of what her reaction would be to his story of the thing which had happened to him in January. If *anything* had happened. Coming in at six and staying in was not so bad, maybe. He could read, watch TV,

(*eat*)

build stuff with his logs and Erector Set. But having to stay in all day as well would be *very* bad . . . and if he told her what he had seen—or thought he had seen—in January, she might make him do just that.

So, for a variety of reasons, Ben withheld the story.

"No, Mamma," he said. "Just Mr. McKibbon rooting around in other people's garbage."

That made her laugh—she didn't like Mr. McKibbon, who was a Republican as well as a "Christer"—and her laugh closed the subject. That night Ben had lain awake late, but no thoughts of being cast adrift and parentless in a hard world troubled him. He felt loved and safe as he lay in his bed looking at the moonlight which came in through the window and spilled across the bed onto the floor. He alternately put his watch to his ear so he could listen to it tick and held it close to his eyes so he could admire its ghostly radium dial.

He had finally fallen asleep and dreamed he was playing baseball with the other boys in the vacant lot behind Tracker Brothers' Truck Depot. He had just hit a bases-clearing home run, swinging from his heels and getting every inch of that little honey, and his cheering teammates met him in a mob at home plate. They pummelled him and clapped him on the back. They hoisted him onto their shoulders and carried him toward the place where their equipment was scattered. In the dream he was almost bursting with pride and happiness . . . and then he had looked out toward center field, where a chainlink fence marked the boundary between the cindery lot and the weedy ground beyond that sloped into the Barrens. A figure was standing in those tangled weeds and low bushes, almost out of sight. It held a clutch of balloons—red, yellow, blue, green—in one white-gloved hand. It beckoned with the other. He couldn't see the figure's face, but he could see the baggy suit with the big orange pompom-buttons down the front and the floppy yellow bow tie.

It was a clown.

Dat's wight, wabbit, a phantom voice agreed.

When Ben awoke the next morning he had forgotten the dream but his pillow was damp to the touch . . . as if he had wept in the night.

He went up to the main desk in the Children's Library, shaking the train of thought the curfew sign had begun as easily as a dog shakes water after a swim.

"Hullo, Benny," Mrs. Starrett said. Like Mrs. Douglas at school, she genuinely liked Ben. Grownups, especially those who sometimes needed to discipline children as part of their jobs, generally liked him, because he was polite, soft-spoken, thoughtful, sometimes even funny in a very quiet way. These were all the same reasons most kids thought he was a puke. "You tired of summer vacation yet?"

Ben smiled. This was a standard witticism with Mrs. Starrett. "Not yet," he said, "since summer vacation's only been going on"—he looked at his watch—"one hour and seventeen minutes. Give me another hour."

Mrs. Starrett laughed, covering her mouth so it wouldn't be too loud. She asked Ben if he wanted to sign up for the summer reading program, and Ben said he did. She gave him a map of the United States and Ben thanked her very much.

He wandered off into the stacks, pulling a book here and there, looking at it, putting it back. Choosing books was serious business. You had to be careful. If you were a grownup you could have as many as you wanted, but kids could only take out three at a time. If you picked a dud, you were stuck with it.

He finally picked out his three—*Bulldozer, The Black Stallion*, and one that was sort of a shot in the dark: a book called *Hot Rod*, by a man named Henry Gregor Felsen.

"You may not like this one," Mrs. Starrett remarked, stamping the book. "It's extremely bloody. I urge it on the teenagers, especially the ones who have just got their driving licenses, because it gives them something to think about. I imagine it slows some of them down for a whole week."

"Well, I'll give it a whirl," Ben said, and took his books over to one of the tables away from Pooh's Corner, where Big Billy Goat Gruff was in the process of giving a double dose of dickens to the troll under the bridge.

He worked on *Hot Rod* for awhile, and it was not too shabby. Not too shabby at all. It was about a kid who was a really great driver, but there was this party-pooper cop who was always trying to slow him down. Ben found out there were no speed limits in Iowa, where the book was set. That was sort of cool.

He looked up after three chapters, and his eye was caught by a brand-new display. The poster on top (the library was gung-ho for posters, all right) showed a happy mailman delivering a letter to a happy kid. LIBRARIES ARE FOR WRITING, TOO, the poster said. WHY NOT WRITE A FRIEND TODAY? THE SMILES ARE GUARANTEED!

Beneath the poster were slots filled with pre-stamped postcards, pre-stamped envelopes, and stationery with a drawing of the Derry Public Library on top in blue ink. The pre-stamped envelopes were a nickel each, the postcards three cents. The paper was two sheets for a penny.

Ben felt in his pocket. The remaining four cents of his bottle money was still there. He marked his place in *Hot Rod* and went back to the desk. "May I have one of those postcards, please?"

"Certainly, Ben." As always, Mrs. Starrett was charmed by his grave politeness and a little saddened by his size. Her mother would have said the boy was digging his grave with a knife and fork. She gave him the card and watched him go back to his seat. It was a table that could seat six, but Ben was the only one there. She had never seen Ben with any of the other boys. It was too bad, because she believed Ben Hanscom had treasures buried inside. He would yield them up to a kind and patient prospector . . . if one ever came along.

"D'Artagnan on Ninth Street: A Brooklyn Boy at the Library" by Pete Hamill

Although he has covered important international events as a reporter, as well as writing six novels, many movie and TV scripts, and more than one hundred short stories, Pete Hamill is perhaps best known for his accounts of life in New York City, published in newspapers and magazines like The New York Post, New York Daily News, The Village Voice, The New York Times Magazine, New York, Playboy, *and* Life. *Hamill has been especially praised for his realism in recording "New York small talk," the voices of people on the streets. Hamill, born in 1935, has come to be associated with the essential spirit of late twentieth-century New York City.*

Hamill's novels include A Killing for Christ (1968); The Gift (1973); Flesh and Blood (1977); Dirty Laundry (1978); The Guns of Heaven (1983); *and* Loving Women: A Novel of the Fifties (1989). *His newspaper columns have been collected in* Irrational Ravings (1971) *and his short stories in* The Invisible City (1980). *He is currently a columnist for* The New York Post.

The library was on Sixth Avenue and Ninth Street on the south slopes of the Brooklyn hills and for a long time in my young life it was the true center of the world.

The formal name, back then, was the Prospect Branch of the Brooklyn Public Library, but to me it was always just The Library and it remains that way in memory. I seem always to have gone there on Saturday mornings, following the same route each time, hurrying past the grocery stores, bakeries, drugstores and bars of Seventh Avenue. At the corner of Ninth Street, I turned left and the broad street dropped away into the distant jumble of the waterfront. On clear mornings, I could see past the elevated tracks of the IND subway and glimpse the Statue of Liberty in the harbor and the vertical smudge of the skyline of Manhattan. But usually I ignored the view. I was locked into a sensuous, almost religious ritual, with the holy sanctuary of the library drawing me like an iron filing to a magnet.

I can feel now the way my blood quickened as I crossed the trolley tracks, passed the stately brownstones and the small synagogue and saw ahead the wild gloomy garden behind the library. As a gesture of support, I would run a finger along the menacing iron pickets of the garden's fence. I wanted that fence to stand forever, holding back the jungle; each spring, the riot of weeds and nameless plants seemed to grow more menacing. I sometimes imagined it spilling into the streets, marching steadily forward to link with Prospect Park. Or it would turn to the nearest target: the library itself. The vengeful blind force of untamed nature would climb those granite walls, seep under the windows and assault the books, those sheaves of murdered trees, sucking them back to the dark earth.

But then I would glance through the immense windows, relieved: the books were still there. Turning at Sixth Avenue, I would look up, feel momentarily dwarfed by the majesty of the mock Corinthian columns that framed the entrance. Then I would take the wide granite steps two at a time. Into my second home. I was 10 the first time I took that journey alone; I kept taking it until I was 17 and went off to the Navy.

Inside, behind walls as thick as any true fortress, I always felt safe. The high-roofed building was warm in winter and cool in summer, and although it seemed built to last forever, and the sense of space was unlike anything I knew except the lobbies of movie houses, the attraction was not merely shelter. I was there on a more exciting mission: the discovery of the world.

In those years during and after the war, I was a citizen of a hamlet we all simply called "the neighborhood" (now cynically renamed the South Slope by real estate developers). There were strict rules (Pay Your Debts, Don't Cross Picket Lines, Don't Squeal to the Cops, Honor the Old) and powerful institutions (the church, the police station and Rattigan's Bar and Grill). There was wisdom in the hamlet, of course, and honor, and the safety of the familiar. But within the boundaries of this working-class parish there were also men who gave it a dangerous edge: sallow-faced characters with gray fedoras and pinkie rings who carried guns under their coats; youth gangs called the Tigers and the South Brooklyn Boys, who wore pegged pants and rolled through the streets with the swagger of victorious armies. There were homeless rummies too, and deranged vets still fighting Tarawa or the Hürtgen Forest, and cops on the take and brawling dock wallopers and apprentice wise guys. As a boy, I was afraid of them, a condition that went beyond the normal fears of childhood. But I knew one big thing: none of them ever came to the library.

So, in one important way, the library was a fortified oasis. At the same time, it alarmed me. The books seemed to look down upon me with a wintry disdain. Most certainly they were adult, and I stood before them as an ignorant child. They knew what I did not know; they were, in some ways, the epitome of the unknowable, full of mystery and challenge and the most scary thing of all, *doubt*. The harder I worked at cracking their codes, the more certain I was that the task was impossible. I will carry that awe before the printed word to my grave.

At first, in my tentative probes of the Caliph's palace, I was condemned to the children's room. I liked the bound volumes of a magazine called St. Nicholas, full of intricate pen drawings and the cheery innocence of the 19th century. I read through most of Robert Louis Stevenson (enthralled by "Treasure Island" and "Kidnapped," disturbed by "Dr. Jekyll and Mr. Hyde," defeated by "The Weir of Hermiston"); Dumas *père* thrilled me with "The Count of Monte Cristo" and "The Three Musketeers"; I consumed "Howard Pyle's Book of Pirates." But the rest of the books meant nothing to me; they all seemed to be about kids living in idyllic country glades, rabbits who talked and an elephant named Babar who had adventures in Africa. Outside the library, I was already traveling through the Africa of Burne Hogarth's comic-strip version of

"Tarzan" and plunging into the South American forests of Bomba the Jungle Boy. When I read "The Count of Monte Cristo," I began to think of the children's room as another version of the Château d'If.

But even in that brightly lit cell, a peculiar process had begun. On the street, I consumed the artifacts of what is now called popular culture: comics, movie serials at the Minerva and the Globe, boys' books that were not in the library (Bomba, the Buddy series, Tom Swift, even G. A. Henty) and radio serials about Captain Midnight, the Green Hornet, Captain Silver and the Sea Hound. Out there, I was swept away by the primary colors of melodrama.

The library took that instinct for the lurid and refined it. The books that were talked about in schoolyards and on rooftops gave me a need for narrative, for removal from the dailiness of my life. But they stood in relation to the books in the library as the raw does to the cooked.

At first, I didn't know one writer from another. It didn't even occur to me that books were actually written by a lone man or woman sitting somewhere at a desk. They were there on the shelf and you took them down and opened them and began to read. To this day, I don't remember learning to read any more than I remember learning how to breathe. And in those years, I read books with a joyous innocence I've only rarely felt in all the years that followed. I had not begun to read, as I do now, as a writer; that is to say (in Stevenson's phrase), I was not reading as a predator.

Looking back, it's clear to me that I was reading as a creator, bringing myself (and comics, radio, movies, the street) to a collaboration with the writer in the invention of an alternate world. These books were not collections of abstract symbols called words, printed on paper; they were real events that had happened to *me*. So I was Jim Hawkins. I was Edmond Dantès. I was D'Artagnan. I hid from Blind Pew. I discovered the hidden grotto. I fought duels with the henchmen of the evil Milady. But alas, I also discovered early that telling these tales to my friends could sometimes provoke boredom or scorn; the stories then became part of my buried private history, another solitary vice.

When I escaped at last from the children's room, I felt like an explorer who had been handed a map written in invisible ink. As in life, one thing always led to another. At 14, I was trying to understand Latin at

Regis High School. In the stacks at the library, this led me to Stevenson's "Virginibus Puerisque," which I still read for pleasure and reward; to Cyril Connolly's "Unquiet Grave" (the byline read "by Palinurus"), and though I surely understood virtually nothing it said, and skipped all the passages in French, I was consumed for a week by its mood of romantic loss. I pored over a translation of Cicero's accounts of murder trials. I took home a book called "Daily Life of the Romans" and copied most of the line drawings of free men and slaves. None of this helped me much with Latin, but the journey did take me to the meditations of Marcus Aurelius, and that splendid book was to help me through the brief anguish of losing all faith in religion.

Other books provoked similar journeys. The Bomba books led me to the geography section of the library, to volumes about South America, to a biography of Simón Bolívar and the fevered discovery of the existence of the great Chilean Bernardo O'Higgins, as Irish as I was, the liberator of his country. In that time, I often rode through the Andes of my imagination, a member of a revolutionary army, about to charge hard upon the hated viceroys in the capital; or I was an old man, seeing the revolution betrayed, saying (with Bolívar): "I have ploughed the seas." These were wars, conflicts, tragedies in the real world, but they were not taught in our schoolbooks, and so they became (I arrogantly thought) my own private discovery. If you lived in Brooklyn in those years, you said words like Caracas and Lima, Cartegena and Bogotá, the Amazon and the Orinoco, as if they were digits on a secular rosary. Years later, I would travel this private tributary to school in Mexico City, to Diego Rivera, David Alfaro Siqueiros and José Clemente Orozco, to Carlos Fuentes and Octavio Paz, Luis Buñuel and José Luis Cuevas, Jorge Luis Borges and Julio Cortázar, the granite of Neruda and the magical groves of Macondo.

The library taught me one other thing that has survived and expanded through the course of my life: the love of books themselves as *objects*. I came to love the feeling of a well-made book, the look of type on fine paper, the leathery worked splendor of certain bindings. I even loved the aroma of certain books, the smell of drying paper, the moldy fragrance of the past. This also has a context. I grew up as the oldest son of seven children of Irish immigrants; we were, I suppose, poor;

there were always books in the house but none of them were very fancy. The library allowed me to borrow the first beautiful things I ever took home. When I was not reading them, I would place them on tables, on the mantelpiece, against a window, just to be able to see them, to turn from dinner and glance at them in the next room. I hated to bring them back, and often borrowed some books three or four times a year, just to have them around. As a result, I am today one of those people with a book jones. There are 10,000 books in my library, and it will keep growing until I die. This has exasperated my daughters, amused my friends and baffled my accountant. If I had not picked up this habit in the library long ago, I would have more money in the bank today; I would not be richer.

In short, the library was a place where most of the things I came to value as an adult had their beginnings. Art was there, poetry, history and words. Millions of words. Trillions. Politicians have come and gone since many of them were written, empires have risen to temporal glory and collapsed into decay. But those words remain as powerful as they were when I was a boy and will be there long after I'm gone. I went to the library in a different time, of course, during the last years before the arrival of the great obliterating force of television. I went to the library in search of entertainment and discovered the world.

Today, kids don't seem to embark on that exhilarating journey as often as they did when I was young. Politicians keep chiseling away at the branch libraries, truncating their hours, reducing their staffs. The dumb forces of darkness still riot in the garden. But there, through the windows, you can still see the shelves. The books stand in eternal wintry challenge, full of wonder, fear, certainty and doubt, just waiting to be opened. Hey, young man, hurrying by, a Walkman plugged into your skull: pause a moment, mount those steps and enter. The world awaits you.

Excerpt from
A Tree Grows in Brooklyn
by Betty Smith

Francie Nolan, the heroine of A Tree Grows in Brooklyn *(1943), became so familiar to American readers that they wrote for years to her creator, Betty Smith (1904–72), to ask what had become of Francie. Had she married? Did she have children? Was she happy? Ms. Smith once reported, "One fifth of my letters start out, 'Dear Francie.' " The novel, described by a reviewer at the time as "a warm, sunny, engaging book as well as a grim one," tells the story of a young girl growing up in a Brooklyn working-class neighborhood. It has sold more than four million copies, been translated into at least sixteen languages, and been made into a movie and a musical comedy on Broadway.*

Ms. Smith's later novels, which never achieved the same success, are Tomorrow Will Be Better *(1948);* Maggie—Now *(1958); and* Joy in the Morning *(1964). She also wrote many one-act plays, mostly with Robert Finch, whom she eventually married. She compiled and edited collections of one-act plays as well, such as* A Treasury of Non-Royalty One-Act Plays *(1958).*

The library was a little old shabby place. Francie thought it was beautiful. The feeling she had about it was as good as the feeling she had about church. She pushed open the door and went in. She liked the combined smell of worn leather bindings, library paste and freshly-inked stamping pads better than she liked the smell of burning incense at high mass.

Francie thought that all the books in the world were in that library and she had a plan about reading all the books in the world. She was reading a book a day in alphabetical order and not skipping the dry ones. She remembered that the first author had been Abbott. She had been reading a book a day for a long time now and she was still in the B's. Already she had read about bees and buffaloes, Bermuda vacations and Byzantine architecture. For all of her enthusiasm, she had to admit that some of the B's had been hard going. But Francie was a reader. She read everything she could find: trash, classics, time tables and the grocer's price list. Some of the reading had been wonderful; the Louisa Alcott books for example. She planned to read all the books over again when she had finished with the Z's.

Saturdays were different. She treated herself by reading a book not in the alphabetical sequence. On that day she asked the librarian to recommend a book.

After Francie had come in and closed the door quietly behind her —the way you were supposed to do in the library—she looked quickly at the little golden-brown pottery jug which stood at the end of the librarian's desk. It was a season indicator. In the fall it held a few sprigs of bittersweet and at Christmas time it held holly. She knew spring was coming, even if there was snow on the ground, when she saw pussy willow in the bowl. And today, on this summer Saturday of 1912, what was the bowl holding? She moved her eyes slowly up the jug past the thin green stems and little round leaves and saw . . . nasturtiums! Red, yellow, gold and ivory-white. A head pain caught her between the eyes at the taking in of such a wonderful sight. It was something to be remembered all her life.

"When I get big," she thought, "I will have such a brown bowl and in hot August there will be nasturtiums in it."

She put her hand on the edge of the polished desk liking the way it felt. She looked at the neat row of freshly-sharpened pencils, the clean green square of blotter, the fat white jar of creamy paste, the precise stack of cards and the returned books waiting to be put back on the shelves. The remarkable pencil with the date slug above its point was by itself near the blotter's edge.

"Yes, when I get big and have my own home, no plush chairs and lace curtains for me. And *no* rubber plants. I'll have a desk like this in my parlor and white walls and a clean green blotter every Saturday night and a row of shining yellow pencils always sharpened for writing and a golden-brown bowl with a flower or some leaves or berries always in it and books . . . books . . . books. . . ."

She chose her book for Sunday; something by an author named Brown. Francie figured she had been reading on the Brown's for months. When she thought she was nearly finished, she noticed that the next shelf started up again with Browne. After that came Browning. She groaned, anxious to get into the C's where there was a book by Marie Corelli that she had peeped into and found thrilling. Would she *ever* get to that? Maybe she ought to read two books a day. Maybe. . . .

She stood at the desk a long time before the librarian deigned to attend to her.

"Yes?" inquired that lady pettishly.

"This book. I want it." Francie pushed the book forward opened at the back with the little card pushed out of the envelope. The librarians had trained the children to present the books that way. It saved them the trouble of opening several hundred books a day and pulling several hundred cards from as many envelopes.

She took the card, stamped it, pushed it down a slot in the desk. She stamped Francie's card and pushed it at her. Francie picked it up but she did not go away.

"Yes?" The librarian did not bother to look up.

"Could you recommend a good book for a girl?"

"How old?"

"She is eleven."

Each week Francie made the same request and each week the librarian asked the same question. A name on a card meant nothing to her and since she never looked up into a child's face, she never did get to know the little girl who took a book out every day and two on Saturday. A smile would have meant a lot to Francie and a friendly comment would have made her so happy. She loved the library and was anxious to worship the lady in charge. But the librarian had other things on her mind. She hated children anyhow.

Francie trembled in anticipation as the woman reached under the desk. She saw the title as the book came up: *If I Were King* by McCarthy. Wonderful! Last week it had been *Beverly of Graustark* and the same two weeks before that. She had had the McCarthy book only twice. The librarian recommended these two books over and over again. Maybe they were the only ones she herself had read; maybe they were on a recommended list; maybe she had discovered that they were sure fire as far as eleven-year-old girls were concerned.

Francie held the books close and hurried home, resisting the temptation to sit on the first stoop she came to, to start reading.

Home at last and now it was the time she had been looking forward to all week: fire-escape-sitting time. She put a small rug on the fire-escape and got the pillow from her bed and propped it against the bars. Luckily there was ice in the icebox. She chipped off a small piece and put it in a glass of water. The pink-and-white peppermint wafers bought that morning were arranged in a little bowl, cracked, but of a pretty blue color. She arranged glass, bowl and book on the window sill and climbed out on the fire-escape. Once out there, she was living in a tree. No one upstairs, downstairs or across the way could see her. But she could look out through the leaves and see everything.

It was a sunny afternoon. A lazy warm wind carried a warm sea smell. The leaves of the tree made fugitive patterns on the white pillowcase. Nobody was in the yard and that was nice. Usually it was pre-empted by the boy whose father rented the store on the ground floor. The boy played an interminable game of graveyard. He dug miniature graves, put live captured caterpillars into little match boxes, buried them with informal ceremony and erected little pebble headstones over the tiny earth mounds. The whole game was accompanied by fake sobbings and heavings of his chest. But today the dismal boy was away visiting an aunt in Bensonhurst. To know that he was away was almost as good as getting a birthday present.

Francie breathed the warm air, watched the dancing leaf shadows, ate the candy and took sips of the cooled water in-between reading the book.

> *If I were King, Love,*
> *Ah, if I were King. . . .*

The story of François Villon was more wonderful each time she read it. Sometimes she worried for fear the book would be lost in the library and she'd never be able to read it again. She had once started copying the book in a two-cent notebook. She wanted to own a book so badly and she had thought the copying would do it. But the penciled sheets did not seem like nor smell like the library book so she had given it up, consoling herself with the vow that when she grew up, she would work hard, save money and buy every single book that she liked.

As she read, at peace with the world and happy as only a little girl could be with a fine book and a little bowl of candy, and all alone in the house, the leaf shadows shifted and the afternoon passed. About four o'clock, the flats in the tenements across from Francie's yard came to life. Through the leaves, she looked into the open uncurtained windows and saw growlers being rushed out and returned overflowing with cool foaming beer. Kids ran in and out, going to and returning from the butcher's, the grocer's and the baker's. Women came in with bulky hock-shop bundles. The man's Sunday suit was home again. On Monday, it would go back to the pawnbroker's for another week. The hock-shop prospered on the weekly interest money and the suit benefited by being brushed and hung away in camphor where the moths couldn't get at it. In on Monday, out on Saturday. Ten cents' interest paid to Uncle Timmy. That was the cycle.

Francie saw young girls making preparations to go out with their fellers. Since none of the flats had bathrooms, the girls stood before the kitchen sinks in their camisoles and petticoats, and the line the arm made, curved over the head while they washed under the arm, was very beautiful. There were so many girls in so many windows washing this way that it seemed a kind of hushed and expectant ritual.

She stopped reading when Fraber's horse and wagon came into the yard next door because watching the beautiful horse was almost as good as reading.

Excerpt from
An American Childhood
by Annie Dillard

Since the publication of her poetic memoir Pilgrim at Tinker's Creek *(1974),
which won a Pulitzer Prize and was favorably compared by critics to Thoreau's*
Walden, *Annie Dillard has been recognized as a major contemporary American
writer. A book of poems,* Tickets for a Prayer Wheel, *also appeared in 1974,
followed by* Holy the Firm *(1978);* Teaching a Stone to Talk *(a collection
of narrative essays) in 1982;* Living by Fiction *(1982);* An American Childhood *(1987); and* The Writing Life *(1989). Ms. Dillard is a regular contributor
to magazines like* The Atlantic Monthly *and* Harper's *as well as to* The New
York Times Book Review. *Born in 1945, she lives with her family in Mid-
dletown, Connecticut.*

*Ms. Dillard once commented to an interviewer that "people want to make you
into a cult figure because of what they fancy to be your life-style, when the truth
of your life is literature!" In the following excerpt from* An American Childhood,
Ms. Dillard talks about discovering that kind of truth in libraries.

The Homewood Library had graven across its enormous stone
facade: FREE TO THE PEOPLE. In the evenings, neighborhood
people—the men and women of Homewood—browsed in the library,

and brought their children. By day, the two vaulted rooms, the adults' and children's sections, were almost empty. The kind Homewood librarians, after a trial period, had given me a card to the adult section. This was an enormous silent room with marble floors. Nonfiction was on the left.

Beside the farthest wall, and under leaded windows set ten feet from the floor, so that no human being could ever see anything from them —next to the wall, and at the farthest remove from the idle librarians at their curved wooden counter, and from the oak bench where my mother waited in her camel's-hair coat chatting with the librarians or reading—stood the last and darkest and most obscure of the tall nonfiction stacks: NEGRO HISTORY and NATURAL HISTORY. It was in Natural History, in the cool darkness of a bottom shelf, that I found *The Field Book of Ponds and Streams*.

The Field Book of Ponds and Streams was a small, blue-bound book printed in fine type on thin paper, like *The Book of Common Prayer*. Its third chapter explained how to make sweep nets, plankton nets, glass-bottomed buckets, and killing jars. It specified how to mount slides, how to label insects on their pins, and how to set up a freshwater aquarium.

One was to go into "the field" wearing hip boots and perhaps a head net for mosquitoes. One carried in a "rucksack" half a dozen corked test tubes, a smattering of screw-top baby-food jars, a white enamel tray, assorted pipettes and eyedroppers, an artillery of cheesecloth nets, a notebook, a hand lens, perhaps a map, and *The Field Book of Ponds and Streams*. This field—unlike the fields I had seen, such as the field where Walter Milligan played football—was evidently very well watered, for there one could find, and distinguish among, daphniae, planaria, water pennies, stonefly larvae, dragonfly nymphs, salamander larvae, tadpoles, snakes, and turtles, all of which one could carry home.

That anyone had lived the fine life described in Chapter 3 astonished me. Although the title page indicated quite plainly that one Ann Haven Morgan had written *The Field Book of Ponds and Streams*, I nevertheless imagined, perhaps from the authority and freedom of it, that its author was a man. It would be good to write him and assure him that someone had found his book, in the dark near the marble floor at the Homewood Library. I would, in the same letter or in a subsequent one, ask him a question outside the scope of his book, which was where I personally might find a pond, or a stream. But I did not know how to address such a letter, of course, or how to learn if he was still alive.

I was afraid, too, that my letter would disappoint him by betraying my ignorance, which was just beginning to attract my own notice. What, for example, was this noisome-sounding substance called cheesecloth, and what do scientists do with it? What, when you really got down to it, was enamel? If candy could, notoriously, "eat through enamel," why would anyone make trays out of it? Where—short of robbing a museum—might a fifth-grade student at the Ellis School on Fifth Avenue obtain such a legendary item as a wooden bucket?

The Field Book of Ponds and Streams was a shocker from beginning to end. The greatest shock came at the end.

When you checked out a book from the Homewood Library, the librarian wrote your number on the book's card and stamped the due date on a sheet glued to the book's last page. When I checked out *The Field Book of Ponds and Streams* for the second time, I noticed the book's card. It was almost full. There were numbers on both sides. My hearty author and I were not alone in the world, after all. With us, and sharing our enthusiasm for dragonfly larvae and single-celled plants, were, apparently, many Negro adults.

Who were these people? Had they, in Pittsburgh's Homewood section, found ponds? Had they found streams? At home, I read the book again; I studied the drawings; I reread Chapter 3; then I settled in to study the due-date slip. People read this book in every season. Seven or eight people were reading this book every year, even during the war.

Every year, I read again *The Field Book of Ponds and Streams*. Often, when I was in the library, I simply visited it. I sat on the marble floor and studied the book's card. There we all were. There was my number. There was the number of someone else who had checked it out more than once. Might I contact this person and cheer him up? For I assumed that, like me, he had found pickings pretty slim in Pittsburgh.

The people of Homewood, some of whom lived in visible poverty, on crowded streets among burned-out houses—they dreamed of ponds and streams. They were saving to buy microscopes. In their bedrooms they fashioned plankton nets. But their hopes were even more vain than mine, for I was a child, and anything might happen; they were adults, living in Homewood. There was neither pond nor stream on the streetcar routes. The Homewood residents whom I knew had little money and little free time. The marble floor was beginning to chill me. It was not fair.

I had been driven into nonfiction against my wishes. I wanted to read fiction, but I had learned to be cautious about it.

"When you open a book," the sentimental library posters said, "anything can happen." This was so. A book of fiction was a bomb. It was a land mine you wanted to go off. You wanted it to blow your whole day. Unfortunately, hundreds of thousands of books were duds. They had been rusting out of everyone's way for so long that they no longer worked. There was no way to distinguish the duds from the live mines except to throw yourself at them headlong, one by one.

The suggestions of adults were uncertain and incoherent. They gave you Nancy Drew with one hand and *Little Women* with the other. They mixed good and bad books together because they could not distinguish between them. Any book which contained children, or short adults, or animals, was felt to be a children's book. So also was any book about the sea—as though danger or even fresh air were a child's prerogative—or any book by Charles Dickens or Mark Twain. Virtually all British books, actually, were children's books; no one understood children like the British. Suited to female children were love stories set in any century but this one. Consequently one had read, exasperated often to fury, *Pickwick Papers*, *Désirée*, *Wuthering Heights*, *Lad, a Dog*, *Gulliver's Travels*, *Gone With the Wind*, *Robinson Crusoe*, Nordhoff and Hall's *Bounty* trilogy, *Moby-Dick*, *The Five Little Peppers*, *Innocents Abroad*, *Lord Jim*, *Old Yeller*.

The fiction stacks at the Homewood Library, their volumes alphabetized by author, baffled me. How could I learn to choose a novel? That I could not easily reach the top two shelves helped limit choices a little. Still, on the lower shelves I saw too many books: Mary Johnson, *Sweet Rocket*; Samuel Johnson, *Rasselas*; James Jones, *From Here to Eternity*. I checked out the last because I had heard of it; it was good. I decided to check out books I had heard of. I had heard of *The Mill on the Floss*. I read it, and it was good. On its binding was printed a figure, a man dancing or running; I had noticed this figure before. Like so many children before and after me, I learned to seek out this logo, the Modern Library colophon.

The going was always rocky. I couldn't count on Modern Library the way I could count on, say, *Mad* magazine, which never failed to slay me. *Native Son* was good, *Walden* was pretty good, *The Interpretation of Dreams* was okay, and *The Education of Henry Adams* was awful. *Ulysses*, a very famous book, was also awful. *Confessions* by Augustine, whose title promised so much, was a bust. *Confessions* by Jean-Jacques Rousseau was much better, though it fell apart halfway through.

In fact, it was a plain truth that most books fell apart halfway through. They fell apart as their protagonists quit, without any apparent reluctance, like idiots diving voluntarily into buckets, the most interesting part of their lives, and entered upon decades of unrelieved tedium. I was forewarned, and would not so bobble my adult life; when things got dull, I would go to sea.

Jude the Obscure was the type case. It started out so well. Halfway through, its author forgot how to write. After Jude got married, his life was over, but the book went on for hundreds of pages while he stewed in his own juices. The same thing happened in *The Little Shepherd of Kingdom Come*, which Mother brought me from a fair. It was simply a hazard of reading. Only a heartsick loyalty to the protagonists of the early chapters, to the eager children they had been, kept me reading chronological narratives to their bitter ends. Perhaps later, when I had become an architect, I would enjoy the latter halves of books more.

This was the most private and obscure part of life, this Homewood Library: a vaulted marble edifice in a mostly decent Negro neighborhood, the silent stacks of which I plundered in deep concentration for many years. There seemed then, happily, to be an infinitude of books.

I no more expected anyone else on earth to have read a book I had read than I expected someone else to have twirled the same blade of grass. I would never meet those Homewood people who were borrowing *The Field Book of Ponds and Streams*; the people who read my favorite books were invisible or in hiding, underground. Father occasionally raised his big eyebrows at the title of some volume I was hurrying off with, quite as if he knew what it contained—but I thought he must know of it by hearsay, for none of it seemed to make much difference to him. Books swept me away, one after the other, this way and that; I made endless vows according to their lights, for I believed them.

"Somebody Always Grabs the Purple" by Henry Roth

Although Henry Roth (born in 1906) published about a dozen short stories, collected in Shifting Landscape *(1987),* Call It Sleep, *a novel first printed in 1934 but which only received widespread attention upon its republication in 1964, is recognized as his major contribution to American literature. One critic has called it "one of the finest American novels of this century, pehaps the best novel about childhood ever written by an American." Some of that power and perceptiveness about the mind of a boy can be felt in "Somebody Always Grabs the Purple," a story that first appeared in* The New Yorker *in 1940.*

Henry Roth has worked as a precision metal grinder, a teacher, an attendant at a state hospital, and a waterfowl farmer. He now lives in Albuquerque, New Mexico.

Up a flight of stairs, past the vases and the clock outside the adult reading room, past cream walls, oak moldings, oak bookcases, and the Cellini statue of Perseus was the children's room of the 123rd Street Branch Library. Young Sammy Farber drew a battered library card out of his pocket and went in. He was a thickset, alert boy, eleven or twelve years old. He flattened his card on the desk and, while he waited for the librarian, gazed about. There were only a few youngsters in the reading room. Two boys in colored jerseys stood whispering at one of the bookcases. On the wall above their heads was a frieze of Grecian urchins blowing trumpets. The librarian approached.

"Teacher," Sammy began, "I just moved, Teacher. You want to change it—the address?"

The librarian, a spare woman, graying and impassive, with a pince-nez, glanced at his card. "Let me see your hands, Samuel," she said.

He lifted his hands. She nodded approvingly and turned his card over. It was well stamped. "You'd better have a new one," she said.

"Can I get it next time, Teacher? I'm in a hurry like."

"Yes. Where do you live now, Samuel?"

"On 520 East 120th Street." He watched her cross out the Orchard Street address and begin writing in the new one. "Teacher," he said, in a voice so low it was barely audible, "you got here the 'Purple Fairy Book'?"

"The what?"

"The 'Purple Fairy Book.' " He knuckled his nose sheepishly. "Everybody says I'm too big to read fairy books. My mother calls 'em stories with a bear."

"Stories with a bear?"

"Yeah, she don't know English good. You got it?"

"Why, yes. I think it's on the shelves."

"Where, Teacher?" He moved instantly toward the aisle.

"Just a moment, Samuel. Here's your card." He seized it. "Now I'll show you where it is."

Together they crossed the room to a bookcase with a brass plate which said "Fairy Tales." Sammy knelt down so that he could read the titles more easily. There were not a great many books in the case—a few legends for boys about Arthur and Roland on the top shelf, then a short row of fairy tales arranged according to countries, and finally, on the bottom shelf, a few fairy books arranged by colors: Blue, Blue, Green. Her finger on the titles wavered. Red . . . Yellow . . . "I'm sorry." She glanced over the books again rapidly. "It's not here."

"Ah!" he said, relaxing. "They grabbed it again!"

"Have you read the others? Have you read the Blue?"

"Yeah, I read the Blue." He stood up slowly. "I read the Blue and the Green and the Yellow. All the colors. And colors that ain't even here. I read the Lilac. But somebody always grabs the Purple."

"I'm pretty sure the 'Purple Fairy Book' hasn't been borrowed," the librarian said. "Why don't you look on the tables? It may be there."

"I'll look," he said. "but I know. Once they grab it, it's goodbye."

Nevertheless he went from table to table, picking up abandoned books, scanning their titles, and putting them down again. His round face was the image of forlorn hope. As he neared one of the last tables, he stopped. A boy was sitting there with a stack of books at his elbow, reading with enormous concentration. Sammy walked behind the boy and peered over his shoulder. On one page there was print, on the other a colored illustration, a serene princeling, hand on the hilt of his sword, regarding a gnarled and glowering gnome. The book was bound in purple. Sammy sighed and returned to the librarian.

"I found it, Teacher. It's over there," he said, pointing. "He's got it."

"I'm sorry, Samuel. That's the only copy we have."

"His hands ain't as clean as mine," Sammy suggested.

"Oh, I'm sure they are. Why don't you try something else?" she urged. "Adventure books are very popular with boys."

"They ain't popular with him." Sammy gazed gloomily at the boy. "That's what they always told me on the East Side—popular. I don't see what's so popular about them. If a man finds a treasure in an adventure book, so right away it's with dollars and cents. Who cares from dollars and cents? I get enough of that in my house."

"There's fiction," she reminded him. "Perhaps you're the kind of boy who likes reading about grownups."

"Aw, them too!" He tossed his head. "I once read a fiction book, it had in it a hero with eyeglasses? Hih!" His laugh was brief and pitying. "How could heroes be with eyeglasses? That's like my father."

The librarian placed her pince-nez a little more securely on her nose. "He may leave it, of course, if you wait," she said.

"Can I ask him?"

"No. Don't disturb him."

"I just want to ask him is he gonna take it or ain't he. What's the use I should hang around all day?"

"Very well. But that's all."

Sammy walked over to the boy again and said, "Hey, you're gonna take it, aintcha?"

Like one jarred out of sleep, the boy started, his eyes blank and wide.

"What d'you want to read from that stuff?" Sammy asked. "Fairy tales!" His lips, his eyes, his whole face expressed distaste. "There's an adventure book here," he said, picking up the one nearest his hand. "Don't you like adventure books?"

The boy drew himself up in his seat. "What're you botherin' me for?" he said.

"I ain't botherin' you. Did you ever read the 'Blue Fairy Book'? That's the best. That's a hard one to get."

"Hey, I'll tell the teacher on you!" The boy looked around. "I'm readin' this!" he said angrily. "And I don't want no other one! Read 'em yourself!"

Sammy waited a moment and then tried again. "You know you shouldn't read fairy books in the liberry."

The boy clutched the book to himself protectingly and rose. "You want to fight?"

"Don't get excited," Sammy waved him back into the chair and retreated a step. "I was just sayin' fairy tales is better to read in the house, ain't it—like when you're sittin' in the front room and your mother's cookin' in the kitchen? Ain't that nicer?"

"Well, what about it?"

"So in the liberry you can read from other things. From King Arthur or from other mitts."

The boy saw through that ruse also. He waved Sammy away. "I'm gonna read it here and I'm gonna read it home too, wise guy."

"All right, that's all I wanted to ask you," said Sammy. "You're gonna take it, aintcha?"

"Sure I'm gonna take it."

"I thought you was gonna take it."

Sammy retreated to one of the central pillars of the reading room and stood there, watching. The same play of wonder and beguilement that animated the boy's thin features while he read also animated Sammy's pudgy ones, as though the enjoyment were being relayed. After a time the boy got up and went to the desk with the book still in his hand. The librarian took the card out of the book and stamped the boy's own card. Then she handed him the book. Sammy's round face dimmed. He waited, however, until the boy had had time to get out of the reading room and down the stairs before he put his worn library card in his pocket and made for the exit.

"The Carnegie Library, Juvenile Division" and "Children Selecting Books in a Library" by Randall Jarrell

Randall Jarrell (1914–65), who died before many critics felt he had fulfilled his great promise as a poet, still left a substantial body of work that continues to be a highly respected contribution to twentieth-century American literature. His criticism, written for such magazines as The Nation, Partisan Review, Yale Review, The New Republic, *and* The New York Times Book Review, *was known for its biting, acerbic quality but also for its passionate belief in high and unalterable standards for poetry. His critical essays were collected in the influential* Poetry and the Age *(1953);* A Sad Heart at the Supermarket *(1962); and several posthumous works, including* Kipling, Auden & Co. *(1980).*

In poetry, Jarrell was both praised and criticized for his plain, colloquial, and clear style. This does not mean that his poems are always simple or instantly accessible. *Fellow poet Karl Shapiro (who is represented elsewhere in this anthology) commented that Jarrell's voice was that of "the poet-professor-critic who refuses to surrender his intelligence and his education to the undergraduate mentality."*

Jarrell's poetry was collected in several books, beginning with Blood for a Stranger *(1942).* The Woman at the Washington Zoo *(1960) won a National Book Award. His last collection was* The Lost World *(1965). Some readers may know Jarrell as the author of children's books,* The Gingerbread Rabbit *(1963) and* The Bat Poet *(1964) among them.*

THE CARNEGIE LIBRARY, JUVENILE DIVISION

The soot drifted from the engines to the marble
The readers climbed to: stone, and the sooty casts
(Dark absent properties confused with crates
And rest-rooms in the darkness of a basement,
And constant in their senseless line, like dates:
A past that puzzles no one, or a child)
All overlooking—as the child too overlooked—
The hills and stone and steeples of the town
Grey in the pure red of the dying sun.

Here under the waves' roof, where the seals are men;
In the rhymes' twilight, where the old cup ticks
Its gnawing lesson; where the beasts loom in the green
Firred darkness of the märchen: country the child thought life
And wished for and crept to out of his own life—
Must you still isle such, raiders from a world
That you so long ago lost heart to represent?
The child tugs the strap tight round four books
To leave the cavern. And the cut-out ornaments
In colors harsh and general as names,
The dolls' scarred furniture, too small
For anything but pity, like the child—
Surely you recognize in these the hole
That widens from the middle of a field
To that one country where the poor see gold?

The woodman dances home, rich, rich; but a shade glides
Into the bright strange sunlight of the world
He owned once; the thaler blur out like a tear,
He knocks like a stranger and a stranger speaks,
And he sees, brass on the knocker, the gnome's joyless smile.

The books too read to ashes——for one owns
Nothing, and finds that there is no exchange
For all the uses lined here, free as air,
Fleeting as air: the sad repeated spell
Of that deep string, half music and half pain——
How many have believed you worth a soul!
How many here will purchase with a world
These worlds still smoldering for the perpetual
Children who haunt this fire-sale of the centuries.
Wandering among so many lives, they too will bear
The life from which they cannot yet escape;
And learn to doubt, with our sad useless smile,
That single universe the living share——
The practice with which even the books are charred.

We learned from you so much about so many things
But never what we were; and yet you made us that.
We found in you the knowledge for a life
But not the will to use it in our lives
That were always, somehow, so different from the books'.
We learn from you to understand, but not to change.

CHILDREN SELECTING BOOKS IN A LIBRARY

With beasts and gods, above, the wall is bright.
The child's head, bent to the book-colored shelves,
Is slow and sidelong and food-gathering,
Moving in blind grace . . . Yet from the mural, Care,
The grey-eyed one, fishing the morning mist,
Seizes the baby hero by the hair

And whispers, in the tongue of gods and children,
Words of a doom as ecumenical as dawn
But blanched, like dawn, with dew. The children's cries
Are to men the cries of crickets, dense with warmth
—But dip a finger into Fafnir, taste it,
And all their words are plain as chance and pain.

Their tales are full of sorcerers and ogres
Because their lives are: the capricious infinite
That, like parents, no one has yet escaped
Except by luck or magic; and since strength
And wit are useless, be kind or stupid, wait
Some power's gratitude, the tide of things.

Read meanwhile . . . hunt among the shelves, as dogs do, grasses,
And find one cure for Everychild's diseases
Beginning: Once upon a time there was
A wolf that fed, a mouse that warned, a bear that rode
A boy. Us men, alas! wolves, mice, bears bore.
And yet wolves, mice, bears, children, gods and men
In slow perambulation up and down the shelves
Of the universe are seeking . . . who knows except themselves?
What some escape to, some escape: if we find Swann's
Way better than our own, and trudge on at the back
Of the north wind to—to—somewhere east
Of the sun, west of the moon, it is because we live

By trading another's sorrow for our own; another's
Impossibilities, still unbelieved in, for our own . . .
"I am myself still"? For a little while, forget:
The world's selves cure that short disease, myself,
And we see bending to us, dewy-eyed, the great
CHANGE, dear to all things not to themselves endeared.

Excerpt from *Half Magic* by Edward Eager

Edward Eager (1911—64) began his writing career as a playwright and lyricist, but when he published **Red Head,** *his first children's book in 1951, he won a wide new audience of enthusiastic young readers and their parents. Through reading to his own son, Eager discovered the magic of E. Nesbit's children's books and began to create magic of his own. (Of Nesbit, he has said: "My own books for children could not even have existed if it were not for her influence. And I am always careful to acknowledge this indebtedness in each of my stories." Watch for just such an acknowledgment in the following excerpt.)*

Eager's first magic book was **Half Magic** *(1954). Others include* **Magic by the Lake** *(1957);* **The Time Garden** *(1958);* **Magic or Not?** *(1959);* **The Well-Wishers** *(1960); and* **Seven-Day Magic** *(1962). Many happy readers have been among those Eager described as "lucky people who never lose the gift of seeing the world as a child sees it, a magic place where anything can happen next minute, and delightful and unexpected things constantly do."*

I. HOW IT BEGAN

It began one day in summer about thirty years ago, and it happened to four children.

Jane was the oldest and Mark was the only boy, and between them they ran everything.

Katharine was the middle girl, of docile disposition and a comfort to her mother. She knew she was a comfort, and docile, because she'd heard her mother say so. And the others knew she was, too, by now, because ever since that day Katharine *would* keep boasting about what a comfort she was, and how docile, until Jane declared she would utter a piercing shriek and fall over dead if she heard another word about it. This will give you some idea of what Jane and Katharine were like.

Martha was the youngest, and very difficult.

The children never went to the country or a lake in the summer, the way their friends did, because their father was dead and their mother worked very hard on the other newspaper, the one almost nobody on the block took. A woman named Miss Bick came in every day to care for the children, but she couldn't seem to care for them very much, nor they for her. And she wouldn't take them to the country or a lake; she said it was too much to expect and the sound of waves affected her heart.

"Clear Lake isn't the ocean; you can hardly hear it," Jane told her.

"It would attract lightning," Miss Bick said, which Jane thought cowardly, besides being unfair arguing. If you're going to argue, and Jane usually was, you want people to line up all their objections at a time; then you can knock them all down at once. But Miss Bick was always sly.

Still, even without the country or a lake, the summer was a fine thing, particularly when you were at the beginning of it, looking ahead into it. There would be months of beautifully long, empty days, and each other to play with, and the books from the library.

In the summer you could take out ten books at a time, instead of three, and keep them a month, instead of two weeks. Of course you could take only four of the fiction books, which were the best, but Jane liked plays and they were non-fiction, and Katharine liked poetry and that was non-fiction, and Martha was still the age for picture-books, and they didn't count as fiction but were often nearly as good.

Mark hadn't found out yet what kind of non-fiction he liked, but he was still trying. Each month he would carry home his ten books and read the four good fiction ones in the first four days, and then read one page each from the other six, and then give up. Next month he would take them back and try again. The non-fiction books he tried were mostly called things like "When I was a Boy in Greece," or "Happy Days on the Prairie"—things that made them sound like stories, only they weren't. They made Mark furious.

"It's being made to learn things not on purpose. It's unfair," he said. "It's sly." Unfairness and slyness the four children hated above all.

The library was two miles away, and walking there with a lot of heavy, already-read books was dull, but coming home was splendid— walking slowly, stopping from time to time on different strange front steps, dipping into the different books. One day Katharine, the poetry-lover, tried to read *Evangeline* out loud on the way home, and Martha sat right down on the sidewalk after seven blocks of it, and refused to go a step farther if she had to hear another word of it. That will tell you about Martha.

After that Jane and Mark made a rule that nobody could read bits out loud and bother the others. But this summer the rule was changed. This summer the children had found some books by a writer named E. Nesbit, surely the most wonderful books in the world. They read every one that the library had, right away, except a book called *The Enchanted Castle*, which had been out.

And now yesterday *The Enchanted Castle* had come in, and they took it out, and Jane, because she could read fastest and loudest, read it out loud all the way home, and when they got home she went on reading, and when their mother came home they hardly said a word to her, and when dinner was served they didn't notice a thing they ate. Bedtime came at the moment when the magic ring in the book changed from a ring of invisibility to a wishing ring. It was a terrible place to stop, but their mother had one of her strict moments; so stop they did.

And so naturally they all woke up even earlier than usual this morning, and Jane started right in reading out loud and didn't stop till she got to the end of the last page.

There was a contented silence when she closed the book, and then, after a little, it began to get discontented.

Martha broke it, saying what they were all thinking.

"Why don't things like that ever happen to *us*?"

"Magic never happens, not really," said Mark, who was old enough to be sure about this.

"How do you know?" asked Katharine, who was nearly as old as Mark, but not nearly so sure about anything.

"Only in fairy stories."

"It *wasn't* a fairy story. There weren't any dragons or witches or poor woodcutters, just real children like us!"

They were all talking at once now.

"They *aren't* like us. We're never in the country for the summer, and walk down strange roads and find castles!"

"We never go to the seashore and meet mermaids and sand-fairies!"

"Or go to our uncle's, and there's a magic garden!"

"If the Nesbit children do stay in the city it's London, and *that's* interesting, and then they find phoenixes and magic carpets! Nothing like that ever happens here!"

"There's Mrs. Hudson's house," Jane said. "That's a *little* like a castle."

"There's the Miss Kings' garden."

"We could *pretend* . . ."

It was Martha who said this, and the others turned on her.

"Beast!"

"Spoilsport!"

Because of course the only way pretending is any good is if you never say right out that that's what you're doing. Martha knew this perfectly well, but in her youth she sometimes forgot. So now Mark threw a pillow at her, and so did Jane and Katharine, and in the excitement that followed their mother woke up, and Miss Bick arrived and started giving orders, and "all was flotsam and jetsam," in the poetic words of Katharine.

Two hours later, with breakfast eaten, Mother gone to work and the dishes done, the four children escaped at last, and came out into the sun. It was fine weather, warm and blue-skied and full of possibilities, and the day began well, with a glint of something metal in a crack in the sidewalk.

"Dibs on the nickel," Jane said, and scooped it into her pocket with the rest of her allowance, still jingling there unspent. She would get round to thinking about spending it after the adventures of the morning.

The adventures of the morning began with promise. Mrs. Hudson's house looked *quite* like an Enchanted Castle, with its stone wall around and iron dog on the lawn. But when Mark crawled into the peony bed and Jane stood on his shoulders and held Martha up to the kitchen window, all Martha saw was Mrs. Hudson mixing something in a bowl.

"Eye of newt and toe of frog, probably," Katharine thought, but Martha said it looked more like simple one-egg cake.

And then when one of the black ants that live in all peony beds bit Mark, and he dropped Jane and Martha with a crash, nothing happened except Mrs. Hudson's coming out and chasing them with a broom the way she always did, and saying she'd tell their mother. This didn't worry them much, because their mother always said it was Mrs. Hudson's own fault, that people who had trouble with children brought it on themselves, but it was boring.

So then the children went farther down the street and looked at the Miss Kings' garden. Bees were humming pleasantly round the columbines, and there were Canterbury bells and purple foxgloves looking satisfactorily old-fashioned, and for a moment it seemed as though anything might happen.

But then Miss Mamie King came out and told them that a dear little fairy lived in the biggest purple foxglove, and this wasn't the kind of talk the children wanted to hear at all. They stayed only long enough to be polite, before trooping dispiritedly back to sit on their own front steps.

They sat there and couldn't think of anything exciting to do, and nothing went on happening, and it was then that Jane was so disgusted that she said right out loud she wished there'd be a fire!

The other three looked shocked at hearing such wickedness, and then they looked more shocked at what they heard next.

What they heard next was a fire-siren!

Fire trucks started tearing past—the engine, puffing out smoke the way it used to do in those days, the Chief's car, the hook-and-ladder, the Chemicals!

Mark and Katharine and Martha looked at Jane, and Jane looked back at them with wild wonder in her eyes. Then they started running.

The fire was eight blocks away, and it took them a long time to get there, because Martha wasn't allowed to cross streets by herself, and couldn't run fast yet, like the others; so they had to keep waiting for her to catch up, at all the corners.

And when they finally reached the house where the trucks had stopped, it wasn't the house that was on fire. It was a playhouse in the back yard, the fanciest playhouse the children had ever seen, two stories high and with dormer windows.

You all know what watching a fire is like, the glory of the flames streaming out through the windows, and the wonderful moment when the roof falls in, or even better if there's a tower and it falls through the roof. This playhouse *did* have a tower, and it fell through the roof most beautifully, with a crash and a shower of sparks.

And the fact that it *was* a playhouse, and small like the children, made it seem even more like a special fire that was planned just for them. And the little girl the playhouse belonged to turned out to be an unmistakably spoiled and unpleasant type named Genevieve, with long golden curls that had probably never been cut; so *that* was all right. And furthermore, the children overheard her father say he'd buy her a new playhouse with the insurance money.

So altogether there was no reason for any but feelings of the deepest satisfaction in the breast of the four children, as they stood breathing heavily and watching the firemen deal with the flames, which they did with that heroic calm typical of fire departments the world over.

And it wasn't until the last flame was drowned, and the playhouse stood there a wet and smoking mess of ashes and charred boards that guilt rose up in Jane and turned her joy to ashes, too.

"Oh, what you did," Martha whispered at her.

"I don't want to talk about it," Jane said. But she went over to a woman who seemed to be the nurse of the golden-haired Genevieve, and asked her how it started.

"All of a piece it went up, like the Fourth of July as ever was," said the nurse. "And it's my opinion," she added, looking at Jane very suspiciously, "that it was *set*! What are *you* doing here, little girl?"

Jane turned right around and walked out of the yard, holding herself as straight as possible and trying to keep from running. The other three went after her.

"Is Jane magic?" Martha whispered to Katharine.

"I don't know. I think so," Katharine whispered back.

Jane glared at them. They went for two blocks in silence.

"Are we magic, too?"

"I don't know. I'm scared to find out."

Jane glared. Once more silence fell.

But this time Martha couldn't hold herself in for more than half a block.

"Will we be burnt as *witches*?"

Jane whirled on them furiously.

"I wish," she started to say.

"Don't!" Katharine almost screamed, and Jane turned white, shut her lips tight, and started walking faster.

Mark made the others run to catch up.

"This won't do any good. We've got to talk it over," he told Jane.

"Yes, talk it over," said Martha, looking less worried. She had great respect for Mark, who was a boy and knew everything.

"The thing is," Mark went on, "was it just an accident, or did we want so much to be magic we *got* that way, somehow? The thing is, each of us ought to make a wish. That'll prove it one way or the other."

But Martha balked at this. You could never tell with Martha. Sometimes she would act just as grown-up as the others, and then suddenly she would be a baby. Now she was a baby. Her lip trembled, and she said she didn't want to make a wish and she *wouldn't* make a wish and she wished they'd never started to play this game in the first place.

After consultation, Mark and Katharine decided this could count as Martha's wish, but it didn't seem to have come true, because if it had they wouldn't remember any of the morning, and yet they remembered it all too clearly. But just as a test Mark turned to Jane.

"What have we been doing?" he asked.

"Watching a fire," Jane said bitterly, and at that moment the fire trucks went by on their way home to the station, to prove it.

So then Mark rather depressedly wished his shoes were seven-league boots, but when he tried to jump seven leagues it turned out they weren't.

Katharine wished Shakespeare would come up and talk to her. She forgot to say exactly *when* she wanted this to happen, but after they waited a minute and he didn't appear, they decided he probably wasn't coming.

So it seemed that if there was any magic among them, Jane had it all.

But try as they might, they couldn't persuade Jane to make another wish, even a little safe one. She just kept shaking her head at all their arguments, and when argument descended to insult she didn't say a word, which was most unlike Jane.

When they got home she said she had a headache, and went out on the sleeping porch, and shut the door. She wouldn't even come downstairs for lunch, but stayed out there alone all the afternoon, moodily eating a whole box of Social Tea biscuits and talking to Carrie, the cat. Miss Bick despaired of her.

When their mother came home she knew something was wrong. But being an understanding parent she didn't ask questions.

At dinner she announced that she was going out for the evening. Jane didn't look up from her brooding silence, but the others were interested. The children always hoped their mother was going on exciting adventures, though she seldom was. Tonight she was going to see Aunt Grace and Uncle Edwin.

"Why?" Mark wanted to know.

"They were very kind to me after your father died. They have been very kind to *you*."

"Useful presents!" Mark was scornful.

"Will Aunt Grace say 'Just a little chocolate cake, best you ever tasted, I made it myself'?" Katharine wanted to know.

"You shouldn't laugh at your Aunt Grace. I don't know what your father would say."

"Father laughed at her, too."

"It isn't the same thing."

"Why?"

This kind of conversation was always very interesting to the children, and could have gone on forever so far as they were concerned, but somehow no grown-ups ever seemed to feel that way about conversations. Their mother put a stop to this one by leaving for Aunt Grace's.

When she had gone things got strange again. Jane kept hovering in and out of the room where the others were playing a half-hearted game of Flinch, until everyone was driven wild.

Finally Mark burst out.

"Why don't you tell us?"

Jane shook her head.

"I can't. You wouldn't understand."

Naturally this made everyone furious.

"Just because she's magic she thinks she's smarter!" Martha said.

"*I* don't think she's magic at all!" This was Katharine. "Only she's afraid to make a wish and find out!"

"I'm not! I *am*!" Jane cried, not very clearly. "Only I don't know why, or how much! It's like having one foot almost asleep, but not quite—you can't use it and you can't enjoy it! I'm afraid to even *think* a wish! I'm afraid to think at *all*!"

If you have ever had magic powers descend on you suddenly out of the blue, you'll know how Jane felt.

When you have magic powers and know it, it can be a fine feeling, like a pleasant tingling inside. But in order to enjoy that tingling, you have to know just how much magic you have and what the rules are for using it. And Jane didn't have any idea how much she had or how to use it, and this made her unhappy and the others couldn't see why, and said so, and Jane answered back, and by the time they went to bed no one was speaking to anyone else.

What bothered Jane most was a feeling that she'd forgotten something, and that if she could remember it she'd know the reason for everything that had happened. It was as if the reason were there in her mind somewhere, if only she could reach it. She leaned into her mind, reaching, reaching . . .

The next thing she knew, she was sitting straight up in bed and the clock was striking eleven, and she had remembered. It was as though she'd gone on thinking in her sleep. Sometimes this happens.

She got up and felt her way to the dresser where she'd put her money, without looking at it, when she came home from the fire. First she felt the top of the dresser. Then she lit the lamp and looked.

The nickel she'd found in the crack in the sidewalk was gone.

And then Jane began thinking really hard.

FIVE

Love in
the Library

J ust as a library invites writers to invent murder mysteries, so it induces them to create love stories. Passion has to be hushed in a library. No one can shout, sing, stamp. Lovers must content themselves with whispers, glances, perhaps a surreptitious touch. But the very difficulties of love in a library seem to inspire writers.

Grace Paley's subtle and poignant story "Wants" uses the library both as setting and as a means of illuminating character. The narrator's exchange with her bitter ex-husband contrasts with the ease of her transaction with the librarian, who, unlike her husband, "trusted me, put my past behind her, wiped the record clean." After returning her library books (overdue eighteen years), the narrator checks them out again, deciding they reflect the changes in her twenty-seven years of marriage. Every line in this tight, ironic story resonates with controlled pain—and, arguably, with love.

In Larry Rubin's "A Note on Library Policy," lust lurks in the stacks. The silence and scholarly concentration of a reading room are also a background for Richard Eberhart's romantic poem "Reading Room, the New York Public Library." The young boys in John Taylor's story, "The Doctors' Club," are using the library to seek knowledge about sex, finding what help they can in the big dictionary in the reference room. Like Grace Paley's story, Sue Kaufman's "Summer Librarian" is about assessing the future, coming to terms with the past, and trying to live in the present. It ends, as perhaps a love story set in a library should, with a passionate affirmation.

"Wants" by Grace Paley

Although Grace Paley has published fewer books than many of her well-known contemporaries, her short stories are so powerful and distinctive that they have won her an extraordinarily high reputation. In 1970 she was awarded the National Institute of Arts and Letters Award for short-story writing.

Born in New York in 1922, with a Russian/Jewish heritage, she has a recognizably New York voice that is still her own as well. That voice, ironic, perceptive, funny and sad by turns, illuminates the stories in The Little Disturbances of Man *(1959);* Enormous Changes at the Last Minute *(1974), from which "Wants" is taken; and* Later the Same Day *(1985). Ms. Paley is currently a member of the literature faculty at Sarah Lawrence College.*

I saw my ex-husband in the street. I was sitting on the steps of the new library.

Hello, my life, I said. We had once been married for twenty-seven years, so I felt justified.

He said, What? What life? No life of mine.

I said, O.K. I don't argue when there's real disagreement. I got up and went into the library to see how much I owed them.

The librarian said $32 even and you've owed it for eighteen years. I didn't deny anything. Because I don't understand how time passes. I have had those books. I have often thought of them. The library is only two blocks away.

My ex-husband followed me to the Books Returned desk. He interrupted the librarian, who had more to tell. In many ways, he said, as I look back, I attribute the dissolution of our marriage to the fact that you never invited the Bertrams to dinner.

That's possible, I said. But really, if you remember: first, my father was sick that Friday, then the children were born, then I had those Tuesday-night meetings, then the war began. Then we didn't seem to know them any more. But you're right. I should have had them to dinner.

I gave the librarian a check for $32. Immediately she trusted me, put my past behind her, wiped the record clean, which is just what most other municipal and/or state bureaucracies will *not* do.

I checked out the two Edith Wharton books I had just returned because I'd read them so long ago and they are more apropos now than ever. They were *The House of Mirth* and *The Children*, which is about how life in the United States in New York changed in twenty-seven years fifty years ago.

A nice thing I do remember is breakfast, my ex-husband said. I was surprised. All we ever had was coffee. Then I remembered there was a hole in the back of the kitchen closet which opened into the apartment next door. There, they always ate sugar-cured smoked bacon. It gave us a very grand feeling about breakfast, but we never got stuffed and sluggish.

That was when we were poor, I said.

When were we ever rich? he asked.

Oh, as time went on, as our responsibilities increased, we didn't go in need. You took adequate financial care, I reminded him. The children went to camp four weeks a year and in decent ponchos with sleeping bags and boots, just like everyone else. They looked very nice. Our place was warm in winter, and we had nice red pillows and things.

I wanted a sailboat, he said. But you didn't want anything.

Don't be bitter, I said. It's never too late.

No, he said with a great deal of bitterness. I may get a sailboat. As a matter of fact I have money down on an eighteen-foot two-rigger. I'm doing well this year and can look forward to better. But as for you, it's too late. You'll always want nothing.

He had had a habit throughout the twenty-seven years of making a narrow remark which, like a plumber's snake, could work its way through the ear down the throat, halfway to my heart. He would then disappear, leaving me choking with equipment. What I mean is, I sat down on the library steps and he went away.

I looked through *The House of Mirth*, but lost interest. I felt extremely accused. Now, it's true, I'm short of requests and absolute requirements. But I do want *something*.

I want, for instance, to be a different person. I want to be the woman who brings these two books back in two weeks. I want to be the effective citizen who changes the school system and addresses the Board of Estimate on the troubles of this dear urban center.

I *had* promised my children to end the war before they grew up.

I wanted to have been married forever to one person, my ex-husband or my present one. Either has enough character for a whole life, which as it turns out is really not such a long time. You couldn't exhaust either man's qualities or get under the rock of his reasons in one short life.

Just this morning I looked out the window to watch the street for a while and saw that the little sycamores the city had dreamily planted a couple of years before the kids were born had come that day to the prime of their lives.

Well! I decided to bring those two books back to the library. Which proves that when a person or an event comes along to jolt or appraise me I *can* take some appropriate action, although I am better known for my hospitable remarks.

"A Note on Library Policy" by Larry Rubin

Larry Rubin (born in 1930) has taught at Georgia Institute of Technology since 1956, where he is now Professor of English. "A Note on Library Policy" was first published in a collection of his poems, The World's Old Way *(1963); other volumes include* Lanced in Light *(1967) and* All My Mirrors Lie *(1975).*

We should never have opened the stacks to the undergraduates.
It's become their favorite trysting place. Like crafty Abelards,
They hide their fingers underneath their books
And pluck at Héloïse.
They swarm; they kiss in cubicles; for all we know
They breed down there in the twelfth century.
(That's where the bulbs are broken; the stack boys
Have to use flashlights on that level.
But they never report anything amiss—
Sworn to secrecy, probably.)
It's most distracting.
How is one to annotate his bibliography
When everywhere he finds these naked couples
Hiding deep in darkened carrels?

I know. They try to be quiet.
But every now and then a girl will laugh;
Warm and moist,
The sound floats up between the cracks of the neoclassic shelves,
And when one is trying to correlate variant versions—
Well, really.

"Reading Room, the New York Public Library" by Richard Eberhart

Richard Eberhart, born in 1904, has won himself a high place in American letters. Many critics regard him as one of the major lyric poets of the twentieth century, and he has received numerous awards for his work, including a shared Bollingen Prize in Poetry, a Pulitzer Prize (1966) for his Selected Poems 1930–1965 *and a National Book Award for* Collected Poems 1930–1976. *Born in Minnesota, he has been for many years associated both with Dartmouth College, where he received his B.A. degree and eventually became a professor of English, and with New Hampshire, where he was appointed the state Poet Laureate in 1979. His books of poetry include* Reading the Spirit *(1936);* Burr Oaks *(1947);* Great Praises *(1957);* The Vastness and Indifference of the World *(1965);* Fields of Grace *(1972);* Ways of Light *(1980). His* Collected Poems 1930–1986 *appeared in 1988, as did* Maine Poems.

In the reading room in the New York Public Library
All sorts of souls were bent over silence reading the past,
Or the present, or maybe it was the future, persons

Devoted to silence and the flowering of the imagination,
When all of a sudden I saw my love,
She was a faun with light steps and brilliant eye
And she came walking among the tables and rows of persons.

Straight from the forest to the center of New York,
And nobody noticed, or raised an eyelash.
These were fixed on imaginary splendours of the past,
Or of the present, or maybe of the future, maybe
Something as seductive as the aquiline nose
Of Eleanor of Aquitaine, or Cleopatra's wrist-locket in Egypt,
Or maybe they were thinking of Juliana of Norwich.

The people of this world pay no attention to the fauns
Whether of this world or of another, but there she was,
All gaudy pelt, and sleek, gracefully moving,
Her amber eye was bright among the porticoes,
Her delicate ears were raised to hear of love,
Her lips had the appearance of green grass
About to be trodden, and her shanks were smooth and sleek.

Everybody was in the splendor of his imagination,
Nobody paid any attention to this splendour
Appearing in the New York Public Library,
Their eyes were on China, India, Arabia, or the Balearics
While my faun was walking among the tables and eyes
Inventing their world of life, invisible and light,
In silence and sweet temper, loving the world.

"The Doctors' Club"
by John Taylor

Born in 1952 in Des Moines, Iowa, John Taylor is a critic of European literature for The Times Literary Supplement *(London) and* The San Francisco Chronicle. *He writes a column for* France *magazine, published in Washington by the French embassy, and he is an associate editor of* The Review of Contemporary Fiction. *Since 1977 he has lived in France.*

His first book, The Presence of Things Past, *was first published in a French translation and in two separate volumes by Les Editions de l'Aube:* Tower Park *(1988);* Présence des Choses Passées *(1990).*

Even after Steve Boyce and I were caught going through his sister's dresser in search of sanitary napkins, my father and mother never mustered the courage to come out straight with the facts about how babies are made. But little matter. I had already learned everything which at eleven must be learned, even much more than is strictly relevant to the labors of love and procreation.

I was schooled in "The Doctors' Club" founded by Dan Cooney, Jon Skidmore and Steve Schmitz at the Byron Rice Elementary School in March, 1964, and of which I became the fourth member shortly before its dissolution, due to summer vacation, in June of that same year. My brief membership permitted me to master the arcana of our club, a long list of dirty medical terms and the secret code we employed to transmit them to each other across the classroom.

The code, devised by Cooney, could be used as a written alphabet or as a sign language. It was never cracked, not even when our gym teacher, a rotund, balding, middle-aged bachelor who encouraged us to call him by his first name, Arnie, confiscated one of Skidmore's pornographic circulars, coded explanations given to him by one of his neighbors, a hoodlum who went to Tech High School. Usually Skidmore's circulars were impeccably clear, and to them I owe my first rudiments of sexual knowledge, but once he misconstrued the hoodlum's teachings and to this day a nauseating image haunts me. In one of those circulars, wrote Skidmore, "If a man's penis is too short, then before copulation he inserts a thin metal straw into it so that the sperm will be able to reach its destination."

We knew such words because every Saturday morning Cooney, Skidmore, Schmitz, and I met downtown at the Des Moines Public Library, where in the middle of the Reference Room, lying open on a wooden reading stand, was *Webster's Third International Dictionary.* Cooney and Schmitz brought the list of words to look up, Cooney culling his off the illustrations in *Gray's Anatomy,* a copy of which he had received for Christmas, and Schmitz having discovered where his parents hid their *Marriage Manual.* After a few Saturdays we had progressed from "testicle," "vagina," and "ovary" to the most esoteric medical terminology. Members of The Doctors' Club knew what "seminal vesicles" and "fallopian tubes" were. A few Saturdays later we giggled over "lactiferous tubules" and "atretic follicles." Anything and everything having to do with the male and female genitalia—a category which, for us, comprised the mammae—was declared a dirty word, and I remember a despondent Cooney appearing one Saturday morning with the announcement that all he had managed to come up with were a few Latin terms for the veins and arteries of the penis. Still the words found their way onto our list.

All the erotic engravings in *Gray's*—of bladders, of testes, of rectums and so forth—were traced by Cooney onto onionskin paper. We stored the sheets in a manila envelope stashed in Skidmore's locker. In that envelope as well was the much sought-after key to The Doctors' Club code. What Annie Peterson would have given to get her hands on it!

I still marvel today that she figured out the note she intercepted was about her. I had written it, in code, to Cooney, folded it twice, printed his name on the outside. Off it went across the classroom, passing from accomplice to accomplice, detouring around teacher's pets, while Mrs. Lawrence droned on about the natural resources of South America. Like all young teachers, Mrs. Lawrence kept her back turned to us too often—writing words on the blackboard, searching for capitals on the wall maps—whence the rapid progress of the note through the first ten hands. There were only five more to go when—Annie unfolded the note to read it!

She must have had an inkling of its contents. Did she then recognize the two n's of her name, our code being alphabetic? A few classes later a similarly passed note arrived at my desk:

"Dear Johnny," she wrote. "I know your note was all about me so why don't you tell me what it says? I'm yours till Niagara Falls drinks Canada Dry! Luv, Annie."

It was just as well that Cooney never received the note. He would have passed it on to Skidmore and Schmitz, who would have made me the laughingstock of the playground. Some sentiments are best kept to oneself; decidedly I had gotten carried away. For how could The Doctors' Club have understood my attempt to describe, with the most beautiful words I knew, Annie Peterson's adorable little face and hands and breasts?

"Summer Librarian" by Sue Kaufman

By the time of her early death, Sue Kaufman (1926–77) had won herself a place among the most widely read and discussed writers who had emerged during the new feminist movement of the 1960s and early 1970s. Her novel Diary of a Mad Housewife *(1967) described the troubles of an upper-middle-class Manhattan wife married to a selfish and demanding tyrant. Kaufman's perceptive and detailed awareness of her heroine's yearnings for a better life made women all over the country respond with angry recognition. The novel became a successful movie in 1970.*

One reviewer wrote in praise of Kaufman's work: "Sue Kaufman does a commendable job in explicating the decadent ethos of contemporary middle-class America," while another noted how "slyly funny" Kaufman was: "It seems to me she has no peer as a recorder of our nickel miseries, anxieties, and hysterics." Her work includes The Happy Summer Days *(1959);* Green Holly *(1962);* The Headshrinker's Test *(1969);* Life with Prudence: A Chilling Tale *(1970); and* Falling Bodies *(1974). "Summer Librarian" is from a collection of her short stories,* The Master, and Other Stories *(1976).*

The little library was set back in a grove of beech and maple, so old, so dense, the tightly meshed leaves gave anyone inside the building the illusion of being in the heart of a forest, rather than just off the main thoroughfare of a busy village. Made of brown shingle, it possessed all the whimsies of a more romantic period in architecture —dormers, porticoes, eaves, gables, dovecotes—and the rumor ran that it had once been the caretaker's cottage on a huge estate. Whatever its original function, it had been the Community Library for over forty years, and in that prospering, burgeoning town was one of the sole remnants of another way of life, now almost extinct.

Cruel Time, Obsolescence, Everything Passes (the Old Order above all)—of such was Mrs. Foss's obsession, and on the dark humid July morning she and her daughter Maria drove through the village in their old gray sedan she held forth, glaring out at chrome-and-glass storefronts and silvery new parking meters, filling the little car with her smoldering comments. Maria, a mildly pretty, unobsessed girl of twenty, who had heard all this too many times, merely nodded as her mother ranted, and with relief finally pulled the car up to the curb fronting the Woman's Exchange. ". . . heaven only knows what next!" concluded Mrs. Foss, getting out and slamming the door for emphasis, but then leaned down and added through the rolled-down window, "I'll be in front of Humbert's at five. Unless, of course, you want to join us for lunch."

"Five," said Maria, answering the luncheon invitation with a vague negative nod, and sat waiting to see if her mother, who was becoming alarmingly absent-minded, had her keys. With detachment she watched the small wiry woman cross the sidewalk, wryly noting how the pastel golf dress, calcimined gumsoles, and visored piqué cap made her look like a clubwoman off for the greens—precisely the desired effect. When she reached the door Mrs. Foss groped for a moment in a purse shaped like a horse's feedbag, but she finally came up with a bunchy key ring and Maria drove off. She proceeded along the still-deserted street for another block and a half, then turned into what seemed a private driveway, but after a few feet opened onto a vast free parking lot neatly bedded with raked gravel and marked off by spanking whitewashed partitions. Neither the lot nor the supermarket which had generously (shrewdly, claimed Mrs. Foss) built it had been there when Maria had been home from college at Christmastime. Because, unlike her mother, Maria loved progress, particularly when it changed the face of this town she had lived in all her life, she ignored her mother's instructions and left the sedan unlocked—one of those small futile gestures that still symbolize so much.

As she hurried out of the lot through another exit, and started down the long block to the library, massed bluegray clouds, already rumbling and shifting with thunder, were heavily pressing down. It had also rained the day before, and when Maria unlocked the glass-paned door she was almost overpowered by the fusty smell of yesterday's dampness, trapped in old boards, moldings, bindings. She rushed about, banging and tugging at all the warped sashes of the windows in the front room. Aside from the new chintz covering the window-seat cushions, and several additional layers of bright blue enamel encrusting the tiny ladder-back chairs, it was a room that had not changed at all since the days Maria had first come there as a child. The four large wicker armchairs and the rack filled with adult magazines were mere tokens, for grown-ups never lingered here. This front room had always been considered a children's reading room, and each time she came in Maria would look at the two long low tables (pocked and incised by two generations of furiously restless little hands), the bookcases crammed with brilliantly colored picture books and primary readers, and she would shiver, briefly haunted by the vision of herself, raptly curled in one of the window seats, lost, lost in a book.

After hanging her raincoat in a closet-bathroom off the back stacks, she came out to the big desk bearing Miss Leonard's brass nameplate. Though Maria was an old favorite of Miss Leonard's, the librarian had made plain her wish to have this part of herself kept intact while she vacationed. So each day Maria was forced to work on a surface cluttered with a heart-shaped faïence penholder from Quimper (stuck with blue and yellow quills), three china bowls of paper clips in three sizes, two jars of rubber bands in two sizes, a family of Doulton scotties, a Lalique bud-vase, and a fistful of jabbing pencils in a Toby mug. Sighing, Maria took a metal file-box and a pack of postcards, mimeographed "Dear————, Your book is overdue!" from a drawer. As she began fingering through the cards in the little file-box, she saw that all the titles were those of current best-sellers, the names of the renters ones she had never seen before, and she knew that her mother would have pounced on this, claiming it as a further piece of circumstantial evidence against the newcomers, who (Mrs. Foss stated) were coarse and vulgar and had no taste. But it only made Maria consider the fate of the books during the heat of the last two weeks—she could see them, lying forsaken, left splayed open on a towel under the shade of an umbrella, or dropped onto the baking sands of one of the new beach clubs—and she sighed again, heavily, with pure envy this time, and dipping her pen into red ink, began.

By eleven, though the rain had still not started, only five people had been in and out of the library. One, a pale lumpish fourteen-year-old named Carol Danziger, had remained, settling herself in one of the wicker armchairs to read her newest selection (Elizabeth Goudge's *City of Bells*) with much noisy turning of pages and sucking of jujubes. In the week and a half Maria had taken over the library the girl had been in five times, clearly protecting herself from something at home by maintaining a careful distance from it, solacing herself with books and a new, instantaneous attachment to Maria she seemed to think secret. Though Maria felt sorry for the poor child—she was so overwhelmingly unattractive—she was more irritated than flattered by all her admiration, and today the creak of that indolent body in straw, the asthmatic breathing and wet sucking noises so set her teeth on edge she was about to do something drastic, when leaf-muffled shouts suddenly came from the front lawn, drowning out the exasperating girl. "Okay, Rourke, okay for *you!*" called someone just beyond the rhododendron bushes screening the front windows, and this was immediately followed by a shrill scream of girlish pain or delight—it was hard to tell which.

With a gritty clomp Carol Danziger brought her size seven-and-a-half moccasins to the floor. "Please, Miss Foss. Won't you tell them to go away?"

"Why?" asked Maria, staring with undisguised dislike into the gray eyes swimming behind lenses.

"Because. Because they're not *supposed* to play here. Miss Leonard always makes them go away."

Frowning, but knowing it would be simpler in the long run, Maria rose and went out on the front porch. Four boys in jeans and a ponytailed girl in tight cotton slacks were ranged out under the roof of leaves, the boys throwing an unraveled baseball back and forth in a magnificently casual game of catch, arcing it tauntingly high and slow while the girl scurried and leapt between them, hopelessly trying to intercept. Delight, thought Maria, diagnosing the girl's screams, and reluctantly started across the spongy lawn; one of the boys caught then held the ball, five pairs of eyes watched her approach—a small long-haired girl in a chambray dress trying to look stern and imposing, but only succeeding in looking what she felt: foolish. Someone gave a long low whistle. Her face burning, looking to neither side, Maria picked the tallest boy, the seeming leader, a grinning rawboned redhead, and marched straight up to him. Politely, but firmly, she asked would he and his friends mind playing ball somewhere else, people in the library were trying to read. In the following silence she heard suppressed sniggers, from the corner of an eye she saw the ponytailed girl sidle up to one of the other boys and meaningfully nudge him in the ribs.

"Ur. Well now, Miss . . . ah Miss? Well. We thought it being vacation and like that nobody studied in there." The redhead's yellow eyes shone insolently, taking her in, while from behind her, from the same spot the whistle had come, a boy's voice soft with wonder said: "Hey. Are you the librarian?"

"I am the *summer* librarian," Maria said with deadly calm, ignoring the speaker and continuing to address the redhead in front of her, "and it just happens that there *are* people who read in the summer. We will all be spared a great deal of unpleasantness if you just move, without further comment."

"Well, now, ya don't say . . ." mincingly began the redhead as she turned to leave, but a husky blond boy now in her line of vision, undoubtedly the whistler (and leader, she belatedly realized), quietly said, "Shove that, Rourke," and the mimicry stopped. In a tense, simmering silence, Maria started back to the porch, rage making her catch her heels in the rain-softened earth, making her clumsily lurch. Once back inside she stood watching at the window—after a dawdling conference, they finally followed the whistler's lead, straggling across the patchy lawn, majestically ignoring the gate and pushing out through the high privet hedge where they left a wounded gap—and she began to tremble with a fury the situation hardly warranted, a fury left over from another time.

"You were just wonderful, Miss Foss," Carol Danziger damply breathed behind her, "just marvelous. Those disgusting boys. Even the teachers are afraid of them. Of course," she added swiftly, daintily, "I've only been *going* to the public school since Miss Maitland's closed last year, and Mummy and Daddy are sending me away to boarding school next year. But I still had to be with them all this past winter. And you know the girls are every bit as disgusting as the boys . . . but then, you wouldn't know." She blushed heavily. "I mean I happen to know you went to Miss Maitland's because I saw you in one of the hockey team pictures hanging in the lunchroom. I remembered because you were by far the prettiest on the team."

Prettiest, thought Maria as she turned from the window and ironically smiled at the girl: the one slender form among eleven beefy ones, all lined up against an ivied gymnasium wall, right hands stolidly clutching hockey sticks, left hands vainly trying to hold down navy serge pinnies whose flapping pleats revealed lumpy, chilblained knees. "Thank you," she said dryly, inclining her head, then could not resist: "Actually I do know about boys and girls like that, and disgusting is an ugly word."

"But how could you possibly know about them?"

"It's quite simple. I went to the high school for my senior year."

"You did?" Gaggling, the girl jabbed her glasses back on the bridge of her unfortunate nose. "But wasn't that silly? I mean, leaving Maitland's in such a *crucial* year. I mean, with Miss Maitland so thick with all the deans at the good colleges?"

"I'm sure it was silly, but it wasn't a question of choice."

"Oh. Dear. I'm terribly sorry, Miss Foss."

"There's no need to be. I really liked the public school very much." As the poor girl, in an anguish of thrashing and swallowing, reached for her book, Maria was filled with remorse—why was she being so cruel?—and in a softer voice said, "I'm going out back for a cigarette, will you rap on the window if anyone comes in?" and hastily went out the back door.

The air was now so thick, so filled with moisture, it was difficult to light a match. Succeeding, she fiercely drew in on her cigarette and with troubled eyes stared out at the library's sad ruin of a backyard: on the left, at the end of an unused driveway, a rotting shingled garage was piled with cartons of moldering junk, its doors coming off the hinges; straight ahead and to the right trees, spaced wider than those out front, had let down enough sunlight to nourish a high wild expanse of grass. Neglect. Decay. Waste. Mostly waste. How vicious and pompous, how ironically like her mother she had just been, and all because the poor girl had unwittingly brought just that back: the waste, the needless waste.

But as overbearing as she had been, she hadn't lied. She *had* liked the public school, the jangle of bells and the shouting and laughter in the halls, the warm density of the overcrowded classrooms, all of it such a relief after the deathly hush of the frame house, and after years of Maitland's chill, sparsely filled rooms. She had also truly liked her wild and noisy schoolmates and had secretly longed to belong, to be taken in, and would have had there been time. For there she had been, a strikingly undistinguished student, suddenly bereft—of a devoted father, of the necessary funds, of the boost of Miss Maitland's invaluable connections—a student who either won a scholarship to college or did not go at all. Since her father had always stressed the importance of college, particularly the right college (though she now did not understand why), she had managed to go; by discovering a dormant "brilliance" of sorts in History, and by living a merciless, constricted life, she had succeeded in winning scholarships for three years at the college her father had most admired. For three winters she had supplemented a meager allowance from her mother by waiting tables, typing manuscripts, doing cataloguing in the library, shortening hems and altering dresses for classmates, and for two summers she had gone off with strange families to be a combination Mother's Helper and tutor in History for their petulant children. She had never complained or considered herself any sort of martyr, but at the same time she never permitted herself to dwell on the dangerous thought: None of this would have been necessary had her mother sold the house.

Maria's father, a Philadelphian, had inherited the pretty white Colonial house from an uncle just shortly after the end of the First World War. After much deliberation, he had accepted a long-standing offer from a New York banking firm, and had come up from Philadelphia with his bride and settled in Marberry Pond Park. Since they already knew many people in the Park, they instantly became a part of its quiet, secluded social life, and lived there happily, and uneventfully, but for the arrival of Maria at a time when they had long reconciled themselves to being childless. Maria's mother passionately loved the Park, her house, her garden, her friends. Maria's father liked the Park well enough, but he was an extremely practical, unsentimental man who, sadly enough, had never prospered, and when the town had begun its sudden violent expansion, he had seen opportunity, and wished to act. He wanted to sell and move to the city nearby: the land had quadrupled its value, he wished to spare himself the exhausting daily commute to the Wall Street banking house where he worked. But his wife was almost hysterical in her opposition. She detested the city. She hated apartment life. Life would be unendurable without her garden, her house, her friends, and the subject of friends brought up the most important thing of all: If they sold they would be the first in the Park to do so, which would amount to a betrayal of the other Park residents, their dear friends, since *he* knew the sort of people ready to jump at the chance to invade their private Park. He did not know, for he was the least snobbish of men, and the fate of "their private Park" did not remotely interest him, but the maintenance of precious peace did. He finally gave it up and soon afterwards succumbed to that strange, terrible exhaustion which it turned out had not been caused by the grinding daily commute at all. He was never told the name of what he had (multiple myeloma), nor did he ever learn that the dread disease which literally ate the marrow out of his poor bones also devoured the hard-won savings of many years. "It would kill him right now if he knew," warned Mrs. Foss. Maria, anguished, deeply loving her father, hardly needed any instructions to be silent. But taking root then, and after her father's death putting out tendrils that were never permitted to break through the surface of her conscious mind, was the ugly suspicion that her mother's real motive for silence had not been compassion, the wish to protect her husband, but fear, the deep well-grounded fear that had the dying man learned the true state of their financial affairs, he would have ordered the house sold from under him. And this spring, when the letter from her mother arrived at college, the suspicion burst out in full bloom at last—proven.

The first sentence in the letter, ending with three exclamation points, stated that the house had been sold. The following staccato sentences explained how it had come about: their house, it seemed, along with four others, had been the last ones left, and the contractor for the middle-income development that was to replace Marberry Pond Park, frantic to get on with things, had in desperation offered unheard-of sums to all of them. Quickly scanning paragraphs documenting betrayal—who had sold out first, who next and next—Maria came to the last and most important page. The house had to be vacated by mid-August, the latest: since there was now not only enough money for Maria to have a "carefree" senior year at college, but also to release her from the hateful summer tutoring, she would expect Maria home. Although, of course, she would need Maria's help in dismantling the house, and moving into the apartment she had leased in one of those new buildings on the station plateau, the rest of Maria's time would be her own—she would have her first real summer of freedom in years. Seeing that she had no choice, she had to go home, and knowing all too well what those hours of "freedom" would be like, Maria quickly made a mental note to write Miss Leonard about working at the library, then sat back to contemplate the enormity of what all this meant. It was not the proof that the house and what it stood for always *had* meant more to her mother than her husband or child, but the dark turn her mother's mind had taken, now that the house was doomed, that chilled Maria through and through. Instead of leaving, clearing out, starting a new life somewhere else, her mother had fanatically encamped on the battlefield, as it were, on the scene of her bitter defeat, and with her few friends rallied round her, clearly intended to make some symbolic sort of Last Stand, pathetic, senseless, yet filled with all the fury of obsessive hate.

Shivering, lighting a fresh cigarette, Maria now heard a ripping swishing sound, and looking to her right she saw a tall blond-haired boy, hands in pockets, striding through the tall tangled grass, making for the porch. The whistler, she remembered, as undaunted by her forbidding glare, he came right up the steps and put out a hand: "Hi. I was just going inside to look for you."

Though she pointedly ignored his extended hand, he was not put off. He let it fall, and continued, smiling: "My name's Harry Strickland and I came back to apologize for Rourke. He's a real wise-guy and doesn't know anything. I mean, you shouldn't mind him."

"I didn't," she said precisely. "And it certainly wasn't necessary to come back and apologize."

This time he reddened and began to blink, and she was instantly sorry, for the handsome face under the inevitable slick haircomb was disarmingly innocent, the blue eyes as clear and candid as a child's. "Well, I didn't really come back for that," he began again, taking courage from the sudden softening he perceived in her face. "The truth is I came back to find out what someone like you's doing here, in a dump like this. This town, I mean."

Because she had to forcibly hold back a smile, she said, almost sternly: "As I told your friend, I'm the summer librarian."

"Well, you talk awful funny. You sure don't *come* from this town and that's what I mean."

"I've lived here all my life."

"Yeah? Then how come I've never seen you before? In the village or anything. You been away?"

"That's right—at college." She flicked her cigarette down into the spongy black loam, and put her cigarettes into the pocket of her cotton shirt-dress.

"College? Phew!" Pursing his lips, he studied her with wide soft eyes; then bent his long neck and watched one of his sneakered feet kick at the rotting top step as though it belonged to someone else. "That must make you about eighteen."

"Twenty," she said with dry finality, and turned and opened the door in the same instant that Carol Danziger began rapping on the window with her garnet ring.

When the firehouse siren went off at noon, she prodded Carol Danziger from her wicker entrenchment, locked the library, and walked into the village for her lunch. Like thousands of growing small towns all over the country, it had completely changed its face in ten years. As low-priced developments mushroomed on its outskirts, and Garden Apartments (restricted to two stories by zoning laws) sprang up in its heart, the merchants had either rallied to the challenge by bravely remodeling and expanding, or had been vanquished by bolder, more inventive new competitors. Maria's route to the drugstore was a purposefully devious one, which took in an extra block of glittering new storefronts, a detour that skirted the Woman's Exchange where her mother's graying sandy head was always visible in the gloom behind the plate glass.

Her first week at the library, to pacify her mother about having arranged for the job in the first place, she had dutifully gone to the Woman's Exchange for lunch every day. The moment she came in her mother, Mrs. Knowles, and Mrs. Hollis stopped whatever they were doing (nothing), and began bustling about like girls, dragging four Hitchcock chairs with peeling gilt stencils (from Mrs. Peterson's dismantled house, and up for sale) into a small alcove formed by a ceiling-to-floor bookcase in the rear of the shop. There, placing them about a beautiful cherry Lazy Susan table (from Mrs. Knowles's dismantled house, and not up for sale), they took out thermoses filled with hot coffee, wrinkled brown paper bags of homemade sandwiches, and sat down to their lunch. When the last sandwich crust was gone, one of them went out front to the case of "home-baked goods" (Mrs. Luther, the cabinet-maker's wife) and brought back a plateful of something crumbling— *Linzer torte, lebkuchen*—or of strudel so damp or brownies so hard they could no longer be decently offered for sale. Maria did not see what they ever *did* sell, since most of the wares were contributed by themselves or by friends who were hardly likely (or able) to repurchase their own handiwork, and since she had witnessed the reception given to strangers, having helplessly watched the whole thing through spaces in the room-divider bookcase that formed the little alcove. The bell over the door would tinkle, there was an aluminum clatter as the young housewife from one of the developments, wearing slacks or shorts, tried to ma-neuver the baby-in-stroller through the door; whoever had risen from the cherry table and gone out—her mother or Mrs. Knowles or Mrs. Hollis—would come to a stop in the center of the front room and remain there, arms crossed, watching but not attempting to assist, airily asking "Yes?" when the complicated entrance-operations were com-pleted; there was the inevitable shy murmur, ending ". . . just like to look around," and whoever had gone out would say "Ah *yes*" like someone successfully grasping a sentence in a difficult foreign language, and would remain there, arms still stolidly crossed, while the stranger explored. The poor self-conscious young woman would then begin to timidly finger and inspect the tin trays decorated with *découpages* of flowers and fruit and the wastepaper baskets glued with hunting scenes and Audubon prints (the work of old Mrs. Davis), the string gloves, potholders, crochet trivets, tea cozies, baby bibs embroidered with bumblebees (all from deaf Mrs. Wade), the little satin pillows filled with sachet, netted bags holding dried potpourri, pomander balls (Mrs. Hammond's specialties)—and finally, since nothing was tagged, would shyly ask some prices. The outrageous sums were always given with a negligible smile, a smile which changed as the stammered explanations began ("didn't dream ... only a tiny present") into a grimace so chilling, accompanied by a murmur of ". . . but of *course*, my dear," so patronizing, that Maria, hidden behind the bookcase, had often trembled with rage. She knew she could not change the three bitter women, but she also knew she did not have to sit and passively witness their senseless games of spite. She managed to stick it out through the first week, but then thought up the lie which would release her for the rest of the summer: on certain days, she told her mother—and she never knew which days they might be—she could not close the library promptly at noontime, for there were people there doing special research with a deadline, or other people who had phoned and asked to come during the lunch hour; since she did not want to hold up their lunches at the Exchange, it was best to count her out from then on; she would grab a sandwich in the village when she could. Though her mother had violently objected—did she realize that would mean needlessly spending at least six dollars a week?—Maria had been happily eating her lunches at a big new air-conditioned drugstore ever since, a wonderful lively place full of clatter and chatter and jukebox din.

Big drops were staining the pastel slates as she hurried back up the library walk after her lunch. She had only been safely inside a few minutes when the rain came down at last, and the whole building began reverberating with cozy pittering sounds. She had finished the "overdue" postcards and dropped them in a mailbox on her way to lunch, so she now went into the musty back stacks and turned on a dim overhead light, browsing in the narrow book-lined aisles which smelled of leather and binder's glue, until at last she found what seemed a light frivolous novel and carried it back inside. To her relief, the rain kept away all comers, even Carol Danziger, and for two hours she traveled about Mayfair, Paris, Rome, worlds away. The library was singingly quiet, the rain closed in the mind. When it finally stopped at four, it lifted the heavy curtain of silence, of rapt peace; tires began wetly cracking out on the boulevard, a horn blew irritably, someone ran thumpingly up the street frantically calling a dog or cat or child named "Kim." Yawning, stretching, she rose and went to the glass-paned door where she stood staring out with amazement at the violent drenched green of the grass, until the front door rattled open behind her and a now-familiar voice said: "Thought I'd see if you drowned."

Without even turning, she put her hand on the knob of the door in front of her and angrily yanked it open. "You leaving just because I came in?" he asked forlornly, and when he got no answer, relentlessly padded across the room and followed her out the door. On the tiny ledge of back porch two colonial settees faced each other, kept dry by the capacious overhang of the roof. When he came out she was sitting resolutely in the dead-center of one of them, but instead of taking the empty bench, he ignored her forbidding glare and jammed himself into a corner of hers. Fury, exasperation—and despite herself, fear—made her fingers so stiff and clumsy she could not light her cigarette. After quietly watching two of her futile attempts, he leaned forward, calmly striking a match from a book he had held hidden and ready in his hand all the time. When a gust of warm damp wind blew it out, he frowned and quickly struck another, cupping big protective hands about the plumy flame. Defeated, Maria bent to light her cigarette, trying to think of something to say that would be so nasty, so cutting, he would go away and never come back, but as she withdrew, puffing on the cigarette, she accidentally glanced into the eyes above the flame. Her face going hot, she hastily retreated to the far corner of the settee: *Never* had any boy, any man, looked at her with such violent worship, such complete and vulnerable surrender, and the sight of these things in his eyes made her almost sick with shame and fear—fear, not of him, but of something struck deep, deep within herself.

"Just tell me one thing," he said in a perfectly ordinary voice that had nothing to do with his swooning eyes, briskly lighting his own cigarette. "It's what we were discussing before. Why aren't you off somewhere on vacation? Why did you come back here?"

"I came back here to help close up the house."

"The house?" he asked in a tone Maria would have recognized as rapture for just this much confidence, had she not been so muddled and distressed by the strange turn of events. "House where?"

"Marberry Pond Road," she snapped tensely and stood up.

"Oh. Where all those fine old houses are coming down for the lousy little ones?"

"They're nothing but white elephants."

"What?"

"Nothing. *Nothing*," she said, finally coming to her senses and realizing she had talked too much. She took a last deep draw on her cigarette.

"Well, why did you have to come? Couldn't your mother and father manage to close the house themselves?"

"My father's dead."

Blinking, mortified by what Maria had deliberately made him feel was a stupid blunder, he fiercely muttered something that sounded like, "You and your big mouth Strickland," and without another glance at her, stood up and went plunging off the porch. As he disappeared around the driveway corner, Maria wondered for the second time that day what was the matter with her—why did she lash out at everyone, particularly at anyone who admired her?—and bewildered, unhappy, stared through tears at a spaniel snuffling among piles of leaves the rain had brought down.

"I got us some pork chops," said Mrs. Foss, putting the brown paper bag between them on the front seat. Saying nothing, Maria started up the car, wanting to say a great deal about the broiler that would have to be lit on such a hot night, the greasy pan *she* would have to scour, not to mention the more appetizing choices they could be having for the same amount of money—frozen crabmeat, African lobstertails, shrimp or chicken salad neatly put up in plastic containers—if her mother and her friends were not crazily involved in a boycott of the new supermarkets, having sworn eternal fealty to Mr. Humbert and his like.

The sun had come back out at four-thirty, bringing a swarm of life to the village. Now, added to the beetling lines of traffic, were the cars coming from the station where the five-seven had just disgorged a load of commuters. At the first chance, Maria took a turnoff to the right, a maneuver which got them out of the honking jam of cars, but which put them on a longer round-about route to their house. "I hear that's coming down in September," said her mother, at last breaking the silence as they passed an ugly turreted building with boarded-up windows, sitting back on several acres of scorched lawn—the remains of Miss Maitland's Country Day.

"Coming down for what?"

"A Recreation Center. Whatever that means." There was a snort.

Maria sighed heavily, but not, as her mother thought, for the soon-to-be-demolished school. She sighed because for the second time that day she was reminded of the waste, of all the money that had been scraped together just so she could walk that building's drafty corridors, sit cheek-by-jowl in its underheated classrooms with girls like herself, daughters of parents not rich enough to manage a good boarding school, yet too proud to consign them to the public high school, parents who fervently hoped that Miss Maitland's one asset—influential connections—would work the saving charm.

The weed-tangled meadow that had once been a neatly taped-off hockey field fell behind, the car sped along roads where the houses became spaced farther and farther apart. Then finally they were on the dirt beginnings of Marberry Pond Road which wound for three mazy miles along the bay's wooded shore. Once a fence with a locked gate had separated Marberry Pond Park from the rest of the world, a gate to which only residents of the Park had possessed keys. Now pointed fence-slats lay fallen, rotting, while the gate itself had been removed from its hinges and carted off, leaving its two fluted supporting pillars standing sentinel on either side of the road, the head of the one on the right nailed with a gaudy green-and-yellow sign shaped like an arrow: MARBERRY ESTATES—$26,500!!! As the old gray car rolled through this doorless portal, sweet earthy smells blew in through the rolled-down windows, sun glanced off Mrs. Hollis's water-beaded trees and shrubs, filling the windshield with glinty brilliance. Then they passed a muddy gouged-out stretch bristling with the toothpick frames of three new houses, the place where the Dixons' lovely old house had once stood surrounded by stately elms, and Maria steeled herself against some remark or gesture from her mother. But tonight her mother was ominously still. And tonight Maria felt a strange and terrible prickling of the skin, for it occurred to her that each evening, as they rolled through that bare and gaping gateway, it was as though they had just passed from the real world of the living into a twilit one like Limbo, all shades of things long dead.

The sun stayed out from that day on. Lawns turned a bleached yellow, leaves hung flaccid on the high old trees. The village was deserted after ten o'clock every morning and all activity at the library stopped. Even Carol Danziger defected, coming by two days after the rain to select three books and to triumphantly announce that Mummy and Daddy were taking her away for two maybe three weeks in the mountains— good-by, good-by, good-*by*!

There was just one daily visitor to the library.

Bent over a book, Maria would first hear him out beyond the high hedge, loudly declaiming to some real or imaginary friend (his way of heralding his impending arrival), and not long after the screen door would twang open, floorboards would creak under sneakered feet. When she finally looked up from her book, he would be standing there all red in the face, wearing a foolish sheepish grin: "Morning. Thought I'd just browse around." Coughing nervously, he would then abruptly turn his back and the game began: for a while he restlessly prowled about the front room, peering at the covers and tables of contents in any new magazines put out in the reading rack, or pulling down children's readers at random, snorting and chuckling at things he found in them; when he tired of this or sensed that she had come to the end of her patience, he padded back into the stacks, and after a long time would emerge carrying something thick and improbable (once, seeing it was Ruskin, she had almost choked) and settle himself in one of the cushioned window seats; there, with much scholarly wetting of thumb and fore-finger, he turned pages at a considered pace, his expression irreproach-ably preoccupied—a deft imitation of the one she wore when she read.

The first few times he came to the library and all this happened, she barely managed to keep from exploding into the green silence of that leaf-shaded room, to keep from asking what on earth was the matter with him, acting like such an idiotic child—had he nothing better to do with his time? Why wasn't he off with his friends, boys and girls his own age, instead of plaguing her? Why wasn't he outside somewhere on such a beautiful hot day, down at the beach like everyone else? As exasperated as she was, she never did explode and ask any of these things, for she knew all the answers. There was nothing the matter with him because he *was* a child, and to his mind there was nothing better to do than hang around the inspiration of his first really serious crush. As for his going to the beach, she had only to look at those carefully mended, washed-thin suntans to see that his family could hardly afford one of the expensive beach clubs commandeering every foot of a shore that had once been free. And after the initial irritation, she began to relax, began to stop being angry and resentful—he was a funny yet somehow pathetic boy—and she even began to enjoy his visits. Not only was the elaborate pantomime he went through rather amusing, it was also strangely touching and even flattering: he was not like the rest of the boorish teenagers who hung about the village, but was a sweet and gentle and well-mannered boy, quite bright, really very bright, and given the proper advantages could do well for himself, a boy whose simple and direct devotion seemed to refresh and restore her, give her a sorely needed lift of the heart. What harm could there be in that?

Too late she saw the harm, saw how much she had come to depend on his visits, when four days went by and he did not come to the library. Despising herself, she nevertheless spent the fourth day listening for the shouts beyond the hedge, waiting, worrying. Was he sick? Had he suddenly gone away? Had he . . . had he found a replacement for herself, someone his own age, someone sensibly accessible to all that adoration?

On the fifth day, a Wednesday, she went to the drugstore later than she ever had, after shamelessly dawdling at the library, waiting. The noontime rush was long over, the place was almost empty, the whirring whoosh of the air-conditioning was the only sound. Without looking around she made straight for a back booth, gave the waitress her order, then sat pushing her leather cigarette case back and forth over the speckled plastic tabletop with her thumbs, wretchedly wondering what had happened to make her sink so low that she fed on the worship of a schoolboy. Had she lost all sense of proportion? When the waitress set down her hamburger and french fries she gave a guilty start. Troubled, dazed, she looked up and immediately saw him beyond the waitress' starched hips, sitting swung around on a stool at the counter, gravely watching her.

As their eyes met he gave one owlish blink, then swung down long legs and nonchalantly sauntered to the booth. "Hello, Maria," he said, towering over the table, sneakered feet planted imperiously wide apart.

It was the first time he had ever dared use her name. "Hello," she said coldly, pointedly not using his.

"Well, isn't this nice," he said with what she guessed to be carefully rehearsed urbanity, lowering himself into the blue leather seat opposite.

She blinked at the trim collegiate haircut replacing the slick blond water-wave and, despite herself, smiled.

"It's cooler this way," he said quickly, blushing as he saw she had guessed the real motive for the visit to the barber.

"I see." To keep from smiling again, she began to eat her hamburger, but found it difficult to chew and swallow under that fixed, rapt gaze. When he finally realized he was making her uncomfortable, he looked away over the low wall of the booth, and keeping his eyes on a tower of Summer Cologne on sale, a tray of Drastically Reduced bathing caps, he began to talk about the beach club where he had spent the last four days as the guest of some well-to-do classmate named Marvin. Maria barely listened to his descriptions of the cabanas with built-in bars and television sets, of the ladies who wore pearls with their bathing suits, but kept covertly glancing at him, with a strange sinking feeling noting the dazzling color changes the sun had wrought in his skin and hair. She also heard the new note of self-assurance in his voice, and from this and his new manner, she realized that he had come to some sort of decision about her—probably that the library relegated him to an insufferably juvenile position, and that he must try to meet her in other places where they would be on a more equal footing. She knew this guess to be correct when he suddenly broke off, got up and went to put a quarter in one of the little chrome machines sitting at each place along the counter, tune-selectors connected to the huge jukebox on the store's back wall. As all the glassy pyramids of bottles and jars began vibrating with the booming bass of some romantic song, he came and sat down with an air of unmistakable satisfaction: Now—they could almost be out on a date together.

Her course clear, she pushed away the plate of untouched french fries. "Exactly how old are you, Harry?"

"Seventeen." He solemnly stared at her, then picked up a paper napkin and began folding it into an airplane. As the eloquent silence from Maria's side of the booth prolonged itself, he glanced up, then down again, sheepishly smiling. "Okay. Sixteen. But seventeen in December . . . and that's the honest to God truth!" He launched the napkin-plane across the booth. It gently nudged her shoulder then fell into her lap. "Four years' difference. Almost three. That isn't much, Maria. That isn't much at all." He spread begging hands flat on the tabletop, and the cold tips of his fingers grazed hers as they nervously toyed with the sugar bowl.

"That's where you're wrong," she said in a choked voice and, trembling, stood up and threw down money for her lunch. "It's all the difference in the world. All the difference there could ever be. And don't you forget it." Then she fled.

A week went by and he did not come to the library. It was their last week in the house on Marberry Pond Road. Since her mother was at the Exchange and she at the library in the daytime, they spent the nights finishing up. Loading the car with cartons of breakable things her mother would not trust with the movers, they shuttled back and forth between the hushed and fragrant cricket-ticking back roads, and the cement station plateau where lighted evening trains clattered emptily in and out, blowing commuter newspapers and chewing-gum wrappers across platforms still hot from the sun.

One stifling night when even this leisurely carting and dumping seemed impossible, they decided to treat themselves to a few hours of relief in one of the new air-conditioned movie houses, and they set off for the village without phoning to see what was playing. They separated in the lobby as they always did, her mother proceeding down a gently inclined aisle to the unpolluted air of the orchestra, Maria climbing a flight of thickly carpeted steps to the smoky balcony. As she settled herself in an empty row, she shivered at icy blasts of air pouring down from a vent above her, and put on the cardigan she had snatched up as they were leaving the house. Then she lit a cigarette and stared hopefully at the screen where multicolored giants moved suavely, their bodiless voices confusingly booming at her from all directions. For a long time she stared and listened, unable to summon any interest, and finally, bored, began glancing about the balcony. Her restless gaze came to a stop on a row two down from hers, where riotous light splashing off the screen variably made silhouettes or bas-reliefs of four long-necked boys and four girls. In a sudden shift to brighter light the head of the boy on the end of the row flashed goldenly, a head, she instantly noted with a sinking feeling, which was not big-eared like the others, and which held nestled, in the hollow between jawbone and clavicle, the tousled dark head of a girl. Going numb with dread and other emotions she could not bear to acknowledge, Maria watched the gold head bend, ministering to the curly one, until, maneuvering to place a more ambitious kiss, the boy turned his head—and revealed a hook-nosed profile with a receding chin.

Rising, Maria stumbled down the steps to the lobby, where she took a seat on a bench next to the soft-drink machine. She stayed there until crashing chords of music announced the end of the film, and her mother, as always, rushed out first to avoid the crush. As she came up to Maria, rising from the bench, she gave a smug little smile: "I see you couldn't even sit it out. Have you *ever* in your life seen such trash?"

Though the moving men were scheduled to come on Monday, they decided to try and finish up the house on Saturday. Late Friday afternoon as Maria was leaving the library, she hung a little wooden sign on the front door—LIBRARY CLOSED TODAY—and told herself it was perfectly all right, Saturdays were always quiet, and one day would hardly matter. But the next morning when she opened her eyes in her stripped bedroom, she saw that the uncurtained windows looked out on a mistfilled garden like blind white eyes, and as she listened to the drops of water softly plopping off the eaves and branches, she knew at once that it was a perfect "library day," it ought to be open, she ought to be there. Groaning, she shut her eyes, trying to postpone the necessity of making a decision, but as she lay there the busy sounds of cupboard doors slamming and quick footsteps on uncarpeted floors made the decision for her: she had to help her mother. She got up at once, threw on a cotton bathrobe, and, as her first move of the day, took the still-warm sheets and pillow and light blanket off the bed where she had slept, and stacked them in a grocery carton in the hall.

At eleven-thirty she methodically went through all the upstairs rooms to make sure none of the small things had been missed, pausing last in the doorway of her father's old room. Light like dark water poured in through the windows over the uneven pegging of the floorboards, the rolled-up mattress on the springs of the bed. A beautiful walnut four-poster, the bed bore blue tags on two of its posts, for it had been sold to a New York dealer for the true and flawless antique it was. As she looked at the bed, and the similarly tagged maple chest-on-chest, Maria thought of how much this would have pleased him, how in fact the sight of that whole dismantled house would have filled him with joy. "Daddy," she said softly to nothing, no one, and fled down the hall, down the stairs.

She went into the living room, filled with crates of books from the shelves on either side of the fireplace, and where the couches, tables, and armchairs were pushed away from the walls in readiness for the movers and stood huddled in the middle of the room like a herd of mute lost beasts. The house was strangely still, still, there was a peculiar smell of sulfur and slate in the air—the dampness in the fireplace, she decided, looking at the charred bricks in the cleaned-out grate. "Mother?" she called uneasily.

"Cooahhh, coo, coo-o-o," answered a mourning dove from the magnolia by the cellar door.

"Mother?" cried Maria on a rising note of fright. "Where are you? Mother? Are you all right?"

She was not. Maria finally found her in the kitchen, sitting in the middle of the floor next to a deep cardboard carton she had been wadding with paper and packing with cooking utensils. She sat holding a cast-iron skillet and a sheet of newspaper in her meager lap, her thin legs pushed straight out in front of her. Though her face, streaming with tears, was strangely calm, the throat beneath the sharp chin was violently working, either in an effort to hold back sobs or to bring out words, which it apparently could not do. Though she was terrified, Maria calmly went up to her mother and, acting as though this were a place she often sat, quietly raised her up and supported her to the benched inglenook where they took most of their meals. Passive as a child, her mother let herself be led and fussed over, and when Maria was finally inspired to ask, "Should I call Myra? Would you like to see Myra?" her mother nodded almost simple-mindedly.

Five minutes after Maria phoned, Myra Hollis came clomping in, wearing a hooded plastic raincoat that made her look like a cellophane-wrapped package, brogue tongues flapping over muddy rubbers, plump cheeks scarlet from her agitated walk down the road. "Well now, Liz," she said heartily. "Having a bit of a crying jag, are you? It's high time —I'd been wondering when you would. Goodness knows, it's only natural after—what—forty years? Have you packed your kettle? Good." She proudly patted her huge shabby tapestry purse. "I stuck in some tea bags and a little nip of brandy as I went out the door. Now all we need is some sugar and cups. Ah lovely, Maria, *that's* the good girl. Now we're all set."

They accepted Maria's story without question: Now that it was raining so hard, she had better go and see if any books had been left in the little wooden box on the library porch. And as long as she was in the village, suggested Myra, she might as well pick up some sandwiches for their lunch—since they had defrosted and cleaned out the icebox after breakfast, it was silly to bring in any other kind of food.

"No need to hurry," said Myra Hollis, winking at Maria going out the door, as if to say the longer she gave them the more likely it was she would find everything restored to normal by the time she got back.

Once off the muddy back roads Maria drove wildly, blindly, trembling with the horror she had so bravely suppressed for the last half hour, the rain streaming and muddling over the windshield like the tears she could not seem to shed. Ignoring the peeling sign that prohibited parking in the library's driveway at all times, Maria turned in the car and parked it halfway up. She crossed the patchy wet grass, looked in the book-deposit box which was empty, then let herself in with her key, leaving the LIBRARY CLOSED TODAY sign hanging on the door. Though the front room was dark with storm light, she did not turn on the desk lamp. Sitting down, she put her throbbing head into clammy hands. Rain slipped down through the maple and beech leaves, slapping the windows, hitting the roof like hail, making such a rushing racket she did not hear the tapping on the door. When she finally did, she knew without lifting her face from its shelter of icy hands just who it was, and she did not move. The tapping on the glass panes continued. Realizing that the desk was plainly visible from the door and that it was impossible to pretend she was not there, she at last rose and went to the door, throwing it open with a violence that rattled the panes. "Can't you read? Don't you see that sign?" she cried through the screen door, glaring at him as he stood pale and blinking on the frayed WELCOME mat.

"Sure. But you're here," he said implacably, and opening the screen door marched in past her.

"I'm the librarian."

"I know," he said softly, without any irony, and stopped in the center of the room, crossing his arms.

"Please, Harry," she whispered, feeling the tears rushing up on her at last. "Please," she begged. "Please go home. I have work I must do."

"I won't bother you if I just sit and read."

"But you *will*."

His face broke up into quivering brilliant planes. "Maria. That's the nicest thing you ever said to me."

"You have *got* to leave. D'you understand?"

"Listen Maria—I can't stand it anymore. I have to know. Is there someone you love?"

"Oh God," she said weakly, taking her hand from the door and passing it over her face. "Don't start being awful, Harry. You're not that way. Don't start now. Just go home."

"Tell me if there's someone else," he whispered, tortured, coming slowly back to the door.

Helpless, she watched him slam the door shut with one shove of his broad palm.

"I'll bet there isn't," he said, forcing a smile, coming so close she could feel his warm breath on her face as he took her elbows into his hands. "I'll bet you don't really even know how to kiss. Maria. I'll bet."

"How horrible you are! How disgusting!" she cried, passionately throwing out her hands to push him away, out of the library, out of her life. But the hands stopped, splayed on the chest, feeling the scudding racking beats of the heart under the ridges of rib, until he took them away and squeezed them, powerless, in his own.

Silenced, they stared, wide-eyed, dazed. Drowning, she thought. Drowning, drowned. As the hands released hers and went under her hair, she shut her eyes, and the hands pressed the nape of her neck until her burning face rested against his burning throat. Tears scalded her lowered lids. Shame, fear, desire and shame—each as she had never known. She jerked back her head to finally speak but "Don't . . ." was all she ever said, for he found her mouth, and then there was only glassy green underwater light, the fleet image of a child curled reading on the window seat, and the sound of a squirrel jumping from a tree, running teeteringly, crazily, across the slippery roof above their heads.

SIX

Mystery and
Murder in
the Library

What could be a more enticing setting to a mystery writer than a library? The hush of a reading room almost invites a bloodcurdling scream; stacks of ordered books provide a backdrop for the startling disorder of a slumped body; a place dedicated to mental activity offers a vivid contrast to the most violent of physical acts. One critic writing on the library in detective fiction commented: "It embodies the quiet, dignity, and inscrutability, but not the tedium, of the tomb."

Many mysteries have been set in libraries, especially the dignified libraries of English country houses. Since our anthology concentrates on the American public library, we regrettably could not include any excerpts from novels set in British libraries. Most full-length murder mysteries do not lend themselves easily to excerpts, so aficionados of the genre may also miss many of their favorites. But our shorter selections do, we believe, convey the chilling atmosphere of violence in a peaceful library. Beware the unlit stacks and stairs.

Not every library mystery is a bloody one, of course; for example, those described in "The Library," by Isaac Asimov, or in the excerpt from *The Treasure of Alpheus Winterborn*. Books and libraries can provide fascinating clues for detective work, and Anthony Boucher's "QL696.C9" is a well-known example. As computerized libraries replace the Dewey decimal system, this story, and others alluding to once-familiar library traditions, may increasingly require some explication.

John D. MacDonald's brief, eerie story "The Reference Room" perhaps belongs more to the genre of science fiction than of mystery. A reader may well debate whether a murder takes place in it at all, though its events are certainly mysterious enough. But in its quick and tense action, its underlying tone of violence, and its extraordinary final scene in a library of the future, it is a fitting climax to "Mystery and Murder in the Library."

"QL696.C9" by Anthony Boucher

Anthony Boucher's influential position as an important critic of mystery and detective fiction, as well as his career as an author, are reflected in the annual convention of mystery enthusiasts called "Bouchercons" held after his death. Anthony Boucher, a pseudonym for William Anthony Parker White (1911–68), also wrote under the names Theo Durrant and H. H. Holmes. Many readers knew him best as the critic who wrote the "Criminals at Large" column in The New York Times Book Review, *for which he contributed more than 850 pieces. He was also a prolific writer of science fiction and fantasy.*

Boucher's mystery novels include The Case of the Seven of Calvary (1937); The Case of the Baker Street Irregulars (1940); The Case of the Solid Key (1941); *and several others. His short stories were collected in* Exeunt Murderers: The Best Mystery Stories of Anthony Boucher (1983).

The librarian's body had been removed from the swivel chair, but Detective Lieutenant Donald MacDonald stood beside the desk. This was only his second murder case, and he was not yet hardened enough to use the seat freshly vacated by a corpse. He stood and faced the four individuals, one of whom was a murderer.

"Our routine has been completed," he said, "and I've taken a statement from each of you. But before I hand in my report, I want to go over those statements in the presence of all of you. If anything doesn't jibe, I want you to say so."

The librarian's office of the Serafin Pelayo branch of the Los Angeles Public Library was a small room. The three witnesses and the murderer (but which was which?) sat crowded together. The girl in the gray dress—Stella Swift, junior librarian—shifted restlessly. "It was all so . . . so confusing and so awful," she said.

MacDonald nodded sympathetically. "I know." It was this girl who had found the body. Her eyes were dry now, but her nerves were still tense. "I'm sorry to insist on this, but . . ." His glance surveyed the other three: Mrs. Cora Jarvis, children's librarian, a fluffy kitten; James Stickney, library patron, a youngish man with no tie and wild hair; Norbert Utter, high-school teacher, a lean, almost ascetic-looking man of forty-odd. One of these . . .

"Immediately before the murder," MacDonald began, "the branch librarian Miss Benson was alone in this office typing. Apparently" (he gestured at the sheet of paper in the typewriter) "a draft for a list of needed replacements. This office can be reached only through those stacks, which can in turn be reached only by passing the main desk. Mrs. Jarvis, you were then on duty at that desk, and according to you only these three people were then in the stacks. None of them, separated as they were in the stacks, could see each other or the door of this office." He paused.

The thin teacher spoke up. "But this is ridiculous, officer. Simply because I was browsing in the stacks to find some fresh ideas for outside reading . . ."

The fuzzy-haired Stickney answered him. "The Loot's right. Put our stories together, and it's got to be one of us. Take your medicine, comrade."

"Thank you, Mr. Stickney. That's the sensible attitude. Now Miss Benson was shot, to judge by position and angle, from that doorway. The weapon was dropped on the spot. All four of you claim to have heard that shot from your respective locations and hurried toward it. It was Miss Swift who opened the door and discovered the body. Understandably enough, she fainted. Mrs. Jarvis looked after her while Mr. Stickney had presence of mind enough to phone the police. All of you watched each other, and no one entered this room until our arrival. Is all that correct?"

Little Mrs. Jarvis nodded. "My, Lieutenant, you put it all so neatly! You should have been a cataloguer like Miss Benson."

"A cataloguer? But she was head of the branch, wasn't she?"

"She had the soul of a cataloguer," said Mrs. Jarvis darkly.

"Now this list that she was typing when she was killed." MacDonald took the paper from the typewriter. "I want you each to look at that and tell me if the last item means anything to you."

The end of the list read:

Davies: MISSION TO MOSCOW (2 cop)

Kernan: DEFENSE WILL NOT WIN THE WAR

FIC

MacInnes: ABOVE SUSP

QL696.C9

The paper went from hand to hand. It evoked nothing but frowns and puzzled headshakings.

"All right." MacDonald picked up the telephone pad from the desk. "Now can any of you tell me why a librarian should have jotted down the phone number of the F.B.I.?"

This question fetched a definite reaction from Stickney, a sort of wry exasperation; but it was Miss Swift who answered, and oddly enough with a laugh. "Dear Miss Benson . . ." she said. "Of course she'd have the F.B.I.'s number. Professional necessity."

"I'm afraid I don't follow that."

"Some librarians have been advancing the theory, you see, that a librarian can best help defense work by watching what people use which books. For instance, if somebody keeps borrowing every work you have on high explosives, you know he's a dangerous saboteur planning to blow up the aqueduct and you turn him over to the G-men."

"Seriously? It sounds like nonsense."

"I don't know, Lieutenant. Aside from card catalogs and bird-study, there was one thing Miss Benson loved. And that was America. She didn't think it was nonsense."

"I see . . . And none of you has anything further to add to this story?"

"I," Mr. Utter announced, "have fifty themes to correct this evening and . . ."

Lieutenant MacDonald shrugged. "O.K. Go ahead. All of you. And remember you're apt to be called back for further questioning at any moment."

"And the library?" Mrs. Jarvis asked. "I suppose I'm the ranking senior in charge now and I . . ."

"I spoke to the head of the Branches Department on the phone. She agrees with me that it's best to keep the branch closed until our investigation is over. But I'll ask you and Miss Swift to report as usual tomorrow; the head of Branches will be here then too, and we can confer further on any matters touching the library itself."

"And tomorrow I was supposed to have a story hour. Well at least," the children's librarian sighed, "I shan't have to learn a new story tonight."

Alone, Lieutenant MacDonald turned back to the desk. He set the pad down by the telephone and dialed the number which had caught his attention. It took time to reach the proper authority and establish his credentials, but he finally secured the promise of a full file on all information which Miss Alice Benson had turned over to the F.B.I.

"Do you think that's it?" a voice asked eagerly.

He turned. It was the junior librarian, the girl with the gray dress and the gold-brown hair. "Miss Swift!"

"I hated to sneak in on you, but I want to know. Miss Benson was an old dear and I . . . I found her and . . . Do you think that's it? That she really did find out something for the F.B.I. and because she did . . . ?"

"It seems likely," he said slowly. "According to all the evidence, she was on the best of terms with her staff. She had no money to speak of, and she was old for a crime-of-passion set-up. Utter and Stickney apparently knew her only casually as regular patrons of this branch. What have we left for a motive, unless it's this F.B.I. business?"

"We thought it was so funny. We used to rib her about being a G-woman. And now . . . Lieutenant, you've got to find out who killed her." The girl's lips set firmly and her eyes glowed.

MacDonald reached a decision. "Come on."

"Come? Where to?"

"I'm going to drive you home. But first we're going to stop off and see a man, and you're going to help me give him all the facts of this screwball case."

"Who? Your superior?"

MacDonald hesitated. "Yes," he said at last. "My superior."

He explained about Nick Noble as they drove. How Lieutenant Noble, a dozen years ago, had been the smartest problem-cracker in the department. How his captain had got into a sordid scandal and squeezed out, leaving the innocent Noble to take the rap. How his wife had needed a vital operation just then, and hadn't got it. How the widowed and disgraced man had sunk until . . .

"Nobody knows where he lives or what he lives on. All we know is that we can find him at a little joint on North Main, drinking cheap sherry by the water glass. Sherry's all that life has left him—that, and the ability to make the toughest problem come crystal clear. Somewhere in the back of that wino's mind is a precision machine that sorts the screwiest facts into the one inevitable pattern. He's the court of last appeal on a case that's nuts, and God knows this one is. QL696.C9 . . . Screwball Division, L.A.P.D., the boys call him."

The girl shuddered a little as they entered the Chula Negra Café. It was not a choice spot for the élite. Not that it was a dive, either. No juke, no B-girls; just a counter and booths for the whole-hearted eating and drinking of the Los Angeles Mexicans.

MacDonald remembered which booth was Nick Noble's sanctum. The little man sat there, staring into a half-empty glass of sherry, as though he hadn't moved since MacDonald last saw him after the case of the stopped timepieces. His skin was dead white and his features sharp and thin. His eyes were of a blue so pale that the irises were almost invisible.

"Hi!" said MacDonald. "Remember me?"

One thin blue-veined hand swatted at the sharp nose. The pale eyes rested on the couple. "MacDonald . . ." Nick Noble smiled faintly. "Glad. Sit down." He glanced at Stella Swift. "Yours?"

MacDonald coughed. "No. Miss Swift, Mr. Noble. Miss Swift and I have a story to tell you."

Nick Noble's eyes gleamed dimly. "Trouble?"

"Trouble. Want to hear it?"

Nick Noble swatted at his nose again. "Fly," he explained to the girl. "Stays there." There was no fly. He drained his glass of sherry. "Give."

MacDonald gave, much the same précis that he had given to the group in the office. When he had finished, Nick Noble sat silent for so long that Stella Swift looked apprehensively at his glass. Then he stirred slightly, beckoned to a waitress, pointed to his empty glass, and said to the girl, "This woman. Benson. What was she like?"

"She was nice," said Stella. "But of course she *was* a cataloguer."

"Cataloguer?"

"You're not a librarian. You wouldn't understand what that means. But I gather that when people go to library school—I never did, I'm just a junior—most of them suffer through cataloguing, but a few turn out to be born cataloguers. Those are a race apart. They know a little of everything, all the systems of classification, Dewey, Library of Congress, down to the last number, and just how many spaces you indent each item on a typed card, and all about bibliography, and they shudder in their souls if the least little thing is wrong. They have eyes like eagles and memories like elephants."

"With that equipment," said MacDonald, "she might really have spotted something for the F.B.I."

"Might," said Nick Noble. Then to the girl, "Hobbies?"

"Miss Benson's? Before the war she used to be a devoted bird-watcher, and of course being what she was she had a positively Kieranesque knowledge of birds. But lately she's been all wrapped up in trying to spot saboteurs instead."

"I'm pretty convinced," MacDonald contributed, "that that's our angle, screwy as it sounds. The F.B.I. lead may point out our man, and there's still hope from the lab reports on prints and the paraffin test."

"Tests," Nick Noble snorted. "All you do is teach criminals what not to do."

"But if those fail us, we've got a message from Miss Benson herself telling us who killed her. And that's what I want you to figure out." He handed over the paper from the typewriter. "It's pretty clear what happened. She was typing, looked up, and saw her murderer with a gun. If she wrote down his name, he might see it and destroy the paper. So she left this cryptic indication. It can't possibly be part of the list she was typing; Mrs. Jarvis and Miss Swift don't recognize it as library routine. And the word above breaks off in the middle. Those letters and figures are her dying words. Can you read them?"

Nick Noble's pallid lips moved faintly. "Q L six nine six point C nine." He leaned back in the booth and his eyes glazed over. "Names," he said.

"Names?"

"Names of four."

"Oh. Norbert Utter, the teacher; James Stickney, the nondescript; Mrs. Cora Jarvis, the children's librarian; and Miss Stella Swift here."

"So." Nick Noble's eyes came to life again. "Thanks, MacDonald. Nice problem. Give you proof tonight."

Stella Swift gasped. "Does that mean that he . . . ?"

MacDonald grinned. "You're grandstanding for the lady, Mr. Noble. You can't mean that you've solved that damned QL business like that?"

"Pencil," Nick Noble said.

Wonderingly, Lieutenant MacDonald handed one over. Nick Noble took a paper napkin, scrawled two words, folded it, and handed it to Stella. "Not now," he warned. "Keep it. Show it to him later. Grand-standing . . . ! Need more proof first. Get it soon. Let me know about tests. F.B.I."

MacDonald rose frowning. "I'll let you know. But how you can . . ."

"Good-bye, Mr. Noble. It's been so nice meeting you."

But Nick Noble appeared not to hear Stella's farewell. He was staring into his glass and not liking what he saw there.

Lieutenant MacDonald drew up before the girl's rooming house. "I may need a lot of help on the technique of librarianship in this case," he said. "I'll be seeing you soon."

"Thanks for the ride. And for taking me to that strange man. I'll never forget how . . . It seems—I don't know—uncanny, doesn't it?" A little tremor ran through her lithe body.

"You know, you aren't exactly what I'd expected a librarian to be. I've run into the wrong ones. I think of them as something with flat shirtwaists and glasses and a bun. Of course Mrs. Jarvis isn't either, but you . . ."

"I do wear glasses when I work," Stella confessed. "And you aren't exactly what I'd expected a policeman to be, or I shouldn't have kept them off all this time." She touched her free flowing hair and punned, "And you should see me with a bun on."

"That's a date. We'll start with dinner and——"

"Dinner!" she exclaimed. "Napkin!" She rummaged in her hand-bag. "I won't tell you what he said, that isn't fair, but just to check on——" She unfolded the paper napkin.

She did not say another word, despite all MacDonald's urging. She waved good-bye in pantomime, and her eyes, as she watched him drive off, were wide with awe and terror.

Lieutenant MacDonald glared at the reports on the paraffin tests of his four suspects. All four negative. No sign that any one of them had recently used a firearm. Nick Noble was right; all you do is teach criminals what not to do. They learn about nitrite specks in the skin, so a handkerchief wrapped over the hand . . . The phone rang.

"Lafferty speaking. Los Angeles Field Office, F.B.I. You wanted the dope on this Alice Benson's reports?"

"Please."

"O.K. She did turn over to us a lot of stuff on a man who'd been reading nothing but codes and ciphers and sabotage methods and ex-plosives and God knows what all. Sounded like a correspondence course for the complete Fifth Columnist. We check up on him, and he's a poor devil of a pulp writer. Sure he wanted to know how to be a spy and a saboteur; but just so's he could write about 'em. We gave him a thorough going over; he's in the clear."

"Name?"

"James Stickney."

"I know him," said MacDonald dryly. "And is that all?"

"We'll send you the file, but that's the gist of it. I gather the Benson woman had something else she wasn't ready to spill, but if it's as much help as that was . . . Keep an eye on that library though. There's something going on."

"How so?"

"Three times in the past two months we've trailed suspects into that Serafin Pelayo branch, and not bookworms either. They didn't do any-thing there or contact anybody, but that's pretty high for coincidence in one small branch. Keep an eye open. And if you hit on anything, maybe we can work together."

"Thanks. I'll let you know." MacDonald hung up. So Stickney had been grilled by the F.B.I. on Miss Benson's information. Revenge for the indignity? Damned petty motive. And still . . . The phone rang again.

"Lieutenant MacDonald? This is Mrs. Jarvis. Remember me?"

"Yes indeed. You've thought of something more about—?"

"I certainly have. I think I've figured out what that QL thing means. At least I think I've figured how we can find out what it means. You see . . ." There was a heavy sound, a single harsh thud. Mrs. Jarvis groaned.

"Mrs. Jarvis! What's the matter? Has anything—"

"Elsie . . ." MacDonald heard her say faintly. Then the line was dead.

"Concussion," the police surgeon said. "She'll live. Not much doubt of that. But she won't talk for several days, and there's no telling how much she'll remember then."

"Elsie," said Lieutenant MacDonald. It sounded like an oath.

"We'll let you know as soon as she can see you. O.K., boys. Get along." Stella Swift trembled as the stretcher bearers moved off. "Poor Cora . . . When her husband comes home from Lockheed and finds . . . I was supposed to have dinner with them tonight and I come here and find you . . ."

Lieutenant MacDonald looked down grimly at the metal statue. "The poor devil's track trophy, and they use it to brain his wife . . . And what the hell brings you here?" he demanded as the lean figure of Norbert Utter appeared in the doorway.

"I live across the street, Lieutenant," the teacher explained. "When I saw the cars here and the ambulance, why naturally I . . . Don't tell me there's been another . . . ?"

"Not quite. So you live across the street? Miss Swift, do you mind staying here to break the news to Mr. Jarvis? It'd come easier from you than from me. I want to step over to Mr. Utter's for a word with him."

Utter forced a smile. "Delighted to have you, Lieutenant."

The teacher's single apartment was comfortably undistinguished. His own books, MacDonald noticed, were chosen with unerring taste; the library volumes on a table seemed incongruous.

"Make yourself at home, Lieutenant, as I have no doubt you will. Now what is it you wanted to talk to me about?"

"First might I use your phone?"

"Certainly. I'll get you a drink meanwhile. Brandy?"

MacDonald nodded as he dialed the Chula Negra. Utter left the room. A Mexican voice answered, and MacDonald sent its owner to fetch Nick Noble. As he waited, he idly picked up one of those incongruous library books. He picked it up carelessly and it fell open. A slip of paper, a bookmark perhaps, dropped from the fluttering pages. MacDonald noticed typed letters:

430945q57w7qoOoqd3 . . .

"Noble here."

"Good." His attention snapped away from the paper. "Listen." And he told the results of the tests and the information from the F.B.I. and ended with the attack on Mrs. Jarvis. Utter came to the door once, looked at MacDonald, at the book, and at the paper. "And so," MacDonald concluded, "we've got a last message again. 'Elsie . . .' "

" 'Elsie . . .' " Nick Noble's voice repeated thoughtfully.

"Any questions?"

"No. Phone me tomorrow morning. Later tonight maybe. Tell you then."

MacDonald hung up frowning. That paper . . . Suddenly he had it. The good old typewriter code, so easy to write and to decipher. For each letter use the key above it. He'd run onto such a cipher in a case recently; he should be able to work it in his head. He visualized a keyboard. The letters and figures shifted into

reportatusualplace . . .

Mr. Utter came back with a tray and two glasses of brandy. His lean face essayed a host's smile. "Refreshments, Lieutenant."

"Thank you."

"And now we can—Or should you care for a cheese cracker?"

"Don't bother."

"No bother." He left the room. Lieutenant MacDonald looked at the cipher, then at the glasses. Deftly he switched them. Then he heard the slightest sound outside the door, a sigh of expectation confirmed, and faint footsteps moving off. MacDonald smiled and switched the glasses back again.

Mr. Utter returned with a bowl of cheese wafers and the decanter. "To the success of your investigations, Lieutenant." They raised their glasses. Mr. Utter took a cautious sip, then coolly emptied his glass out the window. "You outsmarted me, Lieutenant," he announced casually. "I had not expected you to be up to the double gambit. I underrated you, and apologize." He filled his own glass afresh from the decanter, and they drank. It was good brandy, unusually good for a teacher's salary.

"So we're dropping any pretense?" said MacDonald.

Mr. Utter shrugged. "You saw that paper. I was unpardonably careless. You are armed and I am not. Pretense would be foolish when you can so readily examine the rest of those books."

Lieutenant MacDonald's hand stayed near his shoulder holster. "It was a good enough scheme. Certain prearranged books were your vehicles. Any accidental patron finding the messages, or even the average librarian, would pay little attention. Anything winds up as a marker in a library book. A few would be lost, but the safety made up for that. You prepared the messages here at home, returned them in the books so that you weren't seen inserting them in public . . ."

"You reconstruct admirably, Lieutenant."

"And who collected them?"

"Frankly, I do not know. The plan was largely arranged so that no man could inform on another."

"But Miss Benson discovered it, and Miss Benson had to be removed."

Mr. Utter shook his head. "I do not expect you to believe me, Lieutenant. But I have no more knowledge of Miss Benson's death than you have."

"Come now, Utter. Surely your admitted activities are a catamount to a confession of—"

"Is *catamount* quite the word you want, Lieutenant?"

"I don't know. My tongue's fuzzy. So's my mind. I don't know what's wrong . . ."

Mr. Utter smiled, slowly and with great pleasure. "Of course, Lieutenant. Did you really think I had underrated you? Naturally I drugged both glasses. Then whatever gambit you chose, I had merely to refill my own."

Lieutenant MacDonald ordered his hand to move toward the holster. His hand was not interested.

"Is there anything else," Mr. Utter asked gently, "which you should care to hear—while you can still hear anything?"

The room began a persistent circular joggling.

Nick Noble wiped his pale lips, thrust the flask of sherry back into his pocket, and walked into the Main library. At the information desk in the rotunda he handed a slip of paper to the girl in charge. On it was penciled

QL696.C9

The girl looked up puzzled. "I'm sorry, but—"

"Elsie," said Nick Noble hesitantly.

The girl's face cleared. "Oh. Of course. Well, you see, in this library we . . ."

The crash of the door helped to clear Lieutenant MacDonald's brain. The shot set up thundering waves that ripped through the drugwebs in his skull. The cold water on his head and later the hot coffee inside finished the job.

At last he lit a cigarette and felt approximately human. The big man with the moon face, he gathered, was Lafferty, F.B.I. The girl, he had known in the first instant, was Stella Swift.

". . . just winged him when he tried to get out the window," Lafferty was saying. "The doc'll probably want us to lay off the grilling till tomorrow. Then you'll have your murderer, Mac, grilled and on toast."

MacDonald put up a hand to keep the top of his head on. "There's two things puzzle me. A, how you got here?"

Lafferty nodded at the girl.

"I began remembering things," she said, "after you went off with Mr. Utter. Especially I remembered Miss Benson saying just yesterday how she had some more evidence for the F.B.I. and how amazed she was that some people could show such an utter lack of patriotism. Then she laughed and I wondered why and only just now I realized it was because she'd made an accidental pun. There were other things too, and so I—"

"We had a note from Miss Benson today," Lafferty added. "It hadn't reached me yet when I phoned you. It was vaguely promising, no names, but it tied in well enough with what Miss Swift told us to make us check. When we found the door locked and knew you were here . . ."

"Swell. And God knows I'm grateful to you both. But my other puzzle: Just now, when Utter confessed the details of the message scheme thinking I'd never live to tell them, he still denied any knowledge of the murder. I can't help wondering . . ."

When MacDonald got back to his office, he found a memo:

> The Public Library says do you want a book from the Main sent out to the Serafin Pelayo branch tomorrow morning? A man named Noble made the request, gave you as authority. Please confirm.

MacDonald's head was dizzier than ever as he confirmed, wondering what the hell he was confirming.

The Serafin Pelayo branch was not open to the public the next morning, but it was well occupied. Outside in the reading room there waited the bandaged Mr. Utter, with Moon Lafferty on guard; the tousle-haired James Stickney, with a sergeant from Homicide; Hank Jarvis, eyes bleared from a sleepless night at his wife's bedside; and Miss Trumpeter, head of the Branches Department, impatiently awaiting the end of this interruption of her well-oiled branch routine.

Here in the office were Lieutenant MacDonald, Stella Swift, and Nick Noble. Today the girl wore a bright red dress, with a zipper which tantalizingly emphasized the fullness of her bosom. Lieutenant Mac-Donald held the book which had been sent out from the Main. Nick Noble held a flask.

"Easy," he was saying. "Elsie. Not a name. Letters. L. C. Miss Swift mentioned systems of classification. Library of Congress."

"Of course," Stella agreed. "We don't use it in the Los Angeles

Library; it's too detailed for a public system. But you have to study it in library school; so naturally I didn't know it, being a junior, but Mrs. Jarvis spotted it and Miss Benson, poor dear, must have known it almost by heart."

MacDonald read the lettering on the spine of the book. "U. S. Library of Congress Classification Q: Science."

Stella Swift sighed. "Thank Heavens. I was afraid it might be English literature."

MacDonald smiled. "I wonder if your parents knew nothing of literary history or a great deal, to name you Stella Swift."

Nick Noble drank and grunted. "Go on."

MacDonald opened the book and thumbed through pages. "QL: Zoölogy. QL600, Vertebrates. QL696, Birds, systematic list (subdivisions, A–Z)."

"Birds?" Stella wondered. "It was her hobby of course, but . . ." MacDonald's eye went on down the page:

> e.g., .A2, Accipitriformes (Eagles, hawks, etc.)
> .A3, Alciformes (Auks, puffins)
> Alectorides, *see* Gruiformes

"Wonderful names," he said. "If only we had a suspect named Gruiformes . . . Point C seven," he went on, "Coraciiformes, see also. . . . Here we are: Point C nine, Cypseli . . ."

The book slipped from his hands. Stella Swift jerked down her zipper and produced the tiny pistol which had contributed to the fullness of her bosom. Nick Noble's fleshless white hand lashed out, knocking over the flask, and seized her wrist. The pistol stopped halfway to her mouth, twisted down, and discharged at the floor. The bullet went through the volume of L. C. classification, just over the line reading

> .C9, Cypseli (Swifts)

A sober and embittered Lieutenant MacDonald unfolded the paper napkin taken from the prisoner's handbag and read, in sprawling letters:

STELLA SWIFT

"Her confession's clear enough," he said. "A German mother, family in the Fatherland, pressure brought to bear.... She was the inventor of this library-message system and running it unknown even to those using it, like Utter. After her false guess with Stickney, Miss Benson hit the truth with St ... the Swift woman. She had to be disposed of. Then that meant more. Attacking Mrs. Jarvis when she guessed too much and sacrificing Utter, an insignificant subordinate, as a scapegoat to account for Miss Benson's further hints to the F.B.I. But how the hell did you spot it, and right at the beginning of the case?"

"Pattern," said Nick Noble. "Had to fit." His sharp nose twitched, and he brushed the nonexistent fly off it. "Miss Benson was cataloguer. QL business had to be book number. Not system used here or recognized at once, but some system. Look at names: Cora Jarvis, James Stickney, Norbert Utter, Stella Swift. Swift only name could possibly have classifying number."

"But weren't you taking a terrible risk giving her that napkin? What happened to Mrs. Jarvis ..."

Noble shook his head. "She was only one knew you'd consulted me. Attack me, show her hand. Too smart for that. Besides, used to taking risks, when I ..." He left unfinished the reference to the days when he had been the best damned detective lieutenant in Los Angeles.

"We've caught a murderer," said Lieutenant MacDonald, "and we've broken up a spy ring." He looked at the spot where Stella Swift had been standing when she jerked her zipper. The sun from the window had glinted through her hair. "But I'm damned if I thank you."

"Understand," said Nick Noble flatly. He picked up the spilled flask and silently thanked God that there was one good slug of sherry left.

"The Library Book"
by Isaac Asimov

Isaac Asimov's literary output has been so voluminous that merely listing his published works (more than four hundred books, let alone innumerable short stories and nonfiction articles) would be almost a book in itself. He is best known for his novels and stories of science fiction, although he has also written factual books about science, both for adults and for younger readers. He has published many mystery stories and edited mystery anthologies too; the following short story, "The Library," is from his collection The Best Mysteries of Isaac Asimov (1986).

Born in Russia in 1920, Asimov was brought to the United States as a young child and became a naturalized citizen in 1928. He lives in New York City.

When I was young [writes Isaac Asimov], my family could not afford to buy books. Consequently, they managed to get me a library card when I was six years old and for about twenty years or so I visited the library regularly.

After that I found I had a respectable income and could afford to buy books. Now my abode is simply littered with books in every room to the point where one of my big problems is to decide which books to give away and whom to give them to.

And yet, somehow I miss the old days. There was something so delightful about going to the library. The anticipation of wandering through the stacks was so exciting. So was walking home with one book under each arm and a third open *in my hands. (I've never figured out how I avoided being run over while crossing a street.) Anyway, this story is, in a way, a tribute to the old days.*

I looked about at the other three at the Union Club library (Griswold had smoothed his white mustache, taken up his scotch and soda and settled back in his tall armchair) and said rather triumphantly, "I've got a word processor now and, by golly, I can use it."

Jennings said, "One of those typewriter keyboards with a television screen attached?"

"That's right," I said. "You type your material onto a screen, edit it there—adding, subtracting, changing—then print it up, letter-perfect, at the rate of 400-plus words per minute."

"No question," said Baranov, "that if the computer revolution can penetrate your stick-in-the-mud way of life, it is well on the way to changing the whole world."

"And irrevocably," I said. "The odd part of it, too, is that there's no one man to whom we can assign the blame. We know all about James Watt and the steam engine, or Michael Faraday and the electric generator, or the Wright Brothers and the airplane, but to whom do we attribute this new advance?"

"There's William Shockley and the transistor," said Jennings.

"Or Vannevar Bush and the beginnings of electronic computers," I said, "but that's not satisfactory. It's the microchip that's putting the computer onto the assembly line and into the home, and who made that possible?"

It was only then that I was aware that for once Griswold had not closed his eyes but was staring at us, as clearly wide awake as if he were a human being. "I, for one," he said.

"You, for one, what?" I demanded.

"I, for one, am responsible for the microchip," he said haughtily.

It was back in the early 1960's [said Griswold] when I received a rather distraught phone call from the wife of an old friend of mine, who, the morning's obituaries told me, had died the day before.

Oswald Simpson was his name. We had been college classmates and had been rather close. He was extraordinarily bright, was a mathematician, and after he graduated went on to work with Norbert Wiener at M.I.T. He entered computer technology at its beginnings.

I never quite lost touch with him, even though, as I need not tell you, my interests and his did not coincide at all. However, there is a kinship in basic intelligence, however differently it might express itself from individual to individual. This I *do* have to tell you three, as otherwise you would have no way of telling.

Simpson had suffered from rheumatic fever as a child and his heart was damaged. It was a shock, but no real surprise to me, therefore, when he died at the age of forty-three. His wife, however, made it clear that there was something more to his death than mere mortality and I therefore drove upstate to the Simpson home at once. It only took two hours.

Olive Simpson was rather distraught, and there is no use in trying to tell you the story in her words. It took her awhile to tell it in a sensible way, especially since, as you can well imagine, there were numerous distractions in the way of medical men, funeral directors and even reporters, for Simpson, in a limited way, had been well known. Let me summarize, then:

Simpson was not a frank and outgoing person, I recall, even in college. He had a tendency to be secretive about his work, and suspicious of his colleagues. He has always felt people were planning to steal his ideas. That he trusted me and was relaxed with me I attribute entirely to my nonmathematical bent of mind. He was quite convinced that my basic ignorance of what he was doing made it impossible for me to know what notions of his to steal or what to do with them after I had stolen them. He was probably right, though he might have made allowance for my utter probity of character as well.

This tendency of his grew more pronounced as the years passed, and actually stood in the way of his advancement. He had a tendency to quarrel with those about him and to make himself generally detestable in his insistence on maintaining secrecy over everything he was doing. There were even complaints that he was slowing company advances by preventing a free flow of ideas.

This, apparently, did not impress Simpson, who also developed a steadily intensifying impression that the company was cheating him.

Like all companies, they wished to maintain ownership of any discoveries made by their employees, and one can see their point. The work done would not be possible without previous work done by other members of the company and was the product of the instruments, the ambience, the thought processes of the company generally.

Nevertheless, however much this might be true, there were occasionally advances made by particular persons which netted the company hundreds of millions of dollars and the discoverer, mere thousands. It would be a rare person who would not feel ill-used as a result, and Simpson felt more ill-used than anybody.

His wife's description of Simpson's state of mind in the last few years made it clear that he was rather over the line into a definite paranoia. There was no reasoning with him. He was convinced he was being persecuted by the company, that all its success could be attributed to his own work, but that it was intent on robbing him of all credit and financial reward. He was obsessed with that feeling.

Nor was he entirely wrong in supposing his own work to be essential to the company. The company recognized this or they would not have held on so firmly to someone who grew more impossibly difficult with each year.

The crisis came when Simpson discovered something he felt to be fundamentally revolutionary. It was something that he was certain would put his company into the absolute forefront of the international computer industry. It was also something which, he felt, was not likely to occur to anyone else for years, possibly for decades, yet it was so simple that the essence of it could be written down on a small piece of paper. I don't pretend to understand what it was, but I am certain now it was a forerunner of microchip technology.

It occurred to Simpson to hold out the information until the company agreed to compensate him amply, with a sum many times greater than was customary, and with other benefits as well. In this, one can see his motivation. He knew he was likely to die at any time and he wanted to leave his wife and two children well provided for. He kept a record of the secret at home, so that his wife would have something to sell to the company in case he did die before the matter was settled, but it was rather typical of him that he did not tell her where it was. His mania for secrecy passed all bounds.

Then one morning, as he was getting ready to get to work, he said to her in an excited way, "Where's my library book?"

She said, "What library book?"

He said, "*Exploring the Cosmos.* I had it right here."

She said, "Oh. It was overdue. I returned a whole bunch of them to the library yesterday."

He turned so white she thought he was going to collapse then and there. He screamed, "How dare you do that? It was *my* library book. I'll return it when I please. Don't you realize that the company is quite capable of burglarizing the home and searching the whole place? But they wouldn't think of touching a library book. It wouldn't be mine."

He managed to make it clear, without actually saying so, that he had hidden his precious secret in the library book, and Mrs. Simpson, frightened to death at the way he was gasping for breath, said distractedly, "I'll go right off to the library, dear, and get it back. I'll have it here in a minute. Please quiet down. Everything will be all right."

She repeated over and over again that she ought to have stayed with him and seen to it that he was calmed, but that would have been impossible. She might have called a doctor, but that would have done no good even if he had come in time. He was convinced that someone in the library, someone taking out the book, would find his all-important secret and make the millions that should go to his family.

Mrs. Simpson dashed to the library, had no trouble in taking out the book once again and hurried back. It was too late. He had had a heart attack—it was his second, actually—and he was dying. He died, in fact, in his wife's arms, though he did recognize that she had the book again, which may have been a final consolation. His last words were a struggling "Inside—inside—" as he pointed to the book. —And then he was gone.

I did my best to console her, to assure her that what had happened had been beyond her power to control. More to distract her attention than anything else, I asked her if she had found anything in the book.

She looked up at me with eyes that swam in tears. "No," she said, "I didn't. I spent an hour—I thought it was one thing I could do for him—his last wish, you know—I spent an hour looking, but there's nothing in it."

"Are you sure?" I asked. "Do you know what it is you're looking for?"

She hesitated. "I *thought* it was a piece of paper with writing on it. Something he said made me think that. I don't mean that last morning, but before then. He said many times 'I've written it down.' But I don't know what the paper would look like, whether it was large or small, white or yellow, smooth or folded—*anything*! Anyway, I looked through the book. I turned each page carefully, and there was no paper of any kind between any of them. I shook the book hard and nothing fell out. Then I looked at all the page numbers to make sure there weren't two pages stuck together. There weren't.

"Then I thought that it wasn't a paper, but that he had written something in the margin. That didn't seem to make sense, but I thought *maybe*. Or perhaps, he had written between the lines or underlined something in the book. I looked through all of every page. There were one or two stains that looked accidental, but nothing was actually written or underlined."

I said, "Are you sure you took out the same book you had returned, Mrs. Simpson? The library might have had two copies of it, or more."

She seemed startled. "I didn't think of that." She picked up the book and stared at it, then said, "No, it must be the same book. There's that little ink mark just under the title. There was the same ink mark on the book I returned. There couldn't be two like that."

"Are you *sure*?" I said. "About the ink mark, I mean."

"Yes," she said flatly. "I suppose the paper fell out in the library, or someone took it out and probably threw it away. It doesn't matter. I wouldn't have the heart to start a big fight with the company with Oswald dead. —Though it would be nice not to have money troubles and to be able to send the children to college."

"Wouldn't there be a pension from the company?"

"Yes, the company's good that way, but it wouldn't be enough; not with inflation the way it is; and Oswald could never get any reasonable insurance with his history of heart trouble."

"Then let's get you that piece of paper, and we'll find you a lawyer, and we'll get you some money. How's that?"

She sniffed a little as though she were trying to laugh. "Well, that's kind of you," she said, "but I don't see how you're going to do it. You can't make the paper appear out of thin air, I suppose."

"Sure I can," I said, though I admit I was taking a chance in saying so. I opened the book (holding my breath) and it was there all right. I gave it to her and said, "Here you are!"

What followed was long drawn out and tedious, but the negotiations with the company ended well. Mrs. Simpson did not become a trillionaire, but she achieved economic security and both children are now college graduates. The company did well, too, for the microchip was on the way. Without me it wouldn't have gotten the start it did and so, as I told you at the beginning, the credit is mine.

And, to our annoyance, he closed his eyes.

I yelled sharply, "Hey!" and he opened one of them.

"Where did you find the slip of paper?" I said.

"Where Simpson said it was. His last words were 'Inside—inside—' "

"Inside the book. Of course," I said.

"He didn't say 'Inside the book,' " said Griswold. "He wasn't able to finish the phrase. He just said 'Inside—' and it was a library book."

"Well?"

"Well, a library book has one thing an ordinary book does not have. It has a little pocket in which a library card fits. Mrs. Simpson described all the things she did, but she never mentioned the pocket. Well, I remembered Simpson's last words and looked inside the pocket—and that's where it was!"

"The Day of the Bookmobile" by Patricia McGerr

Patricia McGerr (1917–85) was a popular writer of mysteries for more than forty years, beginning with Pick Your Victim *(1947). Her particular contribution to the genre was her skill in writing what has been called a "whodunin?"—a mystery in which the victim of the crime, rather than the murderer, is unknown. She is also known for her original plots. Her many novels include* Fatal in My Fashion *(1955);* For Richer, for Poorer, Till Death *(1969);* Dangerous Landing *(1975). "The Day of the Bookmobile," like many other McGerr stories, first appeared in* Ellery Queen's Mystery Magazine.

Mrs. Moore rolled her wheelchair closer to the window and looked out on her front lawn. It had rained during the night and beads of moisture glistened on the hedge that rimmed the driveway. Across the street a moving van turned into the alley that divided two apartment buildings. Someone coming or going. *Everyone is on the move except me.*

She closed her eyes for a moment, remembering the block as it had been thirty years earlier. All private homes, a community of friends and neighbors. But one by one the houses had been sold to make way for high-rise apartments, parking lots, and a shopping center. Even the

Moore house was not as it had been. Four years ago, after her husband's death, she'd converted the second floor to a separate apartment, keeping the downstairs for herself. And that was fortunate because now, though crippled by arthritis, she was able—with no stairs to climb—to stay alone in her own home and be almost self-sufficient.

Behind the house a wooded area provided, from her kitchen window, a view of the changing seasons. Some day, she told herself, the trees will be cut, the birds and squirrels displaced so more people can huddle in blocks of concrete and glass and park their cars where my house now stands.

She shook off the morbid fancy and looked again out the window. The clouds were thinning, the sun was breaking through. It was not a day for gloom. Besides, she remembered, it's Tuesday, and instantly her spirits rose. For Tuesday was the day of the Bookmobile and always, whatever the weather, Tuesday was a fine day. It was not only the fresh supply of reading matter, though she sometimes wondered how she could endure her disability if she weren't able to lose herself, for hours on end, in a new biography or romance or thriller. Even more welcome than the books was the young woman who brought them. If I had a daughter, Mrs. Moore thought, I'd want her to be like Anne Sheldon.

She let the curtain drop and left the window. Switching on the radio to a news and music station, she learned that the ten A.M. temperature was 58 degrees, the humidity 43 percent. Accompanied by the opening strains of a Mozart concerto, she moved on to the kitchen where she laid a lace-edged cloth with matching napkins on a cart, arranged two gold-rimmed china cups and saucers and small silver spoons on the cart, then filled the sugar bowl and poured cream into the pitcher. Later she'd make fresh coffee and heat the cinnamon buns she'd baked the night before.

When the Bookmobile service began, Anne had arrived soon after breakfast, but after a few months she'd altered her route to make Mrs. Moore's house her last stop. With no one else expecting her, she was able to sit and chat for half an hour or more. And that visit soon became the social highpoint of Mrs. Moore's week.

The coffee service ready, she pushed the cart into a corner and wheeled back into the living room. The four books she was returning were in their usual place on the table near the door. She picked the top one up and leafed through it. It was a life of Queen Victoria that Anne had particularly recommended. Mrs. Moore had enjoyed it, but with reservations, and she anticipated a lively discussion of the book, pro and con.

As she searched for a specific passage, the doorbell rang. A glance at her watch told her that Anne was early. She hoped that didn't mean she was in a hurry. Returning the book to the top of the stack, she went to open the door with a smile of welcome already on her lips.

But it wasn't Anne. Instead a young man stood there, a stranger carrying a black satchel. A salesman was her first thought, though his attire—jeans and dark blue sweater, high boots and tan jacket—hardly fit that image. Before she could frame a question, he gave her wheelchair a hard shove backward and followed her into the room.

"What are you doing?" She put both hands on the wheels to steady herself. "Who are you? You can't—"

"Cool it, granny." He banged the door shut and stood with his back against it.

"Get out," she ordered. "You can't force your way into my house without so much as—"

"This says I can." From a jacket pocket he pulled a snub-nosed gun.

"Oh, no!" Her throat tightened as indignation gave way to fear. "What—what do you want?"

"Do what you're told and you won't get hurt. Who's here with you?"

"No one. I live alone—"

"Yeah?" He flicked her wheelchair with a skeptical glance. "Let's have a look." He went past her into the little hall that opened onto her bedroom and bath. She wheeled toward the phone, trying desperately to recall the emergency number. 911, that was it. If I can dial that, get the police . . . But he was back before she reached it and, darting past her, jerked the telephone cord from the wall.

"No tricks," he snapped. "Not if you want to stay alive. What's back there?"

"The dining room and kitchen."

He made a quick check and, satisfied, returned to her. The gun was out of sight, marked only by a bulge in his pocket.

"How about upstairs?" he asked her.

"That's a separate apartment. It's rented by a young couple—both are at work."

"So it's just you and me." His thin lips twisted in what was meant to be a smile. He was short and stockily built with small, slightly slanted eyes and a nose that looked as if it had once been broken. "Seems like I lucked into a good place to stay."

"Stay? You can't stay here. Do you need money? I haven't much but—"

"Keep your small change, granny. I'm loaded." He carried his bag to the table and set it down beside the pile of books. Opening the clasps he gazed lovingly at its contents for half a minute, then brought it over to wave in front of her. She saw two rows of neatly stacked bills. "Eyeball that," he gloated. "If you're a real good hostess I may leave you a hundred-buck tip."

"You—you stole that money."

"Right out of the First National Bank." He sat down beside the now-useless phone and put the bag on the floor beside him.

"Why did you come here? What do you want from me?"

"A hiding place, that's all. As soon as it's dark I'll be on my way." He leaned back in the chair and released his breath in a long sigh. "I'm bushed. That run took it out of me." His eyelids drooped.

Maybe he'll fall asleep, Mrs. Moore thought. If he does and if I can get to the phone extension in the bedroom ... In the silence she heard the radio. The music had ended and an announcer was giving the news.

"—a bulletin just in. The Valley branch of the First National Bank was held up this morning by a gunman who shot a security guard and escaped with an undisclosed amount of money. We do not yet have a report on the injured man's condition but will bring you more news as we receive it. Now this message—"

"You shot someone!" Mrs. Moore exclaimed.

"The damn fool set off an alarm and spoiled my getaway." He was petulant. "I was going to head for the woods, but the cops came racing up and blocked the way. I was lucky to make it here. Hey, what's happening?" His attention was drawn to the window. "You expecting somebody?"

Mrs. Moore looked past him to see the familiar green and brown station wagon coming up the driveway.

"It's the Bookmobile," she told him.

"Book what?"

"It's a sort of library on wheels for people who can't get out."

"Yeah? That's a nutty idea."

Anne parked the wagon, got out, and walked around to the back to pick out the books. She mustn't walk into danger, Mrs. Moore thought. If only I could signal her to go away, to get help . . .

"Get back out of sight," he said sharply. "And don't start yelling unless you want what I gave the guard. When the book lady rings the bell, don't move. We'll stay under cover until she gives up and goes away."

"I'll be quiet," she promised. And Anne will be safe. She tried not to let her relief show in her voice.

"Hey, wait!" He had a second thought. "She comes here regularly?"

"Once a week."

"And you're always here? Well, where else would you be? Not out for a walk, that's sure. So if you don't answer the bell she'll guess something's wrong and raise an alarm. Smart old lady, aren't you? Thought you could put something over on me. But I'm not that dumb. So here's how it's going to be. You let her in and act natural, the way you do every week. And you can introduce me as—let's see, you got any relations who might come to visit?"

"There's my nephew in Maine. I've talked to her about him."

"That'll do. And don't try to be clever. I'll be standing right here." He posted himself opposite the door. His right hand in his jacket pocket was a silent threat. "If you make a false move or if I get the idea you're trying to give her a message, she'll never leave this house. Understand?"

"Yes, I—I'll do exactly as you say." She took a deep breath. "You're my nephew Cassius who's here for a visit."

"Cajus? What kind of name is that?"

"Italian. His mother is from Rome."

"Yeah?" He grinned crookedly. "I guess I can pass for a spaghetti chomper." The doorbell pealed. He kicked the black bag out of sight under a chair. "Okay, let her in. And remember, Auntie, one word out of line and the two of you will be in big trouble."

She wheeled to the door and opened it. Run, Anne, run, she wanted to shout but, aware of the gun behind her, she held back the words and forced a smile of greeting.

"Good morning, Mrs. M." The girl's voice was vibrant with its usual cheer. "How are you today?"

"I'm fine, dear. And I have company." She turned the wheelchair around to face her captor. For a wild moment she imagined herself rolling forward at top speed to bowl him over. But a bullet can move faster than a wheelchair and she must do nothing that might put Anne in danger. "My nephew is here from Maine. Cassius, this is Miss Sheldon."

"How nice." Anne's smile lighted her face. "Will you be here long?"

"Not very." His hand stayed in his pocket. "I had some business in this area, so I said why not drop in on my aunt."

"I'm sure she's delighted to have you."

"Indeed I am." Mrs. Moore made her voice sound enthusiastic. "I hope he'll stay long enough for me to fatten him up. You've lost weight, Cassius. Doesn't he look lean and hungry, Anne?"

"I'll stay for lunch anyway," he said.

"But we mustn't keep you here talking," Mrs. Moore said quickly. "I know you have other deliveries to make. Last week's books are there on the table. I hope you've brought me some good new ones."

"There's another by the British veterinarian. I know how much you liked his first two." Anne placed her delivery on the table. "And a couple of good mysteries."

"I always enjoy them."

"Is there anything special you'd like me to bring next Tuesday?"

"One of Shakespeare's plays would be nice. Perhaps *Julius Caesar*."

"I'll be sure to get it." She picked up the books to be returned, and nodded to the intruder. "It was very nice to meet you."

"Likewise." His smile was wolfish. "Sorry I won't be here when you come again."

In a moment she was gone. The man stood near the window to watch her go back to the car. Mrs. Moore felt her pulse rate quicken as she waited, almost without breathing, for the sound of the engine. Then he turned from the window and she released her breath. It was all right. Anne at least was out of danger.

"You did good," he complimented her. "Is anybody else coming?"

"Not today."

"Then how about some chow? What you said about me being hungry was dead right. I missed breakfast." He nodded toward the kitchen. "You got food out there, haven't you?"

"I stewed a chicken yesterday. I can reheat it if you like."

"I'll eat it cold. With beer if you've got it."

"I'm afraid there isn't any."

"Then coffee will have to do." He grasped the metal frame of her chair and propelled it toward the kitchen. "Let's see what else you have."

He was indeed hungry. He ate most of the chicken with several slices of bread and butter, drank three cups of coffee, and ate all the sweet buns she'd made for Anne. As he ate he became more relaxed, but he didn't stop watching her. Nor could she forget the gun in his pocket.

"You better eat something too," he suggested.

"No, I couldn't. I never have much appetite."

They returned to the living room in time to hear a noon newscast. The bank guard, it was reported, had been rushed to the hospital and was in critical condition with a bullet in his chest.

"It's his own fault." He answered her unspoken accusation. "He made trouble for you too. If he hadn't tried to be a hero, I'd be long gone. Tell you what, when I get ready to go, you can put the rest of that chicken in a doggy bag."

"I'll be glad to," she assured him.

When I get ready to go. The words hung in her mind as description of a tantalizingly distant future. It was still many hours until dark. And when the time came, was it realistic to hope that he'd take his bag of money and leave her unharmed? If the guard died, he'd be guilty of murder. Why should he let her stay free to put the police on his trail and testify against him?

"Who's that?" He was again at the window, turning back to look at her with suspicion. "Thought you said you weren't expecting anybody else."

"I'm not." A truck stopped in the driveway. The words *United Delivery Service* were lettered on its side panel. "It must be something I ordered from a store."

"Yeah? What?"

"I don't remember."

Two men got out of the van, opened the truck's back doors, and unloaded a large unwieldy object encased in cardboard.

"What the hell is that?"

"It looks like——" She examined it more closely. "Like a mattress."

"You ordered a mattress? That's not something you'd forget."

"No. They must have the wrong address."

"Lamebrains! You'd think they'd make sure they had the right house before they carted that heavy thing up here." He waited for them to ring the bell. "Okay, answer the door and send them away."

Again she was conscious of his standing directly behind her. Again she knew the gun was pointed at her back. She opened the door.

"Good day, ma'am." A tall man in gray coveralls put down his end of the box and touched his cap. "Got a delivery for Whitman, Apartment B."

"That's on the second floor," she told him. "But they're not at home in the daytime."

"Yeah?" He frowned, looked at the paper in his hand, and brightened. "The order says to leave it with the lady downstairs. That must be you. Okay, Joe, let's take it in."

"Wait a minute," the man behind her objected. "You can't fill up her place with that big thing. Bring it back when the people who bought it are home."

"It's all right," she told them. "I often take in the Whitmans' packages."

"Make up your mind." The delivery man was impatient. "If you won't accept it, I'll call the store and ask them what to do. You've got a phone, haven't you?"

"Yes, but——"

"It's all right," the gunman cut her off. "There's no need to make a federal case out of it. Let them bring the damn thing in."

"Excuse me, ma'am." Moving quickly, the man in gray maneuvered the oblong package past her so that she was isolated in a corner, cut off from the rest of the room. A phrase from a novel about gang warfare sprang to her mind. "To the mattresses." It made an effective barricade. Perhaps she might, under its cover, whisper a warning to the second delivery man . . . While her thoughts were still whirling, trying to form a plan, the advance man spoke a sharp command.

"Okay, buster, pull that hand out of your pocket. Slow and easy. And empty. That's the way. Now raise 'em both high."

Resting his burden against the wall, the second man went to join his partner. Mrs. Moore rolled to a spot where she could see round the corner of the box. Her captor was standing with both hands above his head. The advance man kept his gun trained on him while the one called Joe removed the weapon from the intruder's jacket pocket and then clicked on handcuffs that locked his arms behind his back.

"You—" She stared at the two men in gray. "You're police officers."

"That's right, ma'am. Sergeant Cleary. And Detective Williams." He looked at her more closely. "Are you all right?"

"I am now." She put her hand to her throat, finding it hard to breathe as the terror she had so long suppressed suddenly broke free.

"You want me to call a doctor?"

"No, I—I'll be fine." She looked once more at her unwelcome guest. Shackled between the policemen, he was no longer a menacing figure.

"Okay, buster, let's go downtown. The folks there will be mighty pleased to see you." His eyes searched the room, discovering the black bag. "And this too." He picked it up and turned back to Mrs. Moore. "Somebody will be out later to take your statement."

Sullenly the prisoner let himself be hustled through the door. Sergeant Cleary spoke to someone outside.

"All right, miss. You can go in now."

Anne Sheldon came swiftly into the room, dropped to her knees beside the wheelchair, and clasped Mrs. Moore's hand.

"He didn't hurt you, did he?" she asked.

"He only frightened me." She managed a faint smile. "And I'll get over that. I'm very glad you came back."

"I thought you'd want company for a while. The police told me to wait outside until he was in custody."

"It was you who called them?"

"Yes. I phoned from the drugstore on the corner. When I described the man, they were sure it was the one who held up the bank this morning."

"I didn't know whether you got my message. I couldn't be any clearer without making him suspicious."

"You were clear enough." Anne squeezed her hand. "The minute I came in I could tell you were on edge about something. You're not usually in such a rush to get rid of me."

"No." She smiled, returned the pressure. "I look forward to our discussions."

"What clinched it was your asking for a copy of *Julius Caesar*." Her eyes went to the bookcase behind Mrs. Moore. "I know what a fine set of Shakespeare you have. With his complete works on your shelf it didn't make sense to ask for one of his plays. As soon as I got back to the car I was able to put it all together."

" 'Yon Cassius,' " Mrs. Moore quoted, " 'has a lean and hungry look.' "

"With that as a start," Anne said, "it wasn't hard to add the last line of Caesar's speech. 'Such men are dangerous.' "

Excerpt from
The Treasure of Alpheus
Winterborn
by John Bellairs

John Bellairs, who was born in 1938, has created a special niche for himself in the crowded field of children's fiction by writing books that combine humor, suspense, and agreeable shivers of mystery. His titles are like teasing previews: The House with a Clock in Its Walls *(1973);* The Figure in the Shadows

(1975); The Curse of the Blue Figurine (1983); The Dark Secret of Weatherend (1984); The Lamp from the Warlock's Tomb (1987); The Trolley to Yesterday (1989); and many others.

Bellairs has described his books as "a combination of the everyday and the fantastic, like the books of my favorite author, Charles Dickens. The common ordinary stuff—the bullies, the scaredy-cat kid Lewis, the grown-ups, the everyday incidents—all come from my own experience." This enticing mix is evident in the following chapter from The Treasure of Alpheus Winterborn. *("Hoosac," the setting of the story, is modeled on Winona, Minnesota.)*

Bellairs now lives in Haverhill, Massachusetts.

It was a windy night in March. Anthony Monday lay in his bed listening to his heart beat. He was lying on his left side, and the muffled thudding sounded as if it were coming from down inside the mattress. Anthony was scared, but not of the dark. He was scared of what he was listening to. Downstairs, his mother and father were arguing. As usual, they were arguing about money.

"I don't care what you say, Howard. There just isn't enough money coming in, and that's all there is to it. The bills just keep piling up, and I ask myself, 'How are we going to pay them?' How are we going to, Howard? You tell me how!"

"Oh, come on, Ginny. It's not as bad as all that. Why——"

"Not so bad, is it! Not so bad! Well, let me tell you . . ."

And on it went. Mrs. Monday had a thing about money. There was never enough of it around to suit her. She worried so much about money because when she was a little girl, a terrible thing happened to her family. Her father had invested in some stocks that turned out to be fakes, and he lost nearly everything he had. Mrs. Monday had grown up poor, and now she couldn't convince herself that she was well off. The memory of her father's financial disaster haunted her and made her fret and stew about money when there was no reason to worry at all.

Listening to his parents argue made Anthony feel sick to his stomach. He lay there, eyes wide, staring at the dark wall next to his bed. He heard his mother say that if they didn't watch out, they'd all be out in the street. In his mind's eye, Anthony saw his mother and himself standing in the street outside the blackened ruins of their house—this vision always came to him whenever his mother talked that way. It hovered before his eyes like a picture on a movie screen. He wondered if his family really would go broke someday. He worried a lot about money, and considering what his mother was like, this was not very surprising.

Finally, the argument was over. Anthony heard his mother's chair scrape back as she got up and started fixing Mr. Monday's supper. It was almost midnight. Mr. Monday worked late six nights a week. He ran a saloon. In the town where the Mondays lived, nice people didn't run saloons, and the Mondays tried hard to be nice people, so they called their saloon a cigar store: Monday's Cigar Store. And there actually were some dusty glass cases up in the front of the store that had cigars in them. Mostly, though, Monday's Cigar Store sold beer and wine by the glass. Running the place was hard work, and Mr. Monday ran his saloon all by himself. He had hired a helper once, but Mrs. Monday had accused the helper of stealing money out of the cash register, so Mr. Monday had let him go. Anthony often wished he were old enough to help his dad out, but state law said you had to be eighteen to work in a place where liquor was sold, and that was that. Anthony's brother, Keith, who was sixteen, would be able to help their father in two more years. But for now, Mr. Monday had to go it alone.

It was silent downstairs now, except for the sound of bacon sizzling. Anthony rolled over and tried to sleep. Wild shadows, cast by the swinging street lamp on the corner, leaped across the bedroom wall. From across the hall, Anthony could hear the sound of his brother's snoring. Keith was lucky. He could sleep through anything. Meanwhile, Anthony lay awake, worrying. He worried about what would happen if his dad got so sick that he couldn't work. There wasn't much work that a thirteen-year-old boy could do. He could get a paper route, but you hardly made anything at all doing that. . . .

The shelf clock downstairs struck half past twelve. Anthony started to feel drowsy, and as always, his mind drifted from worry into daydream. First he was a diver, stumping across the floor of the ocean in a diving suit, poking among the rotting ribs of a Spanish galleon till he found a chest full of gold coins. Then he imagined himself sitting at his own kitchen table downstairs. The table was covered with a heap of gold coins. Behind him stood his parents. They were smiling as they looked at the glittering mound of wealth. Now his mother would never have to worry about money again, not ever. . . .

And with this pleasant image before his eyes, Anthony fell asleep.

The next day after school, Anthony decided to stop by the library on his way home. He did this a lot, not so much because he was a bookworm, but because he liked the librarian, Miss Eells. Miss Myra Eells was the librarian at the public library in the town of Hoosac, Minnesota, where Anthony lived. Anthony had met her one day when the two of them were browsing at the same magazine rack in a drugstore. They had gotten into a conversation, and after that they had gotten to be friends. Anthony liked Miss Eells. In many ways, she was closer to him than his own mother was. For one thing, he wasn't scared of Miss Eells. He felt comfortable with her. It wasn't the same way with his mother. She always seemed to be bawling him out or telling him that he was worthless and stupid and selfish.

But with Miss Eells it was different. She took Anthony seriously. She listened to him. She took time off from her work to just sit around and be with him, and that meant a lot to Anthony. Miss Eells did other things for him, too. She bought Anthony presents and took him for rides in her car. She had taught him how to play chess, and she had taught him a code that had been used by spies during the Civil War. Anthony and Miss Eells left each other messages in this code because it was fun to do. Sometimes Anthony wondered why she was so nice to him. Anthony didn't have a lot of friends, and he didn't think much of himself—that is, he didn't think he was a very wonderful person— so it was only natural that he would wonder why Miss Eells wanted to be friends with him. Anthony's mother was always telling him to watch out for people who were nice to you because they were only trying to butter you up so they could take advantage. Luckily for Anthony, he didn't always follow his mother's advice. He took Miss Eell's love for what it was and was happy with it.

. . .

Whistling cheerfully, Anthony trotted down Minnesota Avenue, the main street of town, and crossed Levee Park. It was a chilly March day, and Anthony was wearing his brown leather jacket and his red leather cap. He had always worn red leather caps, ever since he could remember, and he had always scrunched the peaks on them so they were curved. He was funny about things like that.

When he got to the far side of the park, he stopped and looked up at the library, a dark shape looming over the bare trees. He always stopped and stared at the library before he went into it. Even people who walked along with their noses to the ground would often look up when they passed it. It was really something to stare at.

The Hoosac Public Library was like a castle out of a fairy tale. Of course, it was a bit smaller than most castles, being only two stories high. But it had battlements like a castle, and funny little bulges here and there with narrow loophole windows, the kind that soldiers might shoot through when they saw the enemy coming. At one corner was a tall round tower with a slate roof and a weather vane with a reindeer on it. Like a castle, the building was made of stone, black stone that glistened when it was wet, and it was covered with fantastic carvings. The carvings nestled in all the angles and corners of the building. They showed stone dwarfs hammering on stone anvils, stone scholars reading stone books, stone dragons breathing curls of stone steam, and many other strange things. Over the main doorway of the library was a carving that showed a half-moon. The moon was the kind that you see in Mother Goose books, with a face and a big, long nose. Under the moon face was a stone banner, and on it these words were carved: BELIEVE ONLY HALF OF WHAT YOU READ.

It was a funny kind of inscription to put over the door of a library. But then, the Hoosac Public Library had been built by a funny kind of man.

The Hoosac Public Library had been designed, built, and paid for back in 1929 by a man named Alpheus T. Winterborn. Mr. Winterborn had been rich—very rich. He had made his money from a company that still employed about half the people in Hoosac—the Winterborn Silverware Company. Winterborn Silverware made silver-plated objects of all kinds—knives, forks, spoons, teapots, percolators, tea strainers and tea balls, and Edam cheese holders—things like that. The company also cast statues in bronze and other metals. In fact, it had cast the small bronze reindeer on the weather vane atop the tower of the library. The company had gotten to be famous nationwide, like the 1847 Rogers Brothers, and it had made Alpheus Winterborn a millionaire.

Millionaires often spend their money in strange ways, but none of them ever spent his more strangely than Alpheus Winterborn did. In the last twenty years of his life, he went from one fad to another. First he decided that he was going to be an inventor. He tried to invent a perpetual-motion machine, a gadget that would run all by itself, without steam or electricity or gasoline or any kind of fuel. He tinkered for years, but all he ever came up with were some funny-looking gadgets that would run for two or three hours and stop. But Alpheus Winterborn wasn't discouraged. He had a lot of money and a lot of time. Next he decided that he would be an archeologist. This was in 1922, when the whole world was talking about King Tut's tomb, which had just been discovered. Alpheus Winterborn didn't see why he couldn't discover something, too, so he bought a pith helmet, a pick, a shovel, and a lot of other gear and went to Egypt. He dug at Luxor, at Karnak, and at some other places on the Upper Nile. Then he went to the Holy Land and did some digging there. When he came back to Hoosac after being away for almost two years, rumors started to fly around. People claimed that old Alpheus had discovered something strange and wonderful, something really valuable. No one knew for sure what the thing was or who it was who had started the rumors, but there were many people in the town of Hoosac who would swear on a stack of Bibles that Alpheus Winterborn had made a find.

Whatever this mysterious treasure was, nobody ever saw it. Alpheus Winterborn remained his usual stolid, uncommunicative self, and after a few months in Hoosac he was off to the Near East again. He made three trips in all to Egypt and Palestine, and every time he returned home, the mysterious rumors started up again. But there are always people in every town who will start rumors, and generally the rumors have no foundation at all.

After his last trip, Alpheus Winterborn came back to Hoosac and shut himself up in his house. He saw no one and talked to no one. He had always been an odd person and the subject of much gossip in the town of Hoosac. But he was odder now than he had ever been, and people began to wonder if maybe they would wake up some morning and find that he had hanged himself from the chandelier in his living room.

Just when public curiosity reached a fever pitch, Alpheus Winterborn came out of hiding. He was nearly seventy, but there was life in the old boy yet. He announced that he would become an architect. What he designed was the Hoosac Public Library. He built it as a kind of shrine to his own memory, just as the Pharaohs of ancient Egypt built their pyramids to house their bodies, their souls, and the record of their accomplishments. On the second floor of the building there was to be an Alpheus Winterborn Reading Room. It was to contain, among other things, a long, windy account, written by himself, of his archeological diggings. No one could figure out why he wanted to leave behind a record of his career as an archeologist, since he had never found anything worth mentioning—except for the mysterious treasure that everyone talked about. But he was a strange man. And because he was rich, he could pretty much do what he pleased.

For the last two years of his life, Alpheus Winterborn was all wrapped up in the library he was building. Day after day he went down to watch the men who were working on it. He would pace back and forth with a roll of blueprints in his hand, carping and making suggestions till the workmen were sick of the sight of him. Finally, though, it was finished in the late fall of 1929. And then Alpheus Winterborn did the strangest thing. The library was to have opened on the first of November, but Alpheus Winterborn ordered that the opening be delayed for a week. Why? Because he wanted to live in the library. To live, as he put it, "inside my own creation," for just seven days.

It was certainly a strange request, but since Alpheus Winterborn was putting up the money for the library, everybody had to do what he wanted. So for a solid week, old Alpheus Winterborn lived in the newly finished Hoosac Library. During that time he never went out. The shades and the drapes on all the windows were pulled tight, but people who passed the library that week thought they could catch glimpses of him going to and fro with a lighted candle in his hand. At the end of the week, he came out and told the mayor and the city council that they could have their grand opening at last. Two weeks later, Alpheus Winterborn was dead.

Anthony stood staring at the library and thinking of all the wild stories he had heard about Alpheus T. Winterborn. He wondered if his mysterious treasure really did exist, and if it did—where? Then he snapped out of his trance and started walking again, and as he walked, he whistled a popular tune that was on the radio a lot. He stopped whistling as soon as he opened the front door of the library because, as he very well knew, you were supposed to be quiet in libraries. He looked around for Miss Eells. Where was she? She wasn't at the main desk, so maybe she was in her office. No, she wasn't there, either. Finally he found her in the West Reading Room. She was standing at the top of a stepladder with a long-handled feather duster in her hand. As she swept the duster back and forth across the faded spines of books, clouds of dust filled the room. Anthony started to call to her, but before he could get anything out, he began to sneeze. Miss Eells stopped dusting and turned around.

Miss Eells was a small, birdlike woman with a wild nest of white hair on her head. Everything about Miss Eells was birdlike. Her eyes, behind her gold-rimmed glasses, were small and bright, like the eyes of a bird, and the quick, darting, side-to-side motions of her head were birdlike, too. The bones of her hands were small and delicate, like the bones of a bird. Her voice was quiet and precise, but oddly enough she had a large vocabulary of curse words. She used these words only on special occasions. Anthony especially remembered the time an entire box of Ohio kitchen matches burst into flame in her hand when she was lighting a fire in one of the library fireplaces at Christmastime. He had been the only one in the library with her, and he still remembered how strange it had been to hear her pour forth a stream of profanity in that well-modulated, ladylike voice of hers.

"Well, hello, Anthony! What brings you to the . . . aah . . . the aaaaaAAAAACHOOOO!" Miss Eells sneezed loudly. Anthony sneezed again, too, and then both of them laughed. "I had better open a few windows," she said as she climbed down from the stepladder. "Otherwise we'll both die of the convulsions."

Anthony followed Miss Eells around the room as she opened the tall windows with transoms at the top. To open the transoms she used a long pole with a hook on the end. Anthony liked to watch her do this. Then Miss Eells went to her office and started making tea.

It took her some time. As Anthony had noticed before, Miss Eells had trouble doing some things, in spite of her brisk, businesslike air. While he sat waiting patiently, she knocked the hot plate halfway off its little table when she tried to turn it on. Finally she got the switch to obey her, and the coil of wire began to glow red. As soon as she had the hot plate set straight on the table, she took a step backward and knocked the teakettle off the corner of her desk. With a sigh, she stooped, picked up the kettle, and carried it into her private bathroom to fill it. Anthony heard the kettle drop into the sink a couple of times, and he heard Miss Eells saying something under her breath.

Now the kettle was warming up on the hot plate. Miss Eells opened a small built-in cupboard in the wall behind her desk and took out two cups, two saucers, and the sugar bowl. She tried to hold them all at once, and she just barely managed to get them all to the desk without dropping them. Then she knocked over the sugar bowl and spent several minutes carefully sweeping the spilled sugar off the desk blotter into the little bowl. Some eraser dust and pencil shavings got mixed in with the sugar, but Miss Eells didn't notice.

By now, Miss Eells was looking flustered and a bit disheveled. She sat down and mopped her face with her pocket handkerchief. "Well now, Anthony! And how is the world treating you these days?"

Anthony frowned. "Not so good, Miss Eells. My folks were arguing again last night. It made me feel real bad."

Miss Eells smiled sympathetically. "Money again?"

"Yeah. My mom thinks that we don't have enough money to live on and that we'll all be out in the street if we don't watch out."

Miss Eells had to bite her tongue to keep from saying that his mother was a worrywart, but of course she couldn't say this, not to Anthony, so she just sat and watched the kettle with a discontented look on her face.

"Miss Eells?"

"Yes, Anthony? What is it?"

"Do you think the man that built this library really did hide a treasure somewheres?"

"Oh, *that* old story! You mean you've heard it, too? Well, who knows if it's true? But I'm afraid the only treasure you and I will ever see, Anthony, is the money we make by working for it."

Anthony said nothing. He just looked gloomy. Miss Eells went back to watching the kettle, but then, quite suddenly, she had an idea. Turning to Anthony, she said, "Do you think you'd be happier if you had a job of some kind?"

Anthony brightened up immediately. "Wow! You bet I would! Do you know about a job I could get?"

"No," said Miss Eells. Anthony's face fell, but she added quickly, "However, and be that as it may, I am the librarian here, and now and then I have a little extra money to play with. And too much work besides. Most people think all a librarian has to do is check out books. How would you like to be a page at this library?"

Anthony was mystified. The only pages he'd ever heard of, aside from the pages in a book, were the little boys in fairy tales who came in and blew horns and announced things. They wore funny-looking costumes and had shoes with long, pointed toes. Anthony wondered if that was the sort of thing Miss Eells had in mind.

Miss Eells smiled. She could tell that Anthony didn't have the faintest idea of what a library page was. She had just opened her mouth to tell him when the kettle started making about-to-boil noises. It trembled and rattled and whined, and little wisps of steam came curling out of the spout. Miss Eells got up and opened the cupboard again. She took out a big brown teapot with a gold band around it, and a yellow box of Lapsang Souchong tea. Then she took the kettle off the hot plate and poured a little of the boiling water into the teapot. She swirled it around and dumped it into a potted geranium in the corner. The geranium was dying, and the hot water wasn't going to help it much. As Miss Eells struggled to get the lid off the tea box, she broke a fingernail, but finally she managed to pry it off. Three spoonfuls went into the pot, and in went the boiling water. They waited for the tea to steep; then Anthony held the strainer as Miss Eells poured it out. It smelled smoky and tasted strange, but Anthony didn't mind. He just liked the idea of having tea with Miss Eells. It was a warm, friendly thing to do.

"Now, then," said Miss Eells as she sipped her tea, "where were we? Oh, yes. A library page has all sorts of duties. He has to take books that have been returned to the library and put them back in their proper places. You'll have to know something about the Dewey decimal system, but that's easy enough to learn. Then you'll have to get books for people, and—"

Anthony looked puzzled. "How come they can't go get them themselves?"

Miss Eells grinned and cocked her head to one side. "Anthony, I know this is hard for you to understand, but most people who come into a library don't have the faintest idea of how to find a book. They don't know how to use the card catalog, and they think the Dewey decimal system is something kids learn in arithmetic class. That's where you come in. You look up the book for them and bring it out to the circulation desk. If you happen to be tending the desk at the time, you stamp the book out for them. Some things, like the back issues of magazines, are kept in a locked room in the basement. If someone wanted one, you would have to go downstairs and get it for them. Then there are all sorts of general tasks, like lighting the fire in the West Reading Room fireplace in the wintertime, and tidying and dusting and things of that sort. Which brings me to something that I feel I have to tell you. If you take the job, you start tomorrow, and tomorrow is the twenty-first of March. Do you know what the twenty-first of March is?"

"Groundhog Day?"

Miss Eells glared at Anthony over the top of her glasses. "Groundhog Day indeed! Go to the foot of the class, as my late father used to say. It's the vernal equinox, the first day of spring! It is also the day when I start the spring cleaning of the library. Do you think you're ready for that?"

"Gee, I dunno. What do I have to do?"

"Oh, not much. You just have to help me polish the woodwork and clean the floors and dust the bric-a-brac and clean the windows and . . ." Miss Eells stopped talking and burst out laughing when she saw the horrified expression on Anthony's face. "Oh, Anthony, come *on*! I'm just kidding! I will have a *few* extra chores for you to do, but

I'm not Simon Legree. You can do what you feel like doing. How about it? Are you interested in the job?"

Anthony grinned and stuck out his hand. "Put 'er there, Miss Eells!" he said.

Miss Eells stuck out her hand, too, and as she did so, she knocked over her cup of tea.

"The Reference Room" by John D. MacDonald

Working out of his Florida houseboat, Travis McGee, John D. MacDonald's sometime-detective, has won a permanent place for himself among American tough-guy heroes, and he has earned an enviable reputation for his creator. In his long career, MacDonald (1916–86) wrote other kinds of novels, including Condominium *(1977) and* Barrier Island *(1986), as well as many mysteries, but he is most widely recognized for his Travis McGee series. Its lurid "color" titles begin with* The Deep Blue Good-by *(1964), continue through such works as* One Fearful Yellow Eye *(1966);* The Dreadful Lemon Sky *(1975); and* The Lonely Silver Rain *(1985).*

MacDonald also wrote over five hundred short stories of mystery and science fiction, one of which is "The Reference Room."

All my warning devices, the nameless things that ring bells in the back of your head, that touch your spine gingerly with ice, they were working. I liked no part of it. He wouldn't tell me who had put him on to me. But he was willing to let me set up the meeting. If the warning system was working properly, that meant that he was willing to sacrifice himself in order to get me. That meant a personal angle. If he was a hired boy, he was out to decoy me into position for the kill.

And I didn't like his voice on the phone.

I told him to call back. Though it worried me, there was high pleasure at getting back into action again. Any kind. Maybe it was entirely on the level. I'd had three months of sloth, living on the fact of the tense three weeks in Yugoslavia, and they had paid me in gold. Gold buys happy amounts of U.S. dollars. And La Mariposa on the California coast is a good place to spend said dollars. The call had come from a pay station in L.A. I'd heard the coins ringing down.

I hadn't liked the voice at all.

He called back the next day. By then I had it set up. In case I had to move fast, I got rid of the girl. She made the usual scene. And learned very quickly that I do not like scenes. And left with white stripes on her cheek, a hastily packed bag, money in her purse and a look of loathing. Which bothered me not.

I protected myself as well as I could. He waited in the last booth of the restaurant for half an hour. By the time I showed up I already knew what he looked like, knew that he had come alone, knew that he was unarmed. I sat opposite him. There was a half bottle of Mexican beer in front of him, a glass half full. The booth table was narrow. I had picked it because it was narrow. I sat and looked mildly at him, and knew he could not see the knife in my hand. It is something I learned a long time ago from the French bayonet drill. A quick half-inch of steel, no more, in the solar plexus, renders a man unconscious at once with no fuss, shout or struggle. If too long unattended, he will die.

I knew at once that I had never seen him before. I would have remembered. He looked at me with recognition. Perhaps he had seen a picture. There are not many pictures. I have seen to that.

"Wilson," he said, no question in his voice, as though labeling a specimen. "Or Willing, or Crandall or Schermer or Fox or Verney."

I do not think my face betrayed the shock. I had not known of a living soul who could link some of those names together. And I knew with a certain sour humor that by reciting that string of names he had committed suicide. He watched me without expression. I would hear what he had to say. First. He had the damndest face. Take a big monkey and starve it to death. Then take a death mask and paint it silver. And fill the eye sockets with flat black lusterless paint. I looked at his hand on the glass. I felt that if I reached over and closed my hand over his, closed down hard, the bones would break like stepping on a matchbox. Nothing hard looking about him. A sort of professional look. But watch that type. Always. They usually have something instead of muscles.

"Nice research, Mr. Smith," I said.

"I'm a trained researcher," he said.

"Collecting names?"

"And dates and places. 1932, Berlin. 1934, Vienna. 1938, Munich. 1939, Warsaw. 1941, Portugal and Tokyo. 1942, Moscow and Chungking. 1943, Argentina. Do I have to go on? Your hand is sweaty on that knife handle, Mr. Wilson. It might slip, you know."

My mouth felt stiff. I felt as if my eyes were open too wide. I moved a bit toward the corner of the booth and glanced toward the bar.

"I'm quite alone, Mr. Wilson. And completely unarmed, as the young man who so clumsily bumped into me probably told you."

There is always a deal. I told myself that. There is always something you can do, some kind of a payoff. "What do you want?" I asked, and the voice didn't sound like my own.

"A most interesting life you've had, Mr. Wilson. Always standing in the alley, within earshot, while history was being made, and helping it along, for pay, with gun and knife, with stealth. And you have a most retentive mind, Mr. Wilson. It was a good life, wasn't it?"

"Past tense?" I tried to say it casually. Something was beating big wings in my chest, trying to fly out.

He leaned forward a little bit. I could see both his hands. They were quite still. They looked frail. He smiled for the first time, a bit sadly, yet proudly. "I've come for you," he said. "Now please get up."

It is something that happens to you when you get very drunk. Your consciousness shrinks down to a little hard bright thing in the back of your head. It switches on and off, like a light. When it goes on again, you are in a new place, not knowing how you got there. It would come on and I would be walking beside him, and then blackness again. And then we were in an old car, heading up into the hills. He drove like an old lady. Then more walking, and the ground was rough. And then a stone room with funny lights. It was like a dream when you know you are dreaming. Yet caught helplessly in the dream. Awaiting the time of awakening.

And the stone room burst inward. Implosion. A quick hammering smash from all sides into a blackness . . .

I was not aware of the moment of awakening. I was upright. There was no feeling in my arms or legs or body. I could not turn my head. I could turn my eyes. It was an enormous room. There were long shafts of sunlight from strange high windows. The walls and the floor seemed to have the texture of dull silver. The room had a look of quietness, of academic peace. And it was like no room in all the world. I tried to move and could not.

About forty feet in front of my eyes I saw a row of objects. They were spaced about ten feet apart. They continued down the length of the room, extending out of the range of my vision on either side. They were the general size and shape of telephone booths, though not quite as tall. The bottom half was the porcelained white of kitchen equipment, with horizontal rows of odd dials. The upper half was glass. Through the glass I could see, in the middle, resting in the center of unbroken white, a round object. Each machine seemed identical. I looked hard at the nearest one, the one directly across from me and I saw, with a feeling of alarm that I did not understand, that the round object was a human head. It faced me. An Oriental head, with hard high cheekbones, cropped skull. It reminded me of General Tsu, and of a deal that was made one rainy afternoon in Peiping.

To his left was the head of a woman, an old woman with a deeply lined face. To his right the head of an Indian, grotesquely out of place with single feather, beaded headband, coarse black braids. I could not make out the others beyond them because something obscured my vision, distorting it a bit. At first I thought it was my eyes and then I saw that it was the distorting effect of a pane of glass some eight inches from my eyes.

I have been in bad spots. There has always been a way out. It is necessary to think, to plan carefully, to avoid panic. It was not difficult, strangely enough, to avoid panic. There was a calmness in my mind that made me feel as though I had been drugged. Yet my mind was working clearly.

There was an eternal quietness in the vast room. Peace and silence. Until they came. Three of them. The frail old man with the starved monkey face. He wore odd clothing. Too bright for his age. Carefully draped. And two girls. The girls had thin, earnest, sexless faces. They stared in at me. I saw their lips move as they talked together. I could not hear them. The old man gestured toward me. He seemed to be explaining something. Their heads were on a level above mine. The old man smiled. He looked proud. He nodded at one of the girls and stepped aside. She reached for something below my line of vision with both hands and then she pulled two objects up. They were little silver cups fastened to thin cables. She looked at me intently and, using both hands, held them against her temples.

You walk slowly through all your days. As though each day is a room, filled with the objects of living. And you go from room to room, opening one door, closing the other behind you. Now all the doors of all the rooms were open, and it was like a great roaring freight train running through all the rooms, though all the days of my life, so quickly that I seemed to get only frozen glimpses of the scenes of my life before they were snatched away and thrown behind me by the great speed. It was a terrifying and weakening thing. When the dizziness stopped, I saw that the girl was handing the silver cups to the other girl. I was given one moment of rest and it occurred again, in precisely the same way as before.

Then, in silence, I saw that the old man was talking to the girls. They seemed to be thanking him. Smiles were exchanged. The girls walked away, looking back over their thin shoulders to smile again. I felt as though I had run a long distance and suddenly I became aware that I was not breathing. There was no discomfort, yet I was not breathing.

The old man looked at me. Sadly, proudly. He leaned forward and made some sort of adjustment. The silence was gone. I heard the fading sound of the steps of the two girls. I heard the murmuring sound of a great city. He took a single silver cup. He spoke.

"You will wish to ask questions. Think your question clearly."

He held the cup against his forehead. I formed the question in my mind. I could not speak. —Where am I?—

He spoke. "In the Historical Section of the Social Research Department of the University of Karachi in the year three thousand two hundred and twelve."

—I cannot move!—It was not a question. It was a cry of fear.

"You are well-mounted, Wilson. Your condition is good. All the circuits have been most carefully checked. The technicians say you will last indefinitely. And stay mentally stable."

A fat owlish boy of about sixteen had come up behind the old man. The old man turned and spoke to him in a language I had never heard before.

—Who are you?— The thought was a scream that seemed to echo in my mind, down the dark rooms of all my days.

The old man stepped back a bit. He handed two silver cups to the boy, who took them with obvious eagerness. The boy stood waiting. The old man bent to make the adjustment to shut out the sound of all the world. And just before he did so, he gave me a look that was somehow aggrieved, as though in some odd way I had offended his professional dignity. Beyond him, at the other row of cabinets, I could see four young people in front of the case containing the Indian head, one of them holding objects against her temples, the others waiting, one of them looking over toward us.

"Why," he said, with a tone of indignation, "I am the librarian."

SEVEN

Laughter
in the Library

People aren't supposed to laugh out loud in libraries. Perhaps because the hush of libraries seems inhospitable to levity, or at least to an open expression of it, library humor is not easy to find. Librarians who are celebrated for being deliberately funny are rare, and so are authors who write funny stories about libraries. But there are exceptions: Richard Armour, for example, wrote an entire humorous book about librarians, *The Happy Bookers*, an excerpt from which is included here.

Writers poke fun at library buildings as well as librarians. Obvious targets are the many Carnegie libraries, which form a recognizable family despite their individual variations. Because those libraries have now become such a treasured part of America's architectural heritage, Finley Peter Dunne's irreverent piece "The Carnegie Libraries" has a surprising sharpness to its satire.

Like Richard Armour, Pyke Johnson, Jr., is clearly fond of libraries and librarians, and his light verse reflects it. The shortest selection in our anthology, "From the Librarian," pinpoints in just two lines the major infuriating weakness of the modern computer-based library.

Decades before computers, another humorist, Sam Walter Foss, gently spoofed librarians in a poem, "The Song of the Library Staff," which gives a fascinating profile of the hierarchy in a 1906 American library. Reading this poem, modern librarians may be surprised to see how little some things have changed.

No representative selection of library humor would be complete without excerpts from two writers, Eleanor Estes and Beverly Cleary, whose books for children delight parents as well. The small hero of Estes's *Rufus M.*, struggling to acquire a library card, finally outlasts the "library lady" in a scene that is one of the funniest in library literature. If a reader comes upon these pages in a silent library reading room, he or she will perhaps find it hard *not* to laugh out loud.

"Library" and excerpt from
The Happy Bookers
by Richard Armour

Richard Armour, born in 1906, has combined careers as a distinguished acade-mician, a popular writer of light verse and humorous prose, and a successful author of children's books. Educated at Pomona College and then at Harvard, he became professor of English and then dean at Scripps College and Claremont Graduate School, as well as holding other posts as professor and writer-in-residence. His many books of light verse include Light Armour *(1954);* Punctured Poems *(1966); and* The Spouse in the House *(1975). Every Armour fan has his or her favorites from a long list of humorous prose works, such as* It All Started with Columbus *(1953);* Through Darkest Adolescence *(1963);* Going Around in Academic Circles *(1965);* English Lit Relit *(1969); and* The Academic Bestiary *(1974). Armour once told an interviewer, "Perhaps because I took a Ph.D. in English philology at Harvard, studying ten dead or deadly languages, I am fascinated by words." He is also fascinated by libraries, as shown in the following excerpt from* The Happy Bookers: A Playful History of Librarians and Their World from the Stone Age to the Present *(1976).*

LIBRARY

Here is where people,
One frequently finds,
Lower their voices
And raise their minds.

LIBRARIANS AFTER THE AMERICAN REVOLUTION

After the Revolution, developments important to librarians came thick and fast, instead of thin and slow. For instance the Library of Congress was established in 1800 so that our nation's leaders could read the latest books and see whether they were mentioned in them. It also enabled them to pick up some good quotes they could use in speeches in the House and Senate.

An ingenious help to librarians in the Library of Congress was a book tunnel and endless-chain system that carried books to and from the Congress. There is no evidence that a librarian ever became entangled in the delivery system and wound up, faithfully clutching the book being delivered, on the floor of the House.

Books burn easily, whether they are burned on purpose or by accident, and librarians are therefore always worried about fires. Nor is a book much helped if a stream of water is played upon it by a fire hose. There are those, notably librarians and bibliophiles, who look back wistfully to the days when books were made of stone or baked clay. The only hope for the future would seem to be printing on waterproof asbestos.

The reason for the above reference to fires is that the Library of Congress was burned by the British in 1814, and all the books were destroyed. One historian says the library was "burned under the administration of James Madison." This would suggest that either (1) Madison supervised the burning or (2) Madison and his cabinet were on the roof of the building at the time. Both possibilities are rather unpleasant and must have lost Madison support among librarians.[1]

---

[1]If the second is correct, Madison undoubtedly lost the support of the library, and one wonders how he and the members of his administration escaped to run the country for three more years.

But all librarians should be grateful to another President, the great Millard Fillmore, who in 1851 helped save the Library of Congress in its second destructive fire. Fillmore, who did not own a book until he was nineteen,[2] formed a bucket brigade with the members of his cabinet and managed to subdue the fire. The expressions "Pass the buck" and "The buck stops here" probably go back to this important event in American history, and should really be "Pass the bucket" and "The bucket stops here," immortal words uttered by President Fillmore at the head of the line.

Madison may have had a hand in framing the United States Constitution, but Fillmore should be held in greater affection by librarians. What good does it do to frame the Constitution if there is no wall in the Library of Congress to hang it on?

It should also be noted that the Library of Congress began the practice of printing and distributing catalog cards. Some ingenious librarian thought of turning the words around, and that gave us the card catalog. Librarians are constantly turning through the cards in a card catalog, which is why one of the requirements for a librarian is sturdy fingernails.

Public libraries in the United States received a boost, and so did the tax rate, when state laws permitted local governments to levy taxes to support public libraries. This began in 1849 in New Hampshire, and soon people in Massachusetts and other states were paying for public libraries whether they used them or not. The tax collector now became as much involved with books as the book collector, and the ordinary citizen became a collector's item.

The first big city library was the Boston City Library, which opened in 1854.[3] Many prominent Bostonians made gifts of books, and the Mayor himself made a cash donation.[4] The library grew so rapidly that it was necessary to engage an experienced librarian, Charles Coffin

[2]The first book he purchased was a dictionary, no doubt to help him read books he borrowed from the library. In case you are interested, Fillmore's father owned two books, a Bible and a hymnal.

[3]This was before the jacket blurb, "Banned in Boston," propelled many a book to the best-seller list.

[4]He may have had no books, or none he cared to have the public know he had been reading.

Jewett, who, according to Elmer D. Johnson, "had made a name for himself as librarian of the Smithsonian Library in Washington."[5]

Even with the involuntary help of taxpayers, there would not have been enough money to build all the libraries needed, and pay librarians, but for gifts from wealthy donors. Some, like John Jacob Astor, remembered libraries in their wills, and librarians went around humming the tune, "Thanks for the Memory." But it remained for one man, Andrew Carnegie, to give to libraries on a large scale (apparently weighing the money rather than counting it) and while he was still alive and might conceivably need to look out for himself in his old age. Moreover, and this is hard to believe, he was born in Scotland.

As a youth, Carnegie was very poor. At one time he worked as a bobbin boy in a cotton factory, perhaps bobbin up and down in front of the loom. He earned $1.20 a week, which was even less than a librarian was paid. But he later went into other enterprises, such as working as a telegraph operator, and by the time he was twenty-four had made a fortune from investments in the Woodruff Sleeping Car Company.[6] Subsequently he went into the steel business, and one biographer says of him that "his steel plants grew rapidly." Librarians and others who have benefited from his wealth should be grateful that he discovered this means of producing steel, perhaps while experimenting with seedlings in his garden.

Carnegie began his philanthropy in 1901, when he donated $5,200,000 to the city of New York for the erection of 65 branch libraries.[7] During his lifetime he gave more than $43,000,000 to establish libraries, and

[5]There is a famous Coffin family in New England. Perhaps Jewett liked to remind the members of his staff, half-jokingly, "You are working under a Coffin." It made them squirm.

[6]"Let sleeping cars lie," said those who counseled Carnegie against taking such a risk. As any Reference Librarian could tell you, you have only to look up "Let" in the index of Bartlett's *Familiar Quotations* and you will learn that the original of this statement, referring to dogs instead of cars, can be found in Chapter 39 of *David Copperfield*.

[7]The idea of branch libraries obviously appealed to Carnegie after his success with steel plants. Since his wealth in 1901 was estimated at around a half billion dollars, he probably carried five million or so around in his pocket as small change.

this was only the beginning. I do not know the cause of his death, in 1919, but suspect he wore himself out trying, unsuccessfully, to give away all his money. However the Carnegie Corporation picked up the ball, or the wallet, and is still trying. Carnegie libraries now number nearly 3000 in the English-speaking world, and some librarians are said to have amended their prayers slightly, saying "Carnegie be thy name."

By the latter part of the nineteenth century, if not earlier, women greatly outnumbered men as librarians. Indeed the librarian as a woman became a Stereotype, which has nothing to do with typography. However men continued to occupy certain positions, notably those that were (1) at the upper administrative level, whether or not actually on the level, (2) higher salaried, and (3) with shorter working hours. Increasingly, women objected to what they considered discrimination, but they were so well schooled (in Library School) that they raised their voices only outside the library, where readers would not be distracted.

With growing specialization, special libraries have developed in the past century which provide unusual opportunities for librarians who are qualified. A few examples of such libraries are the New York State Lunatic Asylum Library, the Sing Sing Prison Library, the International Ladies' Garment Workers' Union Library, and the National Livestock and Meat Board Library.[8]

There are also newspaper libraries, the most interesting part of which is the morgue, which is not quite so gruesome as its name would suggest. Indeed it contains much more than information for future obituaries, and a librarian can work there alone, well into the night, without getting goosepimples.

Even more important, associations of librarians began in 1876[9] with the founding of the American Library Association. It sets standards, issues publications, and, most important, holds conventions where librarians can temporarily forget their troubles by hearing of the worse troubles of others. The A.L.A., as it is known by librarians, was followed

[8]Any applicant for a library position at Sing Sing must be able to carry a tune as well as a book. As for the Meat Board Library, it would be interesting to attend a board meating.

[9]This is not to say that librarians did not associate with one another previously.

by such organizations as the Special Libraries Association and the Osteopathic Library Association.[10]

A few years later, in 1887, the first library school in the United States was organized at Columbia University. Eventually it became necessary for anyone going into library work to obtain a graduate degree in Library Science. What was really needed, of course, was a degree in Library Science Fiction, and this may come yet.

One of the courses in Library School is The History of the Book, in which it is hoped this book, which could not have been written had the author not read books written by authors who had read more books than the author of this book, will be required reading.

"The Carnegie Libraries"
by Finley Peter Dunne

"Mr. Dooley," an Irish saloon keeper who holds forth about Carnegie libraries in the following short prose piece, has been called "the most popular literary comedian and crackerbox philosopher between Artemus Ward and Will Rogers." His creator, Finley Peter Dunne (1867–1936), was a Chicago journalist who wrote more than seven hundred dialect essays. Many were republished in a series of books in which Dooley talks with a character called Mr. Hennessey, created to represent someone with the prejudices and passions of an ignorant day laborer.

[10]Whether there is also an Extra-Special Libraries Association I do not know, nor whether there is an Association of Library Associations.

Mr. Dooley in Peace and in War *(1898) was the first of this series;* Mr. Dooley on Making a Will *(1919) was the last.*

"Has Andhrew Carnaygie given ye a libry yet?" asked Mr. Dooley. "Not that I know iv," said Mr. Hennessy.

"He will," said Mr. Dooley. "Ye'll not escape him. Befure he dies he hopes to crowd a libry on ivry man, woman, an' child in th' counthry. He's given thim to cities, towns, villages, an' whistlin' stations. They're tearin' down gas-houses an' poor-houses to put up libries. Befure another year, ivry house in Pittsburg that ain't a blast-furnace will be a Carnaygie libry. In some places all th' buildin's is libries. If ye write him f'r an autygraft he sinds ye a libry. No beggar is iver turned impty-handed fr'm th' dure. Th' pan-handler knocks an' asts f'r a glass iv milk an' a roll. 'No, sir,' says Andhrew Carnaygie. 'I will not pauperize this on-worthy man. Nawthin' is worse f'r a beggar-man thin to make a pauper iv him. Yet it shall not be said iv me that I give nawthin' to th' poor. Saunders, give him a libry, an' if he still insists on a roll tell him to roll th' libry. F'r I'm humorous as well as wise,' he says."

"Does he give th' books that go with it?" asked Mr. Hennessy.

"Books?" said Mr. Dooley. "What ar-re ye talkin' about? D'ye know what a libry is? I suppose ye think it's a place where a man can go, haul down wan iv his fav'rite authors fr'm th' shelf, an' take a nap in it. That's not a Carnaygie libry. A Carnaygie libry is a large, brown-stone, impenethrible buildin' with th' name iv th' maker blown on th' dure. Libry, fr'm th' Greek wurruds, libus, a book, an' ary, sildom— sildom a book. A Carnaygie libry is archytechoor, not lithrachoor. Lith-rachoor will be riprisinted. Th' most cillybrated dead authors will be honored be havin' their names painted on th' wall in distinguished comp'ny, as thus: Andhrew Carnaygie, Shakespeare; Andhrew Carnaygie, Byron; Andhrew Carnaygie, Bobby Burns; Andhrew Carnaygie, an' so on. Ivry author is guaranteed a place next to pure readin' matther like a bakin'-powdher advertisment, so that whin a man comes along that niver heerd iv Shakespeare he'll know he was somebody, because there he is on th' wall. That's th' dead authors. Th' live authors will stand outside an' wish they were dead.

"He's havin' gr-reat spoort with it. I r-read his speech th' other day, whin he laid th' corner-stone iv th' libry at Pianola, Ioway. Th' entire popylation iv this lithry cinter gathered to see an' hear him. There was th' postmaster an' his wife, th' blacksmith an' his fam'ly, the station agent, mine host iv th' Farmers' Exchange, an' some sthray live stock. 'Ladies an' gintlemen,' says he. 'Modesty compels me to say nawthin' on this occasion, but I am not to be bulldozed,' he says. 'I can't tell ye how much pleasure I take in disthributin' monymints to th' humble name around which has gathered so manny hon'rable associations with mesilf. I have been a very busy little man all me life, but I like hard wurruk, an' givin' away me money is th' hardest wurruk I iver did. It fairly makes me teeth ache to part with it. But there's wan consolation. I cheer mesilf with th' thought that no matther how much money I give it don't do anny particular person anny good. Th' worst thing ye can do fr anny man is to do him good. I pass by th' organ-grinder on th' corner with a savage glare. I bate th' monkey on th' head whin he comes up smilin' to me window, an' hurl him down on his impecyoon-yous owner. None iv me money goes into th' little tin cup. I cud kick a hospital, an' I lave Wall Sthreet to look afther th' widow an' th' orphan. Th' submerged tenth, thim that can't get hold iv a good chunk iv th' goods, I wud cut off fr'm th' rest iv th' wurruld an' prevint fr'm bearin' th' haughty name iv papa or th' still lovelier name iv ma. So far I've got on'y half me wish in this matther.

" 'I don't want poverty an' crime to go on. I intind to stop it. But how? It's been holdin' its own fr cinchries. Some iv th' gr-reatest iv former minds has undertook to prevint it an' has failed. They didn't know how. Modesty wud prevint me agin fr'm sayin' that I know how, but that's nayether here nor there. I do. Th' way to abolish poverty an' bust crime is to put up a brown-stone buildin' in ivry town in th' counthry with me name over it. That's th' way. I suppose th' raison it wasn't thried befure was that no man iver had such a name. 'Tis thrue me efforts is not apprecyated ivrywhere. I offer a city a libry, an' oftentimes it replies an' asks me fr something to pay off th' school debt. I rayceive degraded pettyshuns fr'm so-called proud methropolises fr a gas-house in place iv a libry. I pass thim by with scorn. All I ask iv a city in rayturn fr a fifty-thousan'-dollar libry is that it shall raise wan millyon dollars to maintain th' buildin' an' keep me name shiny, an' if it won't do that much fr lithrachoor, th' divvle take it, it's onworthy iv th' name iv an American city. What ivry community needs is taxes an' lithrachoor. I give thim both. Three cheers fr a libry an' a bonded debt! Lithrachoor, taxation, an' Andhrew Carnaygie, wan an' insiprable, now an' foriver! They'se nawthin' so good as a good book. It's betther thin food; it's better thin money. I have made money an' books, an' I like me books betther thin me money. Others don't, but I do. With these few wurruds I will con-clude. Modesty wud prevint me fr'm sayin' more, but I have to catch a thrain, an' cannot go on. I stake ye to this libry, which ye will have as soon as ye raise th' money to keep it goin'. Stock it with useful readin', an' some day ye're otherwise pauper an' criminal childher will come to know me name whin I am gone an' there's no wan left to tell it thim.'

"Whin th' historyan comes to write th' histhry iv th' West he'll say: 'Pianola, Ioway, was a prosperous town till th' failure iv th' corn crop in nineteen hundherd an' wan, an' th' Carnaygie libry in nineteen hundherd an' two. Th' govermint ast fr thirty dollars to pave Main Sthreet with wooden blocks, but th' gr-reat philanthropist was firm, an' the libry was sawed off on th' town. Th' public schools, th' wur-rukhouse, th' wather wurruks, an' th' other penal instichoochions was at wanst closed, an' th' people begun to wurruk to support th' libry. In five years th' popylation had deserted th' town to escape taxation, an' now, as Mr. Carnaygie promised, poverty an' crime has been abol-ished in th' place, th' janitor iv th' buildin' bein' honest an' well paid.'

"Isn't it good fr lithrachoor, says ye? Sure, I think not, Hinnissy. Libries niver encouraged lithrachoor anny more thin tombstones en-courage livin'. No wan iver wrote annythin' because he was tol' that a hundherd years fr'm now his books might be taken down fr'm a shelf in a granite sepulcher an' some wan wud write 'Good' or 'This man is crazy' in th' margin. What lithrachoor needs is fillin' food. If Andhrew wud put a kitchen in th' libries an' build some bunks or even swing a few hammocks where livin' authors cud crawl in at night an' sleep while waitin' fr this enlightened nation to wake up an' discover th' Shake-speares now on th' turf, he wud be givin' a rale boost to lithrachoor. With th' smoke curlin' fr'm th' chimbley, an' hundherds iv potes settin' aroun' a table loaded down with pancakes an' talkin' pothry an' prize-fightin', with hundherds iv other potes stacked up nately in th' sleepin'-rooms an' snorin' in wan gran' chorus, with their wives holdin' down good-payin' jobs as libraryans or cooks, an' their happy little childher playin' through th' marble corrydors, Andhrew Carnaygie wud not have lived in vain. Maybe that's th' on'y way he knows how to live. I don't believe in libries. They pauperize lithrachoor. I'm fr helpin' th' boys that's now on th' job. I know a pote in Halsted Sthreet that wanst wrote a pome beginnin', 'All th' wealth iv Ind,' that he sold to a magazine fr two dollars, payable on publycation. Lithrachoor don't need advancin'. What it needs is advances fr th' lithrachoors. Ye can't shake down posterity fr th' price.

"All th' same, I like Andhrew Carnaygie. Him an' me ar-re agreed on that point. I like him because he ain't shamed to give publicly. Ye don't find him puttin' on false whiskers an' turnin' up his coat-collar whin he goes out to be benivolent. No, sir. Ivry time he dhrops a dollar it makes a noise like a waither fallin' down-stairs with a tray iv dishes. He's givin' th' way we'd all like to give. I niver put annything in th' poor-box, but I wud if Father Kelly wud rig up like wan iv thim slot-machines, so that whin I stuck in a nickel me name wud appear over th' altar in red letthers. But whin I put a dollar in th' plate I get back about two yards an' hurl it so hard that th' good man turns around to see who done it. Do good be stealth, says I, but see that th' burglar-alarm is set. Anny benivolent money I hand out I want to talk about me. Him that giveth to th' poor, they say, lindeth to th' Lord; but in these days we look fr quick returns on our invistmints. I like Andhrew Carnaygie, an', as he says, he puts his whole soul into th' wurruk."

"What's he mane be that?" asked Mr. Hennessy.

"He manes," said Mr. Dooley, "that he's gin'rous. Ivry time he gives a libry he gives himsilf away in a speech."

"Please Do Not Feed the Librarians," "Take a Librarian to Lunch," and "From the Librarian" by Pyke Johnson, Jr.

Pyke Johnson, Jr., was born in Denver, Colorado, and raised in Washington, DC. He holds degrees from the University of Maryland and George Washington University. After serving in the Navy in World War II, he worked in book publishing and retired as Managing Editor at Doubleday after more than thirty years with that publishing house. He now lives in Old Greenwich, Connecticut, and is a columnist for Greenwich Time. *He has been on the Board of Directors of the Perrot Memorial Library in Old Greenwich for over twenty-five years. His poetry has appeared in magazines like* Harper's *and* Saturday Review *as well as in anthologies.*

PLEASE DO NOT FEED THE LIBRARIANS

> Do not feed Librarians.
> They have a special diet.
> Taboo for them are crunchy foods,
> Which tend to mar the quiet.
> We know you want to pamper them,

But, please, we ask, don't do it.
They simply can't chew noisy food;
Instead, they must eschew it.

So do not toss them peanuts—
Or lobsters—in the shell.
Raw carrots are off-limits
And celery stalks, as well.
Hard candy is forbidden
Or gum that they can pop.
And as for any kind of snack,
Don't pass it out, please. Stop.

And when it comes to liquids,
We ask that you think twice.
Don't give them drinks to suck with straws,
And never ones with ice.
And since the cans are drippy,
Don't ever stand them beers.
Do not feed Librarians.
(But do feed Volunteers.)

TAKE A LIBRARIAN TO LUNCH

Take a Librarian to lunch.
You know that she deserves it.
Ascertain her favorite food,
Then find a place that serves it.

Seek out, too, an ambience
That you are sure will suit her:
Some place that bans all little kids
And where there's no computer.

Serve her with her favorite drink:
Champagne? Or something diet?
And make it clear that, at this meal,
There are no rules on quiet.

But do leave promptly when you've shared
Good talk and drink and food.
Librarians must be back when due,
*And may not be renewed.**

FROM THE LIBRARIAN

Annual report to the heads of the town:
Circulation is up. Computer is down.

*N.B. Nothing here should be construed as precluding the taking of a male Librarian to lunch.

"The Interest Gauge"
by Edmund Lester Pearson

*Edmund Lester Pearson (1880–1937) was both a New York librarian and an author of books and essays. Some of his stories, like "The Interest Gauge," focus on libraries (*The Old Librarian's Almanack, *1909;* The Librarian at Play, *1911). Others investigate murders and oddities in the past, like* Studies in Murder *(1924);* Queer Books *(1928);* Instigation of the Devil *(1930);* The Trial of Lizzie Borden *(1937). Norman D. Stevens, an authority on library humor and himself an accomplished library humorist, has stated that "Pearson's work, especially in his column 'The Librarian' that appeared weekly for almost 15 years, is one of the few solid bodies of library humor by a single*

American librarian." Pearson *edited the* Bulletin of the New York Public Library *from 1914 to 1927.*

"**W**e are thinking of calling them 'interest gauges,' " said the agent, "but perhaps you can suggest a better name."

I took one of the little instruments and examined it. Hardly over an inch long, with its glass tube and scale, it resembled a tiny thermometer. The figures and letters were so small that I could not make them out, though they became clear enough through a reading-glass.

"Interest gauges," I remarked, "sounds like something connected with banks. I should think you could find a better name. Who invented them?"

The agent looked important.

"They were invented," he explained, "by Professor Dufunnie, the great psychologist. They are a practical application of psychology. Let me show you how they are used. Allow me—I will take this book— the 'Letters of Junius,' and attach the interest gauge. Here in the back, you see, the gauge is invisible to the reader. You will notice now, if you look through the glass, that the gauge marks zero. No one is reading the book, we have not even opened it, and the human mind is not acting upon the book. If you will take it into your hand, and look down at the gauge through the glass, you will see probably some little agitation of the liquid within the tube. You do, do you not? I thought so. That is because you are probably already familiar, to some extent, with the 'Letters of Junius' and the recollections that they arouse in your mind are exerting themselves upon the fluid. Now, if you will oblige me, open the book and read attentively for a few moments."

I did so, and then handed it back to the agent.

"Look," he cried, "as soon as you cease reading, the fluid sinks back to zero. But the little aluminum arrow remains at the highest point which the fluid reached—that is, the highest point of interest which you felt in the book. Ah, yes—40 degrees—a faint interest. You will notice that the degree-points are marked at intervals with descriptive phrases—40 is 'faint interest,' 30 is 'indifference,' 20 is 'would not keep you awake after 9 P.M.,' and so on."

The thing was very fascinating.

"It is astounding," I said, "for that is exactly my feeling towards Junius, and yet I tried to get more interested in him than usual."

The agent laughed.

"You can't fool the gauges," he said. "You can't do it, even when you know one is attached to your book. I need not say that it is absolutely correct when the reader is not aware that there is a gauge upon his book. You must see the value of these to a librarian. Let me show you how incorruptible they are. Have you something there in which you have absolutely no interest—some book or article that is dry as dust?"

I looked about.

"This pretty nearly fills the bill," I said, and I handed him a copy of a library magazine with an article by Dr. Oscar Gustafsen on "How to Make the Workingman Read the Greek Tragedies."

The agent attached an interest gauge, and told me to read Dr. Gustafsen's article, and to try as hard as I could to become interested; to pretend, if I could not feel, the greatest excitement over it. I did so, and strained every muscle in my brain, so to speak, to find something in it to interest or attract me. It was no use—the fluid gave a few convulsive wabbles, but at the end the little arrow had not even reached 10; or "Bored to Death."

Then the agent took a copy of "The Doctor's Dilemma," and putting an interest gauge on the volume, asked me to read a few pages, and to remain as indifferent as possible. I read it calmly enough, but the liquid in the tube mounted slow and sure, and when we examined the arrow it pointed to 80.

"Try it on this," said the agent, handing me Conan Doyle's "Round the Fire Stories."

I put on an interest gauge and read the tale of "The Lost Special." The arrow shot up to 98 before I had half finished the yarn.

"The highest that the gauge will record, you see, is 140, though we guarantee them to stand a pressure of 165. They are not often subjected to anything like that. The average novel or short story to-day does not put them under a very severe strain. The greatest risk we run is from authors reading their own books. We had an especially dangerous case the other day, during some tests in the laboratory. We had a young author reading the proofs of his first book, and we put on a high pressure scale, capable of recording up to 210, and even then we took off the gauge only just in time. It had reached the limit, and there were danger signs."

"What are danger signs?" I asked.

"The liquid begins to boil," he said, "and then you have to look out for trouble. Now how many of these will you take? I can let you have a trial dozen for $4, or two dozen for $7.50. Two dozen? Thank you. You attach them in the back of the book—so fashion—or if the book is bound with a loose back, then you put them down here. There is no danger of their being seen, in either case. Here is our card, we shall be very pleased to fill any further orders. Thank you. Good day!"

As soon as he had gone I left my office, and went out into the public part of the library. I had started for the reading room, when I heard my name called. It was Professor Frugles, the well-known scientific historian. He is giving his course of lectures on "The Constitutional Development of Schleswig-Holstein" and I had attended one or two of them. They had already been going on for two months—and although he lectured four times a week, he hadn't progressed beyond the intro- duction and preliminaries. Both of the lectures I had heard were long wrangles in which the professor devoted his energies to proving that some writer on this subject (a German whose name I did not catch) was wholly untrustworthy. I was told by some of the most patient listeners that so far no single thing about Schleswig-Holstein itself had been mentioned, and that it did not appear to be in sight. The course consisted merely of Frugles' opinions of the authorities.

Now the professor came slowly toward me, wiping his face with a large red handkerchief and waving his cane.

"Got any new books?" he shouted.

I told him we had a few, and took him back into one of the workrooms. He examined them.

"This will do; I'll look this over," and he picked up something in German.

I offered him another—in English, and, as I thought, rather interesting in appearance.

"Pah!" he ejaculated, as if I had put some nauseous thing under his nose, "popular!"

He exploded this last word, which was his most violent term of condemnation, and ran through the rest of the books.

"Well, I'll take this into the reading room and look it through," and he started with the German book.

I prevailed upon him to take the other as well, and he consented, with a grunt. He did not notice that I had slipped an interest gauge into both of them.

After a bit, I followed him into the reading room. He was in a far corner, hard at work. Mrs. Cornelia Crumpet was engaged in conversation with Miss Bixby, the reference librarian, when I came in.

"Oh, here's Mr. Edwards!" she exclaimed. "Why, what a library you have! I can't find anything at all about the Flemish Renaissance and I do not know what I shall do, for I have to read a paper on it tomorrow afternoon before the Twenty-Minute Culture Club. Miss Bixby was just saying she would get me something. Now what would you advise? There is nothing at all in the books I looked at."

"Perhaps you looked in the wrong books," I suggested, observing that she had a copy of "Thelma" under her arm.

"Oh, Mr. Edwards, how ridiculous of you! I'm carrying this book home for the housemaid; she's sick in bed, and the cook said she was homesick and threatened to leave. So I said I would get her something to read to occupy her mind. This is fearful trash, I suppose, but I thought it would keep her contented until she got well. But I do wish you would tell me what to consult about the Flemish Renaissance."

"Mrs. Crumpet," I said, "Miss Bixby knows more about that subject in one minute than I do all day, and I advise you to let her prescribe."

Mrs. Crumpet agreed to wait, while Miss Bixby went for the books.

"Where's that copy of 'Thelma'? I put it down here. Oh, you have it, Mr. Edwards! Well, you had better let me take it; I'm sure it is too frivolous for you serious-minded librarians to read. I'll sit here and look it over until she comes back with those books."

She took it, interest gauge and all, and sat down.

Miss Larkin came into the room just then and asked me to come over to the children's department.

"I want to show you," she said, "what an interest these children take in serious reading and non-fiction. It is most encouraging."

When we arrived at the children's room she had two or three small persons arranged about the desks.

"Now, Willie," she said, "which do you like best, story-books or nature books?"

Willie answered with great promptness: "Nacher books."

The others all confessed to an extraordinary fondness for "hist'ry" or "biography" or "nacher."

I asked Miss Larkin's leave to try a little experiment, and then explained to her the workings of the interest gauges. We chose Willie as a subject for our investigations, and gave him a copy of one of his beloved "nacher" books, with a gauge attached. Five minutes' reading by Willie sent the arrow up to 30, but the same time on "The Crimson Sweater" sent it up to 110.

"He seems to like Mr. Barbour better than the Rev. Dr. Fakir, Miss Larkin—I'm afraid that his enthusiasm for 'nacher' is in accordance with what he knows will please you. Why don't you use your influence with him to lead him toward truthfulness? It's a better quality, even, than a fondness for nonfiction."

As I went back I met Professor Frugles.

"Let me have this, as soon as it is ready to go out," he said, brandishing the German work; "this other—trifling, sir, trifling!"

And away he went.

But I noticed that the German book had only sent the gauge up to 40, while the "trifling" work, which had caused him to express so much contempt, had registered 75.

At the issue desk was Mrs. Crumpet, having her books charged. As there were no gauges on the books about the Flemish Renaissance, I had no data to go on, except the fact that although she declared she had "skimmed through" them all and found them "very helpful," she had not, so far, cut any of the pages. I did not mention this to her, as she might have retorted that we ought to have cut them ourselves. Which was quite true.

But while she talked with Miss Carey, I managed to extract the gauge from "Thelma." At least, I took away the fragments of it. The arrow had gone up to 140, and trying to get still higher the little glass tube had been smashed to bits.

"Song of the Library Staff" by Sam Walter Foss

Sam Walter Foss (1858–1911), wrote several humorous poems about libraries, one of which is reprinted here. Born and raised in New Hampshire, after graduation from Brown University Foss became an editor and journalist, eventually writing for various papers in Massachusetts. His best-known poem is "The House by the Side of the Road." Many of his poems were collected in Back Country Poems *(1892) and* Songs of the Average Man *(1907).*

(Read at the annual meeting of the American Library Association,
Narragansett Pier, July 6, 1906.)

Oh, joy! to see the Library staff perpetually jogging,
And to see the Cataloguer in the act of cataloguing.
("Catalogs—Log-books for cattle," was the school-boy's definition,—
A statement not to be despised for insight and precision.)
Every language spoke at Babel in the books that pile her table,
Every theme discussed since Adam—song or story, fact or fable!
And she sweetly takes all knowledge for her province, as did Bacon,
All the fruit that's dropped and mellowed since the Knowledge tree was shaken,
All the ologies of the colleges, all the isms of the schools,
All the unassorted knowledges she assorts by Cutter's rules;

Or tags upon each author in large labels that are gluey
Their place in Thought's great Pantheon in decimals of Dewey;
Oh, joy! to see the Library staff perpetually jogging,
And to see the Cataloguer in the act of cataloguing.

See the Reference Librarian and the joys that appertain to her;
Who shall estimate the contents and the area of the brain to her?
See the people seeking wisdom from the four winds ever blown to her,
For they know there is no knowledge known to mortals but is known to her;
See this flower of perfect knowledge, blooming like a lush geranium,
All converging rays of wisdom focussed just beneath her cranium:
She is stuffed with erudition as you'd stuff a leather cushion,
And wisdom is her specialty——it's marketing her mission.
How they throng to her, all empty, grovelling in their insufficience;
How they come from her, o'erflooded by the sea of her omniscience!
And they know she knows she knows things,——while she drips her
    learned theses
The percentage of illiteracy perceptibly decreases.
Ah, they know she knows she knows things, and her look is education;
And to look at her is culture, and to know her is salvation.

See the Children's gay Librarian! Oh, what boisterous joys are hers
As she sits upon her whirl-stool, throned amid her worshippers,
Guiding youngsters seeking wisdom through Thought's misty morning
    light;
Separating Tom and Billy as they clinch in deadly fight;
Giving lavatory treatment to the little hand that smears
With the soil of crusted strata laid by immemorial years;
Teaching critical acumen to the youngsters munching candy,
To whom books are all two classes——they are either "bum" or
    "dandy";
Dealing out to Ruths and Susies, or to Toms and Dicks and Harrys,
Books on Indians or Elsie, great big bears, or little fairies;
For the Children's gay Librarian passes out with equal pains
Books on Indians or Elsie, satisfying hungering brains;
Dealing Indians or Elsie, each according to his need,
Satisfying long, long longings for an intellectual feed.

See the gleeful Desk Attendants ever dealing while they can
The un-inspected canned beef of the intellect of man;
Dealing out the brains of sages and the poet's heart divine
(Receiving for said poet's heart ofttimes a two-cent fine);
Serene amid the tumult for new novels manifold,——
For new novels out this afternoon but thirty minutes old;——
Calm and cool amid the tumult see the Desk Attendant stand
With contentment on her features and a date-stamp in her hand.
As they feed beasts at the circus to appease their hungering rage,
So she throws this man a poet and she drops that man a sage;
And her wild beasts growl in fury when they do not like her
    meat,——
When the sage is tough and fibrous and the bard not over-sweet;
And some retire in frenzy, lashing wrathfully about,
When the intellectual spare-rib that they most affect is out.
But she feeds 'em, and she leads 'em, and beguiles 'em with sweet
    guile,
And wounds 'em with her two-cent fine and heals 'em with her
    smile.

Oh, the gleesome Desk Attendant—who shall estimate her glee?
Get some mightier bard to sing it—'tis a theme too big for me!

Now, my Muse, prepare for business. Plume your wings for loftier
    flight
Through the circumambient ether to a superlunar height,
Then adown the empyrean from the heights where thou hast risen
Sing, O Muse! the Head Librarian and the joy that's her'n or his'n.
See him, see her, his or her head weighted with the lore of time,
Trying to expend a dollar when he only has a dime;
Tailoring appropriations—and how deftly he succeeds,
Fitting his poor thousand dollars to his million dollar needs.
How the glad book agents cheer him—and he cannot wish them
    fewer
With "their greatest work yet published since the dawn of literature."
And he knows another agent, champing restive to begin
With another work still greater, will immediately come in.
So perfection on perfection follows more and more sublime

And the line keeps on forever down the avenues of time—
So they travel on forever, stretching far beyond our ken,
Lifting demijohns of wisdom to the thirsty lips of men.

See him 'mid his myriad volumes listening to the gladsome din
Of the loud vociferant public that no book is ever "in";
And he hears the fierce taxpayer evermore lift up the shout
That the book he needs forever is the book forever "out."
How they rage, the numerous sinners, when he tries to please the
saints;
When he tries to please the sinners, hear the numerous saints' com-
plaints;
And some want a Bowdlered Hemans and an expurgated Watts;
Some are shocked beyond expression at the sight of naked thoughts,
And he smooths their fur the right way, and he placates him or her,
And those who come to snarl and scratch remain behind to purr.
Oh, the gamesome glad Librarian gushing with his gurgling glee!—
Here I hand my resignation,—'tis a theme too big for me.

Excerpt from *Beezus and Ramona* by Beverly Cleary

Beverly Cleary's warm and funny books about Ramona Quimby, as well as her other books for children, are now contemporary classics that appear in over ten countries in a variety of languages. Born in 1916, Ms. Cleary has won many awards, such as the 1984 John Newbery Medal for Dear Mr. Henshaw *and the 1975 Laura Ingalls Wilder Award from the American Library Association.*

Ramona and Her Father and Ramona Quimby, Age 8 *were named 1978 and 1982 Newbery Honor Books, respectively.*

Ms. Cleary has said that she spent much of her childhood either with books or on her way to and from the public library. She later became a librarian and specialized in library work with children. Her affectionate familiarity with libraries is evident in the following selection from Beezus and Ramona.

The best thing to do with Ramona, Beezus had learned, was to think up something to take the place of whatever her mind was fixed upon. And what could take the place of *The Littlest Steam Shovel*? Another book, of course, a better book, and the place to find it was certainly the library.

"Ramona, how would you like me to take you to the library to find a different book?" Beezus asked. She really enjoyed taking Ramona places, which, of course, was quite different from wanting to go someplace herself and having Ramona insist on tagging along.

For a moment Ramona was undecided. Plainly she was torn between wanting *The Littlest Steam Shovel* read aloud again and the pleasure of going out with Beezus. "O.K.," she agreed at last.

"Get your sweater while I tell Mother," said Beezus.

"Clunk! Clunk!" shouted Ramona happily.

When Ramona appeared with her sweater Beezus stared at her in dismay. Oh, no, she thought. She can't wear those to the library.

On her head Ramona wore a circle of cardboard with two long paper ears attached. The insides of the ears were colored with pink crayon, Ramona's work at nursery school. "I'm the Easter bunny," announced Ramona.

"Mother," wailed Beezus. "You aren't going to let her wear those awful ears to the library!"

"Why, I don't see why not." Mother sounded surprised that Beezus should object to Ramona's ears.

"They look so silly. Whoever heard of an Easter bunny in September?" Beezus complained, as Ramona hopped up and down to make her ears flop. I just hope we don't meet anybody we know, Beezus thought, as they started out the front door.

But the girls had no sooner left the house when they saw Mrs. Wisser, a lady who lived in the next block, coming toward them with a friend. It was too late to turn back. Mrs. Wisser had seen them and was waving.

"Why, hello there, Beatrice," Mrs. Wisser said, when they met. "I see you have a dear little bunny with you today."

"Uh . . . yes." Beezus didn't know what else to say.

Ramona obligingly hopped up and down to make her ears flop.

Mrs. Wisser said to her friend, as if Beezus and Ramona couldn't hear, "Isn't she adorable?"

Both children knew whom Mrs. Wisser was talking about. If she had been talking about Beezus, she would have said something quite different. Such a nice girl, probably. A sweet child, perhaps. Adorable, never.

"Just look at those eyes," said Mrs. Wisser.

Ramona beamed. She knew whose eyes they were talking about. Beezus knew too, but she didn't care. Mother said blue eyes were just as pretty as brown.

Mrs. Wisser leaned over to Ramona. "What color are your eyes, sweetheart?" she asked.

"Brown and white," said Ramona promptly.

"Brown and white eyes!" exclaimed the friend. "Isn't that cunning?"

Beezus had thought it was cunning the first time she heard Ramona say it, about a year ago. Since then she had given up trying to explain to Ramona that she wasn't supposed to say she had brown and white eyes, because Ramona always answered, "My eyes *are* brown and white," and Beezus had to admit that, in a way, they were.

"And what is the little bunny's name?" asked Mrs. Wisser's friend.

"My name is Ramona Geraldine Quimby," answered Ramona, and then added generously, "My sister's name is Beezus."

"Beezus!" exclaimed the lady. "What an odd name. Is it French?"

"Oh, no," said Beezus. Wishing, as she so often did, that she had a more common nickname, like Betty or Patsy, she explained as quickly as she could how she happened to be called Beezus.

Ramona did not like to lose the attention of her audience. She hitched up the leg of her overalls and raised her knee. "See my scab?" she said proudly. "I fell down and hurt my knee and it bled and bled."

"Ramona!" Beezus was horrified. "You aren't supposed to show people your scabs."

"Why?" asked Ramona. That was one of the most exasperating things about Ramona. She never seemed to understand what she was not supposed to do.

"It's a very nice scab," said Mrs. Wisser's friend, but she did not look as if she really thought it was nice.

"Well, we must be going," said Mrs. Wisser.

"Good-bye, Mrs. Wisser," said Beezus politely, and hoped that if they met anyone else they knew she could somehow manage to hide Ramona behind a bush.

"Bye-bye, Ramona," said Mrs. Wisser.

"Good-bye," said Ramona, and Beezus knew that she felt that a girl who was four years old was too grown-up to say bye-bye.

Except for holding Ramona's hand crossing streets, Beezus lingered behind her the rest of the way to the library. She hoped that all the people who stooped and smiled at Ramona would not think they were together. When they reached the Glenwood Branch Library, she said, "Ramona, wouldn't you like me to carry your ears for you now?"

"No," said Ramona flatly.

Inside the library, Beezus hurried Ramona into the boys' and girls' section and seated her on a little chair in front of the picture books. "See, Ramona," she whispered, "here's a book about a duck. Wouldn't you like that?"

"No," said Ramona in a loud voice.

Beezus' face turned red with embarrassment when everyone in the library looked at Ramona's ears and smiled. "Sh-h," she whispered, as Miss Greever, the grownups' librarian, frowned in their direction. "You're supposed to speak quietly in the library."

Beezus selected another book. "Look, Ramona. Here's a funny story about a kitten that falls into the goldfish bowl. Wouldn't you like that?"

"No," said Ramona in a loud whisper. "I want to find my own book."

If only Miss Evans, the children's librarian, were there! She would know how to select a book for Ramona. Beezus noticed Miss Greever glance disapprovingly in their direction while the other grownups watched Ramona and smiled. "All right, you can look," Beezus agreed, to keep Ramona quiet. "I'll go find a book for myself."

When Beezus had selected her book, she returned to the picture-book section, where she found Ramona sitting on the bench with both arms clasped around a big flat book. "I found my book," she said, and held it up for Beezus to see. On the cover was a picture of a steam shovel with its jaws full of rocks. The title was *Big Steve the Steam Shovel*.

"Oh, Ramona," whispered Beezus in dismay. "You don't want that book."

"I do, too," insisted Ramona, forgetting to whisper. "You told me I could pick out my own book."

Under the disapproving stare of Miss Greever, Beezus gave up. Ramona was right. Beezus looked with distaste at the big orange-colored book in its stout library binding. At least it would be due in two weeks, but Beezus did not feel very happy at the thought of two more weeks of steam shovels. And it just went to show how Ramona always got her own way.

Beezus took her book and Ramona's to Miss Greever's desk.

"Is this where you pay for the books?" asked Ramona.

"We don't have to pay for the books," said Beezus.

"Are you going to charge them?" Ramona asked.

Beezus pulled her library card out of her sweater pocket. "I show this card to the lady and she lets us keep the books for two weeks. A library isn't like a store, where you buy things."

Ramona looked as if she did not understand. "I want a card," she said.

"You have to be able to write your own name before you can have a library card," Beezus explained.

"I can write my name," said Ramona.

"Oh, Ramona," said Beezus, "you can't either."

"Perhaps she really does know how to write her name," said Miss Greever, as she took a card out of her desk. Beezus watched doubtfully while Miss Greever asked Ramona her name and age. Then the librarian asked Ramona what her father's occupation was. When Ramona didn't understand, she asked, "What kind of work does your father do?"

"He mows the lawn," said Ramona promptly.

The librarian laughed. "I mean, how does he earn his living?"

Somehow Beezus did not like to have Miss Greever laugh at her little sister. After all, how could Ramona be expected to know what Father did? "He works for the Pacific Gas and Electric Company," Beezus told the librarian.

Miss Greever wrote this down on the card and shoved it across the desk to Ramona. "Write your name on this line," she directed.

Nothing daunted, Ramona grasped the pencil in her fist and began to write. She bore down so hard that the tip snapped off the lead, but she wrote on. When she laid down the pencil, Beezus picked up the card to see what she had written. The line on the card was filled with

"That's my name," said Ramona proudly.

"That's just scribbling," Beezus told her.

"It is too my name," insisted Ramona, while Miss Greever quietly dropped the card into the waste-basket. "I've watched you write and I know how."

"Here, Ramona, you can hold my card." Beezus tried to be comforting. "You can pretend it's yours."

Ramona brightened at this, and Miss Greever checked out the books on Beezus' card. As soon as they got home, Ramona demanded, "Read my new book to me."

And so Beezus began. "Big Steve was a steam shovel. He was the biggest steam shovel in the whole city . . ." When she finished the book she had to admit she liked Big Steve better than Scoopy. His only sound effects were tooting and growling. He tooted and growled in big letters on every page. Big Steve did not shed tears or want to be a pile driver. He worked hard at being a steam shovel, and by the end of the book Beezus had learned a lot about steam shovels. Unfortunately, she did not want to learn about steam shovels. Oh, well, she guessed she could stand two weeks of Big Steve.

"Read it again," said Ramona enthusiastically. "I like Big Steve. He's better than Scoopy."

"How would you like me to show you how to really write your name?" Beezus asked, hoping to divert Ramona from steam shovels.

"O.K.," agreed Ramona.

Beezus found pencil and paper and wrote *Ramona* in large, careful letters across the top of the paper.

Ramona studied it critically. "I don't like it," she said at last.

"But that's the way your name is spelled," Beezus explained.

"You didn't make dots and lines," said Ramona. Seizing the pencil, she wrote,

"But, Ramona, you don't understand." Beezus took the pencil and wrote her own name on the paper. "You've seen me write *Beatrice*, which has an *i* and a *t* in it. See, like that. You don't have an *i* or a *t* in your name, because it isn't spelled that way."

Ramona looked skeptical. She grabbed the pencil again and wrote with a flourish.

"That's my name, because I like it," she announced. "I like to make dots and lines." Lying flat on her stomach on the floor she proceeded to fill the paper with *i*'s and *t*'s.

"But, Ramona, nobody's name is spelled with just . . ." Beezus stopped. What was the use? Trying to explain spelling and writing to Ramona was too complicated. Everything became difficult when Ramona was around, even an easy thing like taking a book out of the library.

Well, if Ramona was happy thinking her name was spelled with *i*'s and *t*'s, she could go ahead and think it.

The next two weeks were fairly peaceful. Mother and Father soon tired of tooting and growling and, like Beezus, they looked forward to the day *Big Steve* was due at the library. Father even tried to hide the book behind the radio, but Ramona soon found it. Beezus was happy that one part of her plan had worked—Ramona had forgotten *The Littlest Steam Shovel* now that she had a better book. On Ramona's second trip to the library, perhaps Miss Evans could find a book that would make her forget steam shovels entirely.

As for Ramona, she was perfectly happy. She had three people to read aloud a book she liked, and she spent much of her time covering sheets of paper with *i*'s and *t*'s. Sometimes she wrote in pencil, sometimes she wrote in crayon, and once she wrote in ink until her mother caught her at it.

Finally, to the relief of the rest of the family, the day came when *Big Steve* had to be returned. "Come on, Ramona," said Beezus. "It's time to go to the library for another book."

"I have a book," said Ramona, who was lying on her stomach writing her version of her name on a piece of paper with purple crayon.

"No, it belongs to the library," Beezus explained, glad that for once Ramona couldn't possibly get her own way.

"It's my book," said Ramona, crossing several *t*'s with a flourish.

"Beezus is right, dear," observed Mother. "Run along and get *Big Steve*."

Ramona looked sulky, but she went into the bedroom. In a few minutes she appeared with *Big Steve* in her hand and a satisfied expression on her face. "It's my book," she announced. "I wrote my name in it."

Mother looked alarmed. "What do you mean, Ramona? Let me see." She took the book and opened it. Every page in the book was covered with enormous purple *i*'s and *t*'s in Ramona's very best handwriting.

"Mother!" cried Beezus. "Look what she's done! And in crayon so it won't erase."

"Ramona Quimby," said Mother. "You're a very naughty girl! Why did you do a thing like that?"

"It's my book," said Ramona stubbornly. "I like it."

"Mother, what am I going to do?" Beezus demanded. "It's checked out on my card and I'm responsible. They won't let me take any more books out of the library, and I won't have anything to read, and it will all be Ramona's fault. She's always spoiling my fun and it isn't fair!" Beezus didn't know what she would do without her library card. She couldn't get along without library books. She just couldn't, that was all.

"I do *not* spoil your fun," stormed Ramona. "You have all the fun. I can't read and it isn't fair." Ramona's words ended in a howl as she buried her face in her mother's skirt.

"I couldn't read when I was your age and I didn't have someone to read to me all the time, so it is too fair," argued Beezus. "You always get your own way, because you're the youngest."

"I do not!" shouted Ramona. "And you don't read all the time. You're mean!"

"I am *not* mean," Beezus shouted back.

"Children!" cried Mother. "Stop it, both of you! Ramona, you were a very naughty girl!" A loud sniff came from Ramona. "And, Beezus," her mother continued, "the library won't take your card away from you. If you'll get my purse I'll give you some money to pay for the damage to the book. Take Ramona along with you, explain what happened, and the librarian will tell you how much to pay."

This made Beezus feel better. Ramona sulked all the way to the library, but when they got there Beezus was pleased to see that Miss Evans, the children's librarian, was sitting behind the desk. Miss Evans was the kind of librarian who would understand about little sisters.

"Hello, Beatrice," said Miss Evans. "Is this your little sister I've heard so much about?"

Beezus wondered what Miss Evans had heard about Ramona. "Yes, this is Ramona," she said and went on hesitantly, "and, Miss Evans, she—"

"I'm a bad girl," interrupted Ramona, smiling winningly at the librarian.

"Oh, you are?" said Miss Evans. "What did you do?"

"I wrote in a book," said Ramona, not the least ashamed. "I wrote in purple crayon and it will never, never erase. Never, never, never."

Embarrassed, Beezus handed Miss Evans *Big Steve the Steam Shovel*. "Mother gave me the money to pay for the damage," she explained.

The librarian turned the pages of the book.

"Well, you didn't miss a page, did you?" she finally said to Ramona.

"No," said Ramona, pleased with herself. "And it will never, never—"

"I'm awfully sorry," interrupted Beezus. "After this I'll try to keep our library books where she can't reach them."

Miss Evans consulted a file of little cards in a drawer. "Since every page in the book was damaged and the library can no longer use it, I'll have to ask you to pay for the whole book. I'm sorry, but this is the rule. It will cost two dollars and fifty cents."

Two dollars and fifty cents! What a lot of things that would have bought, Beezus reflected, as she pulled three folded dollar bills out of her pocket and handed them to the librarian. Miss Evans put the money in a drawer and gave Beezus fifty cents in change.

Then Miss Evans took a rubber stamp and stamped something inside the book. By twisting her head around, Beezus could see that the word was *Discarded*. "There!" Miss Evans said, pushing the book across the desk. "You have paid for it, so now it's yours."

Beezus stared at the librarian. "You mean . . . to keep?"

"That's right," answered Miss Evans.

Ramona grabbed the book. "It's mine. I told you it was mine!" Then she turned to Beezus and said triumphantly, "You said people didn't buy books at the library but you just bought one!"

"Buying a book and paying for damage are not the same thing," Miss Evans pointed out to Ramona.

Beezus could see that Ramona didn't care. The book was hers, wasn't it? It was paid for and she could keep it. And that's not fair, thought Beezus. Ramona shouldn't get her own way when she had been naughty.

"But, Miss Evans," protested Beezus, "if she spoils a book she shouldn't get to keep it. Now every time she finds a book she likes she will . . ." Beezus did not go on. She knew very well what Ramona would do, but she wasn't going to say it out loud in front of her.

"I see what you mean." Miss Evans looked thoughtful. "Give me the book, Ramona," she said.

Doubtfully Ramona handed her the book.

"Ramona, do you have a library card?" Miss Evans asked.

Ramona shook her head.

"Then Beezus must have taken the book out on her card," said Miss Evans. "So the book belongs to Beezus."

Why, of course! Why hadn't she thought of that before? It was her book, not Ramona's. "Oh, thank you," said Beezus gratefully, as Miss Evans handed the book to her. She could do anything she wanted with it.

For once Ramona didn't know what to say. She scowled and looked as if she were building up to a tantrum. "You've got to read it to me," she said at last.

"Not unless I feel like it," said Beezus. "After all, it's my book," she couldn't resist adding.

"That's not fair!" Ramona looked as if she were about to howl.

"It is too fair," said Beezus calmly. "And if you have a tantrum I won't read to you at all."

Suddenly, as if she had decided Beezus meant what she said, Ramona stopped scowling. "O.K.," she said cheerfully.

Beezus watched her carefully for a minute. Yes, she really was being agreeable, thought Beezus with a great feeling of relief. And now that she did not have to read *Big Steve* unless she wanted to, Beezus felt she would not mind reading it once in a while. "Come on, Ramona," she said. "Maybe I'll have time to read to you before Father comes home."

"O.K.," said Ramona happily, as she took Beezus' hand.

Miss Evans smiled at the girls as they started to leave. "Good luck, Beatrice," she said.

Excerpt from *Rufus M.* by Eleanor Estes

Like Beverly Cleary, another much-loved writer of children's books, Eleanor Estes (1906–88), was trained as a librarian. Her earliest books chronicled the lives of the Moffat family, beginning with The Moffats *(1941) and including* Rufus M. *(1943), from which the following excerpt is taken. These stories are fiction-alizations of the author's memories of her own growing up in the town of West Haven, Connecticut, the fictional "Cranbury." Also residents of Cranbury are members of the Pye family, who appeared in the Newbery award–winning* Ginger Pye *(1951). Estes's other popular books include* Miranda the Great *(1967);* The Lost Umbrella of Kim Chu *(1978); and* The Curious Adventures of Jimmy McGee *(1987).*

Rufus M. That's the way Rufus wrote his name on his heavy arith-metic paper and on his blue-lined spelling paper. Rufus M. went on one side of the paper. His age, seven, went on the other. Rufus had not learned to write his name in school, though that is one place for learning to write. He had not learned to write his name at home either, though that is another place for learning to write. The place where he had learned to write his name was the library, long ago before he ever went to school at all. This is the way it happened.

One day when Rufus had been riding his scooter up and down the street, being the motorman, the conductor, the passengers, the steam, and the whistle of a locomotive, he came home and found Joey, Jane, and Sylvie, all reading in the front yard. Joey and Jane were sitting on the steps of the porch and Sylvie was sprawled in the hammock, a book in one hand, a chocolate-covered peppermint in the other.

Rufus stood with one bare foot on his scooter and one on the grass and watched them. Sylvie read the fastest. This was natural since she was the oldest. But Joey turned the pages almost as fast and Jane went lickety-cut on the good parts. They were all reading books and he couldn't even read yet. These books they were reading were library books. The library must be open today. It wasn't open every day, just a few days a week.

"I want to go to the library," said Rufus. "And get a book," he added.

"We all just came home from there," said Jane, while Joey and Sylvie merely went on reading as though Rufus had said nothing. "Besides," she added, "why do you want a book anyway? You can't even read yet."

This was true and it made Rufus mad. He liked to do everything that they did. He even liked to sew if they were sewing. He never thought whether sewing was for girls only or not. When he saw Jane sewing, he asked Mama to let him sew too. So Mama tied a thread to the head of a pin and Rufus poked that in and out of a piece of goods. That's the way he sewed. It looked like what Jane was doing and Rufus was convinced that he was sewing too, though he could not see much sense in it.

Now here were the other Moffats, all with books from the library. And there were three more books stacked up on the porch that looked like big people's books without pictures. They were for Mama no doubt. This meant that he was the only one here who did not have a book.

"I want a book from the library," said Rufus. A flick of the page as Sylvie turned it over was all the answer he got. It seemed to Rufus as though even Catherine-the-cat gave him a scornful glance because he could not read yet and did not have a book.

Rufus turned his scooter around and went out of the yard. Just wait! Read? Why, soon he'd read as fast if not faster than they did. Reading looked easy. It was just flipping pages. Who couldn't do that?

Rufus thought that it was not hard to get a book out of the library. All you did was go in, look for a book that you liked, give it to the lady to punch, and come home with it. He knew where the library was for he had often gone there with Jane and some of the others. While Jane went off to the shelves to find a book, he and Joey played the game of Find the Duke in the Palmer Cox Brownie books. This was a game that the two boys had made up. They would turn the pages of one of the Brownie books, any of them, and try to be the first to spot the duke, the brownie in the tall hat. The library lady thought that this was a noisy game, and said she wished they would not play it there. Rufus hoped to bring a Brownie book home now.

"Toot-toot!" he sang to clear the way. Straight down Elm Street was the way to the library; the same way that led to Sunday School, and Rufus knew it well. He liked sidewalks that were white the best for he could go the fastest on these.

"Toot-toot!" Rufus hurried down the street. When he arrived at the library, he hid his scooter in the pine trees that grew under the windows beside the steps. Christmas trees, Rufus called them. The ground was covered with brown pine needles and they were soft to walk upon. Rufus always went into the library the same way. He climbed the stairs, encircled the light on the granite arm of the steps, and marched into the library.

Rufus stepped carefully on the strips of rubber matting that led to the desk. This matting looked like dirty licorice. But it wasn't licorice. He knew because once when Sylvie had brought him here when he was scarcely more than three he had tasted a torn corner of it. It was not good to eat.

The library lady was sitting at the desk playing with some cards. Rufus stepped off the matting. The cool, shiny floor felt good to his bare feet. He went over to the shelves and luckily did find one of the big Palmer Cox Brownie books there. It would be fun to play the game of Find the Duke at home. Until now he had played it only in the library. Maybe Jane or Joey would play it with him right now. He laughed out loud at the thought.

"Sh-sh-sh, quiet," said the lady at the desk.

Rufus clapped his chubby fist over his mouth. Goodness! He had forgotten where he was. Do not laugh or talk out loud in the library. He knew these rules. Well, he didn't want to stay here any longer today anyway. He wanted to read at home with the others. He took the book to the lady to punch.

She didn't punch it though. She took it and she put it on the table behind her and then she started to play cards again.

"That's my book," said Rufus.

"Do you have a card?" the lady asked.

Rufus felt in his pockets. Sometimes he carried around an old playing card or two. Today he didn't have one.

"No," he said.

"You'll have to have a card to get a book."

"I'll go and get one," said Rufus.

The lady put down her cards. "I mean a library card," she explained kindly. "It looks to me as though you are too little to have a library card. Do you have one?"

"No," said Rufus. "I'd like to though."

"I'm afraid you're too little," said the lady. "You have to write your name to get one. Can you do that?"

Rufus nodded his head confidently. Writing. Lines up and down. He'd seen that done. And the letters that Mama had tied in bundles in the closet under the stairs were covered with writing. Of course he could write.

"Well, let's see your hands," said the lady.

Rufus obligingly showed this lady his hands, but she did not like the look of them. She cringed and clasped her head as though the sight hurt her.

"Oh," she gasped. "You'll just have to go home and wash them before we can even think about joining the library and borrowing books."

This was a complication upon which Rufus had not reckoned. However, all it meant was a slight delay. He'd wash his hands and then he'd get the book. He turned and went out of the library, found his scooter safe among the Christmas trees, and pushed it home. He surprised Mama by asking to have his hands washed. When this was done, he mounted his scooter again and returned all the long way to the library. It was not just a little trip to the library. It was a long one. A long one and a hot one on a day like this. But he didn't notice that. All he was bent on was getting his book and taking it home and reading with the others on the front porch. They were all still there, brushing flies away and reading.

Again Rufus hid his scooter in the pine trees, encircled the light, and went in.

"Hello," he said.

"Well," said the lady. "How are they now?"

Rufus had forgotten he had had to wash his hands. He thought she was referring to the other Moffats. "Fine," he said.

"Let me see them," she said, and she held up her hands.

Oh! His hands! Well, they were all right, thought Rufus, for Mama had just washed them. He showed them to the lady. There was a silence while she studied them. Then she shook her head. She still did not like them.

"Ts, ts, ts!" she said. "They'll have to be cleaner than that."

Rufus looked at his hands. Supposing he went all the way home and washed them again, she still might not like them. However, if that is what she wanted, he would have to do that before he could get the Brownie book . . . and he started for the door.

"Well now, let's see what we can do," said the lady. "I know what," she said. "It's against the rules but perhaps we can wash them in here." And she led Rufus into a little room that smelled of paste where lots of new books and old books were stacked up. In one corner was a little round sink and Rufus washed his hands again. Then they returned to the desk. The lady got a chair and put a newspaper on it. She made Rufus stand on this because he was not big enough to write at the desk otherwise.

Then the lady put a piece of paper covered with a lot of printing in front of Rufus, dipped a pen in the ink well and gave it to him.

"All right," she said. "Here's your application. Write your name here."

All the writing Rufus had ever done before had been on big pieces of brown wrapping paper with lots of room on them. Rufus had often covered those great sheets of paper with his own kind of writing at home. Lines up and down.

But on this paper there wasn't much space. It was already covered with writing. However, there was a tiny little empty space and that was where Rufus must write his name, the lady said. So, little space or not, Rufus confidently grasped the pen with his left hand and dug it into the paper. He was not accustomed to pens, having always worked with pencils until now, and he made a great many holes and blots and scratches.

"Gracious," said the lady. "Don't bear down so hard! And why don't you hold it in your right hand?" she asked, moving the pen back into his right hand.

Rufus started again scraping his lines up and down and all over the page, this time using his right hand. Wherever there was an empty space he wrote. He even wrote over some of the print for good measure. Then he waited for the lady, who had gone off to get a book for some man, to come back and look.

"Oh," she said as she settled herself in her swivel chair, "is that the way you write? Well . . . it's nice, but what does it say?"

"Says Rufus Moffat. My name."

Apparently these lines up and down did not spell Rufus Moffat to this lady. She shook her head.

"It's nice," she repeated. "Very nice. But nobody but you knows what it says. You have to learn to write your name better than that before you can join the library."

Rufus was silent. He had come to the library all by himself, gone back home to wash his hands, and come back because he wanted to take books home and read them the way the others did. He had worked hard. He did not like to think he might have to go home without a book.

The library lady looked at him a moment and then she said quickly before he could get himself all the way off the big chair, "Maybe you can *print* your name."

Rufus looked at her hopefully. He thought he could write better than he could print, for his writing certainly looked to him exactly like all grown people's writing. Still he'd try to print if that was what she wanted.

The lady printed some letters on the top of a piece of paper. "There," she said. "That's your name. Copy it ten times and then we'll try it on another application."

Rufus worked hard. He worked so hard the knuckles showed white on his brown fist. He worked for a long, long time, now with his right hand and now with his left. Sometimes a boy or a girl came in, looked over his shoulder and watched, but he paid no attention. From time to time the lady studied his work and she said, "That's fine. That's fine." At last she said, "Well, maybe now we can try." And she gave him another application.

All Rufus could get, with his large generous letters, in that tiny little space where he was supposed to print his name, was R-U-F. The other letters he scattered here and there on the card. The lady did not like this either. She gave him still another blank. Rufus tried to print smaller and this time he got RUFUS in the space, and also he crowded an M at the end. Since he was doing so well now the lady herself printed the *offat* part of Moffat on the next line.

"This will have to do," she said. "Now take this home and ask your mother to sign it on the other side. Bring it back on Thursday and you'll get your card."

Rufus's face was shiny and streaked with dirt where he had rubbed it. He never knew there was all this work to getting a book. The other Moffats just came in and got books. Well, maybe they had had to do this once too.

Rufus held his hard-earned application in one hand and steered his scooter with the other. When he reached home Joey, Jane and Sylvie were not around any longer. Mama signed his card for him, saying, "My! So you've learned how to write!"

"Print," corrected Rufus.

Mama kissed Rufus and he went back out. The lady had said to come back on Thursday, but he wanted a book today. When the other Moffats came home, he'd be sitting on the top step of the porch, reading. That would surprise them. He smiled to himself as he made his way to the library for the third time.

Once his application blew away. Fortunately it landed in a thistle bush and did not get very torn. The rest of the way Rufus clutched it carefully. He climbed the granite steps to the library again only to find that the big round dark brown doors were closed. Rufus tried to open them but he couldn't. He knocked at the door, even kicked it with his foot, but there was no answer. He pounded on the door but nobody came.

A big boy strode past with his newspapers. "Hey, kid," he said to Rufus. "Library's closed!" And off he went, whistling.

Rufus looked after him. The fellow said the library was closed. How could it have closed so fast? He had been here such a little while ago. The lady must still be here. He did want his Brownie book. If only he could see in, he might see the lady and get his book. The windows were high up but they had very wide sills. Rufus was a wonderful climber. He could shinny up trees and poles faster than anybody on the block. Faster than Joey. Now, helping himself up by means of one of the pine trees that grew close to the building, and by sticking his toes in the ivy and rough places in the bricks, he scrambled up the wall. He hoisted himself up on one of the sills and sat there. He peered in. It was dark inside, for the shades had been drawn almost all the way down.

"Library lady!" he called, and he knocked on the windowpane. There was no answer. He put his hands on each side of his face to shield his eyes, and he looked in for a long, long time. He could not believe that she had left. Rufus was resolved to get a book. He had lost track of the number of times he had been back and forth from home to the library, and the library home. Maybe the lady was in the cellar. He climbed down, stubbing his big toe on the bricks as he did so. He stooped down beside one of the low dirt-spattered cellar windows. He couldn't see in. He lay flat on the ground, wiped one spot clean on the window, picked up a few pieces of coal from the sill and put them in his pocket for Mama.

"Hey, lady," he called.

He gave the cellar window a little push. It wasn't locked so he opened it a little and looked in. All he could see was a high pile of coal reaching up to this window. Of course he didn't put any of that coal in his pocket for that would be stealing.

"Hey, lady," he yelled again. His voice echoed in the cellar but the library lady did not answer. He called out, "Hey, lady," every few seconds, but all that answered him was an echo. He pushed the window open a little wider. All of a sudden it swung wide open and Rufus slid in, right on top of the coal pile, and crash, clatter, bang! He slid to the bottom, making a great racket.

A little light shone through the dusty windows, but on the whole it was very dark and spooky down here and Rufus really wished that he was back on the outside looking in. However, since he was in the library, why not go upstairs quick, get the Brownie book, and go home? The window had banged shut, but he thought he could climb up the coal pile, pull the window up, and get out. He certainly hoped he could anyway. Supposing he couldn't and he had to stay in this cellar! Well, that he would not think about. He looked around in the dusky light and saw a staircase across the cellar. Luckily his application was still good. It was torn and dirty but it still had his name on it, RUFUS M., and that was the important part. He'd leave this on the desk in exchange for the Brownie book.

Rufus cautiously made his way over to the steps but he stopped halfway across the cellar. Somebody had opened the door at the top of the stairs. He couldn't see who it was, but he did see the light reflected and that's how he knew that somebody had opened the door. It must be the lady. He was just going to say, "Hey, lady," when he thought, "Gee, maybe it isn't the lady. Maybe it's a spooky thing."

Then the light went away, the door was closed, and Rufus was left in the dark again. He didn't like it down here. He started to go back to the coal pile to get out of this place. Then he felt of his application. What a lot of work he had done to get a book and now that he was this near to getting one, should he give up? No. Anyway, if it was the lady up there, he knew her and she knew him and neither one of them was scared of the other. And Mama always said there's no such thing as a spooky thing.

So Rufus bravely made his way again to the stairs. He tiptoed up them. The door at the head was not closed tightly. He pushed it open and found himself right in the library. But goodness! There in the little sink room right opposite him was the library lady!

Rufus stared at her in silence. The library lady was eating. Rufus had never seen her do anything before but play cards, punch books, and carry great piles of them around. Now she was eating. Mama said not to stare at anybody while they were eating. Still Rufus didn't know the library lady ate, so it was hard for him not to look at her.

She had a little gas stove in there. She could cook there. She was reading a book at the same time that she was eating. Sylvie could do that too. This lady did not see him.

"Hey, lady," said Rufus.

The librarian jumped up out of her seat. "Was that you in the cellar? I thought I heard somebody. Goodness, young man! I thought you had gone home long ago."

Rufus didn't say anything. He just stood there. He had gone home and he had come back lots of times. He had the whole thing in his mind; the coming and going, and going and coming, and sliding down the coal pile, but he did not know where to begin, how to tell it.

"Didn't you know the library is closed now?" she demanded, coming across the floor with firm steps.

Rufus remained silent. No, he hadn't known it. The fellow had told him but he hadn't believed him. Now he could see for himself that the library was closed so the library lady could eat. If the lady would let him take his book, he'd go home and stay there. He'd play the game of Find the Duke with Jane. He hopefully held out his card with his name on it.

"Here this is," he said.

But the lady acted as though she didn't even see it. She led Rufus over to the door.

"All right now," she said. "Out with you!" But just as she opened the door the sound of water boiling over on the stove struck their ears, and back she raced to her little room.

"Gracious!" she exclaimed. "What a day!"

Before the door could close on him, Rufus followed her in and sat down on the edge of a chair. The lady thought he had gone and started to sip her tea. Rufus watched her quietly, waiting for her to finish.

After a while the lady brushed the crumbs off her lap. And then she washed her hands and the dishes in the little sink where Rufus had washed his hands. In a library a lady could eat and could wash. Maybe she slept here too. Maybe she lived here.

"Do you live here?" Rufus asked her.

"Mercy on us!" exclaimed the lady. "Where'd you come from? Didn't I send you home? No, I don't live here and neither do you. Come now, out with you, young man. I mean it." The lady called all boys "young man" and all girls "Susie." She came out of the little room and she opened the big brown door again. "There," she said. "Come back on Thursday."

Rufus's eyes filled up with tears.

"Here's this," he said again, holding up his application in a last desperate attempt. But the lady shook her head. Rufus went slowly down the steps, felt around in the bushes for his scooter, and with drooping spirits he mounted it. Then for the second time that day, the library lady changed her mind.

"Oh, well," she said, "come back here, young man. I'm not supposed to do business when the library's closed, but I see we'll have to make an exception."

So Rufus rubbed his sooty hands over his face, hid his scooter in the bushes again, climbed the granite steps and, without circling the light, he went back in and gave the lady his application.

The lady took it gingerly. "My, it's dirty," she said. "You really ought to sign another one."

"And go home with it?" asked Rufus. He really didn't believe this was possible. He wiped his hot face on his sleeve and looked up at the lady in exhaustion. What he was thinking was: All right. If he had to sign another one, all right. But would she just please stay open until he got back?

However, this was not necessary. The lady said, "Well now, I'll try to clean this old one up. But remember, young man, always have everything clean—your hands, your book, everything, when you come to the library."

Rufus nodded solemnly. "My feet too," he assured her.

Then the lady made Rufus wash his hands again. They really were very bad this time, for he had been in a coal pile, and now at last she gave Rufus the book he wanted—one of the Palmer Cox Brownie books. This one was "The Brownies in the Philippines."

And Rufus went home.

When he reached home, he showed Mama his book. She smiled at him, and gave his cheek a pat. She thought it was fine that he had gone to the library and joined all by himself and taken out a book. And she thought it was fine when Rufus sat down at the kitchen table, was busy and quiet for a long, long time, and then showed her what he had done.

He had printed RUFUS M. That was what he had done. And that's the way he learned to sign his name. And that's the way he always did sign his name for a long, long time.

But, of course, that was before he ever went to school at all, when the Moffats still lived in the old house, the yellow house on New Dollar Street; before this country had gone into the war; and before Mr. Abbot, the curate, started leaving his overshoes on the Moffats' front porch.

EIGHT

Reading-Room
Reveries

Who hasn't been stirred to a reverie in a library reading room? It is an appealing place to let one's odd thoughts wander. Unless a reader is really engrossed in a riveting book, the quiet, bookish atmosphere of the reading room, broken only by the soft rustle of turning pages, easily leads to a dreamy state of mind. (With some people, it soon leads to sleep!) Pausing from the book, looking toward the window or across the table or around the room, almost dozing, one can begin to imagine the gentlest, or wildest, or strangest things. No wonder so many writers have reported that they have written their manuscripts at reading-room tables.

In this section, we include a sampling of just such reading-room reveries, some inspired by a writer's glimpses of other readers, some by a writer's musings on the nature of the library itself. Robert Pinsky's poem suggests something of the peculiar power that reading brings. Marsden Hartley, in "Daily Library Visitor," observes an older man, probably once a sailor, then a farmer, for whom the library is a final gift. Dannye Romine Powell's playful poem "In the Periodical Room" goes beyond recording and valuing the presence of another library patron. She invites us to join the speaker of the poem, a reader perhaps bored with her book, who is cheerfully inventing a past for the middle-aged woman at the next table. In "Now Adam," the writer's imagination works on a plaster statue, a reproduction she has borrowed from the public library. (Modern libraries lend many things besides books.)

Like Hartley and Powell, Randall Jarrell fantasizes about a nearby reader, a sleepy young girl. She is a sturdy student with straight brown bangs, braids, and glasses, but Jarrell sees more. Louis Jenkins also lets his mind carry him far from the reading-room table. The reader whom Howard Nemerov describes is a scholar, a man of dedication, determination, and even daring. What does the scholar find in his deep journey? What has he lost?

Novelist Steven Millhauser's excursion into the dream world of the library is very different from all of these poems. It is a high fantasy in prose, a long riff on the idea of a dream library. Nancy Willard is also interested in magic, in flying through space and time on the wings of words. A very special librarian once took her seriously enough to guide her to just the right kind of books. Ms. Willard learned—at least in part through her library books—that "there was also an order of life that, like the angel's, was not bound by the laws of the physical universe. And I came to believe that there were two kinds of people in the world, those who believed in tables and those who believed in angels."

In the solid, matter-of-fact world of the public library, it is possible, as these writers so marvelously demonstrate, to believe in both.

"Library Scene" by Robert Pinsky

In a time when poets have an increasingly difficult time finding an audience, Robert Pinsky continues to attract readers who relish his intelligence, grace, fluidity of verse, and clarity—all virtues to be found in the following poem, "Library Scene," from Sadness and Happiness (1975). *Pinsky's other collections of poetry include* An Explanation of America (1979); History of My Heart (1984); *and* The Want Bone (1990).

A teacher and critic, Pinsky has been since 1980 a professor of English at University of California (Berkeley); since 1978, he has served as poetry editor of The New Republic. *His critical work* The Situation of Poetry: Contemporary Poetry and Its Traditions *(1976) is now a classic in its field. A collection of his reviews and essays,* Poetry and the World, *appeared in 1988.*

TO P.M.S.

Under the ceiling of metal stamped like plaster
And below the ceiling fan, in the brown lustre

Someone is reading, in the sleepy room
Alert, her damp cheek balanced on one palm,

With knuckles loosely holding back the pages
Or fingers waiting lightly at their edges.

Her eyes are like the eyes of someone attending
To a fragile work, familiar and demanding—

Some work of delicate surfaces or threads.
Someone is reading the way a rare child reads,

A kind of changeling reading for love of reading,
For love and for the course of something leading

Her child's intelligent soul through its inflection:
A force, a kind of loving work or action.

Someone is reading in a deepening room
Where something happens, something that will come

To happen again, happening as many times
As she is reading in as many rooms.

What happens outside that calm like water braiding
Over green stones? The ones of little reading

Or who never read for love, are many places.
They are in the house of power, and many houses

Reading as they do, doing what they do.
Or it happens that they come, at times, to you

Because you are somehow someone that they need:
They come to you and you tell them how you read.

"Daily Library Visitor"
by Marsden Hartley

Although Marsden Hartley (1877–1943) is best known as a modern painter,
especially for studies of his native Maine landscape, he practiced poetry as well.
Gail Scott, who published an edition of his essays, On Art *(1982), and his*
Collected Poems 1904–1943 *(1987), states that "he took his writing—both*
poetry and essays—as seriously as his painting." He even divided his working
day between the two arts, "writing in the morning and painting in the afternoon
when the light suited his needs."

  Hartley's poetry and essays appeared in many leading periodicals, The Dial,
The Little Review, *and others. Three volumes of poetry appeared during his*
lifetime: Twenty-five Poems *(1925);* Androscoggin *(1940); and* Sea Burial
(1941).

> *I seem to hear winches and peaveys*
> *and capstans as he walks,*
> *the great rumblings of a quiet man put*
> *to good use—*

he sits him down——reads nothing in particular
but looks like a monument of fine conduct
as he does it——
his field has been ploughed——he knows this
better than anyone else how many rocks he
took out of it
and how many worms came up for the robins
he has seen clouds of frozen breath rise
from oxen nostrils
and heard often the click of iron shoe
against broken rifts of granite,
and perhaps the impertinent laughter
of herring gulls above his blueberry fields
the laughter is not respectable which steals——
once it was anchor chains probably, then it
was ploughs,
now it is just fixing things up around the
house,
now it is the quiet look of a mystic in love
with a simple theme,
for the beautiful mask is utterly unruffled——
and the huge hands seem to say, we have earned
a little respite now, and can afford to hold
a book.

"In the Periodical Room" and "Now Adam" by Dannye Romine Powell

Dannye Romine Powell was born in Miami, Florida, in 1941. "I fell in love with public libraries in the children's room of the Miami Public Library, where you could stand at the window and watch boats sail Biscayne Bay," she reports. She is Book Review Editor and a feature writer for The Charlotte Observer *in Charlotte, North Carolina. Her poems have recently appeared in* Shenandoah *and* Gettysburg Review *and are forthcoming in* Prairie Schooner. *"Now Adam" first appeared in* The Little Magazine *and "In the Periodical Room" in* The Paris Review.

IN THE PERIODICAL ROOM

> *At the next table*
> *a woman in patent shoes,*
> *blue summer shift*
> *flips through* House Beautiful.
> *On her arm the flat oval*
> *of a small pox vaccination*
> *gleams like egg yolk.*
> *I feel it is my duty*

to reduce her age.
First I tuck her several chins
into her neck,
smooth the fan of wrinkles
from her cheek,
prune all flesh
so bones protrude.
At last she is thirteen,
wears middy blouse
and pleated navy skirt.
Later she will play croquet
on her grandfather's lawn.
A balding man in nylon socks,
khaki shorts
approaches her table.
He smoothes the space
between the tufts of gray,
checks his watch.
He told his wife
to meet him here
at exactly half past three.
Now all he can find
is this ridiculous girl
swinging her legs
and licking a peppermint stick.

NOW ADAM

You can borrow "Adam" from the public library
for six weeks at a time, free of charge,
no renewals. I tried it as an experiment,
lugged him home, settled his lusty weight
upon my bureau. He didn't turn his head
when I undressed, but kept his chin
solidly pressed into his shoulder. Relax,
I whispered into his plastered ear.
The world's undone, we all fell long ago.

He didn't flinch. It's not your rib
I'm after, I insisted, just some sign
you're aware that I exist. He didn't bat
a lash, but gazed, gazed his steady gaze
out my window.

Next I offered apples, first whole,
then sliced, finally pan fried with cinnamon.
He didn't give a tendon. Out of wiles,
I told him straight: Look, Adam, if you
want the cubic truth, unless you can take
some affirmative action, you're out of fashion,
a mass of idle weight. There are numerous
committees, you know, for just such flagrant
refusals. He didn't budge, but gazed, gazed
his steady gaze out my window until dusk fell
thick as fig leaves about our naked feet.

"A Girl in a Library"
by Randall Jarrell

For a brief biographical sketch of Randall Jarrell (1914–65), see page 232.

An object among dreams, you sit here with your shoes off
And curl your legs up under you; your eyes
Close for a moment, your face moves toward sleep . . .
You are very human.

                    But my mind, gone out in tenderness,
Shrinks from its object with a thoughtful sigh.
This is a waist the spirit breaks its arm on.
The gods themselves, against you, struggle in vain.
This broad low strong-boned brow; these heavy eyes;
These calves, grown muscular with certainties;
This nose, three medium-sized pink strawberries
—But I exaggerate. In a little you will leave:
I'll hear, half squeal, half shriek, your laugh of greeting—
Then, decrescendo, *bars of that strange speech*
In which each sound sets out to seek each other,
Murders its own father, marries its own mother,
And ends as one grand transcendental vowel.
(Yet for all I know, the Egyptian Helen spoke so.)
As I look, the world contracts around you:
I see Brünnhilde had brown braids and glasses
She used for studying; Salome straight brown bangs,
A calf's brown eyes, and sturdy light-brown limbs
Dusted with cinnamon, an apple-dumpling's . . .
Many a beast has gnawn a leg off and got free,
Many a dolphin curved up from Necessity—
The trap has closed about you, and you sleep.
If someone questioned you, What doest thou here?
You'd knit your brows like an orangoutang
(But not so sadly; not so thoughtfully)
And answer with a pure heart, guilelessly:
I'm studying. . . .
                              If only you were not!
Assignments,
              recipes,
                    the Official Rulebook
Of Basketball—*ah, let them go; you needn't mind.*
The soul has no assignments, neither cooks
Nor referees: it wastes its time.
                              It wastes its time.
Here in this enclave there are centuries
For you to waste: the short and narrow stream
Of Life meanders into a thousand valleys

Of all that was, or might have been, or is to be.
The books, just leafed through, whisper endlessly . . .
Yet it is hard. One sees in your blurred eyes
The "uneasy half-soul" Kipling saw in dogs'.
One sees it, in the glass, in one's own eyes.
In rooms alone, in galleries, in libraries,
In tears, in searchings of the heart, in staggering joys
We memorize once more our old creation,
Humanity: with what yawns the unwilling
Flesh puts on its spirit, O my sister!

So many dreams! And not one troubles
Your sleep of life? no self stares shadowily
From these worn hexahedrons, beckoning
With false smiles, tears? . . .
                  Meanwhile Tatyana
Larina (gray eyes nickel with the moonlight
That falls through the willows onto Lensky's tomb;
Now young and shy, now old and cold and sure)
Asks, smiling: "But what is she dreaming of, fat thing?"
I answer: She's not fat. She isn't dreaming.
She purrs or laps or runs, all in her sleep;
Believes, awake, that she is beautiful;
She never dreams.
             Those sunrise-colored clouds
Around man's head—that inconceivable enchantment
From which, at sunset, we come back to life
To find our graves dug, families dead, selves dying:
Of all this, Tanya, she is innocent.
For nineteen years she's faced reality:
They look alike already.
                They say, man wouldn't be
The best thing in this world—and isn't he?—
If he were not too good for it. But she
—She's good enough for it.
               And yet sometimes
Her sturdy form, in its pink strapless formal,
Is as if bathed in moonlight—modulated

Into a form of joy, a Lydian mode;
This Wooden Mean's a kind, furred animal
That speaks, in the Wild of things, delighting riddles
To the soul that listens, trusting . . .

                                        Poor senseless Life:

When, in the last light sleep of dawn, the messenger
Comes with his message, you will not awake.
He'll give his feathery whistle, shake you hard,
You'll look with wide eyes at the dewy yard
And dream, with calm slow factuality:
"Today's Commencement. My bachelor's degree
In Home Ec., my doctorate of philosophy
In Phys. Ed.

                [Tanya, they won't even scan]
Are waiting for me. . . ."

                     Oh, Tatyana,

The Angel comes: better to squawk like a chicken
Than to say with truth, "But I'm a good girl,"
And Meet his Challenge with a last firm strange
Uncomprehending smile; and—then, then!—see
The blind date that has stood you up: your life.
(For all this, if it isn't, perhaps, life,
Has yet, at least, a language of its own
Different from the books'; worse than the books'.)
And yet, the ways we miss our lives are life.
Yet . . . yet . . .

                 to have one's life add up to yet!

You sigh a shuddering sigh. Tatyana murmurs,
"Don't cry, little peasant"; leaves us with a swift
"Good-bye, good-bye . . . Ah, don't think ill of me . . ."
Your eyes open: you sit here thoughtlessly.

I love you—and yet—and yet—I love you.

Don't cry, little peasant. Sit and dream.
One comes, a finger's width beneath your skin,
To the braided maidens singing as they spin;

There sound the shepherd's pipe, the watchman's rattle
Across the short dark distance of the years.
I am a thought of yours: and yet, you do not think . . .
The firelight of a long, blind, dreaming story
Lingers upon your lips; and I have seen
Firm, fixed forever in your closing eyes,
The Corn King beckoning to his Spring Queen.

"Library" by Louis Jenkins

Louis Jenkins, born in Oklahoma in 1942, worked for several years as a clerk in libraries in Kansas and Colorado. He now lives in Duluth, Minnesota. Jenkins's first book of poetry was The Well Digger's Wife *(1973); others have included* The Wrong Tree *(1980);* The Water's Easy Reach *(1985); and* An Almost Human Gesture *(1987). He has also contributed poetry to magazines and to several other collections. "Library" was reprinted in* News of the Universe: Poems of Twofold Consciousness, *edited by Robert Bly (1980).*

I sit down at a table and open a book of poems and move slowly into the shadows of tall trees. They are white pines I think. The ground is covered with soft brown needles and there are signs that animals have come here silently and vanished before I could catch sight of them. But here the trail edges into a cedar swamp; wet ground, deadfall and rotting leaves. I move carefully but rapidly, pleased with myself.

Someone else comes and sits down at the table, a serious looking young man with a large stack of books. He takes a book from the top of the stack and opens it. The book is called How to Get a High Paying Job. *He flips through it and lays it down and picks up another and pages through it quickly. It is titled* Moving Ahead.

We are moving ahead very rapidly now, through a second growth of popple and birch, our faces scratched and our clothes torn by the underbrush. We are moving even faster now, marking the trail, followed closely by bulldozers and crews with chain saws and representatives of the paper company.

"To a Scholar in the Stacks" by Howard Nemerov

Howard Nemerov, born in 1920, occupies a distinguished and much-honored position among contemporary American poets. Although he has maintained a belief in what one critic calls "the traditional means of poetry, such as full rhyme and a well-established and sustained metrical pattern," Nemerov is also known for his intelligent and imaginative complexities. "To a Scholar in the Stacks," for example, demands more than one careful reading.

Nemerov has won virtually all the awards America can bestow upon its poets, including a Pulitzer Prize and National Book Award in 1978 (following publication of The Collected Poems *in 1977); a Bollingen Prize in 1981; many honorary degrees; and election to the American Academy. He is currently a Distinguished Professor of English at Washington University.*

Nemerov's books of poetry include: The Image and the Law *(1947);* The Salt Garden *(1955);* The Painter Dreaming in the Scholar's House *(1968);* Sentences *(1980);* Inside the Onion *(1984);* War Stories: Poems About

Long Ago and Now *(1987). He has also received acclaim for his volumes of collected essays,* Figures of Thought: Speculations on the Meaning of Poetry and Other Essays *(1978) and* New and Selected Essays *(1985), and others, as well as for several novels and many short stories.*

When you began your story all its words
Had long been written down, its elements
Already so cohered in such exact
Equations that there should have seemed to be
No place to go, no entrance to the maze.
A heart less bold would have refused to start,
A mind less ignorant would have stayed home.

For Pasiphaë already had conceived
And borne her bully boy, and Daedalus
Responding had designed the darkness in
Its mystical divisions; Theseus,
Before you came, descended and returned,
By means of the thread, many and many a time.
What was there that had not been always done?

And still, when you began, only because
You did begin, the way opened before you.
The pictured walls made room, received your life;
Pasiphaë frowned, the Sea King greeted you,
And sighing Ariadne gave the thread
As always; in that celebrated scene
You were alone in being alone and new.

And now? You have gone down, you have gone in,
You have become incredibly rich and wise
From wandering underground. And yet you weary.
And disbelieve, daring the Minotaur
Who answers in the echoes of your voice,
Holding the thread that has no other end,
Speaking her name whom you abandoned long ago.

Then out of this what revelation comes?
Sometimes in darkness and in deep despair
You will remember, Theseus, that you were
The Minotaur, the Labyrinth and the thread
Yourself; even you were that ingener
That fled the maze and flew—so long ago—
Over the sunlit sea to Sicily.

"The Library of Morpheus," from *From the Realm of Morpheus,* by Steven Millhauser

Novelist and short-story writer Steven Millhauser was born in 1943 in New York City and educated at Columbia College and Brown University. He received much acclaim for his fictional biography, Edwin Mullhouse: The Life & Death of an American Writer 1943–1954, by Jeffrey Cartwright, *published in 1972, which won the Prix Medicis Étranger.* Portrait of a Romantic, *which focused on the boredom of adolescence, appeared in 1977. Millhauser has contributed fiction to* The New Yorker, The Hudson Review, Antaeus, *and other magazines. A collection of his stories,* In the Penny Arcade, *appeared in 1986.*

I found myself in what appeared to be a dimlit library, stretching away on all sides and into the distance. It was not like any library I had ever seen. The wooden shelves did not extend in straight perspectives but meandered lazily, forming sinuous and alluring aisles that turned out of sight like forest paths. The shelves were irregular in height, ranging from about ten to fifteen feet, though occasionally soaring out of sight into the upper darkness. The aisles were dimly illuminated by small flames enclosed in cylinders of glass, attached to wooden pegs projecting from the vertical divisions between shelves. Here and there among the books occurred gaps of about six feet, and in most of these spaces a person lay upon a pillow, reading or sleeping. The air was filled with a soft sound of breathing and of pages gently turning. The shelf-people lay stretched out on their backs with their arms over their eyes, or their books held open upon their chests. Sometimes they leaned on an elbow as they read in the glow of the flaming shelf-lights, or lay on their stomachs with one arm dangling. And here and there among the books a couple lay entwined in a languorous embrace.

As we advanced in silence along a winding aisle, from which other winding aisles continually branched, I noticed that at intervals there extended from each shelf-edge a small horizontal grip or bar. These wooden grips rose above one another like a series of steps, and now and then I saw someone by this means ascending or descending to another shelf. I glanced at titles as we passed, but they were always unfamiliar. The aisles narrowed and widened as we advanced, sometimes coming so close together that it was necessary for us to squeeze sideways or even to stop and seek out another aisle; occasionally the highest shelves leaned toward one another at the top, forming picturesque archways. Sometimes, when aisles crossed, an open place like a plaza was formed. In one such place I saw a great tree with spreading leafy branches hung with lanterns, under which soft reading-chairs were disposed upon a carpet. In another place I saw a scattering of simple beds, where people lay reading, or lay fast asleep, their books open beside them.

As we continued along the hushed and winding aisles I stopped from time to time to examine one of the strange volumes. One winding aisle contained books upon each of whose dark bindings was neither title nor author but only a Roman numeral. The volumes were in disorder and numbered in the thousands, although I was not certain what to make of barred numerals such as $\overline{\text{CXVIII}}\text{CCXLI}$. I examined several of these volumes, which began with chapters having even higher Roman numerals. It seemed to be a vast connected story of some sort, with much attention to genealogy and the minutiae of social custom; a few dim black-and-white illustrations showed battles and voyages. The alien and unfamiliar quality of all these books did not excite my imagination but rather oppressed and irritated me, and it was not until I turned with Morpheus into still another aisle that I first felt a stirring of interest.

As soon as we turned the corner I detected familiar names on book-spines. We seemed to have come to a random section of classics, for I saw such names as Spenser, Dickens, Byron, Stendhal, Chaucer. With mild curiosity I took down a volume entitled SPENSER, VII–XII. Upon opening it, I saw that it contained Books VII–XII of *The Faerie Queene*. Nearby was a slim volume entitled DICKENS, which proved to contain the final chapters of *Edwin Drood*. I looked up in surprise and said: "But I thought *Edwin Drood*——" "Aye, lad: woefully unfinished, there in thy lax realm." Clearly pleased, he indicated three thick dusty volumes on another shelf; they contained, in closely printed double columns, Chaucer's completion of *The Canterbury Tales*. Leaning close to me, Morpheus whispered that the Miller's second and third tales were something of a disappointment but that his fourth tale was remarkable for its blend of the sublime and the obscene, though even that paled in comparison with the second appearance of the Pardoner; and the Epilogue was one of the high points in the history of English literature. Yet even as he was speaking he had already removed from the shelf a matching set in red leather, containing completions by Keats of *Hyperion* and *The Fall of Hyperion*, respectively. Nearby stood a slender volume, in which I found the final chapter of *The Castle*, translated by Willa and Edwin Muir. Morpheus, moving along, pointed out Sir Walter Ralegh's completion of *The History of the World* and Gottfried von Strassburg's completion of *Tristan*. In quick succession he showed me Marlowe's completion of *Hero and Leander*, Flaubert's completion of *Bouvard et Pecuchet*, Byron's completion of *Don Juan*——Morpheus called the Italian cantos "a triumph" ——and Stevenson's completion of *Weir of Hermiston*. The books seemed arranged in no particular order, and as Morpheus urged me forward I thumbed hastily through a number of completions, not all of whose titles I recognized: *Jean Santeuil*, *Kubla Khan*, *The Man Without Qualities*,

The Triumph of Life, *The Legend of Good Women*, *Orlando Innamorato*, *Christabel*, *Lucien Leuwen*, *Sanditon*, and *Septimus Felton*.

I turned now into the next winding aisle, where I saw several half-familiar names which I could not quite place. I had picked up a volume of poems by the vaguely familiar Jeffrey Aspern, and was reading one called "Venetian Impressions," when Morpheus handed me a slim volume by Tonio Kröger: bound in morocco and printed on fine paper, it bore the date 1899. I was still unable to grasp the nature of this section of the library, and my perplexity only grew when, happening to turn to the shelves across the aisle, I saw a great number of novels by David Copperfield. They bore such titles as *The Personal History and Adventures of Walter Worthington*, *The Life and Times of Edward Thrush*, *Little Em'ly*, *A Word to the Wise*, *Greymanse*, *Eugene Pemberton: Bart.*, *A Year and a Day*, *Agnes Foster*, *Is She Right?*, *Cora Broughton*, *The Lily and the Rose*, *The Chimney Corner*, *Once and for All*, *Wriothesley Wold*, and *Lucy Dearheart*. "Why, look thee, blinking lad, canst not see? Here hast thou the works of all those sweet scribblers, whom scribblers in thy realm have wantonly imagined." And now among writers whose names I did not recognize I began to find familiar and less familiar ones, as well as odd, elusive names that hovered between the half-familiar and the unknown; and among the many writers of that aisle were Enoch Soames, Gustav von Aschenbach, Seamus Earwicker, Pierre Glendinning, Arthur Pendennis, Hugh Verecker, Stephen Dedalus, Edwin Mullhouse, Sebastian Knight, Martin Eden, Pierre Delalande, Roman Bonavena, Edwin Reardon, Mark Ambient, and Bergotte.

Scarcely had I run my eye along these shelves when at the turning of the aisle I came to an extensive section of texts in Latin and Greek, as well as translations into many languages, which stretched on and on for many aisles in all directions, and whose principle of unification eluded me. Here the shelves rose tier on tier to a height of thirty feet or more. Most of the authors were entirely unknown to me and even the names I recognized did not yield a clue. I noticed an Elizabethan translation of Ovid's *Medea*, a Latin translation in thirty-seven books of *On Nature* by Epicurus, a play by Euripides entitled *Bellerophon*. Without much interest I noted a collection of the complete works of Naevius, a biography of Pomponius Secundus by Pliny the Elder, an epic called the *Titanomachy*. I had no knowledge of Greek and a mere smattering of Latin, and my knowledge of even the translated classics was shamefully slight. Looking up in perplexity I asked in a whisper what these books were. Morpheus looked at me with disappointment or disdain and said in a stern undertone: "Know'st thou not thy classics?" Then I felt my cheeks burn; and raising his arm, and making a grand sweeping gesture, Morpheus said:

" 'Tis all the lost books o' th'ancient world. Here be the seventy-two lost plays of Aeschylus, the hundred lost plays of Sophocles, the eighty lost plays of Euripides. Here be the thirty lost plays of that sweet rogue Aristophanes. Here wilt thou find the lost satires of Menippus of Gadara, among the which I would commend to thy rapt attention his wondrous journey to the lower world. Here be the lost philosophies of Thales, of Anaximander, of Anaximenes, of Xenophanes, of Parmenides, of Empedocles, of Democritus, and of Diogenes of Apollonia. Here be the lost histories of a mouthful o' names that be sweet to sound on the tongue, among the which there be Eugeon of Samoa, Deiochus of Proconessus, Eudemus of Paros, Democles of Phigalia, the Argive Acusilaus, Hellanicus of Lesbos, and Xanthus the Lydian, to name only them. Here wilt thou find the two hundred thirty-seven lost books of Theophrastus, the lost *Republic* of Zeno, the one hundred five lost plays of Menander. Here wilt thou find the incomparable lost works o' the Alexandrian pornographers. Here be the lost tragedies of Neophron of Sicyon and the lost comedies of Plato Comicus, and here be the lost epics o' the Cyclic poets, among the which Morpheus doth commend the *Little Iliad*, the *Iliupersis*, and the *Theogony*. These be but a few o' the motes i' the mighty moonbeam o' the lost works of ancient Greece, yet here wilt thou find as well all the lost works of Rome, among the which I would mention in especial Suetonius his *Lives of Famous Whores* and sweet Ovid his *Gigantomachy*, his *Medea*, and his *Triumph of Tiberius*. Here be the seventy-two lost works of Varro and that instructive treatise on the use o' the javelin by Pliny the Elder. Here be—'sblood, ancient mariner, an thou not stick to thy alphabet I'll break thy neck."

This last remark was flung at a scholarly man lying on an upper shelf, who had been directing irritated glances at Morpheus and had begun to hiss out shushes. I quickly led Morpheus into another aisle, where the lost literature of the ancient world continued, winding into the distance and towering overhead; and awed by the sight of all the books that had disappeared from the upper world I said in hushed tones: "I hadn't known how many had been lost." "Aye," said Morpheus loudly, "there's no end of scribbling."

He led me through many winding aisles, where the lost literature of Greece and Rome continued unabated, and as I followed I began to feel we would never emerge from the heavyladen shelves that soared out of sight into the upper darkness and turned and twisted relentlessly into the distance: and as we advanced I saw in the trembling haloes of the flamelights a fine dust falling, sifting down through the empty spaces, falling onto the shelves and into my hair, settling in the crevices of my shirt, falling upon the backs of my hands and the tips of my shoes, falling like a scarcely perceptible snow, covering everything.

After a while I became aware of a change. The shelves still soared high above, but now we were passing books of a different kind, and I realized we had entered an extensive section of medieval texts in many languages. This section appeared to stretch on in many directions and I felt relieved when at the turning of an aisle I saw titles in English. Here Morpheus paused to show me *The Book of the Leoun* by Chaucer and a thick collection of lost fourteenth-century lyrics. In a nearby aisle he pointed to shelf after shelf of Anglo-Saxon epics, among which he said were many that were far superior to Beowulf, especially *Wada* and the delightful *Offa*.

From here Morpheus led me into the aisles of the Renaissance, where the shelves were no more than fifteen feet high, and where he paused for a moment in the Elizabethan section before what he called his favorite play, *The Isle of Dogs* by Ben Jonson and Thomas Nashe. "Aye, lad, there's life in it yet, and in many another lost play o' that sweet-tongued time. And I do have a love for that dark devil Ralegh, whose *Cynthia* here's found complete, the which Spenser hath so highly praised. Here be those works Ben Jonson lost i' the fire, the which he doth enumerate in his 'Execration upon Volcan,' and here be those lost works of sweet Jack Skelton, the which he doth mention in his *Garlande of Lawrell*, of which the best is 'The Balade of the Mustarde Tarte.' And here too wilt thou find the lost verses of gentle and honey-flowing Spenser, among the which old Morpheus doth commend for pleasant and delightsome reading *The Dying Pellicane*, *The Court of Cupide*, *My Slomber*, and *The English Poet*."

Despite my keen interest in these books my mind was beginning to feel overburdened with the weight of the lost literature of the upper world, and I asked Morpheus whether anything of value had been lost in more recent centuries. In reply he led me along winding aisles until he stopped suddenly and removed from the shelves a book that resembled a journal. This proved to be the celebrated *Memoirs* of Lord Byron. Morpheus said that it contained several amusing anecdotes of erotic adventures in Spain and Milan, and a short but lively account of the deflowering of Lady Byron on a sofa before dinner on their wedding day, but that on the whole it was disappointing, for it omitted all mention of that delightful and instructive subject, incest. Of modern books in general he said there were few losses of interest, by far the greater part being the private correspondence of great men, which had been deliberately destroyed by upright friends and relations; yet in the matter of fiction he confessed to a fondness for the second half of *Dead Souls*, and a remarkable novel called *The Messiah*, by Bruno Schulz.

Upon my exclaiming once again how many books had been lost, Morpheus laughed and said we had glimpsed but a few, for the section of lost books spread out in many directions we had not followed; for we had not seen the lost literature of China, of Persia, of Arabia; and there were to be found as well the complete collections once housed in the lost libraries of Alexandria and Pergamum; for all books that had been lost in the upper world, and now led a phantom existence in the minds of men, here had their residence.

But at last leaving the maze of lost books, we came to an aisle that contained many names familiar to me, yet whose principle of organization I could not grasp. There I found a book by Lewis Carroll, entitled *Alice's Shadow*, with illustrations by John Tenniel. The first illustration showed Alice standing by a stream with her hands clasped behind her, while her shadow was sitting against a tree on the other side of the stream. There were many poems scattered throughout, among them a poem of two verses entitled "The Muffin and the Bandbox":

Said the muffin to the bandbox,
 "Won't you come and dine with me?
I will serve you cabbage sandwiches
 And turtles in your tea."

Said the bandbox to the muffin,
 "I am sorry to decline,
But turtles are not tortoises,
 Though both are fond of wine."

Nearby was a slender black volume on which were the words JAMES JOYCE. The book was untitled and unpaginated; it was written entirely without punctuation or capitalization, in a style of childlike simplicity. Beside it was a volume entitled THE POETICAL WORKS OF JOHN KEATS, vol. 3. To my surprise the volume contained not a single poem I recognized; yet as I read here and there, I heard unmistakably the music of Keats. There was a long poem in blank verse entitled *The Dream of Apollo*, a scattering of sonnets ("If to be heard . . . ," "To ————"), several short pieces in a variety of forms, such as *Mirabel* and "Puck's Song," and a deeply felt poem in ottava rima called "Lines on the Death of Shelley." In perplexity I turned to the title page, which read: THE POETICAL WORKS OF JOHN KEATS. VOLUME III: 1822–1827. " 'Tis a somewhat uneven collection, with no strong burst like unto the summer of 1819 or the autumn of 1831; there's a backsliding here and there to the candied sweetness of wanton Madeline, and methinks there be overmuch solemnity in his Miltonic mouthings; yet hath an errant stanza hither and yon such melancholy-gay music as to draw marrow out of mortal bones and hale the soul out of a wanton roving god. Yet 'tis in his thirty-sixth autumn that he doth reach such heights as few have eyes to see; for many are the miles, and weary the way, 'twixt pissing and Parnassus. 'Tis in that youthful-ripe year that he doth learn to mingle the stately measure wi' the sweet and wild to make such music as the Nine Sisters joy to dance to, on the holy hill."

"But what are these books?" I asked softly, after a pause in which his words were borne away by the silence.

"Why, canst not see? Here be all those books that in thy world have been desired, yet by some caprice or oversight came not to be written. Here be the late poems of poets dying young, the books after the final books, the great works after the last great works. Here wilt thou find the novel after *Finnegans Wake*, the poem after *The Aeneid*, the play after *The Tempest*. And here wilt thou find the desired books of an age or nation, among the which there be the great American novel and the great French epic."

"And still the library goes on and on."

"Aye, that it does. For there be many aisles, and many turnings, in the library of Morpheus. Thou hast had a glimpse of those books not completed i' th'upper realm, and those books penned by imaginary scribblers, and those books lost in the careless way o' thy world, and those books yearned-for yet unscribbled. Yet here's many a sweet book more than thou mayst chance to think on. Here be those books seen i' the fancy by scribblers o' th'upper world, but not edited, and among these the greatest is John Milton's epic of King Arthur, in especial the ninth book, though some there be that do prefer that *Life of a Great Sinner* the which was mused upon by that great sinner Dostoyevsky in the last years of his life. Here be the books of all those who dreamed of turning author, but through lack of faith, or will, or talent, or lucre, did not; and this is the great literature of unpursued careers, extending farther than thou couldst walk in a week of time. Here be the completer hist'ries of all th'imaginary heroes o' thy realm, wherein thou canst read of Don Quixote his childhood and of that course of study which young Hamlet did idle his time away withal at the University of Wittenberg. Here be the books of all th'imaginary races of all th'imaginary islands o' thy realm. There be books of silver and books of gold, books of glass and books of snow. There be books that grow on the branches of trees, and planted give birth to new trees bearing new fruit of books. There be books nourished by the mind of a reader, the which do grow pale, and wither away, and die, an they be not read. And there be divisions and subdivisions, categories and subcategories, to stretch out a god's speech beyond enduring; for in the library of Morpheus wilt thou find all those books which are imaginary in thy realm. Such, and many more, be the sweet books o' the library of Morpheus, which is to the libraries o' th'upper world as the sun to a candle, the moon to a peeled potato, all Eden to a flowerpot, and Mount Helicon to the mole on the rump of Calliope."

We now continued through the library, and as we advanced I noticed that the books were growing larger. In one aisle they were two feet high; in the next the bottommost books came up to my chin; and we turned into an aisle in which vast shelves soared out of sight, and the books were twelve feet high. Morpheus paused before one of these great tomes and together we slowly and laboriously pulled it out. The cumbrous volume was three feet thick, and very heavy; it was with no small difficulty that we managed to lean it like an immense door against the base of the towering bookshelves. The cover was thickly overlaid with figured bronze. Morpheus pulling and I pushing, slowly we opened the heavy cover, walking in a long semicircle and at last leaning it against the shelves. We then walked back and proceeded to turn the blank inner leaf, which proved much easier to handle. The paper was strong and flexible though coarse-grained in quality; here and there a brown fleck the size of a thumbtack appeared. Upon the title page was the word BRILDGRULL, in thick black letters larger than my hand. We next opened to the first page, on which the text was printed in smaller letters, the capital A's being about the size of an ordinary pair of compasses and the small o's about the size of a silver dollar. The language itself, although printed in Roman characters, was not known to me; Morpheus revealed that it was Brobdingnagian, and that we had wandered into the portion of his library which housed the books of that great kingdom. I expressed awe at their great size, but Morpheus replied that giants came in many sizes, and that in remote aisles which we would not follow there were books four times the size, with letters one foot high; and he knew of one race of giants whose books were so large that the letter t was the size of a telephone pole.

Morpheus now led me to an aisle where the books resumed their normal size, but as we advanced through the winding aisles I became aware that the library was changing. The darkness had increased, the books were becoming tattered and stained, here and there small puddles appeared in the aisles. The paths became more tortuous, new aisles appeared with every turning, and entire aisles lay in darkness. Here and there grassclumps, ferns, and twisting weeds sprouted between books,

and even from the books themselves. I heard dim mutterings and whis-
perings in the darkened aisles and now and then faint laughter. In the
dim reddish glow of a guttering flame I removed a book. The binding
was damp and stained, and when I opened it I saw that the pages were
mottled with brownish spots; a wettish wormlike creature crawled
slowly across the page, leaving a trail of slime. The cracked and brown-
stained words appeared to be rotting on the page; they were difficult
to decipher but seemed to be about a redfaced man doing something
to a female corpse. When I thrust the book back on its shelf my hand
touched something soft; a small animal scampered across my hand and
vanished in the dark. I stayed close to Morpheus as we continued along
still darker aisles; a strong odor of urine rose to my nostrils and here
and there on the edges of shelves I saw damp dripping clots of dung.
On one shelf-space I saw a man with a sickly pallor and a soft loose
mouth, who smiled at me as I passed; from his open trouserfly hung a
small limp penis. Here and there in the darkness of shelves I heard the
squeak and scamper of rats and saw the gleam of rat-eyes. A woman
with lank damp hair lay on her back staring up as if in a trance; her
knees were raised, causing her dress to fall along her slowly opening
and closing thighs, between which protruded a stained book. Nearby,
one open book lay face downward upon another open book that lay on
its spine. The fetid odor of wet excrement increased as we advanced,
until I could scarcely breathe; books lay moldering in dark yellow puddles
in the aisles; books rotting on the shelves were riddled with holes and
covered with soft growths resembling fungi. One book lying flat had
rotted so thoroughly that it was little more than a hollow box filled
with brown malodorous matter, round which sluggish fat flies buzzed,
tinged with green. Some books in their decay had taken on a sinister
beauty, and glowed with melting reds, greens, and purples. Still others
seemed to be afflicted with diseases: one binding was covered with
scablike scales, another was covered with red sores from which leaked
yellowish extrusions of pus, from another oozed a thick sticky liquid
that dripped down to the next shelf. As I passed one book a thick,
sluggish snake slowly slithered out. Turning behind Morpheus into
another aisle I was plunged into blackness; soft grunts and hisses issued
from the shelves, there was a sound of oozing and dripping; my foot

stepped on something soft that burst. In the distance I heard a sound of water. Turning into the next aisle I could see a faint lightness ahead, and after a few more turnings we came to a marble fountain bursting into white plumes.

Beyond the fountain the library resumed its former healthy appearance and even took on a pleasing pastoral air. The winding aisles began to rise and dip, and here and there arched bridges of stone appeared above, connecting the upper shelves. People strolled across the bridges or stood leaning on their elbows on the parapets, gazing down. Along the center of one wide and winding aisle a small brook in a stream-bed bubbled over stones. Open places at the junction of aisles appeared frequently; at one such place was a small and mazy wood, with benches set among the winding paths. Here and there in the shelves a rough-hewn opening would appear, which proved to be the entrance to a dark, booklined tunnel that wound through the heart of the thick shelves and finally emerged in the opposite aisle. At one open place a wooded hill rose up. At the base of the hill was a tunnel that led after numerous windings to a high cavern hung with torches and fitted with bookshelves adapted to the uneven formation of the interior. At the other side of the cave a tunnel led to an arched opening which admitted one to another winding aisle.

Gradually as we advanced the library lost its pastoral quality and took on a playful, even impish air. Soft conversation was audible in the aisles, and as I looked about I was surprised to find that the words were issuing from the books themselves. Some books were talking quietly, others appeared to be engaged in argument. I paused before two large and weighty tomes, who were debating the relative merits of Classic and Modern authors, while a third volume tried to gain their attention by insisting that those two categories were far from sufficient and that the worth of a book depended solely on its imaginative truth. This position was in turn derided by a thick and fierce-looking book on a nearby shelf, who maintained that "imagination" and "truth" were contradictory terms. A slender, delicate book, who coughed frequently, began to argue in feverish tones that the truth of a book lay in the degree to which it refused to be related to any world whatever, but a fit of coughing overtaking him he was obliged to break off.

These arguments held a strong interest for me, but my attention was distracted by a conversation taking place on a shelf several feet above my head. There a young man lying on his stomach was speaking in low, intense tones to a book that lay open before him. A feminine voice answered softly, and lightly laughed. Intrigued by this odd method of reading, I chose a book at random from an upper shelf. When I opened it I heard a soft though distinct conversation between a man and a woman. The conversation quickly became an argument; the man rose angrily; a door slammed; the woman wept softly. Suddenly she addressed me, and asked if I knew why he had so changed of late. I assured her I had no idea. She asked if I would help her, and promising her that everything would soon be all right I softly closed the book.

Morpheus seemed impatient to leave the aisle of talking books, and we passed now into an aisle where men and women stood leaning indolently against the shelves, talking lightly to one another, and occasionally taking small bites out of the books they held in their hands. A foppish youth, chewing thoughtfully, and brushing crumbs from his waistcoat with languorous flicks of his long white fingers, remarked to a young woman: "Rather heavy, don't you know," whereupon she replied: "Oh, but I do find him so absolutely delicious." Upon the partially chewed volume I noticed the words: ARCEL OUST. Several eater-readers appeared surfeited, and held their bloated stomachs in evident discomfort. One gaunt youth with black burning eyes and fever-flushed cheeks walked rapidly along the aisle, biting hungrily into each book in turn, swallowing pieces in great gulps and moving on to the next. I noticed a volume entitled DICKENS, and giving way to curiosity I removed it from the shelf and took a small bite. It had the taste of roast lamb, peas, and mashed potatoes with gravy. Nearby I saw a volume entitled KAFKA, which I also had the curiosity to sample. It had the taste of pure, burning-cold water, which seemed to cut into my throat. I next tried a volume entitled POPE, and was astonished to find that it tasted like a gumdrop. I looked hungrily at volumes entitled JOYCE and MELVILLE and SWIFT and MILTON but Morpheus seemed impatient to continue, and we turned into another aisle.

Here books were fluttering across the aisle from one shelf to another, gently flapping their pages. Some of these books hovered uncertainly about the shelves, as if searching for a place to rest; others inserted themselves between books in rows, and appeared to sleep. Now and then the air became so thick with flying books that it became necessary for me to raise an arm before my face and with my other hand to push the sharp-edged books carefully aside as I passed. Once a book landed lightly on my shoulder and after a few steps rose with gentle flapping sounds and flew to a higher shelf.

We next came to an aisle crowded with people, whom I could see emerging from various books. These characters talked among themselves, strolled about, or entered other books. A woman who reminded me of Catherine Earnshaw stood talking to a man who bore a curious resemblance to Leopold Bloom. A beautiful young woman and a dashing young man emerged simultaneously from books in opposite rows; they walked off arm in arm, she fanning herself and lowering her eyes, he talking heatedly and stealing glimpses of her heaving bosom.

As I passed along this aisle I could not help being struck by the curious method of reading practiced by those lying on the shelves. One young man carefully opened a book and holding it upright advanced the top of his head slowly toward the pages. As his head reached the pages it met with no resistance but continued to advance, as if he were entering a tunnel. In this manner he slowly disappeared into the book. On an upper shelf I saw a volume lying open beside a pair of black high-heeled shoes.

As I passed a volume lying on its side, the cover opened slightly and a white arm emerged. It appeared to beckon to me. On an impulse I reached over and touched the soft hand, which instantly closed around my hand and began pulling me into the book. As my head passed through a substance that parted like mist I felt another hand grasp my ankle, for a moment I stared down at a rolling green countryside with a castle in the distance, then I felt myself being pulled by the ankle up through the book and Morpheus said sternly: "Beware." Grasping me firmly by the arm he led me through this dangerous aisle, at one point rudely knocking aside a fellow with waxed mustaches who fell so violently against the shelves that books came tumbling down on him, and still keeping his grip on me he then led me through several whimsical and fantastical aisles, where prickly books hung on branches growing from the shelves and clung to me like burrs, or where ghostly and insubstantial books lurked on mist-haunted shelves in the hooting dark. He did not release me until we had emerged in a more sober portion of the library. I wanted to study this new group of books but Morpheus strode swiftly and I had to hurry to keep track of his robe-ends disappearing around the bends of the aisles. Around one turning a great door loomed before me; the center of the door was closing over a black-slippered foot. Pushing through the heavy curtain I found myself at the top of a circular stairway, down which Morpheus was already pattering.

I hurried down after him. At the bottom I came to an arch that opened onto a crevice-passageway, and turning right I hurried behind Morpheus along the dark and winding way.

All at once the passage ended, and I entered a great cavern-chamber.

Listless figures lay drowsily about. Before me loomed the black bed. We had entered facing a new angle of the bed and I felt confused and a trifle giddy as I followed Morpheus up the little stairway of crimson velvet and through the black velvet curtains onto the soft and sagging floor of his chamber. At the far end my forgotten lamp still burned on the shelf. I followed with a feeling of faint dizziness as Morpheus trod heavily toward the head of the bed, knocking over objects that fell softly. When he reached the pillows he flung out an arm and said: "Hail, Bed, haven of heroes, womb of wanderers, sweet swan of the River Morpheus. Take me to thy soft bosom, Bed, and wrap me round with thy sweet arms. Ope wide thy downy thighs, and admit me to thy most dark delights, O thou of the white belly, thou of the lush lap. And thou, soft Pillow, kiss my tir'd eyelids shut, for I'm a-weary, and fain would rest." With that he tumbled heavily into bed and I lay down beside my chair on the soft velvety bedspread. Despite my weariness I did not fall readily asleep but lay tiredly awake with my arm over my eyes as confused images sprang into my mind and melted away. I saw Ignotus walking up and down before the sluggish black lake which then became a black velvet curtain that parted suddenly to reveal a winding stairway. Books fluttered from the stairs and began to swirl about me and I had to knock them aside as I wandered lost among high pillars. After a while I felt myself drifting toward sleep. Wearily I turned onto my side, and as I pressed my cheek against the velvet dark, all at once I saw the empty bench, the bright-green grass, the silver backstop, the blue nylon jacket with one arm dangling, but already they had begun to turn like objects on a merry-go-round, turning faster and faster to a whistling carousel melody, turning faster and faster until all outline was blurred away, turning and turning and whirling and spinning until they were a spinning wheel of dreams on the mighty canopy of Morpheus.

Excerpt from *Angel in the Parlor* by Nancy Willard

Nancy Willard's imaginative books for children have become modern classics. A Visit to William Blake's Inn (1981) won a John Newbery Medal; it was also a Caldecott Honor Book. Her other recent books include Night Story *(1986);* The Mountains of Quilt *(1987);* The Voyage of the Ludgate Hill *(1987); and* East of the Sun & West of the Moon *(1989). She is also known as a poet, a literary critic, and a short-story writer. Her short stories have appeared in* The Lively Anatomy of God *(1968) and* Childhood of the Magician *(1973), as well as in other publications. Ms. Willard teaches at Vassar College and lives in Poughkeepsie, New York.*

In the following excerpt from her collection of stories and essays Angel in the Parlor, *Willard describes how the library contributed to her love of the reading and writing of fantasy.*

The house where I grew up had squirrels in the attic, mice in the pantry, and an angel in the parlor. I never saw the angel, and I only found out about it by accident. My mother had two sisters, both divorced, who hated to cook and who dropped by our house every Sunday for dinner. They never came alone. They brought their boyfriends. Aunt Jessie brought her daughter. Aunt Nellie brought her son and four Baptist missionaries from Detroit bent on saving our comfortable Presbyterian souls. It was not to them that the angel appeared, however, but to the kindly schoolmaster whom my Aunt Jessie had dated for so long that I called him Uncle Bill and assumed that somewhere in the roots of the tree of life we were related.

I remember the first time the angel appeared. We had just sat down to Sunday dinner when my mother, who had been cooking all morning, counted heads and made a perilous discovery.

"There are thirteen at the table," she said. "If we sit down with thirteen at the table, one of us will die within the year."

And she carried her plate to the sideboard. We all knew better than to try to change her mind. So over the clatter of silverware we shouted to her how delicious the chicken tasted, and she shouted back that there were more mashed potatoes in the kitchen, and nobody heard a word.

Then suddenly, for no reason, everyone stopped talking at once. Uncle Bill closed his eyes. Then he glanced at his watch and looked past the dining room into the parlor.

"Ah!" he murmured. "An angel has flown through the room."

I followed his gaze. I, too, looked into the parlor but saw no angel. I could tell from the astonished faces around me that no one else had seen it either. Why, I wondered, would an angel choose Uncle Bill? Why not me? Or the four Baptist missionaries?

Years later I discovered that the angel that flew through the room on that day was a figure of speech, acknowledging the blessing of silence in a room full of voices.

But even after my mother enlightened me about the angel, I still talked about it, still joked about it, and finally, by paying it so much attention, I came to believe in it. That is to say, I came to believe that our house was more than a collection of people, tables, chairs, lost pocketbooks, misplaced spectacles, and back issues of the National Geographic. All these things I could see and hear and touch. But there was also an order of life that, like the angel's, was not bound by the laws of the physical universe. And I came to believe that there were two kinds of people in the world, those who believed in tables and those who believed in angels.

In our public library I met representatives of both. There was the plump lady, who worked on Mondays, Wednesdays, and Fridays, and who gave me books on dinosaurs and Abraham Lincoln. The covers of the books she chose bore the label, "This is a Read-It-Yourself Book." That meant I knew all the words and did not have to ask my mother what, for example, a hippodrome was. Then there was the thin lady, who worked on Tuesdays, Thursdays, and Saturdays and gave me books about talking animals and giants and countries at the back of the north wind. The books she recommended had more words I didn't know than words I did, but I felt rather privileged carrying them home, as if I'd just checked out the Rosetta stone.

I do not remember what books I was carrying the afternoon I walked home from the library and saw, high in the clear October sky, a flock of geese winging south over the city. It was their plaintive cry that made me turn, startled at the wild sound over the hum of traffic. Thanks to the plump librarian's selection of books on the migration of birds, I knew how long a journey lay before them. I also knew I would never be happy until I too learned to fly as they did.

Monday afternoon I went to the library and asked the plump librarian for a book on flying. She nodded agreeably. She prided herself on filling all requests, be they ever so peculiar. She gave me a handsomely illustrated book on the Wright brothers. Leafing through it, I could see at once that it did not speak to my condition. So I handed it back and said, "Have you any books on how I can make my own wings and fly like a bird?"

The plump librarian looked distressed but not defeated.

"It is not possible for you to fly like a bird," she answered.

I thanked her and returned to the library on Tuesday. I told the thin librarian I wanted a book on flying but I did not want a book on airplanes. She looked hurt that I should think her capable of so gross a gesture, and after a moment's thought she plucked a small book from the shelving truck. It had only two pictures, neither of them in color. It was the story of Icarus.

I read the story very carefully. I paid special attention to the construction of the wings, but the drawings were not detailed enough to be very useful. I needed a working plan, with measurements. And where on earth could I find so many feathers?

I checked out the book, however, and as the thin librarian was stamping my card I said, "Have you any books that will teach me to fly?"

She considered my question very seriously.

"You want a book on magic," she answered.

"Have you books on magic?" I asked.

She pointed to a section at the back of the room.

"We have plenty of books on how to do magic tricks. However, there is a great difference between mere sleight-of-hand and real magic."

And she waved her hand at the whole section, as if conjuring it to disappear, and led me over to a cupboard. In the cupboard behind windowed doors, which were not locked but looked as if they might be, stood the fairy tales. Here I discovered stories of wizards, witches, shamans, soldiers, fools, and saints who flew by means of every imaginable conveyance, including carpets, trunks, horses, ships, and even bathtubs. It showed me that luck, a virtuous life, or both had something to do with one's ability to fly. As I was born under a mischievous star, I would have to count on luck; virtue would get me nowhere.

It was around this time that I made a curious discovery about my father. He was, by profession, a chemist. For him, to see was to believe. One afternoon I discovered on his bedside table two books I had never noticed before. One was the notebook where he wrote down solutions to scientific problems as they occurred to him during the night. The second was an account of an island called Atlantis, located west of Gibraltar and said by Plato to have sunk into the sea. I sat down on my father's bed and started reading the account of Atlantis, written, according to the title page, by an Englishman who claimed that unbeknownst to geographers the lost island had not sunk but had merely become invisible to ordinary sight. The author knew this for a fact; indeed, he had actually visited Atlantis. In his introduction he took pains to assure his readers that he was telling the truth. He was not, he explained, writing science fiction. A photograph of the island, opposite the title page, showed a woman wearing a snake headdress and a sequined tunic. The caption read, "Queen of Atlantis, taken by the author with a Leica M-1." I thought she looked like a tired Hedy Lamarr.

This book, I discovered, was part of a secret library my father kept hidden in the springs of his bed, a library that made his mattress so lumpy that no guests ever slept in it and thus no one else except my mother knew about his passion for the fantastic and the occult. In my father's bedspring library I found numerous books on Atlantis, Shangri-La, flying saucers, and reincarnation. I pored over a book of fuzzy images purported to be the souls of famous men and women photographed during a séance by one Madame Ugo Ugo. These volumes appalled my mother and confused me. They sounded like fairy tales, yet their authors claimed to be telling the truth. Were these books true and my fairy tales false? Were they all false? I knew that the fantasies I read could not be scientifically true. Fantasy, therefore, must be a literature of lies.

I am sure we have all met people who would agree with this view. Fantasy, they will tell you, is a literature of escape from the real world. By the real world they mean the physical world of tables and chairs. A man once asked me if I didn't agree with him that fantasy should be forbidden to children, as it is so difficult for them to unlearn the lies that it teaches. And unlearning, he reminded me, is a painful process, almost as painful as losing one's faith. I thought of my father's books and wondered what this man would make of them. I had long ago decided that my father's books were false because their authors recognized only one kind of truth, the truth of science. Of course, fairy tales are not literally true; their authors make no such claims. But taken as a record of what some call our psychological experience and others call our spiritual history, fantasy at its best is one of the truest forms of fiction we have. Many people have committed the error of taking literally what was meant to be taken metaphorically. Some of the most famous victims of this misunderstanding are those alchemists who tried, several hundred years ago, to turn lead into gold.

I want to look briefly at that lost science, for it is closer to the art of writing than you may have imagined. Surely it is no accident that in ancient Egypt the god of alchemy was also the god of writing. Every Christmas my father received at least a dozen cards showing pictures of alchemists. The details never varied. A man sits in his study, surrounded by beakers, alembics, and the assorted apparatus of scientific discovery. A skull and an hourglass stand on his desk to remind him that he is mortal. A lion dozes at his feet, but the alchemist is not afraid of the lion. Indeed, he seems to have made a pet of it.

Now take away the scientific apparatus. The alchemist undergoes a remarkable change. Posed beside his skull, his hourglass, and his lion, he looks less like a scientist than a saint, meditating on human frailty. Or like an eccentric writer, awaiting the arrival of the muse.

Many years after my interest in flying waned, I came across a chapter on alchemy in a book on magic. It was Albertus Magnus, alchemist par excellence, who kindled my imagination. I particularly liked the story in which he invites a group of churchmen to a garden party in the middle of winter. Albertus Magnus turns winter to summer and the guests dine among blossoms and trees laden with fruit. When they have finished the last course, winter returns. That struck me as rather a neat trick. I went to the public library and asked for a book on alchemy. Alchemy made plain.

The plump librarian gave me an encyclopedia of chemistry. Of alchemy she seemed never to have heard. The thin librarian gave me a book called *Remarks upon Alchemy and the Alchemists* and warned me not to blow myself up with crazy experiments. The book contained directions for turning base metals into gold. But I found these directions quite impossible to follow. How could anyone set up an experiment from the following passages:

> You must so join or mix gold and silver that they may not, by any possible means whatever, be separated. The reader, surely, need not be told that this is not a work of the hands. If you know not how to do this, you know nothing truly in our Art.
>
> Farewell, dilligent reader. In reading these things, invocate the Spirit of Eternal Light; speak little, meditate much, and judge aright.

Further reading gave me the key to this secret language. What many alchemists took to be the science of turning ordinary metal into gold was really a way of describing the spiritual disciplines that turn ordinary people into heroes and saints.

Now think for a moment what we as writers do. We transmute our personal experiences into works of art, which are impersonal and far more orderly and permanent than the lives that created them. The notebook I found by my father's bed testified to his faith in the mystery of this process. He went to bed with the broken pieces of a problem in his head. By what alchemy did he wake in the night with the pieces gathered into a neat solution? By what alchemy do our stories, gathered from our experiences at diverse times and distant places, rise up in our imaginations mended and whole?

NINE

Democracy in
the Library

F ree and open access to libraries, which represent knowledge, is so important to a democracy that our title for this section seems almost redundant. Library and democracy: one implies the other, for at its best, a democracy is governed by educated citizens who are chosen by other educated citizens.

America is a nation of immigrants, and for them the public library has often been a crucial resource. Bel Kaufman remembers herself as a twelve-year-old girl, newly arrived in New York from Russia "groping toward the mastery of the English language." On the other side of the continent, eight-year-old Amy Tan, a Chinese-American who thirty years later became a best-selling author, entered a local contest on "What the Library Means to Me." With simple directness, the young Amy stated her pride and pleasure in being able to use the library of Santa Rosa, California.

The library has helped some writers to place themselves, to feel they belong somewhere, to begin to understand their part in American life and history. Alfred Kazin recalls how he used the library as a way to learn about New York's past, which in turn might teach him about how he fit into the present. Not every American, however, has found easy entry into the world of books offered by libraries. James Baldwin describes the painful walk taken by John, a dreamy and unhappy black boy, toward midtown Manhattan. After a long meditation on the glories of the city, and how inaccessible they seem, John ends up at the pinnacle of desire: the public library. But he is too afraid to enter. John's experience echoes that of another black writer, Richard Wright, who tells in bitter detail how he had to scheme to find a way to use a Memphis library.

The issue of who should be allowed to use a library emerges as a kind of reflective subplot in Philip Roth's *Goodbye, Columbus*. While Neil, the narrator, struggles to fit into the upper-middle-class world of Short Hills, he works in a library that does not welcome the surrounding black community.

Not only do some libraries not welcome everyone, not every community welcomes a library. Democracy functions at its lowest ebb in John Cheever's "The Trouble of Marcie Flint," when the suburb of Shady Hill decides not to plan for a public library because certain members of the Village Council believe that a library might make their exclusive domain "attractive to a development."

But, despite occasional flaws and failings, the public library remains a symbol of America's proudest democratic aspirations and institutions. In 1875, John Greenleaf Whittier eulogized the opening of a new library, with lofty rhetoric: "The lords of thought await our call!" A century later, Archibald MacLeish also celebrated the opening of a new library: "The library, almost alone of the great monuments of civilization, stands taller now than it ever did before. The city—our American city at least—decays. The nation loses its grandeur. . . . The university is no longer always certain what it is. But the library remains. . . ." His words are a credo for all lovers of libraries.

"The Liberry" by Bel Kaufman

Born in Germany and raised in Russia, Bel Kaufman came to the United States at the age of twelve. Her awareness of an immigrant's feelings is evident in the following essay, "The Liberry."

Ms. Kaufman taught in New York City schools for twenty years, an experience reflected in her best-selling novel Up the Down Staircase *(1964), the story of a young English teacher in a contemporary big-city high school. Its phenomenal success led* Time *magazine to comment that it was "easily the most popular novel about U.S. public schools in history."*

Ms. Kaufman's second novel, Love, Etc., *appeared in 1979. She has also written lyrics for musicals and contributed to many periodicals and newspapers, including* The New York Times, *in which "The Liberry" was first published.*

A small boy in one of William Saroyan's stories finds himself in the public library for the first time. He looks around in awe: "All them books," he says, "and something written in each one!"

I remember myself as a 12-year-old, newly arrived from Russia, groping toward the mastery of the English language in my neighborhood library. Guided by no reading lists, informed by no book reviews, I had no use for the card catalogue, since I worked each shelf alphabetically, burrowing my way from one end of the stacks to the other, relentless as a mole. I read by trial and error, through trash and treasure; like a true addict, I was interested not so much in quality as in getting the stuff.

Sometimes I would stumble upon a book that was special; a book unrequired, unrecommended, unspoiled by teacher-imposed chores— "Name 3 . . . Answer the following . . ."—a book to be read for sheer pleasure.

Where else was it allowed, even encouraged, to thumb through a book, to linger on a page without being shooed away from handling the merchandise? This was merchandise to be handled. I was not fooled by the stiff, impassive maroon and dark-green library bindings; I nosed out the good ones. If the pages were worn and dog-eared, if the card tucked into its paper pocket inside the cover was stamped with lots of dates, I knew I had a winner.

Those dates linked me to the anonymous fellowship of other readers whose hands had turned the pages I was turning, who sometimes left penciled clues in the margins: a philosophic "How True!"—a succinct "Stinks."

Here, within walls built book by solid book, we sat in silent kinship, the only sounds shuffling of feet, scraping of chairs, an occasional loud whisper, and the librarian's stern "Shhh!"

The librarian was always there, unobtrusive and omniscient, ready for any question: Where to find a book about Eskimos? A history of submarines? A best-selling novel?—unruffled even by a request I once overheard in the children's section: "Have you got a book for an eight-year-old with tonsils?"

I am remembering this because today the public libraries are becoming less and less available to the people who need them most. Already shut part of the time, their hours reduced by 50 percent in the last five years, their budgets further curtailed as of July 1, and still threatened with continued cuts in staff and services, the public libraries have suffered more in the city's financial squeeze than any other major public-service agencies.

The first priority of our nation, according to former New York State Commissioner of Education, James E. Allen, is the right to read. Educators are inundating our schools with massive surveys, innovative techniques and expensive gimmicks to combat illiteracy and improve the reading skills of our children—at the same time that our public libraries are gradually closing their doors.

What are our priorities? Name 3.

It seems to me that especially now, when there are so many people in our city whose language is not English, whose homes are barren of books, who are daily seduced by clamorous offers of instant diversion, especially now we must hold on to something that will endure when the movie is over, the television set broken, the class dismissed for the last time.

For many, the public library is the only quiet place in an unquiet world; a refuge from the violence and ugliness outside; the only space available for privacy of work or thought. For many it is the only exposure to books waiting on open shelves to be taken home, free of charge.

As a former student put it: "In a liberry it's hard to avoid reading."

When I taught English in high school, I used to ask my students to bring a library card to class, on the chance that if they had one they might use it. One boy brought in his aunt's. "Aw, I ain't gonna *use* it," he cheerfully assured me, "I just brought it to *show* you!"

Still—some did make use of their cards, if only because they were *there*. Some enter the library today because it is *there*. Inside are all them books, and something written in each one. How sad for our city if the sign on the door should say CLOSED.

"What the Library Means to Me"
by Amy Tan

Amy Tan wrote this very short essay when she was eight years old for a contest sponsored by the Citizens Committee for the Santa Rosa (California) Library. It was published in the Santa Rosa Press-Democrat *under the headline, "Santa Rosa's School Children Tell What Library Means To Them."*

Ms. Tan reached a far wider audience when she was published again in her thirties: her first novel, The Joy Luck Club, *about the struggle for understanding between Chinese mothers and their Americanized children, became an instant best-seller in 1989 and made statistical history with its high sale price (over $1 million) for paperback rights. In* The New York Times Book Review, *a critic praised Ms. Tan for her "wonderful eye for what is telling, a fine ear for dialogue, a deep empathy for her subject matter and a guilelessly straightforward way of writing." Ms. Tan, who was born in Oakland, California, now lives in San Francisco.*

My name is Amy Tan, 8 years old, a third grader in Matanzas School. It is a brand new school and everything is so nice and pretty. I love school because the many things I learn seem to turn on a light in the little room in my mind. I can see a lot of things I have never seen before. I can read many interesting books by myself now. I love to read. My father takes me to the library every two weeks, and I check five or six books each time. These books seem to open many windows in my little room. I can see many wonderful things outside. I always look forward to go the library.

Once my father did not take me to the library for a whole month. He said, the library was closed because the building is too old. I missed it like a good friend. It seems a long long time my father took me to the Library again just before Christmas. Now it is on the second floor of some stores. I wish we can have a real nice and pretty library like my school. I put 18 cents in the box and signed my name to join Citizens of Santa Rosa Library.

"A Summer's Reading"
by Bernard Malamud

When Bernard Malamud, novelist and short-story writer, died in 1986 at the age of seventy-one, this loss to American literature was front-page news. Winner of two National Book Awards and a Pulitzer Prize, Malamud was highly respected by other writers and critics. At his death The New York Times *said that Malamud "was considered by many critics to be one of the finest contemporary American writers." The* Times *summarized his accomplishment: "Mr. Malamud's work showed a regard for Jewish tradition and the plight of ordinary men, and was imbued with the theme of moral wisdom gained through suffering." Critic*

Alan Lelchuk praised Malamud for surpassing skill in "the ancient art of basic storytelling in a modern voice." In the clarity, pain, and sympathy of "A Summer's Reading," a reader can hear that powerful voice.

Malamud's first novel, The Natural *(1952), was made into a popular movie starring Robert Redford in 1984. It was followed by other novels:* The Assistant *(1957);* A New Life *(1961);* The Fixer *(1966), which won a National Book Award and a Pulitzer Prize;* Pictures of Fidelman *(1969);* The Tenants *(1971);* Dubin's Lives *(1979); and* God's Grace *(1982). His stories appeared in several volumes, including* The Magic Barrel *(1958), which won another National Book Award, and* The Stories of Bernard Malamud *(1983).* The People: And Uncollected Stories *was published posthumously in 1989.*

George Stoyonovich was a neighborhood boy who had quit high school on an impulse when he was sixteen, run out of patience, and though he was ashamed everytime he went looking for a job, when people asked him if he had finished and he had to say no, he never went back to school. This summer was a hard time for jobs and he had none. Having so much time on his hands, George thought of going to summer school, but the kids in his classes would be too young. He also considered registering in a night high school, only he didn't like the idea of the teachers always telling him what to do. He felt they had not respected him. The result was he stayed off the streets and in his room most of the day. He was close to twenty and had needs with the neighborhood girls, but no money to spend, and he couldn't get more than an occasional few cents because his father was poor, and his sister Sophie, who resembled George, a tall bony girl of twenty-three, earned very little and what she had she kept for herself. Their mother was dead, and Sophie had to take care of the house.

Very early in the morning George's father got up to go to work in a fish market. Sophie left at about eight for her long ride in the subway to a cafeteria in the Bronx. George had his coffee by himself, then hung around in the house. When the house, a five-room railroad flat above a butcher store, got on his nerves he cleaned it up—mopped the floors with a wet mop and put things away. But most of the time he sat in his room. In the afternoons he listened to the ball game. Otherwise he had a couple of old copies of the *World Almanac* he had bought long ago, and he liked to read in them and also the magazines and newspapers that Sophie brought home, that had been left on the tables in the cafeteria. They were mostly picture magazines about movie stars and sports figures, also usually the *News* and *Mirror*. Sophie herself read whatever fell into her hands, although she sometimes read good books.

She once asked George what he did in his room all day and he said he read a lot too.

"Of what besides what I bring home? Do you ever read any worthwhile books?"

"Some," George answered, although he really didn't. He had tried to read a book or two that Sophie had in the house but found he was in no mood for them. Lately he couldn't stand made-up stories, they got on his nerves. He wished he had some hobby to work at—as a kid he was good in carpentry, but where could he work at it? Sometimes during the day he went for walks, but mostly he did his walking after the hot sun had gone down and it was cooler in the streets.

In the evening after supper George left the house and wandered in the neighborhood. During the sultry days some of the storekeepers and their wives sat in chairs on the thick, broken sidewalks in front of their shops, fanning themselves, and George walked past them and the guys hanging out on the candy store corner. A couple of them he had known his whole life, but nobody recognized each other. He had no place special to go, but generally, saving it till the last, he left the neighborhood and walked for blocks till he came to a darkly lit little park with benches and trees and an iron railing, giving it a feeling of privacy. He sat on a bench here, watching the leafy trees and the flowers blooming on the inside of the railing, thinking of a better life for himself. He thought of the jobs he had had since he had quit school—delivery boy, stock clerk, runner, lately working in a factory—and he was dissatisfied with all of them. He felt he would someday like to have a good job and live in a private house with a porch, on a street with trees. He wanted to have some dough in his pocket to buy things with, and a girl to go with, so as not to be so lonely, especially on Saturday nights. He wanted people to like and respect him. He thought about these things often but mostly when he was alone at night. Around midnight he got up and drifted back to his hot and stony neighborhood.

One time while on his walk George met Mr. Cattanzara coming home very late from work. He wondered if he was drunk but then could tell he wasn't. Mr. Cattanzara, a stocky, bald-headed man who worked in a change booth on an IRT station, lived on the next block after George's, above a shoe repair store. Nights, during the hot weather, he sat on his stoop in an undershirt, reading the *New York Times* in the light of the shoemaker's window. He read it from the first page to the last, then went up to sleep. And all the time he was reading the paper, his wife, a fat woman with a white face, leaned out of the window, gazing into the street, her thick white arms folded under her loose breast, on the window ledge.

Once in a while Mr. Cattanzara came home drunk, but it was a quiet drunk. He never made any trouble, only walked stiffly up the street and slowly climbed the stairs into the hall. Though drunk, he looked the same as always, except for his tight walk, the quietness, and that his eyes were wet. George liked Mr. Cattanzara because he remembered him giving him nickels to buy lemon ice with when he was a squirt. Mr. Cattanzara was a different type than those in the neighborhood. He asked different questions than the others when he met you, and he seemed to know what went on in all the newspapers. He read them, as his fat sick wife watched from the window.

"What are you doing with yourself this summer, George?" Mr. Cattanzara asked. "I see you walkin' around at nights."

George felt embarrassed. "I like to walk."

"What are you doin' in the day now?"

"Nothing much just right now. I'm waiting for a job." Since it shamed him to admit he wasn't working, George said, "I'm staying home—but I'm reading a lot to pick up my education."

Mr. Cattanzara looked interested. He mopped his hot face with a red handkerchief.

"What are you readin'?"

George hesitated, then said, "I got a list of books in the library once, and now I'm gonna read them this summer." He felt strange and a little unhappy saying this, but he wanted Mr. Cattanzara to respect him.

"How many books are there on it?"

"I never counted them. Maybe around a hundred."

Mr. Cattanzara whistled through his teeth.

"I figure if I did that," George went on earnestly, "it would help me in my education. I don't mean the kind they give you in high school. I want to know different things than they learn there, if you know what I mean."

The change maker nodded. "Still and all, one hundred books is a pretty big load for one summer."

"It might take longer."

"After you're finished with some, maybe you and I can shoot the breeze about them?" said Mr. Cattanzara.

"When I'm finished," George answered.

Mr. Cattanzara went home and George continued on his walk. After that, though he had the urge to, George did nothing different from usual. He still took his walks at night, ending up in the little park. But one evening the shoemaker on the next block stopped George to say he was a good boy, and George figured that Mr. Cattanzara had told him all about the books he was reading. From the shoemaker it must have gone down the street, because George saw a couple of people smiling kindly at him, though nobody spoke to him personally. He felt a little better around the neighborhood and liked it more, though not so much he would want to live in it forever. He had never exactly disliked the people in it, yet he had never liked them very much either. It was the fault of the neighborhood. To his surprise, George found out that his father and Sophie knew about his reading too. His father was too shy to say anything about it—he was never much of a talker in his whole life—but Sophie was softer to George, and she showed him in other ways she was proud of him.

As the summer went on George felt in a good mood about things. He cleaned the house every day, as a favor to Sophie, and he enjoyed the ball games more. Sophie gave him a buck a week allowance, and though it still wasn't enough and he had to use it carefully, it was a helluva lot better than just having two bits now and then. What he bought with the money—cigarettes mostly, an occasional beer or movie ticket—he got a big kick out of. Life wasn't so bad if you knew how to appreciate it. Occasionally he bought a paperback book from the newsstand, but he never got around to reading it, though he was glad to have a couple of books in his room. But he read thoroughly Sophie's magazines and newspapers. And at night was the most enjoyable time, because when he passed the storekeepers sitting outside their stores, he could tell they regarded him highly. He walked erect, and though he did not say much to them, or they to him, he could feel approval on all sides. A couple of nights he felt so good that he skipped the park at the end of the evening. He just wandered in the neighborhood, where people had known him from the time he was a kid playing punchball whenever there was a game of it going; he wandered there, then came home and got undressed for bed, feeling fine.

For a few weeks he had talked only once with Mr. Cattanzara, and though the change maker had said nothing more about the books, asked no questions, his silence made George a little uneasy. For a while George didn't pass in front of Mr. Cattanzara's house anymore, until one night, forgetting himself, he approached it from a different direction than he usually did when he did. It was already past midnight. The street, except for one or two people, was deserted, and George was surprised when he saw Mr. Cattanzara still reading his newspaper by the light of the street lamp overhead. His impulse was to stop at the stoop and talk to him. He wasn't sure what he wanted to say, though he felt the words would come when he began to talk; but the more he thought about it, the more the idea scared him, and he decided he'd better not. He even considered beating it home by another street, but he was too near Mr. Cattanzara, and the change maker might see him as he ran, and get annoyed. So George unobtrusively crossed the street, trying to make it seem as if he had to look in a store window on the other side, which he did, and then went on, uncomfortable at what he was doing. He feared Mr. Cattanzara would glance up from his paper and call him a dirty rat for walking on the other side of the street, but all he did was sit there, sweating through his undershirt, his bald head shining in the dim light as he read his *Times*, and upstairs his fat wife leaned out of the window, seeming to read the paper along with him. George thought she would spy him and yell out to Mr. Cattanzara, but she never moved her eyes off her husband.

George made up his mind to stay away from the change maker until he had got some of his softback books read, but when he started them and saw they were mostly story books, he lost his interest and didn't bother to finish them. He lost his interest in reading other things too. Sophie's magazines and newspapers went unread. She saw them piling up on a chair in his room and asked why he was no longer looking at them, and George told her it was because of all the other reading he had to do. Sophie said she had guessed that was it. So for most of the day, George had the radio on, turning to music when he was sick of the human voice. He kept the house fairly neat, and Sophie said nothing on the days when he neglected it. She was still kind and gave him his extra buck, though things weren't so good for him as they had been before.

But they were good enough, considering. Also his night walks invariably picked him up, no matter how bad the day was. Then one night George saw Mr. Cattanzara coming down the street toward him. George was about to turn and run but he recognized from Mr. Cattanzara's walk that he was drunk, and if so, probably he would not even bother to notice him. So George kept on walking straight ahead until he came abreast of Mr. Cattanzara and though he felt wound up enough to pop into the sky, he was not surprised when Mr. Cattanzara passed him without a word, walking slowly, his face and body stiff. George drew a breath in relief at his narrow escape, when he heard his name called, and there stood Mr. Cattanzara at his elbow, smelling like the inside of a beer barrel. His eyes were sad as he gazed at George, and George felt so intensely uncomfortable he was tempted to shove the drunk aside and continue on his walk.

But he couldn't act that way to him, and, besides, Mr. Cattanzara took a nickel out of his pants pocket and handed it to him.

"Go buy yourself a lemon ice, Georgie."

"It's not that time anymore, Mr. Cattanzara," George said, "I am a big guy now."

"No, you ain't," said Mr. Cattanzara, to which George made no reply he could think of.

"How are all your books comin' along now?" Mr. Cattanzara asked. Though he tried to stand steady, he swayed a little.

"Fine, I guess," said George, feeling the red crawling up his face.

"You ain't sure?" The change maker smiled slyly, a way George had never seen him smile.

"Sure I'm sure. They're fine."

Though his head swayed in little arcs, Mr. Cattanzara's eyes were steady. He had small blue eyes which could hurt if you looked at them too long.

"George," he said, "name me one book on that list that you read this summer, and I will drink to your health."

"I don't want anybody drinking to me."

"Name me one so I can ask you a question on it. Who can tell, if it's a good book maybe I might wanna read it myself."

George knew he looked passable on the outside, but inside he was crumbling apart.

Unable to reply, he shut his eyes, but when—years later—he opened them, he saw that Mr. Cattanzara had, out of pity, gone away, but in his ears he still heard the words he had said when he left: "George, don't do what I did."

The next night he was afraid to leave his room, and though Sophie argued with him he wouldn't open the door.

"What are you doing in there?" she asked.

"Nothing."

"Aren't you reading?"

"No."

She was silent a minute, then asked, "Where do you keep the books you read? I never see any in your room outside of a few cheap trashy ones."

He wouldn't tell her.

"In that case you're not worth a buck of my hard-earned money. Why should I break my back for you? Go on out, you bum, and get a job."

He stayed in his room for almost a week, except to sneak into the kitchen when nobody was home. Sophie railed at him, then begged him to come out, and his old father wept, but George wouldn't budge, though the weather was terrible and his small room stifling. He found it very hard to breathe, each breath was like drawing a flame into his lungs.

One night, unable to stand the heat anymore, he burst into the street at one A.M, a shadow of himself. He hoped to sneak to the park without being seen, but there were people all over the block, wilted and listless, waiting for a breeze. George lowered his eyes and walked, in disgrace, away from them, but before long he discovered they were still friendly to him. He figured Mr. Cattanzara hadn't told on him. Maybe when he woke up out of his drunk the next morning, he had forgotten all about meetng George. George felt his confidence slowly come back to him.

That same night a man on a street corner asked him if it was true that he had finished reading so many books and George admitted he had. The man said it was a wonderful thing for a boy his age to read so much.

"Yeah," George said, but he felt relieved. He hoped nobody would mention the books anymore, and when, after a couple of days, he accidentally met Mr. Cattanzara again, *he* didn't, though George had the idea he was the one who had started the rumor that he had finished all the books.

One evening in the fall, George ran out of his house to the library, where he hadn't been in years. There were books all over the place, wherever he looked, and though he was struggling to control an inward trembling, he easily counted off a hundred, then sat down at a table to read.

Excerpt from *A Walker in the City* by Alfred Kazin

For a biographical sketch of Alfred Kazin see pages 74–75, the introduction to an excerpt from his book New York Jew. *In the selection that follows, a reader can walk with Kazin toward the library.*

There was a new public library I liked to walk out to right after supper, when the streets were still full of light. It was to the north of the Italians, just off the El on Broadway, in the "American" district of old frame houses and brownstones and German ice-cream parlors and quiet tree-lined streets where I went to high school. Everything about that library was good, for it was usually empty and cool behind its awnings, and the shelves were packed with books that not many people ever seemed to take away. But even better was the long walk out of Brownsville to reach it.

How wonderful it was in the still suspended evening light to go past the police station on East New York and come out into the clinging damp sweetness of Italian cheese. The way to the borders of Brownsville there was always heavy with blocks of indistinguishable furniture stores, monument works, wholesale hardware shops. Block after block was lined with bedroom sets, granite tombstones, kitchen ranges, refrigerators, store fixtures, cash registers. It was like taking one last good look around before you said good-by. As the sun bore down on new kitchen ranges and refrigerators, I seemed to hear the clang of all those heavily smooth surfaces against the fiery windows, to feel myself pulled down endless corridors of tombstones, cash registers, maple beds, maple love seats, maple vanity tables. But at the police station, the green lamps on each side of the door, the detectives lounging along the street, the smell from the dark, damp, leaky steps that led down to the public toilets below, instantly proclaimed the end of Brownsville.

Ahead, the Italians' streets suddenly reared up into hills, all the trolley car lines flew apart into wild plunging crossroads—the way to anywhere, it seemed to me then. And in the steady heat, the different parts of me racing each other in excitement, the sweat already sweet on my face, still tasting on my lips the corn and salt and butter, I would dash over the tree-lined island at the crossroads, and on that boulevard so sharp with sun that I could never understand why the new red-brick walls of the Catholic church felt so cool as I passed, I crossed over into the Italian district.

I still had a certain suspicion of the Italians—surely they were all Fascists to a man? Every grocery window seemed to have a picture of Mussolini frowning under a feather-tipped helmet, every drugstore beneath the old-fashioned gold letters pasted on the window a colored lithograph of the Madonna with a luminescent heart showing through a blue gown. What I liked best in the windows were the thickly printed opera posters, topped by tiny photographs of singers with olive-bronze faces. Their long straight noses jutted aloofly, defying me to understand them. But despite the buzz of unfamiliar words ending in the letter *i*, I could at least make contact with LA FORZA DEL DESTINO. In the air was that high overriding damp sweetness of Italian cheese, then something peppery. In a butcher shop window at the corner of Pacific Street long incredibly thin sausage rings were strung around a horizontal bar. The clumps of red and brown meat dripping off those sausage rings always stayed with me until I left the Italians at Fulton Street—did they eat such things?

Usually, at that hour of the early evening when I passed through on my way to the new library, they were all still at supper. The streets were strangely empty except for an old man in a white cap who sat on the curb sucking at a twisted Italian cigar. I felt I was passing through a deserted town and knocking my head against each door to call the inhabitants out. It was a poor neighborhood, poor as ours. Yet all the houses and stores there, the very lettering of the signs AVVOCATO FARMACIA LATTERIA tantalized me by their foreignness. Everything there looked smaller and sleepier than it did in Brownsville. There was a kind of mild, infinitely soothing smell of flour and cheese mildly rotting in the evening sun. You could almost taste the cheese in the sweat you licked off your lips, could feel your whole body licking and tasting at the damp inner quietness that came out of the stores. The heat seemed to melt down every hard corner in sight.

Beyond Atlantic Avenue the sun glared and glared on broken glass lining the high stone walls of a Catholic reformatory that went all around the block. Barbed wire rose up on the other side of the wall, and oddly serene above the broken glass, very tall trees. Behind those walls, I had always heard, lived "bad girls" under the supervision of nuns. We knew what all that broken glass meant. The girls stole out every night and were lifted over the walls every morning by their laughing boy friends. We knew. The place was a prison house of the dark and hypocritical Catholic religion. Whenever I heard the great bell in the yard clanging for prayers as I passed, I had the same image in my mind of endless barren courts of narrow rooms, in each of which a girl in a prison smock looked up with pale hatred at a nun.

> And priests in black gowns were walking their rounds
> And binding with briars my joys and desires

Jesus! I would say to myself with hoped-for scorn, *look at my Yeshua!* How I wanted to get on to my library, to get on beyond that high stone wall lined with the jagged ends of broken milk bottles; never to have to look back at that red-brick church that reared itself up across from the borders of Brownsville like a fortress. Once, on the evening before an examination, I had gone into that church, had tried vaguely to pray, but had been so intimidated by the perpetual twilight, the remoteness of the freezing white altar and the Italian women in kerchiefs around me, that at a low murmuring out of a confession box near the door I had run away. Yet how lonely it always was passing under the wall—as if I were just about to be flung against it by a wave of my own thought.

Ahead of me now the black web of the Fulton Street El. On the other side of the BANCA COMMERCIALE, two long even pavements still raw with sunlight at seven o'clock of a summer evening take me straight through the German and Irish "American" neighborhoods. I could never decide whether it was all those brownstones and blue and gray frame houses or the sight of the library serenely waiting for me that made up the greatest pleasure of that early evening walk. As soon as I got out from under the darkness of the El on Fulton Street, I was catapulted into tranquillity.

Everything ahead of me now was of a different order—wide, clean, still, every block lined with trees. I sniffed hungrily at the patches of garden earth behind the black iron spikes and at the wooden shutters hot in the sun—there where even the names of the streets, Macdougal, Hull, Somers, made me humble with admiration. The long quiet avenues rustled comfortably in the sun; above the brownstone stoops all the yellow striped awnings were unfurled. Every image I had of peace, of quiet shaded streets in some old small-town America I had seen dreaming over the ads in the *Saturday Evening Post*, now came back to me as that proud procession of awnings along the brownstones. I can never remember *walking* those last few blocks to the library; I seemed to float along the canvas tops. Here were the truly American streets; here was where they lived. To get that near to brownstones, to see how private everything looked in that world of cool black painted floors and green walls where on each windowsill the first shoots of Dutch bulbs rose out of the pebbles like green and white flags, seemed to me the greatest privilege I had ever had. A breath of long-stored memory blew out at me from the veranda of Oyster Bay. Even when I visited an Irish girl from my high school class who lived in one of those brownstones, and was amazed to see that the rooms were as small as ours, that a Tammany court attendant's family could be as poor as we were, that behind the solid "American" front of fringed shawls, Yankee rocking chairs, and oval daguerreotypes on the walls they kept warm in winter over an oil stove—even then, I could think of those brownstone streets only as my great entrance into America, a half-hour nearer to "New York."

I had made a discovery; I had stumbled on a connection between myself and the shape and color of time in the streets of New York. Though I knew that brownstones were old-fashioned and had read scornful references to them in novels, it was just the thick, solid way in which they gripped to themselves some texture of the city's past that now fascinated me. There was one brownstone on Macdougal Street I would stop and brood over for long periods every evening I went to the library for fresh books—waiting in front of it, studying every crease in the stone, every line in the square windows jutting out above the street, as if I were planning its portrait. I had made a discovery: walking could take me back into the America of the nineteenth century.

On those early summer evenings, the library was usually empty, and there was such ease at the long tables under the plants lining the windowsills, the same books of American history lay so undisturbed on the shelves, the wizened, faintly smiling little old lady who accepted my presence without questions or suggestions or reproach was so delightful as she quietly, smilingly stamped my card and took back a batch of new books every evening, that whenever I entered the library I would walk up and down trembling in front of the shelves. For each new book

I took away, there seemed to be ten more of which I was depriving myself. Everything that summer I was sixteen was of equal urgency— Renan's *Life of Jesus*; the plays of Eugene O'Neill, which vaguely depressed me, but were full of sex; Galsworthy's *The Forsyte Saga*, to which I was so devoted that even on the day two years later Hitler came to power I could not entirely take it in, because on the same day John Galsworthy died; anything about Keats and Blake; about Beethoven; the plays of W. Somerset Maugham, which I could not relate to the author of *Of Human Bondage*; *The Education of Henry Adams*, for its portrait of John Quincy Adams leading his grandson to school; Lytton Strachey's *Eminent Victorians*, for its portrait of Cardinal Newman, the beautiful Newman who played the violin and was seen weeping in the long sad evening of his life; Thomas Mann's *Death in Venice*, which seemed to me vaguely sinister and unbearably profound; Turgenev's *Fathers and Sons*, which I took away one evening to finish on my fire escape with such a depth of satisfaction that I could never open the book again, for fear I would not recapture that first sensation.

The automatic part of all my reading was history. The past, the past was great: anything American, old, glazed, touched with dusk at the end of the nineteenth century, still smoldering with the fires lit by the industrial revolution, immediately set my mind dancing. The present was mean, the eighteenth century too Anglo-Saxon, too far away. Between them, in the light from the steerage ships waiting to discharge my parents onto the final shore, was the world of dusk, of rust, of iron, of gaslight, where, I thought, I would find my way to that fork in the road where all American lives cross. The past was deep, deep, full of solitary Americans whose careers, though closed in death, had woven an arc around them which I could see in space and time—"lonely Americans," it was even the title of a book. I remember that the evening I opened Lewis Mumford's *The Brown Decades* I was so astonished to see a photograph of Brooklyn Bridge, I so instantly formed against that brownstone on Macdougal Street such close and loving images of Albert Pinkham Ryder, Charles Peirce, Emily Dickinson, Thomas Eakins, and John August Roebling, that I could never walk across Roebling's bridge, or pass the hotel on University Place named Albert, in Ryder's honor, or stop in front of the garbage cans at Fulton and Cranberry Streets in

Brooklyn at the place where Whitman had himself printed *Leaves of Grass,* without thinking that I had at last opened the great trunk of forgotten time in New York in which I, too, I thought, would someday find the source of my unrest.

I felt then that I stood outside all that, that I would be alien forever, but that I could at least keep the trunk open by reading. And though I knew somewhere in myself that a Ryder, an Emily Dickinson, an Eakins, a Whitman, even that fierce-browed old German immigrant Roebling, with his flute and his metaphysics and his passionate love of suspension bridges, were alien, too, alien in the deepest way, like my beloved Blake, my Yeshua, my Beethoven, my Newman—nevertheless I still thought of myself then as standing outside America. I read as if books would fill my every gap, legitimize my strange quest for the American past, remedy my every flaw, let me in at last into the great world that was anything just out of Brownsville.

So that when, leaving the library for the best of all walks, to Highland Park, I came out on Bushwick Avenue, with its strange, wide, sun-lit spell, a thankfulness seized me, mixed with envy and bitterness, and I waited against a hydrant for my violence to pass. Why were these people *here*, and we *there*? Why had I always to think of insider and outsider, of their belonging and our not belonging, when books had carried me this far, and when, as I could already see, it was myself that would carry me farther—beyond these petty distinctions I had so long made in loneliness?

Excerpt from
Go Tell It on the Mountain
by James Baldwin

When James Baldwin died in 1987 at the age of sixty-three, The New York Times *said in a front-page story that Baldwin's "passionate, intensely personal essays in the 1950s and '60s made him an eloquent voice of the civil-rights movement." The most important collections of Baldwin's essays are* Notes of a Native Son *(1955);* Nobody Knows My Name *(1961); and* The Fire Next Time *(1963), whose very titles hold something of the ringing, almost apocalyptic, and yet fiercely colloquial tone of Baldwin's prose.*

Baldwin's novels and plays did not receive the unqualified praise accorded his essays. Among the best-reviewed was Go Tell It on the Mountain *(1953), his first book and first novel, an autobiographical account of a poor boy growing up in the 1930s under the tyrannical domination of his father, who was a Harlem preacher. The following excerpt is taken from this novel.*

Baldwin's other works include the novels Giovanni's Room *(1956);* Another Country *(1962);* Tell Me How Long the Train's Been Gone *(1968); If Beale Street Could Talk *(1974);* Just Above My Head *(1979); several plays, such as* Blues for Mister Charlie *(1964); an essay about blacks and American films,* The Devil Finds Work *(1976); a long essay on the murder of twenty-eight black children in Atlanta,* Evidence of Things Not Seen *(1985); and a collection of stories,* Going to Meet the Man *(1964).*

Then he remembered his father and his mother, and all the arms stretched out to hold him back, to save him from this city where, they said, his soul would find perdition.

And certainly perdition sucked at the feet of the people who walked there; and cried in the lights, in the gigantic towers; the marks of Satan could be found in the faces of the people who waited at the doors of movie houses; his words were printed on the great movie posters that invited people to sin. It was the roar of the damned that filled Broadway, where motor cars and buses and the hurrying people disputed every inch with death. *Broadway:* the way that led to death *was* broad, and many could be found thereon; but narrow was the way that led to life eternal, and few there were who found it. But he did not long for the narrow way, where all his people walked; where the houses did not rise, piercing, as it seemed, the unchanging clouds, but huddled, flat, ignoble, close to the filthy ground, where the streets and the hallways and the rooms were dark, and where the unconquerable odor was of dust, and sweat, and urine, and homemade gin. In the narrow way, the way of the cross, there awaited him only humiliation forever; there awaited him, one day, a house like his father's house, and a church like his father's, and a job like his father's, where he would grow old and black with hunger and toil. The way of the cross had given him a belly filled with wind and had bent his mother's back; they had never worn fine clothes, but here, where the buildings contested God's power and where the men and women did not fear God, here he might eat and drink to his heart's content and clothe his body with wondrous fabrics, rich to the eye and pleasing to the touch. And then what of his soul, which would one day come to die and stand naked before the judgment bar? What would his conquest of the city profit him on that day? To hurl away, for a moment of ease, the glories of eternity!

These glories were unimaginable—but the city was real. He stood for a moment on the melting snow, distracted, and then began to run down the hill, feeling himself fly as the descent became more rapid, and thinking: "I can climb back up. If it's wrong, I can always climb back up." At the bottom of the hill, where the ground abruptly leveled off onto a gravel path, he nearly knocked down an old white man with a white beard, who was walking very slowly and leaning on his cane.

They both stopped, astonished, and looked at one another. John struggled to catch his breath and apologize, but the old man smiled. John smiled back. It was as though he and the old man had between them a great secret; and the old man moved on. The snow glittered in patches all over the park. Ice, under the pale, strong sun, melted slowly on the branches and the trunks of trees.

He came out of the park at Fifth Avenue where, as always, the old-fashioned horse-carriages were lined along the curb, their drivers sitting on the high seats with rugs around their knees, or standing in twos and threes near the horses, stamping their feet and smoking pipes and talking. In summer he had seen people riding in these carriages, looking like people out of books, or out of movies in which everyone wore old-fashioned clothes and rushed at nightfall over frozen roads, hotly pursued by their enemies who wanted to carry them back to death. *"Look back, look back,"* had cried a beautiful woman with long blonde curls, *"and see if we are pursued!"*—and she had come, as John remembered, to a terrible end. Now he stared at the horses, enormous and brown and patient, stamping every now and again a polished hoof, and he thought of what it would be like to have one day a horse of his own. He would call it Rider, and mount it at morning when the grass was wet, and from the horse's back look out over great, sun-filled fields, his own. Behind him stood his house, great and rambling and very new, and in the kitchen his wife, a beautiful woman, made breakfast, and the smoke rose out of the chimney, melting into the morning air. They had children, who called him Papa and for whom at Christmas he bought electric trains. And he had turkeys and cows and chickens and geese, and other horses besides Rider. They had a closet full of whisky and wine; they had cars—but what church did they go to and what would he teach his children when they gathered around him in the evening? He looked straight ahead, down Fifth Avenue, where graceful women in fur coats walked, looking into the windows that held silk dresses, and watches, and rings. What church did they go to? And what were their houses like when in the evening they took off these coats, and these silk dresses, and put their jewelry in a box, and leaned back in soft beds to think for a moment before they slept of the day gone by? Did they read a verse from the Bible every night and fall on their knees to pray? But no, for their thoughts were not of God, and their way was not God's way. They were in the world, and of the world, and their feet laid hold on Hell.

Yet in school some of them had been nice to him, and it was hard to think of them burning in Hell forever, they who were so gracious and beautiful now. Once, one winter when he had been very sick with a heavy cold that would not leave him, one of his teachers had bought him a bottle of cod liver oil, especially prepared with heavy syrup so that it did not taste so bad: this was surely a Christian act. His mother had said that God would bless that woman; and he had got better. They were kind—he was sure that they were kind—and on the day that he would bring himself to their attention they would surely love and honor him. This was not his father's opinion. His father said that all white people were wicked, and that God was going to bring them low. He said that white people were never to be trusted, and that they told nothing but lies, and that not one of them had ever loved a nigger. He, John, was a nigger, and he would find out, as soon as he got a little older, how evil white people could be. John had read about the things white people did to colored people; how, in the South, where his parents came from, white people cheated them of their wages, and burned them, and shot them—and did worse things, said his father, which the tongue could not endure to utter. He had read about colored men being burned in the electric chair for things they had not done; how in riots they were beaten with clubs; how they were tortured in prisons; how they were the last to be hired and the first to be fired. Niggers did not live on these streets where John now walked; it was forbidden; and yet he walked here, and no one raised a hand against him. But did he dare to enter this shop out of which a woman now casually walked, carrying a great round box? Or this apartment before which a white man stood, dressed in a brilliant uniform? John knew he did not dare, not today, and he heard his father's laugh: *"No, nor tomorrow neither!"* For him there was the back door, and the dark stairs, and the kitchen or the basement. This world was not for him. If he refused to believe, and wanted to break his neck trying, then he could try until the sun refused to shine; they would never let him enter. In John's mind then, the people and the avenue underwent a change, and he feared them and knew that one day he could hate them if God did not change his heart.

He left Fifth Avenue and walked west towards the movie houses.

Here on 42nd Street it was less elegant but no less strange. He loved this street, not for the people or the shops but for the stone lions that guarded the great main building of the Public Library, a building filled with books and unimaginably vast, and which he had never yet dared to enter. He might, he knew, for he was a member of the branch in Harlem and was entitled to take books from any library in the city. But he had never gone in because the building was so big that it must be full of corridors and marble steps, in the maze of which he would be lost and never find the book he wanted. And then everyone, all the white people inside, would know that he was not used to great buildings, or to many books, and they would look at him with pity. He would enter on another day, when he had read all the books uptown, an achievement that would, he felt, lend him the poise to enter any building in the world.

Excerpt from *Black Boy* by Richard Wright

After publication in 1940 of his powerful novel Native Son, *Richard Wright (1908–60) was long considered the leading black author of the United States. Born in Mississippi, he left for Chicago at age nineteen (the setting of* Native Son*) and then, after World War II, became an expatriate in Paris. Although Wright is best known today for* Native Son *and for* Black Boy *(1945), an autobiography of his childhood and youth (from which the following excerpt is taken), he published several other notable books.* Uncle Tom's Children *(1938, enlarged 1940) is a collection of four long stories; other novels include* The Outsider *(1953),* Black Power *(1954);* The Color Curtain *(1956);* Pagan

Spain (1957); and a few works published posthumously, including an autobiographical sequel to Black Boy, American Hunger *(1977).*

One morning I arrived early at work and went into the bank lobby where the Negro porter was mopping. I stood at a counter and picked up the Memphis *Commercial Appeal* and began my free reading of the press. I came finally to the editorial page and saw an article dealing with one H. L. Mencken. I knew by hearsay that he was the editor of the *American Mercury*, but aside from that I knew nothing about him. The article was a furious denunciation of Mencken, concluding with one, hot, short sentence: Mencken is a fool.

I wondered what on earth this Mencken had done to call down upon him the scorn of the South. The only people I had ever heard denounced in the South were Negroes, and this man was not a Negro. Then what ideas did Mencken hold that made a newspaper like the *Commercial Appeal* castigate him publicly? Undoubtedly he must be advocating ideas that the South did not like. Were there, then, people other than Negroes who criticized the South? I knew that during the Civil War the South had hated northern whites, but I had not encountered such hate during my life. Knowing no more of Mencken than I did at that moment, I felt a vague sympathy for him. Had not the South, which had assigned me the role of a non-man, cast at him its hardest words?

Now, how could I find out about this Mencken? There was a huge library near the riverfront, but I knew that Negroes were not allowed to patronize its shelves any more than they were the parks and playgrounds of the city. I had gone into the library several times to get books for the white men on the job. Which of them would now help me to get books? And how could I read them without causing concern to the white men with whom I worked? I had so far been successful in hiding my thoughts and feelings from them, but I knew that I would create hostility if I went about this business of reading in a clumsy way.

I weighed the personalities of the men on the job. There was Don, a Jew; but I distrusted him. His position was not much better than mine and I knew that he was uneasy and insecure; he had always treated me in an offhand, bantering way that barely concealed his contempt. I was afraid to ask him to help me to get books; his frantic desire to demonstrate a racial solidarity with the whites against Negroes might make him betray me.

Then how about the boss? No, he was a Baptist and I had the suspicion that he would not be quite able to comprehend why a black boy would want to read Mencken. There were other white men on the job whose attitudes showed clearly that they were Kluxers or sympathizers, and they were out of the question.

There remained only one man whose attitude did not fit into an anti-Negro category, for I had heard the white men refer to him as a "Pope lover." He was an Irish Catholic and was hated by the white Southerners. I knew that he read books, because I had got him volumes from the library several times. Since he, too, was an object of hatred, I felt that he might refuse me but would hardly betray me. I hesitated, weighing and balancing the imponderable realities.

One morning I paused before the Catholic fellow's desk.

"I want to ask you a favor," I whispered to him.

"What is it?"

"I want to read. I can't get books from the library. I wonder if you'd let me use your card?"

He looked at me suspiciously.

"My card is full most of the time," he said.

"I see," I said and waited, posing my question silently.

"You're not trying to get me into trouble, are you, boy?" he asked, staring at me.

"Oh, no, sir."

"What book do you want?"

"A book by H. L. Mencken."

"Which one?"

"I don't know. Has he written more than one?"

"He has written several."

"I didn't know that."

"What makes you want to read Mencken?"

"Oh, I just saw his name in the newspaper," I said.

"It's good of you to want to read," he said. "But you ought to read the right things."

I said nothing. Would he want to supervise my reading?

"Let me think," he said. "I'll figure out something."

I turned from him and he called me back. He stared at me quizzically.

"Richard, don't mention this to the other white men," he said.

"I understand," I said. "I won't say a word."

A few days later he called me to him.

"I've got a card in my wife's name," he said. "Here's mine."

"Thank you, sir."

"Do you think you can manage it?"

"I'll manage fine," I said.

"If they suspect you, you'll get in trouble," he said.

"I'll write the same kind of notes to the library that you wrote when you sent me for books," I told him. "I'll sign your name."

He laughed.

"Go ahead. Let me see what you get," he said.

That afternoon I addressed myself to forging a note. Now, what were the names of books written by H. L. Mencken? I did not know any of them. I finally wrote what I thought would be a foolproof note: *Dear Madam: Will you please let this nigger boy*—I used the word "nigger" to make the librarian feel that I could not possibly be the author of the note—*have some books by H. L. Mencken?* I forged the white man's name.

I entered the library as I had always done when on errands for whites, but I felt that I would somehow slip up and betray myself. I doffed my hat, stood a respectful distance from the desk, looked as unbookish as possible, and waited for the white patrons to be taken care of. When the desk was clear of people, I still waited. The white librarian looked at me.

"What do you want, boy?"

As though I did not possess the power of speech, I stepped forward and simply handed her the forged note, not parting my lips.

"What books by Mencken does he want?" she asked.

"I don't know, ma'am," I said, avoiding her eyes.

"Who gave you this card?"

"Mr. Falk," I said.

"Where is he?"

"He's at work, at the M——— Optical Company," I said. "I've been in here for him before."

"I remember," the woman said. "But he never wrote notes like this."

Oh, God, she's suspicious. Perhaps she would not let me have the books? If she had turned her back at that moment, I would have ducked out the door and never gone back. Then I thought of a bold idea.

"You can call him up, ma'am," I said, my heart pounding.

"You're not using these books, are you?" she asked pointedly.

"Oh, no, ma'am. I can't read."

"I don't know what he wants by Mencken," she said under her breath.

I knew now that I had won; she was thinking of other things and the race question had gone out of her mind. She went to the shelves. Once or twice she looked over her shoulder at me, as though she was still doubtful. Finally she came forward with two books in her hand.

"I'm sending him two books," she said. "But tell Mr. Falk to come in next time, or send me the names of the books he wants. I don't know what he wants to read."

I said nothing. She stamped the card and handed me the books. Not daring to glance at them, I went out of the library, fearing that the woman would call me back for further questioning. A block away from the library I opened one of the books and read a title: *A Book of Prefaces*. I was nearing my nineteenth birthday and I did not know how to pronounce the word "preface." I thumbed the pages and saw strange words and strange names. I shook my head, disappointed. I looked at the other book; it was called *Prejudices*. I knew what that word meant; I had heard it all my life. And right off I was on guard against Mencken's books. Why would a man want to call a book *Prejudices*? The word was so stained with all my memories of racial hate that I could not conceive of anybody using it for a title. Perhaps I had made a mistake about Mencken? A man who had prejudices must be wrong.

When I showed the books to Mr. Falk, he looked at me and frowned.

"That librarian might telephone you," I warned him.

"That's all right," he said. "But when you're through reading those books, I want you to tell me what you get out of them."

That night in my rented room, while letting the hot water run over my can of pork and beans in the sink, I opened *A Book of Prefaces* and began to read. I was jarred and shocked by the style, the clear, clean, sweeping sentences. Why did he write like that? And how did one write like that? I pictured the man as a raging demon, slashing with his pen, consumed with hate, denouncing everything American, extolling everything European or German, laughing at the weaknesses of people, mocking God, authority. What was this? I stood up, trying to realize what reality lay behind the meaning of the words ... Yes, this man was fighting, fighting with words. He was using words as a weapon, using them as one would use a club. Could words be weapons? Well, yes, for here they were. Then, maybe, perhaps, I could use them as a weapon? No. It frightened me. I read on and what amazed me was not what he said, but how on earth anybody had the courage to say it.

Occasionally I glanced up to reassure myself that I was alone in the room. Who were these men about whom Mencken was talking so passionately? Who was Anatole France? Joseph Conrad? Sinclair Lewis, Sherwood Anderson, Dostoevski, George Moore, Gustave Flaubert, Maupassant, Tolstoy, Frank Harris, Mark Twain, Thomas Hardy, Arnold Bennett, Stephen Crane, Zola, Norris, Gorky, Bergson, Ibsen, Balzac, Bernard Shaw, Dumas, Poe, Thomas Mann, O. Henry, Dreiser, H. G. Wells, Gogol, T. S. Eliot, Gide, Baudelaire, Edgar Lee Masters, Stendhal, Turgenev, Huneker, Nietzsche, and scores of others? Were these men real? Did they exist or had they existed? And how did one pronounce their names?

I ran across many words whose meanings I did not know, and I either looked them up in a dictionary or, before I had a chance to do that, encountered the word in a context that made its meaning clear. But what strange world was this? I concluded the book with the conviction that I had somehow overlooked something terribly important in life. I had once tried to write, had once reveled in feeling, had let my crude imagination roam, but the impulse to dream had been slowly beaten out of me by experience. Now it surged up again and I hungered for books, new ways of looking and seeing. It was not a matter of believing or disbelieving what I read, but of feeling something new, of being affected by something that made the look of the world different.

As dawn broke I ate my pork and beans, feeling dopey, sleepy. I went to work, but the mood of the book would not die; it lingered, coloring everything I saw, heard, did. I now felt that I knew what the white men were feeling. Merely because I had read a book that had spoken of how they lived and thought, I identified myself with that book. I felt vaguely guilty. Would I, filled with bookish notions, act in a manner that would make the whites dislike me?

I forged more notes and my trips to the library became frequent. Reading grew into a passion. My first serious novel was Sinclair Lewis's *Main Street*. It made me see my boss, Mr. Gerald, and identify him as an American type. I would smile when I saw him lugging his golf bags into the office. I had always felt a vast distance separating me from the boss, and now I felt closer to him, though still distant. I felt now that I knew him, that I could feel the very limits of his narrow life. And this had happened because I had read a novel about a mythical man called George F. Babbitt.

The plots and stories in the novels did not interest me so much as the point of view revealed. I gave myself over to each novel without reserve, without trying to criticize it; it was enough for me to see and feel something different. And for me, everything was something different. Reading was like a drug, a dope. The novels created moods in which I lived for days. But I could not conquer my sense of guilt, my feeling that the white men around me knew that I was changing, that I had begun to regard them differently.

Whenever I brought a book to the job, I wrapped it in newspaper —a habit that was to persist for years in other cities and under other circumstances. But some of the white men pried into my packages when I was absent and they questioned me.

"Boy, what are you reading those books for?"

"Oh, I don't know, sir."

"That's deep stuff you're reading, boy."

"I'm just killing time, sir."

"You'll addle your brains if you don't watch out."

I read Dreiser's *Jennie Gerhardt* and *Sister Carrie* and they revived in me a vivid sense of my mother's suffering; I was overwhelmed. I grew silent, wondering about the life around me. It would have been impossible for me to have told anyone what I derived from these novels, for it was nothing less than a sense of life itself. All my life had shaped me for the realism, the naturalism of the modern novel, and I could not read enough of them.

Steeped in new moods and ideas, I bought a ream of paper and tried to write; but nothing would come, or what did come was flat beyond telling. I discovered that more than desire and feeling were necessary to write and I dropped the idea. Yet I still wondered how it was possible to know people sufficiently to write about them? Could I ever learn about life and people? To me, with my vast ignorance, my Jim Crow station in life, it seemed a task impossible of achievement. I now knew what being a Negro meant. I could endure the hunger. I had learned to live with hate. But to feel that there were feelings denied me, that the very breath of life itself was beyond my reach, that more than anything else hurt, wounded me. I had a new hunger.

In buoying me up, reading also cast me down, made me see what was possible, what I had missed. My tension returned, new, terrible, bitter, surging, almost too great to be contained. I no longer *felt* that the world about me was hostile, killing; I *knew* it. A million times I asked myself what I could do to save myself, and there were no answers. I seemed forever condemned, ringed by walls.

I did not discuss my reading with Mr. Falk, who had lent me his library card; it would have meant talking about myself and that would have been too painful. I smiled each day, fighting desperately to maintain my old behavior, to keep my disposition seemingly sunny. But some of the white men discerned that I had begun to brood.

"Wake up there, boy!" Mr. Olin said one day.

"Sir!" I answered for the lack of a better word.

"You act like you've stolen something," he said.

I laughed in the way I knew he expected me to laugh, but I resolved to be more conscious of myself, to watch my every act, to guard and hide the new knowledge that was dawning within me.

If I went north, would it be possible for me to build a new life then? But how could a man build a life upon vague, unformed yearnings? I wanted to write and I did not even know the English language. I bought English grammars and found them dull. I felt that I was getting a better sense of the language from novels than from grammars. I read hard, discarding a writer as soon as I felt that I had grasped his point of view. At night the printed page stood before my eyes in sleep.

Mrs. Moss, my landlady, asked me one Sunday morning:

"Son, what is this you keep on reading?"

"Oh, nothing. Just novels."

"What you get out of 'em?"

"I'm just killing time," I said.

"I hope you know your own mind," she said in a tone which implied that she doubted if I had a mind.

I knew of no Negroes who read the books I liked and I wondered if any Negroes ever thought of them. I knew that there were Negro doctors, lawyers, newspapermen, but I never saw any of them. When I read a Negro newspaper I never caught the faintest echo of my preoccupation in its pages. I felt trapped and occasionally, for a few days, I would stop reading. But a vague hunger would come over me for books, books that opened up new avenues of feeling and seeing, and again I would forge another note to the white librarian. Again I would read and wonder as only the naïve and unlettered can read and wonder, feeling that I carried a secret, criminal burden about with me each day.

That winter my mother and brother came and we set up housekeeping, buying furniture on the installment plan, being cheated and yet knowing no way to avoid it. I began to eat warm food and to my surprise found that regular meals enabled me to read faster. I may have lived through many illnesses and survived them, never suspecting that I was ill. My brother obtained a job and we began to save toward the trip north, plotting our time, setting tentative dates for departure. I told none of the white men on the job that I was planning to go north; I knew that the moment they felt I was thinking of the North they would change toward me. It would have made them feel that I did not like the life I was living, and because my life was completely conditioned by what they said or did, it would have been tantamount to challenging them.

I could calculate my chances for life in the South as a Negro fairly clearly now.

I could fight the southern whites by organizing with other Negroes, as my grandfather had done. But I knew that I could never win that way; there were many whites and there were but few blacks. They were strong and we were weak. Outright black rebellion could never win. If I fought openly I would die and I did not want to die. News of lynchings was frequent.

I could submit and live the life of a genial slave, but that was impossible. All of my life had shaped me to live by my own feelings and thoughts. I could make up to Bess and marry her and inherit the house. But that, too, would be the life of a slave; if I did that, I would crush to death something within me, and I would hate myself as much as I knew the whites already hated those who had submitted. Neither could I ever willingly present myself to be kicked, as Shorty had done. I would rather have died than do that.

I could drain off my restlessness by fighting with Shorty and Harrison. I had seen many Negroes solve the problem of being black by transferring their hatred of themselves to others with a black skin and fighting them. I would have to be cold to do that, and I was not cold and I could never be.

I could, of course, forget what I had read, thrust the whites out of my mind, forget them; and find release from anxiety and longing in sex and alcohol. But the memory of how my father had conducted himself made that course repugnant. If I did not want others to violate my life, how could I voluntarily violate it myself?

I had no hope whatever of being a professional man. Not only had I been so conditioned that I did not desire it, but the fulfillment of such an ambition was beyond my capabilities. Well-to-do Negroes lived in a world that was almost as alien to me as the world inhabited by whites.

What, then, was there? I held my life in my mind, in my consciousness each day, feeling at times that I would stumble and drop it, spill it forever. My reading had created a vast sense of distance between me and the world in which I lived and tried to make a living, and that sense of distance was increasing each day. My days and nights were one long, quiet, continuously contained dream of terror, tension, and anxiety. I wondered how long I could bear it.

Excerpt from *Goodbye, Columbus* by Philip Roth

Philip Roth, born in New Jersey in 1933, has made himself one of the most visible and articulate novelists of contemporary American life, particularly of urban, Eastern and Jewish culture. Readers who have never read Roth may still have heard of his comic novel Portnoy's Complaint *(1969), which shocked (and delighted) a wide audience with its relentlessly frank discussion of male sexuality.* Goodbye, Columbus *(1959), from which the following excerpt is taken, contained the title novella and five short stories; it won Roth a National Book Award. His other novels, almost always best-sellers, include* Letting Go *(1962);* Our Gang *(1971);* The Breast *(1972);* The Great American Novel *(1973);* The Professor of Desire *(1977);* The Ghost Writer *(1979);* Zuckerman Unbound *(1981);* Zuckerman Bound *(1985); and* The Counterlife *(1987).*

In this excerpt from Goodbye, Columbus, *Neil, who works as a librarian in the downtown Newark Public Library, has fallen in love with Brenda Patimkin, who lives in the inaccessible suburban splendor of Short Hills. The contrast between Neil's life and Brenda's is heightened by Neil's experience with a small black boy in the library. This boy's world is even farther removed from Neil's than Neil's is from Brenda's.*

The next morning I found a parking space on Washington Street directly across from the library. Since I was twenty minutes early

I decided to stroll in the park rather than cross over to work; I didn't particularly care to join my colleagues, who I knew would be sipping early morning coffee in the binding room, smelling still of all the orange crush they'd drunk that weekend at Asbury Park. I sat on a bench and looked out towards Broad Street and the morning traffic. The Lackawanna commuter trains were rumbling in a few blocks to the north and I could hear them, I thought—the sunny green cars, old and clean, with windows that opened all the way. Some mornings, with time to kill before work, I would walk down to the tracks and watch the open windows roll in, on their sills the elbows of tropical suits and the edges of briefcases, the properties of businessmen arriving in town from Maplewood, the Oranges, and the suburbs beyond.

The park, bordered by Washington Street on the west and Broad on the east, was empty and shady and smelled of trees, night, and dog leavings; and there was a faint damp smell too, indicating that the huge rhino of a water cleaner had passed by already, soaking and whisking the downtown streets. Down Washington Street, behind me, was the Newark Museum—I could see it without even looking: two oriental vases in front like spittoons for a rajah, and next to it the little annex to which we had traveled on special buses as schoolchildren. The annex was a brick building, old and vine-covered, and always reminded me of New Jersey's link with the beginning of the country, with George Washington, who had trained his scrappy army—a little bronze tablet informed us children—in the very park where I now sat. At the far end of the park, beyond the Museum, was the bank building where I had gone to college. It had been converted some years before into an extension of Rutgers University; in fact, in what once had been the bank president's waiting room I had taken a course called Contemporary Moral Issues. Though it was summer now, and I was out of college three years, it was not hard for me to remember the other students, my friends, who had worked evenings in Bamberger's and Kresge's and had used the commissions they'd earned pushing ladies' out-of-season shoes to pay their laboratory fees. And then I looked out to Broad Street again. Jammed between a grimy-windowed bookstore and a cheesy luncheonette was the marquee of a tiny art theater—how many years had passed since I'd stood beneath that marquee, lying about the year of my birth so as to see Hedy Lamarr swim naked in *Ecstasy*; and then, having slipped the ticket taker an extra quarter, what disappointment I had felt at the frugality of her Slavic charm . . . Sitting there in the park, I felt a deep knowledge of Newark, an attachment so rooted that it could not help but branch out into affection.

Suddenly it was nine o'clock and everything was scurrying. Wobbly-heeled girls revolved through the doors of the telephone building across the way, traffic honked desperately, policeman barked, whistled, and waved motorists to and fro. Over at St. Vincent's Church the huge dark portals swung back and those bleary-eyes that had risen early for Mass now blinked at the light. Then the worshipers had stepped off the church steps and were racing down the streets towards desks, filing cabinets, secretaries, bosses, and—if the Lord had seen fit to remove a mite of harshness from their lives—to the comfort of air-conditioners pumping at their windows. I got up and crossed over to the library, wondering if Brenda was awake yet.

The pale cement lions stood unconvincing guard on the library steps, suffering their usual combination of elephantiasis and arteriosclerosis, and I was prepared to pay them as little attention as I had for the past eight months were it not for a small colored boy who stood in front of one of them. The lion had lost all of its toes the summer before to a safari of juvenile delinquents, and now a new tormentor stood before him, sagging a little in his knees, and growling. He would growl, low and long, drop back, wait, then growl again. Then he would straighten up, and, shaking his head, he would say to the lion, "Man, you's a coward . . ." Then, once again, he'd growl.

The day began the same as any other. From behind the desk on the main floor, I watched the hot high-breasted teen-age girls walk twitch-ingly up the wide flight of marble stairs that led to the main reading room. The stairs were an imitation of a staircase somewhere in Versailles, though in their toreador pants and sweaters these young daughters of Italian leatherworkers, Polish brewery hands, and Jewish furriers were hardly duchesses. They were not Brenda either, and any lust that sparked inside me through the dreary day was academic and time-passing. I looked at my watch occasionally, thought of Brenda, and waited for lunch and then for after lunch, when I would take over the Information Desk upstairs and John McKee, who was only twenty-one but wore elastic bands around his sleeves, would march starchily down the stairs to work assiduously at stamping books in and out. John McRubberbands was in his last year at Newark State Teachers College where he was studying at the Dewey Decimal System in preparation for his lifework. The library was not going to be my lifework, I knew it. Yet, there had been some talk—from Mr. Seapello, an old eunuch who had learned somehow to disguise his voice as a man's—that when I returned from my summer vacation I would be put in charge of the Reference Room, a position that had been empty ever since that morning when Martha Winney had fallen off a high stool in the Encyclopedia Room and shattered all those frail bones that come together to form what in a woman half her age we would call the hips.

I had strange fellows at the library and, in truth, there were many hours when I never quite knew how I'd gotten there or why I stayed. But I did stay and after a while waited patiently for that day when I would go into the men's room on the main floor for a cigarette and, studying myself as I expelled smoke into the mirror, would see that at some moment during the morning I had gone pale, and that under my skin, as under McKee's and Scapello's and Miss Winney's, there was a thin cushion of air separating the blood from the flesh. Someone had pumped it there while I was stamping out a book, and so life from now on would be not a throwing off, as it was for Aunt Gladys, and not a gathering in, as it was for Brenda, but a bouncing off, a numbness. I began to fear this, and yet, in my muscleless devotion to my work, seemed edging towards it, silently, as Miss Winney used to edge up to the *Britannica*. Her stool was empty now and awaited me.

Just before lunch the lion tamer came wide-eyed into the library. He stood still for a moment, only his fingers moving, as though he were counting the number of marble stairs before him. Then he walked creepily about on the marble floor, snickering at the clink of his taps and the way his little noise swelled up to the vaulted ceiling. Otto, the guard at the door, told him to make less noise with his shoes, but that did not seem to bother the little boy. He clacked on his tiptoes, high, secretively, delighted at the opportunity Otto had given him to practice his posture. He tiptoed up to me.

"Hey," he said, "where's the heart section?"

"The what?" I said.

"The heart section. Ain't you got no heart section?"

He had the thickest sort of southern Negro dialect and the only word that came clear to me was the one that sounded like heart.

"How do you spell it?" I said.

"*Heart.* Man, pictures. Drawing books. Where you got them?"

"You mean art books? Reproductions?"

He took my polysyllabic word for it. "Yea, they's them."

"In a couple places," I told him. "Which artist are you interested in?"

The boy's eyes narrowed so that his whole face seemed black. He started backing away, as he had from the lion. "All of them . . ." he mumbled.

"That's okay," I said. "You go look at whichever ones you want. The next flight up. Follow the arrow to where it says Stack Three. You remember that? Stack Three. Ask somebody upstairs."

He did not move; he seemed to be taking my curiosity about his taste as a kind of poll-tax investigation. "Go ahead," I said, slashing my face with a smile, "right up there . . ."

And like a shot he was scuffling and tapping up towards the heart section.

After lunch I came back to the in-and-out desk and there was John McKee, waiting, in his pale blue slacks, his black shoes, his barber-cloth shirt with the elastic bands, and a great knit tie, green, wrapped into a Windsor knot, that was huge and jumped when he talked. His breath smelled of hair oil and his hair of breath and when he spoke, spittle cobwebbed the corners of his mouth. I did not like him and at times had the urge to yank back on his armbands and slingshoot him out past Otto and the lions into the street.

"Has a little Negro boy passed the desk? With a thick accent? He's been hiding in the art books all morning. You know what those boys *do* in there."

"I saw him come in, John."

"So did I. Has he gone *out* though."

"I haven't noticed. I guess so."

"Those are *very* expensive books."

"Don't be so nervous, John. People are supposed to touch them."

"There is touching," John said sententiously, "and there is touching. Someone should check on him. I was afraid to leave the desk here. You know the way they treat the housing projects we give them."

"*You* give them?"

"The city. Have you seen what they do at Seth Boyden? They threw *beer* bottles, those big ones, on the *lawn*. They're taking over the city."

"Just the Negro sections."

"It's easy to laugh, you don't live near them. I'm going to call Mr. Scapello's office to check the Art Section. Where did he ever find out about art?"

"You'll give Mr. Scapello an ulcer, so soon after his egg-and-pepper sandwich. I'll check, I have to go upstairs anyway."

"You know what they do in there," John warned me.

"Don't worry, Johnny, *they're* the ones who'll get warts on their dirty little hands."

"Ha ha. Those books happen to cost—"

So that Mr. Scapello would not descend upon the boy with his chalky fingers, I walked up the three flights to Stack Three, past the receiving room where rheumy-eyed Jimmy Boylen, our fifty-one-year-old boy, unloaded books from a cart; past the reading room, where bums off Mulberry Street slept over *Popular Mechanics*; past the smoking corridor where damp-browed summer students from the law school relaxed, some smoking, others trying to rub the colored dye from their tort texts off their fingertips; and finally, past the periodical room, where a few ancient ladies who'd been motored down from Upper Montclair now huddled in their chairs, pince-nezing over yellowed, fraying society pages in old old copies of the Newark *News*. Up on Stack Three I found the boy. He was seated on the glass brick floor holding an open book in his lap, a book, in fact, that was bigger than his lap and had to be propped up by his knees. By the light of the window behind him I could see the hundreds of spaces between the hundreds of tiny black corkscrews that were his hair. He was very black and shiny, and the flesh of his lips did not so much appear to be a different color as it looked to be unfinished and awaiting another coat. The lips were parted, the eyes wide, and even the ears seemed to have a heightened receptivity. He looked ecstatic—until he saw me, that is. For all he knew I was John McKee.

"That's okay," I said before he could even move, "I'm just passing through. You read."

"Ain't nothing *to* read. They's pictures."

"Fine." I fished around the lowest shelves a moment, playing at work.

"Hey, mister," the boy said after a minute, "where is this?"

"Where is what?"

"Where is these pictures? These people, man, they sure does look cool. They ain't no yelling or shouting here, you could just see it."

He lifted the book so I could see. It was an expensive large-sized edition of Gauguin reproductions. The page he had been looking at showed an $8\frac{1}{2} \times 11$ print, in color, of three native women standing knee-high in a rose-colored stream. It *was* a silent picture, he was right.

"That's Tahiti. That's an island in the Pacific Ocean."

"That ain't no place you could go, is it? Like a ree-*sort*?"

"You could go there, I suppose. It's very far. People live there . . ."

"Hey, *look*, look here at this one." He flipped back to a page where a young brown-skinned maid was leaning forward on her knees, as though to dry her hair. "Man," the boy said, "that's the fuckin life." The euphoria of his diction would have earned him eternal banishment from the Newark Public Library and its branches had John or Mr. Scapello—or, God forbid, the hospitalized Miss Winney—come to investigate.

"Who took these pictures?" he asked me.

"Gauguin. He didn't take them, he painted them. Paul Gauguin. He was a Frenchman."

"Is he a white man or a colored man?"

"He's white."

"Man," the boy smiled, chuckled almost, "I knew that. He don't *take* pictures like no colored men would. He's a good picture taker . . . *Look, look*, look here at this one. Ain't that the fuckin *life*?"

I agreed it was and left.

Later I sent Jimmy Boylen hopping down the stairs to tell McKee that everything was all right. The rest of the day was uneventful. I sat at the Information Desk thinking about Brenda and reminding myself that that evening I would have to get gas before I started up to Short Hills, which I could see now, in my mind's eye, at dusk, rose-colored, like a Gauguin stream.

"The Trouble of Marcie Flint" by John Cheever

John Cheever (1912–82) wrote such memorable stories and novels about spiritually impoverished life in prosperous New York and Connecticut suburbs that Walter Clemons, a Newsweek *critic, once said, "There is by now a recognizable landscape that can be called Cheever country." His novels include* The Wapshot Chronicle *(1957);* The Wapshot Scandal *(1964);* Bullet Park *(1969); and* Falconer *(1977). Many of his stories appeared originally in* The New Yorker, *and his collection* The Stories of John Cheever *(1978) won him a Pulitzer Prize, National Book Critics Circle Award, and an American Book Award. Among other awards, he received the National Medal for Literature for his "distinguished and continuing contribution to American letters."*

This is being written aboard the S.S. *Augustus*, three days at sea. My suitcase is full of peanut butter, and I am a fugitive from the suburbs of all large cities. What holes! The suburbs, I mean. God preserve me from the lovely ladies taking in their asters and their roses at dusk lest the frost kill them, and from ladies with their heads whirling with civic zeal. I'm off to Torino, where the girls love peanut butter and the world is a man's castle and . . ." There was absolutely nothing wrong with the suburb (Shady Hill) from which Charles Flint was fleeing, his age is immaterial, and he was no stranger to Torino, having been there for three months recently on business.

"God preserve me," he continued, "from women who dress like *toreros* to go to the supermarket, and from cowhide dispatch cases, and from flannels and gabardines. Preserve me from word games and adulterers, from basset hounds and swimming pools and frozen canapés and Bloody Marys and smugness and syringa bushes and P.T.A. meetings." On and on he wrote, while the *Augustus*, traveling at seventeen knots, took a course due east; they would raise the Azores in a day.

Like all bitter men, Flint knew less than half the story and was more interested in unloading his own peppery feelings than in learning the truth. Marcie, the wife from whom he was fleeing, was a dark-haired, dark-eyed woman—not young by any stretch of the imagination but gifted with great stores of feminine sweetness and gallantry. She had not told her neighbors that Charlie had left her; she had not even called her lawyer; but she had fired the cook, and she now took a south-south-west course between the stove and the sink, cooking the children's supper. It was not in her to review the past, as her husband would, or to inspect the forces that could put an ocean between a couple who had been cheerfully married for fifteen years. There had been, she felt, a slight difference in their points of view during his recent absence on business, for while he always wrote that he missed her, he also wrote that he was dining at the Superga six nights a week and having a wonderful time. He had only planned to be away for six weeks, and when this stretched out to three months, she found that it was something to be borne.

Her neighbors had stood by her handsomely during the first weeks, but she knew, herself, that an odd woman can spoil a dinner party, and as Flint continued to stay away, she found that she had more and more lonely nights to get through. Now, there were two aspects to the night life of Shady Hill; there were the parties, of course, and then there was another side—a regular Santa Claus's workshop of madrigal singers, political discussion groups, recorder groups, dancing schools, confirmation classes, committee meetings, and lectures on literature, philosophy, city planning, and pest control. The bright banner of stars in heaven has probably never before been stretched above such a picture of nocturnal industry. Marcie, having a sweet, clear voice, joined a madrigal group that met on Thursdays and a political workshop that met on Mondays. Once she made herself available, she was sought as a committeewoman, although it was hard to say why; she almost never opened her mouth. She finally accepted a position on the Village Council, in the third month of Charlie's absence, mostly to keep herself occupied.

Virtuousness, reason, civic zeal, and loneliness all contributed to poor Marcie's trouble. Charlie, far away in Torino, could imagine her well enough standing in their lighted doorway on the evening of his return, but could he imagine her groping under the bed for the children's shoes or pouring bacon fat into an old soup can? "Daddy has to stay in Italy in order to make the money to buy the things we need," she told the children. But when Charlie called her from abroad, as he did once a week, he always seemed to have been drinking. Regard this sweet woman, then, singing "Hodie Christus Natus Est," studying Karl Marx, and sitting on a hard chair at meetings of the Village Council.

If there was anything really wrong with Shady Hill, anything that you could put your finger on, it was the fact that the village had no public library—no foxed copies of Pascal, smelling of cabbage; no broken sets of Dostoevski and George Eliot; no Galsworthy, even; no Barrie and no Bennett. This was the chief concern of the Village Council during Marcie's term. The library partisans were mostly newcomers to the village; the opposition whip was Mrs. Selfredge, a member of the Council and a very decorous woman, with blue eyes of astonishing brilliance and inexpressiveness. Mrs. Selfredge often spoke of the chosen quietness of their life. "We never go out," she would say, but in such a way that she seemed to be expressing not some choice but a deep vein of loneliness. She was married to a wealthy man much older than herself, and they had no children; indeed, the most indirect mention of sexual fact brought a deep color to Mrs. Selfredge's face. She took the position that a library belonged in that category of public service that might make Shady Hill attractive to a development. This was not blind prejudice. Carsen Park, the next village, had let a development inside its boundaries, with disastrous results to the people already living there. Their taxes had been doubled, their schools had been ruined. That there was any connection between reading and real estate was disputed by the partisans of the library, until a horrible murder—three murders, in fact—took place in one of the cheese-box houses in the Carsen Park development, and the library project was buried with the victims.

From the terraces of the Superga you can see all of Torino and the snow-covered mountains around, and a man drinking wine there might not think of his wife attending a meeting of the Village Council. This was a board of ten men and two women, headed by the Mayor, who screened the projects that came before them. The Council met in the Civic Center, an old mansion that had been picked up for back taxes. The board room had been the parlor. Easter eggs had been hidden here, children had pinned paper tails on paper donkeys, fires had burned on the hearth, and a Christmas tree had stood in the corner; but once the house had become the property of the village, a conscientious effort seems to have been made to exorcise these gentle ghosts. Raphael's self-portrait and the pictures of the Broken Bridge at Avignon and the Avon at Stratford were taken down and the walls were painted a depressing shade of green. The fireplace remained, but the flue was sealed up and the bricks were spread with green paint. A track of fluorescent tubing across the ceiling threw a withering light down into the faces of the Village Council members and made them all look haggard and tired. The room made Marcie uncomfortable. In its harsh light her sweetness was unavailing, and she felt not only bored but somehow painfully estranged.

On this particular night they discussed water taxes and parking meters, and then the Mayor brought up the public library for the last time. "Of course, the issue is closed," he said, "but we've heard everyone all along, on both sides. There's one more man who wants to speak to us, and I think we ought to hear him. He comes from Maple Dell." Then he opened the door from the board room into the corridor and let Noel Mackham in.

Now, the neighborhood of Maple Dell was more like a development than anything else in Shady Hill. It was the kind of place where the houses stand cheek by jowl, all of them white frame, all of them built twenty years ago, and parked beside each was a car that seemed more substantial than the house itself, as if this were a fragment of some nomadic culture. And it was a kind of spawning ground, a place for bearing and raising the young and for nothing else—for who would ever come back to Maple Dell? Who, in the darkest night, would ever think with longing of the three upstairs bedrooms and the leaky toilet and the sour-smelling halls? Who would ever come back to the little living room where you couldn't swing a cat around without knocking down the colored photograph of Mount Rainier? Who would ever come back to the chair that bit you in the bum and the obsolete TV set and the bent ashtray with its pressed-steel statue of a naked woman doing a scarf dance?

"I understand that the business is closed," Mackham said, "but I just wanted to go on record as being in favor of a public library. It's been on my conscience."

He was not much of an advocate for anything. He was tall. His hair had begun an erratic recession, leaving him with some sparse fluff to comb over his bald brow. His features were angular; his skin was bad. There were no deep notes to his voice. Its range seemed confined to a delicate hoarseness—a monotonous and laryngitic sound that aroused in Marice, as if it had been some kind of Hungarian music, feelings of irritable melancholy. "I just wanted to say a few words in favor of a public library," he rasped. "When I was a kid we were poor. There wasn't much good about the way we lived, but there was this Carnegie Library. I started going there when I was about eight. I guess I went there regularly for ten years. I read everything—philosophy, novels, technical books, poetry, ships' logs. I even read a cookbook. For me, this library amounted to the difference between success and failure. When I remember the thrill I used to get out of cracking a good book, I just hate to think of bringing my kids up in a place where there isn't any library."

"Well, of course, we know what you mean," Mayor Simmons said. "But I don't think that's quite the question. The question is not one of denying books to children. Most of us in Shady Hill have libraries of our own."

Mark Barrett got to his feet. "And *I'd* like to throw in a word about poor boys and reading, if I might," he said, in a voice so full of color and virility that everyone smiled. "I was a poor boy myself," he said cheerfully, "and I'm not ashamed to say so, and I'd just like to throw in—for what it's worth—that I never put my nose inside a public library, except to get out of the rain, or maybe follow a pretty girl. I just don't want anybody to be left with the impression that a public library is the road to success."

"I didn't say that a public library was the road to——"

"Well, you *implied* it!" Barrett shouted, and he seated himself with a big stir. His chair creaked, and by bulging his muscles a little he made his garters, braces, and shoes all sound.

"I only wanted to say——" Mackham began again.

"You *implied* it!" Barrett shouted.

"Just because *you* can't read," Mackham said, "it doesn't follow——"

"Damn it, man, I didn't say that I couldn't read!" Barrett was on his feet again.

"Please, gentlemen. Please! Please!" Mayor Simmons said. "Let's keep our remarks temperate."

"I'm not going to sit here and have someone who lives in Maple Dell tell me the reason he's such a hot rock is because he read a lot of books!" Barrett shouted. "Books have their place. I won't deny it. But no book ever helped me to get where I am, and from where I am I can spit on Maple Dell. As for my kids, I want them out in the fresh air playing ball, not reading cookbooks."

"Please, Mark. Please," the Mayor said. And then he turned to Mrs. Selfredge and asked her to move that the meeting be adjourned.

"My day, my hour, my moment of revelation," Charlie wrote, in his sun-deck cabin on the *Augustus*, "came on a Sunday, when I had been home eight days. Oh God, was I happy! I spent most of the day putting up storm windows, and I like working on my house. Things like putting up storm windows. When the work was done, I put the ladder away and grabbed a towel and my swimming trunks and walked over to the Townsends' swimming pool. They were away, but the pool hadn't been drained. I put on my trunks and dove in and I remember seeing—way, way up in the top of one of the pine trees—a brassiere that I guess the Townsend kids had snitched and heaved up there in midsummer, the screams of dismay from their victim having long since been carried away on the west wind. The water was very cold, and blood pressure or some other medical reason may have accounted for the fact that when I got out of the pool and dressed I was nearly busting with happiness. I walked back to the house, and when I stepped inside it was so quiet that I wondered if anything had gone wrong. It was not an ominous silence—it was just that I wondered why the clock should sound so loud. Then I went upstairs and found Marcie asleep in her bedroom. She was covered with a light wrap that had slipped from her shoulders and breasts. Then I heard Henry and Katie's voices, and I went to the back bedroom window. This looked out onto the garden, where a gravel path that needed weeding went up a little hill. Henry and Katie were there. Katie was scratching in the gravel with a stick —some message of love, I guess. Henry had one of those broad-winged planes—talismanic planes, really—made of balsa wood and propelled by a rubber band. He twisted the band by turning the propeller, and I could see his lips moving as he counted. Then, when the rubber was taut, he set his feet apart in the gravel, like a marksman—Katie watched none of this—and sent the plane up. The wings of the plane were pale in the early dark, and then I saw it climb out of the shade up to where the sun washed it with yellow light. With not much more force than a moth, it soared and circled and meandered and came slowly down again into the shade and crashed on the peony hedge. 'I got it up again!' I heard Henry shout. 'I got it up into the light.' Katie went on writing her message in the dirt. And then, like some trick in the movies, I saw myself as my son, standing in a like garden and sending up out of the dark a plane, an arrow, a tennis ball, a stone—anything—while my sister drew hearts in the gravel. The memory of how deep this impulse to reach into the light had been completely charmed me, and I watched the boy send the plane up again and again.

"Then, still feeling very springy and full of fun, I walked back toward the door, stopping to admire the curve of Marcie's breasts and deciding, in a blaze of charity, to let her sleep. I felt so good that I needed a drink—not to pick me up but to dampen my spirits—a libation, anyhow—and I poured some whiskey in a glass. Then I went into the kitchen to get some ice, and I noticed that ants had got in somehow. This was surprising, because we never had much trouble with ants. Spiders, yes. Before the equinoctial hurricanes—even before the barometer had begun to fall—the house seemed to fill up with spiders, as if they sensed the trouble in the air. There would be spiders in the bathtubs and spiders in the living room and spiders in the kitchen, and walking down the long upstairs hallway before a storm, you could sometimes feel the thread of a web break against your face. But we had had almost no trouble with ants. Now, on this autumn afternoon, thousands of ants broke out of the kitchen woodwork and threw a double line across the drainboard and into the sink, where there seemed to be something they wanted.

"I found some ant poison at the back of the broom-closet shelf, a little jar of brown stuff that I'd bought from Timmons in the village years ago. I put a generous helping of this into a saucer and put it on the drainboard. Then I took my drink and a piece of the Sunday paper out onto the terrace in front of the house. The house faced west, so I had more light than the children, and I felt so happy that even the news in the papers seemed cheerful. No kings had been assassinated in the rainy black streets of Marseille; no storms were brewing in the Balkans; no clerkly Englishman—the admiration of his landlady and his aunts—had dissolved the remains of a young lady in an acid bath; no jewels, even, had been stolen. And that sometime power of the Sunday paper to evoke an anxious, rain-wet world of fallen crowns and inevitable war seemed gone. Then the sun withdrew from my paper and from the chair where I sat, and I wished I had put on a sweater.

"It was late in the season—the salt of change was in the air—and this tickled me, too. Last Sunday, or the Sunday before, the terrace would have been flooded with light. Then I thought about other places where I would like to be—Nantucket, with only a handful of people left and the sailing fleet depleted and the dunes casting, as they never do in the summer, a dark shadow over the bathing beach. And I thought about the Vineyard and the farina colored bluffs and the purple autumn sea and that stillness in which you might hear, from way out in the Sound, the rasp of a block on a traveler as a sailboard there came about. I tasted my whiskey and gave my paper a shake, but the view of the golden light on the grass and the trees was more compelling than the news, and now mixed up with my memories of the sea islands, was the whiteness of Marcie's thighs.

"Then I was seized by some intoxicating pride in the hour, by the joy and the naturalness of my relationship to the scene, and by the ease with which I could put my hands on what I needed. I thought again of Marcie sleeping and that I would have my way there soon—it would be a way of expressing this pride. And then, listening for the voices of my children and not hearing them, I decided to celebrate the hour as it passed. I put the paper down and ran up the stairs. Marcie was still sleeping and I stripped off my clothes and lay down beside her, waking her from what seemed to be a pleasant dream, for she smiled and drew me to her."

. . .

To get back to Marcie and her trouble: She put on her coat after the meeting was adjourned and said, "Good night. Good night . . . I'm expecting him home next week." She was not easily upset, but she suddenly felt that she had looked straight at stupidity and unfairness. Going down the stairs behind Mackham, she felt a powerful mixture of pity and sympathy for the stranger and some clear anger toward her old friend Mark Barrett. She wanted to apologize, and she stopped Mackham in the door and said that she had some cheerful memories of her own involving a public library.

As it happened, Mrs. Selfredge and Mayor Simmons were the last to leave the board room. The Mayor waited, with his hand on the light switch, for Mrs. Selfredge, who was putting on her white gloves. "I'm glad the library's over and done with," he said. "I have a few misgivings, but right now I'm against anything public, anything that would make this community attractive to a development." He spoke with feeling, and at the word "development" a ridge covered with identical houses rose in his mind. It seemed wrong to him that the houses he imagined should be identical and that they should be built of green wood and false stone. It seemed wrong to him that young couples should begin their lives in an atmosphere that lacked grace, and it seemed wrong to him that the rows of houses could not, for long, preserve their slender claim on propriety and would presently become unsightly tracts. "Of course, it isn't a question of keeping children from books," he repeated. "We all have libraries of our own. There isn't any problem. I suppose you were brought up in a house with a library?"

"Oh yes, yes," said Mrs. Selfredge. The Mayor had turned off the light, and the darkness covered and softened the lie she had told. Her father had been a Brooklyn patrolman, and there had not been a book in his house. He had been an amiable man—not very sweet-smelling —who talked to all the children on his beat. Slovenly and jolly, he had spent the years of his retirement drinking beer in the kitchen in his underwear, to the deep despair and shame of his only child.

The Mayor said good night to Mrs. Selfredge on the sidewalk, and standing there she overheard Marcie speaking to Mackham. "I'm terribly sorry about Mark, about what he said," Marcie said. "We've all had to put up with him at one time or another. But why don't you come back to my house for a drink? Perhaps we could get the library project moving again."

So it wasn't over and done with, Mrs. Selfredge thought indignantly. They wouldn't rest until Shady Hill was nothing but developments from one end to the other. The colorless, hard-pressed people of the Carsen Park project, with their flocks of children, and their monthly interest payments, and their picture windows, and their view of identical houses and treeless, muddy, unpaved streets, seemed to threaten her most cherished concepts—her lawns, her pleasures, her property rights, even her self-esteem.

Mr. Selfredge, an intelligent and elegant old gentleman, was waiting up for his Little Princess and she told him her troubles. Mr. Selfredge had retired from the banking business—mercifully, for whenever he stepped out into the world today he was confronted with the deterioration of those qualities of responsibility and initiative that had made the world of his youth selective, vigorous, and healthy. He knew a great deal about Shady Hill—he even recognized Mackham's name. "The bank holds the mortgage on his house," he said. "I remember when he applied for it. He works for a textbook company in New York that has been accused by at least one Congressional committee of publishing subversive American histories. I wouldn't worry about him, my dear, but if it would put your mind at ease, I could easily write a letter to the paper."

"But the children were not as far away as I thought," Charlie wrote, aboard the *Augustus*. "They were still in the garden. And the significance of that hour for them, I guess, was that it was made for stealing food. I have to make up or imagine what took place with them. They may have been drawn into the house by a hunger as keen as mine. Coming into the hall and listening for sounds, they would hear nothing, and they would open the icebox slowly, so that the sound of the heavy latch wouldn't be heard. The icebox must have been disappointing, because Henry wandered over to the sink and began to eat the sodium arsenate. 'Candy,' he said, and Katie joined him, and they had a fight over the remaining poison. They must have stayed in the kitchen for quite a while, because they were still in the kitchen when Henry began to retch. 'Well, don't get it all *over* everything,' Katie said. 'Come on outside.' She was beginning to feel sick herself, and they went outside and hid under a syringa bush, which is where I found them when I dressed and came down.

"They told me what they had eaten, and I woke Marcie up and then ran downstairs again and called Doc Mullens. 'Jesus Christ!' he said. 'I'll be right over.' He asked me to read the label on the jar, but all it said was sodium arsenate; it didn't say the percentage. And when I told him I had bought it from Timmons, he told me to call and ask Timmons who the manufacturer was. The line was busy and so, while Marcie was running back and forth between the two sick children, I jumped into the car and drove to the village. There was a lot of light in the sky, I remember, but it was nearly dark in the streets. Timmons' drugstore was the only place that was lighted, and it was the kind of place that seems to subsist on the crumbs from other tradesmen's tables. This late hour when all the other stores were shut was Timmons' finest. The crazy jumble of displays in his windows—irons, ashtrays, Venus in a truss, ice bags, and perfumes—was continued into the store itself, which seemed like a pharmaceutical curiosity shop or funhouse: a storeroom for cardboard beauties anointing themselves with sun oil; for cardboard mountain ranges in the Alpine glow, advertising pine-scented soap; for bookshelves, and bins filled with card-table covers, and plastic water pistols. The drugstore was a little like a house, too, for Mrs. Timmons stood behind the soda fountain, a neat and anxious-looking woman, with photographs of her three sons (one dead) in uniform arranged against the mirror at her back, and when Timmons himself came to the counter, he was chewing on something and wiped the crumbs of a sandwich off his mouth with the back of his hand. I showed him the jar and said, 'The kids ate some of this about an hour ago. I called Doc Mullens, and he told me to come and see you. It doesn't say what the percentage of arsenate is, and he thought if you could remember where you got it, we could telephone the manufacturer and find out.'

" 'The children are poisoned?' Timmons asked.

" 'Yes!' I said.

" 'You didn't buy this merchandise from me,' he said.

"The clumsiness of his lie and the stillness in that crazy store made me feel hopeless. 'I *did* buy it from you, Mr. Timmons,' I said. 'There's no question about that. My children are deathly sick. I want you to tell me where you got the stuff.'

" 'You didn't buy this merchandise from me,' he said.

"I looked at Mrs. Timmons, but she was mopping the counter; she was deaf. 'God damn it to hell, Timmons!' I shouted, and I reached over the counter and got him by the shirt. 'You look up your records! You look up your God-damned records and tell me where this stuff came from.'

" 'We know what it is to lose a son,' Mrs. Timmons said at my back. There was nothing full to her voice; nothing but the monotonous, the gritty, music of grief and need. 'You don't have to tell us anything about that.'

" 'You didn't buy this merchandise from me,' Timmons said once more, and I wrenched his shirt until the buttons popped, and then I let him go. Mrs. Timmons went on mopping the counter. Timmons stood with his head so bent in shame that I couldn't see his eyes at all, and I went out of the store.

"When I got back, Doc Mullens was in the upstairs hall, and the worst was over. 'A little more or a little less and you might have lost them,' he said cheerfully. 'But I've used a stomach pump, and I think they'll be all right. Of course, it's a heavy poison, and Marcie will have to keep specimens for a week—it's apt to stay in the kidneys—but I think they'll be all right.' I thanked him and walked out to the car with him, and then I came back to the house and went upstairs to where the children had been put to bed in the same room for company and made some foolish talk with them. Then I heard Marcie weeping in our bedroom, and I went there. 'It's all right, baby,' I said. 'It's all right now. They're all right.' But when I put my arms around her, her wailing and sobbing got louder, and I asked her what she wanted.

" 'I want a divorce,' she sobbed.

" 'What?'

" 'I want a divorce. I can't bear living like this any more. I can't bear it. Every time they have a head cold, every time they're late from school, whenever anything bad happens, I think it's retribution. I can't stand it.'

" 'Retribution for what?'

" 'While you were away, I made a mess of things.'

" 'What do you mean?'

" 'With somebody.'

" 'Who?'

" 'Noel Mackham. You don't know him. He lives in Maple Dell.'

"Then for a long time I didn't say anything—what could I say? And suddenly she turned on me in fury.

" 'Oh, I knew you'd be like this, I knew you'd be like this, I knew you'd blame me!' she said. 'But it wasn't my fault, it just wasn't my fault. I knew you'd blame me, I knew you'd blame me, I knew you'd be like this, and I . . .'

"I didn't hear much else of what she said, because I was packing a suitcase. And then I kissed the kids goodbye, caught a train to the city, and boarded the *Augustus* next morning."

What happened to Marcie was this: The evening paper printed Selfredge's letter, the day after the Village Council meeting, and she read it. She called Mackham on the telephone. He said he was going to ask the editor to print an answer he had written, and that he would stop by her house at eight o'clock to show her the carbon copy. She had planned to eat dinner with her children, but just before she sat down, the bell rang, and Mark Barrett dropped in. "Hi, honey," he said. "Make me a drink?" She made him some Martinis, and he took off his hat and topcoat and got down to business. "I understand you had that meatball over here for a drink last night."

"Who told you, Mark? Who in the world told you?"

"Helen Selfredge. It's no secret. She doesn't want the library thing reopened."

"It's like being followed. I hate it."

"Don't let that bother you, sweetie." He held out his glass, and she filled it again. "I'm just here as a neighbor—friend of Charlie's—and what's the use of having friends and neighbors if they can't give you advice? Mackham is a meatball, and Mackham is a wolf. With Charlie away, I feel kind of like an older brother—I want to keep an eye on you. I want you to promise me that you won't have that meatball in your house again."

"I can't, Mark. He's coming tonight."

"No, he isn't, sweetie. You're going to call him up and tell him not to come."

"He's human, Mark."

"Now, listen to me, sweetie. You listen to me. I'm about to tell you something. Of course he's human, but so is the garbage man and the cleaning woman. I'm about to tell you something very interesting. When I was in school, there was a meatball just like Mackham. Nobody liked him. Nobody spoke to him. Well, I was a high-spirited kid, Marcie, with plenty of friends, and I began to wonder about this meatball. I began to wonder if it wasn't my responsibility to befriend him and make him feel that he was a member of the group. Well, I spoke to him, and I wouldn't be surprised if I was the first person who did. I took a walk with him. I asked him up to my room. I did everything I could to make him feel accepted.

"It was a terrible mistake. First, he began going around the school telling everybody that he and I were going to do this and he and I were going to do that. Then he went to the Dean's office and had himself moved into my room without consulting me. Then his mother began to send me these lousy cookies, and his sister—I'd never laid eyes on her—began to write me love letters, and he got to be such a leech that I had to tell him to lay off. I spoke frankly to him; I told him the only reason I'd ever spoken to him was because I pitied him. This didn't make any difference. When you're stuck with a meatball, it doesn't matter what you tell them. He kept hanging around, waiting for me after classes, and after football practice he was always down in the locker room. It got so bad that we had to give him the works. We asked him up to Pete Fenton's room for a cup of cocoa, roughed him up, threw his clothes out the window, painted his rear end with iodine, and stuck his head in a pail of water until he damned near drowned."

Mark lighted a cigarette and finished his drink. "But what I mean to say is that if you get mixed up with a meatball you're bound to regret it. Your feelings may be kindly and generous in the beginning, but you'll do more harm than good before you're through. I want you to call up

Mackham and tell him not to come. Tell him you're sick. I don't want him in your house."

"Mackham isn't coming here to visit me, Mark. He's coming here to tell me about the letter he wrote for the paper."

"I'm ordering you to call him up."

"I won't, Mark."

"You go to that telephone."

"Please, Mark. Don't shout at me."

"You go to that telephone."

"Please get out of my house, Mark."

"You're an intractable, weak-headed, God-damned fool!" he shouted. "That's the trouble with you!" Then he went.

She ate supper alone, and was not finished when Mackham came. It was raining, and he wore a heavy coat and a shabby hat—saved, she guessed, for storms. The hat made him look like an old man. He seemed heavy-spirited and tired, and he unwound a long yellow woolen scarf from around his neck. He had seen the editor. The editor would not print his answer. Marcie asked him if he would like a drink, and when he didn't reply, she asked him a second time. "Oh, no, thank you," he said heavily, and he looked into her eyes with a smile of such engulfing weariness that she thought he must be sick. Then he came up to her as if he were going to touch her, and she went into the library and sat on the sofa. Halfway across the room he saw that he had forgotten to take off his rubbers.

"Oh, I'm sorry," he said. "I'm afraid I've tracked mud——"

"It doesn't matter."

"It would matter if this were *my* house."

"It doesn't matter here."

He sat in a chair near the door and began to take off his rubbers, and it was the rubbers that did it. Watching him cross his knees and remove the rubber from one foot and then the other so filled Marcie with pity at this clumsy vision of humanity and its touching high purpose in the face of adversity that he must have seen by her pallor or her dilated eyes that she was helpless.

The sea and the decks are dark. Charlie can hear the voices from the bar at the end of the passageway, and he has told his story, but he does not stop writing. They are coming into warmer water and fog, and the foghorn begins to blow at intervals of a minute. He checks it against his watch. And suddenly he wonders what he is doing aboard the *Augustus* with a suitcase full of peanut butter. "Ants, poison, peanut butter, foghorns," he writes, "love, blood pressure, business trips, inscrutability. I know that I will go back." The foghorn blasts again, and in the held note he sees a vision of his family running toward him up some steps—crumbling stone, wild pinks, lizards, and their much-loved faces. "I will catch a plane in Genoa," he writes. "I will see my children grow and take up their lives, and I will gentle Marcie—sweet Marcie, dear Marcie, Marcie my love. I will shelter her with the curve of my body from all the harms of the dark."

"Seth Compton" and "Rhoda Pitkin" by Edgar Lee Masters

Edgar Lee Masters (1868–1950) is remembered by many older readers who encountered in school (and perhaps memorized) poems from his Spoon River Anthology *(1915), from which the following two selections are taken. Ever since its publication,* Spoon River Anthology *has been a classic of American literature. It contains a fascinating series of brief, often bitter, verse epitaphs, which describe not only individuals but the communal life of their small Midwestern town. Masters wrote many other volumes of poetry, such as* Domesday Book *(1920);* Lichee Nuts *(1930);* The New World *(1937); and* Illinois Poems *(1941). His prose works include novels, biographical studies like* Lincoln, the Man *(1931) and* Mark Twain *(1938), and an autobiography,* Across Spoon River *(1936).*

SETH COMPTON

When I died, the circulating library
Which I built up for Spoon River,
And managed for the good of inquiring minds,
Was sold at auction on the public square,
As if to destroy the last vestige
Of my memory and influence.
For those of you who could not see the virtue
Of knowing Volney's "Ruins" as well as Butler's "Analogy"
And "Faust" as well as "Evangeline,"
Were really the power in the village,
And often you asked me,
"What is the use of knowing the evil in the world?"
I am out of your way now, Spoon River,
Choose your own good and call it good.
For I could never make you see
That no one knows what is good
Who knows not what is evil;
And no one knows what is true
Who knows not what is false.

RHODA PITKIN

Seth Compton died, and by that alone
We banished Volney, Haeckel and Darwin;
And then came Carnegie, who gave us a building,
And Ezra Fink, who gave us the books.
And think! I was Ezra's boyhood teacher,
And helped to make him the man he became.
How proud I was to be the librarian!
For due to Ezra's power and care
He chose the committee that bought the books,
And thus we started to mould our children
On history, religion and pure fiction,
And make them patriots, law abiders,
The builders of homes, and true Americans!

For what you feed them determines people:
Meat for muscle, and truth for brains.
And who can tell what youth will arise,
To be the president, run the country,
And keep it prosperous, safe and pure,
Out of the books which Ezra Fink
Gave and controlled for Spoon River?

"The Library"
by John Greenleaf Whittier

For generations, American schoolchildren dutifully read, memorized, and recited poems by John Greenleaf Whittier (1807–92), poems of heartfelt moral sentiment like "Barefoot Boy," "Maud Muller," "Skipper Ireson's Ride," "Telling the Bees," and "Barbara Frietchie." Another schoolroom classic, the New England winter idyll Snow-Bound, *is considered Whittier's greatest work. Whittier was born in Massachusetts of Quaker stock, and his love for rural New England life and his commitment to causes of social justice are evident in almost all his work. "The Library" was written to commemorate the opening of the Haverhill, Massachusetts, library in 1875.*

(Sung at the opening of the Haverhill Library, November 11, 1875.)

"Let there be light!" God spake of old,
Aud over chaos dark and cold,
And through the dead and formless frame
Of nature, life and order came.

Faint was the light at first that shone
On giant fern and mastodon,
On half-formed plant and beast of prey,
And man as rude and wild as they.

Age after age, like waves, o'erran
The earth, uplifting brute and man;
And mind, at length, in symbols dark
Its meanings traced on stone and bark.

On leaf of palm, on sedge-wrought roll;
On plastic clay and leathern scroll,
Man wrote his thoughts; the ages passed,
And lo! the Press was found at last!

Then dead souls woke; the thoughts of men
Whose bones were dust revived again;
The cloister's silence found a tongue,
Old prophets spake, old poets sung.

And here, to-day, the dead look down,
The kings of mind again we crown;
We hear the voices lost so long,
The sage's word, the sibyl's song.

Here Greek and Roman find themselves
Alive along these crowded shelves;
And Shakespeare treads again his stage,
And Chaucer paints anew his age.

As if some Pantheon's marbles broke
Their stony trance, and lived and spoke,
Life thrills along the alcoved hall,
The lords of thought await our call!

"Libraries" by Karl Shapiro

Karl Shapiro's long career as poet and critic has been marked by his sense of adventure and innovation and by many prestigious awards for his achievements. His early, more traditional work appeared in collections like Person, Place and Thing *(1942) and* Essay on Rime *(1945);* The Bourgeois Poet *(1964) (in which "Libraries" was reprinted) moved into free verse.* The Poetry Wreck: Selected Essays 1950–1970 *(1975) and his* Collected Poems 1940–1978 *(1978) were followed by* Love and War, Art and God *(1984). The Younger Son, first volume of an autobiography,* Poet, *appeared in 1988, and* New and Selected Poems: 1940–1986 *in 1987. Shapiro, a Fellow in American Letters, Library of Congress, and a member of the American Academy of Arts and Sciences, has received, among other honors, a Pulitzer Prize and a Bollingen Prize.*

Libraries, where one takes on the smell of books, stale and attractive. Service with no motive, simple as U.S. mail. Fountains and palms, armchairs for smokers. Incredible library where ideas run for safety, place of rebirth of forgotten anthems, modern cathedral for lovers. Library, hotel lobby for the unemployed, the failure, the boy afraid to go home, penniless. Switchboards for questioners: what do you know about unicorns? How do you address a duchess? Palladian architecture of gleaming glass and redwood. Window displays of this week's twelve bestsellers. Magnificent quarters of the director, who dines with names of unknown fame. Lavatories, rendezvous of desperate homosexuals. In the periodical room the newspapers bound with a stick, carried like banners of surrender to pale oak tables. Library, asylum, platform for uninhibited leaps.

In the genealogy room the delicate perspiration of effete brains. Room also of the secret catalogue, room of unlisted books, those sought by police, manuscript room with the door of black steel, manuscripts stolen in delicate professional theft from abroad, sealed for seventy-five years. Sutras on spools of film. And all this courtesy and all this trust, tons of trash and tons of greatness, burning in time with the slow cool burning, burning in the fires of poems that gut libraries, only to rebuild them, more grand and palladian, freer, more courteous, with cornerstones that say: Decide for yourself.

"The Premise of Meaning," by Archibald MacLeish

As this thoughtful and eloquent essay shows, Archibald MacLeish (1892–1982) was deeply concerned with the ultimate meaning of literature. In his poetry and prose, he tangled with the most difficult issues that human beings confront, and he eschewed easy answers. One of his best-known works was a verse play, J.B., *exploring Job's trials in a modern setting and idiom; it won a Pulitzer Prize in 1958.*

MacLeish's work spanned almost a century. His early volumes of poetry began with Tower of Ivory *(1917) and continued through, among others,* New Found Land *(1930) and* Conquistador *(1932), a Pulitzer Prize–winning epic of the conquest of Mexico. He began to write so-called "public verse," poetry about social ideas and current political events, in volumes like* Colloquy for the States *(1943). His* Collected Poems 1917–1952 *won another Pulitzer Prize in 1953. His essays, speeches, and memoirs appeared in* Poetry *and* Experience *(1961) and* Riders on the Earth *(1978), among others.*

MacLeish, educated as a lawyer, held many important nonlegal posts: Librarian of Congress (1939–44), Assistant Secretary of State (1944–45), and Boylston Professor at Harvard (1949–62).

This essay is adapted from an address delivered at the opening of the Scott Library at York University in Toronto.

What is a collection of books? Which can be reversed to read: what is a book in a collection?—a book to a library?—to a librarian? Is it merely the unit of collection, a more or less fungible (as the lawyers put it) object made of paper, print and protective covering that fulfills its bibliographical destiny by being classified as to subject and catalogued by author and title and properly shelved? Or is it something very different? Is it still a book? Is it, indeed, something more now than a book, being a book selected to compose with other books a library? But, if so, what has it become?

When he was seventy-four years old the Cretan novelist Nikos Kazantzakis began a book. He called it *Report to Greco*, Greco being, of course, the older and even more famous Cretan who painted the *Burial of Count Orgaz* and other canvases. *Report* is the operative word in this title: Kazantzakis thought of himself as a soldier reporting to his commanding officer on a mortal mission—his life. "I collect my tools: sight, smell, touch, taste, hearing, intellect ... I call upon my memory to remember, I assemble my life from the air, place myself soldier-like before the general and make my report ... For Greco is kneaded from the same Cretan soil as I and is able to understand me better than all the strivers of past and present. Did he not leave the same red track upon the stones?"

Well, there is only one *Report to Greco*, but no true book—no book truly part of a true library—was ever anything else than a report. Shakespeare used a different—and, being Shakespeare, a better—metaphor but it comes to the same thing. Lear speaks it to Cordelia at that sunshine moment toward the play's end before the deluge of the dark. They will go off, says Lear, the two of them, to their prison cell and "take upon's the mystery of things/ As though we were God's spies." All poems worthy to be preserved as poems are written so—by God's spies beneath the burden of the mystery—and so are all other gathered writings of whatever kind however we may classify them, whether as fictions or as science, as history or philosophy or whatever. A true book is a report upon the mystery of existence; it tells what has been seen in a man's life in the world—touched there, thought of, tasted.

But it does more, too, as Kazantzakis' *Report* does more: it interprets the signs, brings word back from the frontiers, from the distances. Whether it offers its news in a live voice or is left, like Emily Dickinson's snippets of paper tied up with loops of thread, to be found by an astonished sister afterward in a little drawer, it speaks of the world, of our life in the world. Everything we have in the books on which our libraries are founded—Euclid's figures, Leonardo's notes, Newton's explanations, Cervantes' myth, Sappho's broken songs, even the vast surge of Homer—everything is a report of one kind or another and the sum of all of them together is our little knowledge of our world and of ourselves. Call a book Das Kapital or The Voyage of the Beagle or Theory of Relativity or Alice in Wonderland or Moby Dick, it is still what Kazantzakis called his book—what Shakespeare intended by that immortal metaphor—it is still a "report"—upon the "mystery of things."

But if this is what a book is in a library, then a library, considered not as a collection of objects that happen to be books but as a number of books that have been chosen to constitute a library, is an extraordinary thing. It is not at all what it is commonly supposed to be even by men who describe themselves as intellectuals—perhaps I should say particularly by men who describe themselves as intellectuals. It is not a sort of scholarly filling station where students of all ages can repair to get themselves supplied with a tankful of titles: not an academic facility to be judged by the quantity of its resources and the promptness of its services. On the contrary it is an achievement in and of itself—one of the greatest of human achievements because it combines and justifies so many others. That its card catalogues and bibliographical machinery are useful no one doubts: modern scholarship would be impossible without them. That its housing and safekeeping arrangements are vital, essential, necessary goes without saying. But what is more important in a library than anything else—than everything else—is the fact that it exists.

For the existence of a library, the fact of its existence, is, in itself and of itself, an assertion—a proposition nailed like Luther's to the door of time. By standing where it does at the center of the university—which is to say at the center of our intellectual lives—with its books in a certain order on its shelves and its cards in a certain structure in their cases, the true library asserts that there is indeed a "mystery of things." Or, more precisely, it asserts that the reason why the "things" compose a mystery is that they seem to mean: that they fall, when gathered together, into a kind of relationship, a kind of wholeness, as though all these different and dissimilar reports, these bits and pieces of experience, manuscripts in bottles, messages from long before, from deep within, from miles beyond, belonged together and might, if understood together, spell out the meaning which the mystery implies.

For the point is that without the implication of meaning, which is to say the premise of meaning, there can be no mystery anywhere. The dark is not mysterious: it is merely dark. Even the greatest of physicists, even Einstein himself, when he wished to speak of the universe as science observes it, spoke of it as standing before us "like a great, eternal riddle." And a riddle, needless to say, even a scientist's riddle, even a scientist's eternal riddle, even a scientist's eternal riddle of the dimensions of the universe, is something which, by hypothesis, exists to be solved.

It is this fact—the fact of the library's implicit assertion of the possibility of meaning—which provides the drama of the dedication of a new library in a world like ours. Whatever the opening of a library may have been back in the days of Mr. Carnegie's kindness when all good Scots believed that reading resulted in understanding and the rest of the world believed the Scots—whatever the opening of a new library may have been in those days there is a taste of irony about it now and more than a stir of drama. Our world—at least that part of our world which we call the West—no longer hopes for meanings. Even the philosophers, whose goal was once what they called A Final Explanation, concern themselves these days with something less—with a process. And as for the intellectuals, more numerous as confidence in the intellect declines, their shuttling caravan has almost come to rest at the last oasis on the road to Prester John—the sandy spring of the absurd. Their leaders may desert them. Ionesco himself, author of *The Bald Soprano*, may regret the disappearance of meaning from the world. But the caravan holds firm beneath the dying date trees. "There was a time, long, long ago," says Ionesco, "when the world seemed to man to be so charged with meaning that he didn't have time to ask himself questions . . . The whole world was like a theater in which the elements, the forests, the oceans, the rivers, the mountains and the plains, the bushes and each plant played an incomprehensible role that man tried to understand, tried to explain to himself . . . Exactly when," says Ionesco, "was the world emptied of substance, exactly when were the signs no longer signs?" To which the caravan responds with a single voice that there was a time long, long ago when Ionesco's answer to all those draughty questions would have been "Who cares?" Certainly the caravan doesn't care. Meanings went out for it with Hiroshima. All that's left us is absurdity. Unless you count despair.

But if Ionesco's complaint is out of fashion, what shall we say of the Great Affirmation spelled out in almost visible letters above the door of a new library? Those Reports to Greco on its shelves exist in a relationship which implies that the library's business is relationship. But the generation the library is to serve has been raised in the belief that what matters is not the relationships which compose our lives but something very different—something called relevance—the relevance of each aspect of existence to ourselves. Not the weft and weave that surrounds us, the mystery of things, the riddle of the universe, the implicitness of meaning, but an immediate identification of each thing with each self on the assumption that there is no meaning and that only self is real. Love, for example, which is all relationship, total relationship, infinite connection, is made relevant by turning it to sex which is connection and nothing more. Death, which was once, in the old world of relationship, the perspective of everything, the distance that turns the mountains blue, becomes relevant by becoming conclusion: not even exit—just an end.

And life itself, once that infinite possibility, that prison cell where the defeated king could take upon himself and his mild daughter the vastness of our human wonder, is made a prison cell and nothing more—the ultimate relevance—in a solitary and absurd confinement where nothing, not even Godot, ever comes and nothing answers but the idiot whimper of self-pity.

Oh, there is drama enough on this occasion, irony enough, but which way truly does the irony cut? Is it the library's implicit assertion of the immanence of meaning that has become ridiculous in our fuddled time, or is it the tired caravan of intellectual fashion stumbling toward the Mountains of the Moon? I do not know the answer but I know something that can learn the answer. I know that meaninglessness is just as much a matter of belief as meaning. The caravan of the intellectuals would have you think that someone has discovered meaninglessness out there beyond us in the desert—in the infinities of space—and brought it home like a phoenix egg to prove the world is void. Nothing could be more childish. Meaninglessness, like meaning, is a conclusion in the mind, a reading, an interpretation.

And science—honest science—knows it. Jacques Monod, the French biochemist who sees living beings as chemical machines that construct themselves out of chemical chance, concludes that the process of life is blind and man an accident. But he reaches this conclusion, as he himself acknowledges, by way of his belief in theories of quantum mechanics in which other scientists, Einstein among the lot, are unable to believe. "A mutation," writes M. Monod, "is in itself a microscopic event, a quantum event, to which the principle of uncertainty consequently applies." But to Einstein the consequence does not apply because the assumption is unsound. Einstein, as Gerald Holton puts it, was a scientist "fighting for a causal physics" who assumed "a rational God of causal laws who would not play dice with the universe." Whether Einstein's assumption is right or M. Monod's, is not, perhaps, for us, and certainly not for me, to say, but one thing is clear even to a scientific illiterate like myself: the issue between M. Monod and Einstein, or between their positions, is an issue of belief. Einstein makes that clear enough. Quantum physics was to him a "false religion." And he said so. In so many words.

It would be helpful to us, with a library to open and a question to answer, if there were an Einstein of the world of letters to match that explicit Einstein in the world of science. For it is in the world of letters that the contemporary taste for meaninglessness has presented itself most flagrantly as something more than a taste, more than an opinion: as an established fact to be accepted with despair. And it is in the world of letters that this masquerade can do most damage. Critics may pursue the meaningless relentlessly, as they may pursue anything else that moves, without damage to their reputations or themselves. And playwrights, ambiguous reporters, may make their fortunes by it—they have. But the poor devil of a poet lives by meanings if he lives at all. Relationship is all he has to work with: that *analogie universelle* which Baudelaire discovered in the poems of two thousand years and which the poems not yet written still must seek. For the poet, the novelist—the artist in letters—to assert the meaninglessness of the world is the ultimate act of human folly, the act that ridicules itself. Even if the "principle of uncertainty" were established to the satisfaction of all science and M. Monod were right in his finding that no "master plan" exists for the construction of his "chemical machines," man would still exist. And it is precisely man who, through his arts, through his thought, through his Reports to Greco, has constructed meanings over millennia of time, whether the universe has confirmed them or not. Job's demand for justice was shouted down by the voice from the whirlwind but Job, because he was a man, took back his life and lived it notwithstanding.

No, it is not the library, I think, that has become ridiculous by standing there against the dark with its books in order on its shelves. On the contrary the library, almost alone of the great monuments of civilization, stands taller now than it ever did before. The city—our American city at least—decays. The nation loses its grandeur, becomes what we call a "power," a Pentagon, a store of missiles. The university is no longer always certain what it is. But the library remains: a silent and enduring affirmation that the great Reports still speak, and not alone but somehow all together—that, whatever else is chance and accident, the human mind, that mystery, still seems to mean.